UTOPIA

A REVISED TRANSLATION
BACKGROUNDS
CRITICISM

SECOND EDITION

Norton Critical Editions in the
History of Ideas

For a complete list of Norton Critical Editions, visit
www.wwnorton.com/college/english/nce.welcome.htm

A NORTON CRITICAL EDITION

Sir Thomas More

UTOPIA

A REVISED TRANSLATION

BACKGROUNDS

CRITICISM

SECOND EDITION

Translated and Edited by

ROBERT M. ADAMS
LATE OF
UNIVERSITY OF CALIFORNIA AT LOS ANGELES

W · W · NORTON & COMPANY · *New York* · *London*

Printed in the United States of America.

The text of this book is composed in Electra,
with the display set in Bernhard Modern.
Composition and manufacturing by The Maple-Vail Book Manufacturing Group.
Book design by Antonina Krass

Library of Congress Cataloging in Publication Data

More, Thomas, Sir, Saint, 1478–1535.
[Utopia. English]
Utopia : a revised translation, backgrounds, criticism Sir
Thomas More ; translated and edited by Robert M. Adams. — 2nd ed.
p.   cm. — (A Norton critical edition)
Includes bibliographical references (p.   ) and index.
1. Utopias.   I. Adams, Robert Martin, 1915–   .   II. Title.
HX810.5.E54   1991
321'.07–dc20   91-17730

ISBN 0-393-96145-1

W. W. Norton & Company, Inc., 500 Fifth Avenue, New York, N.Y. 10110
www.wwnorton.com

W. W. Norton & Company Ltd., Castle House, 75/76 Wells Street,
London W1T 3QT

5 6 7 8 9 0

Contents

Preface to the Second Edition

Utopia is one of those mercurial, jocoserious writings that turn a new profile to every advancing generation, and respond in a different way to every set of questions addressed to them. Though small in size and flippant in tone, it is in fact two very heavy books. The first part propounds a set of riddles such as every sincere man who enters public life is bound to ask himself, whether he is living in early-capitalist England, late-capitalist America, or any other society dominated by the money-mad and the authority-intoxicated. He must think, What good can I do as an honorable man in a society of power-hungry individuals? What evil will I have to condone as the price of the good I accomplish? And how can I tell when the harm I am doing, by acting as window-dressing for evil, outweighs my potential for good? The second part of *Utopia* offers a set of no less disturbing questions. For example, Can a community be organized for the benefit of all, and not to satisfy the greed, lust, and appetite for domination of a few? How much repression is a good society justified in exercising in order to retain its goodness? And finally, When we give some persons power in our society (as we must), and appoint others to watch them (as we'd better), who is going to watch the watchers? Can we really stand a society in which everybody watches everybody?

Almost everyone has seen that these are some of the major questions the *Utopia* raises; they include many of the classical questions of political economy and social organization. As for what answers the author of *Utopia* provided, we are still in dispute; he was a complex man who understood very well that it is not always safe or politic to speak one's entire mind—even supposing it is ever possible. Most of the authorities whose essays are assembled at the back of the book try to calculate the answers. More gave to his questions by studying the way in which they are framed or the context in which they occurred to him. Some see him as a man modern far beyond his era, proposing prophetic remedies for the problems of an outworn social system; others see him as a conservative, medieval-minded man whose ideal community was patterned on that of the monastery. Still others deny that he meant anything at all, preferring to describe his book as a joke. Some feel that the book can be understood in terms of its literary form or genre, in terms of its predecessors among the imaginary commonwealths, or in terms of the ideals prevalent among More's literary friends on the Continent. Some find the key to its equivocal patterns of meaning in an equivocal pattern of syntax; it has been argued that Utopia was a real place located in Peru, and Hythloday a real man who had visited it and talked with More. In "modern times" (which seems now to mean mostly the age of mass production, mass mental-control, and mass murder), speculative thinkers have played variations, mostly sardonic, on themes sounded half a millennium ago by Thomas More. A gamut of speculation is thus offered to the reader, spreading, if not from the sublime to the ridiculous, at least from the plausible to the improbable.

But, whatever the book "really" meant when it was written, one aspect of it that our materials do not properly emphasize (simply because of lack of space) is the enormous influence it had on men's minds. It had this influence not only on socialist Utopians of the nineteenth century like William Morris and Edward Bellamy, but on men of its own time, that is, the sixteenth century. America had been discovered for fewer than twenty-five years when the *Utopia* appeared in print. Europeans knew very little about the new land beyond the ocean, and what information they got from the first explorers was sparse, ill-written, and, worst of all, not very interesting, especially when it was accurate. Just at this moment, More appeared with a finished and elegant literary production, describing some enchanting people who, in addition to all the "natural" virtues like innocence, simplicity, and native honor, had some very sophisticated institutions perfectly suited to comment on the most notorious abuses of contemporary Europe. No wonder the book took European readers by storm. Naive folk of the early sixteenth century swallowed More's account of Utopia as a fair description of the New World; tougher and more practical men still tended, when they came to America, to see the natives as potential Utopians or ex-Utopians. In Mexico and South America the best and most generous of the explorers tried to form the tribes and pueblos they discovered into little Amaurots. These, of course, disintegrated; but throughout the centuries and across most of the American latitudes, there have rarely failed to be found little groups of true believers whose social ideals owed something to the inspiration of More's *Utopia*. The book is thus of special interest to Americans, North and South; it helped to make us what we are today by determining, not our immediate institutions, but the level of our expectations. And in the long run that may be the most important, though the least formal, of our institutions.

If, then, it was a mere joke, More's book was one of the most appealing and influential jokes ever made—consequently, one of the cruelest. And that, I think, takes it outside the limits of More's character. The power of the book's idealism is a real ingredient of its structure; that fact has been demonstrated, not in a learned article, but by the testimony of history. We may interpret it as we will, but the way a book like *Utopia* has been read and lived across the centuries is an authentic part of its nature. However we choose to read it, we cannot deprive it of qualities it has proved on the pulses of mankind. On these terms it cannot be other than a compassionate and generous book, as well as a witty one—that is, a book interested in living people and the way they live, not just in verbal phantoms and personae. To read it is a test of one's own temper. We in the United States should be particularly aware of this book as we move beyond the two hundredth anniversary of our own generous, perilous experiment.

ROBERT M. ADAMS

1991

Translator's Note

Translations, according to a cynical, sexist wheeze, are like mistresses; the faithful ones are apt to be ugly, and the beautiful ones false. This glib cliché can be supplemented by another one, declaring that the translator's game always involves an effort to have his cake and eat it too. He wants to catch, to savor, to crystallize in his mind the special qualities of his original, and at the same time to transfuse them into an entirely different medium, readable modern English. Thomas More's *Utopia* is not cast in artificial or ornate literary language, as his age understood it. The Latin More uses is simple, conversational, everyday prose such as a lawyer, a diplomat, or a humanist might employ about the normal occasions and business of daily existence. But it is quite unlike modern English in several important respects. The sentences are longer and less tightly knit in patterns of subordination. The main idea of a sentence may be hidden in an ablative absolute, or hung out at a considerable distance in space and syntax. Because it is an inflected language, Latin can scatter the ingredients of a sentence about more loosely than English does, in the assurance that a reader will be able to assemble them within his own mind. An English sentence is expected to do more of the reader's work for him. At the same time, Latin, or at least More's lawyerly Latin, has a whole mass of delicate innuendoes and qualifications at its disposal— double negatives, ironic appositives, pseudo-antitheses, and formal (but only formal) correlatives. To represent the structure of More's Latin syntax in English would create the impression of a whirling chaos; reproducing his stylistic nuances would give rise to a mincing and artificial English, as of a rhetorical sophist. And in either case, the real flavor of More's book, which is casual and colloquial, would be lost completely.

A constant temptation of the translator is to go for one quality of his original at the expense of all the others. More's long, loosely articulated sentences can be made swift and clear by rearranging some of their parts and omitting others; his rhetorical structure can be retained, at the cost of sacrificing the colloquial and conversational flavor of his book. In trying to respond to all four demands (for clarity, completeness, colloquial ease, and a sense of contour in the prose), I have consulted from time to time the work of my predecessors. Three in particular proved suggestive and challenging. Ralph Robynson's 1551 rendering is a superb achievement; it still withstands the severest test of any translation, close comparison with the original. To be sure, Robynson is so anxious to squeeze out every drop of More's meaning, that he sometimes translates one word by two or four or more; and his language, after more than four hundred years, requires no less glossing and translation than the original text. H. V. S. Ogden (1949) is swift, deft, and modern; but to gain these qualities, he omits not only elements of More's meaning but most of the nuances of More's expression. It is an extraordinary *flat* translation, as if written for someone in a great hurry; and it occasionally misrepresents to odd effect the actual sense of the Latin. Finally, Father Edward Surtz's (1965) recension of the (1923) translation by G. C. Richards strives as earnestly as Robynson for completeness of expression. But, following a Latinate word order, this version is generally stiff and sometimes wooden; its sentences, with their intricate turnings and grammatical suspensions, often defy articulation by the mouth of anyone who knows and cares for English idiom. Yet all three translations catch intersecting and overlapping sectors of an original that is richer than any of them. In the process of making my own text, I consulted these various versions freely, and even when dissatisfied with the work of one of my predecessors, drew from it the stimulus of disagreement. A. E. Housman dedicated his great edition of Manillius *in usu editorum*—for the use of those future editors who, he supposed, would *really* study the complexities of a text to which he had merely indicated the first approaches. Less formidably, any "new" translation of a much-translated text can best define itself as a temporary trial balance, for the guidance of future translators in their search for a miracle capable of reversing the action of the old philosopher's stone. For where the alchemist's dream was of turning lead to precious gold, the translator's dream is that he may somehow be kept from reducing gold to common lead.

This translation is dedicated to the memory of Mr. William Nagel of the Horace Mann School for Boys, who more than forty years ago taught me—reluctant and ungrateful infant that I was—the rudiments of the Latin tongue.

R.M.A.

The Text of
UTOPIA

This woodcut image of Utopia is from the March 1518 edition printed in Basel by John Froben. It was the work of Ambrosius Holbein (brother of the more famous Hans Holbein the Younger). There had been a different and much simpler (yet in some ways more literal) image of the island before the first (1516) edition printed at Louvain. For analysis and discussion of these illustrations, see W. W. Wooden and John N. Wall, Jr., "Thomas More and the Painter's Eye," in *Journal of Medieval and Renaissance Studies* 15 (1985): 231–63.

CONCERNING THE BEST
STATE OF A COMMONWEALTH
AND THE NEW ISLAND
OF UTOPIA

A Truly Golden Handbook
No Less Beneficial Than Entertaining
by the Most Distinguished and Eloquent Author
THOMAS MORE
Citizen and Sheriff of the Famous City
of London

BOOK ONE

The most invincible King of England, Henry the Eighth of that name, a prince adorned with the royal virtues beyond any other, had recently some differences of no slight import with Charles, the most serene Prince of Castille,[1] and sent me into Flanders as his spokesman to discuss and settle them. I was companion and associate to that incomparable man Cuthbert Tunstall,[2] whom the King has recently created Master of the Rolls, to everyone's great satisfaction. I will say nothing in praise of this man, not because I fear the judgment of a friend might be questioned, but because his learning and integrity are greater than I can describe and too well-known everywhere to need my commendation—unless I would, according to the proverb, "Light up the sun with a lantern."[3]

[The word "Utopia" is compounded from Greek *ou* and *topos*, meaning "no place"; there may also be a pun on *eutopos*, meaning "good place." More sometimes spoke of his book by a Latin equivalent, Nusquama, from *nusquam*, nowhere. This whole ornate title is translated from the title page of the March 1518 edition—the third—published by Froben at Basle.]

1. The Prince of Castille is the future Charles V (Carlos Quinto), as yet only fifteen years old and under the guardianship of his grandfather, but about to be come King of Castille, then King of Spain, and, before he was twenty-one, Holy Roman Emperor. As part of his royal possessions, he inherited the Low Countries. The matters in dispute between him and Henry were certain Dutch import duties, against which the English government protested by declaring an embargo on all exports of wool to Holland. In retaliation for this act Charles was hinting at an expropriation of the English fleet, or such parts of it as he could get his hands on.

2. An admired scholar and influential cleric, though not yet a bishop, Cuthbert Tunstall (1474–1559) was appointed Ambassador to Brussels in May 1515, and a year later became Master of the Rolls.

3. Analogues of this saying are scattered through the *Adagia* of Erasmus, an immense collection of proverbs and popular sayings: see especially No. 1407 in the *Opera* (Leyden, 1703–6) 2, 556.

Those appointed by the prince to deal with us, all excellent men, met us at Bruges by prearrangement. Their head and leader was the Margrave, so called, of Bruges,[4] a most distinguished person. But their main speaker and guiding spirit was Georges de Themsecke, the Provost of Cassel,[5] a man eloquent by nature as well as by training, very learned in the law, and most skillful in diplomatic affairs through his ability and long practice. After we had met several times, certain points remained on which we could not come to agreement; so they adjourned the meetings and went to Brussels for some days to consult their prince in person.

Meanwhile, since my business permitted it, I went to Antwerp.[6] Of those who visited me while I was there, Peter Giles[7] was more welcome to me than any of the others. He was a native of Antwerp, a man of high reputation, already appointed to a good position and worthy of the very best: I hardly know a young man more learned or of better character. Apart from being cultured, virtuous, and courteous to all, with his intimates he is so open, trustworthy, loyal and affectionate that it would be hard to find another friend like him anywhere. No man is more modest or more frank; none better combines simplicity with wisdom. His conversation is so merry, and so witty without malice, that the ardent desire I felt to see my native country, my wife and my children (from whom I had been separated more than four months) was much eased by his agreeable company and pleasant talk.

One day after I had heard mass at Nôtre Dame, the most beautiful and most popular church in Antwerp, I was about to return to my quarters when I happened to see him talking with a stranger, a man of quite advanced years. The stranger had a sunburned face, a long beard, and a cloak hanging loosely from his shoulders; from his appearance and dress, I took him to be a ship's captain. When Peter saw me, he approached and greeted me. As I was about to return his greeting, he drew me aside, and, indicating the stranger, said, "Do you see that man? I was just on the point of bringing him to you."

"He would have been very welcome on your behalf," I answered.

"And on his own too, if you knew him," said Peter, "for there is no man alive today can tell you so much about unknown peoples and lands; and I know that you're always greedy for such information."

"In that case," said I, "my guess wasn't a bad one, for at first glance I supposed he was a skipper."

4. J. (for Jean or Jacques) de Halewyn, Seigneur de Maldeghem, was Margrave of Bruges. Bruges itself, after a rich commercial flowering in the fourteenth century (when it was the central distributing point and an important manufacturing center for English wool), was losing some of its commercial clout in the early sixteenth century, partly because its harbor was silting up. Like the town itself, the title "Margrave of Bruges" was mostly vestigial but still impressive.

5. Georges de Themsecke, Provost of Cassel, was a native of Bruges, author of a regional history, and chief magistrate of Cassel, a small town between Dunkirk and Lille.
6. Antwerp and Brussels are about equidistant (sixty miles) from Bruges.
7. Peter Giles (1486?–1533) had been a star pupil of Erasmus, and was now (1515) town clerk of his native Antwerp, as well as a poet and editor of Latin texts.

"Then you're not quite right," he replied, "For his sailing has not been like that of Palinurus,[8] but more that of Ulysses, or rather of Plato. This man, who is named Raphael—his family name is Hythloday[9]— knows a good deal of Latin, and is particularly learned in Greek. He studied Greek more than Latin because his main interest is philosophy, and in that field he found that the Romans have left us nothing very valuable except certain works of Seneca and Cicero. Being eager to see the world, he left to his brothers the patrimony to which he was entitled at home (he is a native of Portugal), and took service with Amerigo Vespucci.[1] He accompanied Vespucci on the last three of his four voyages, accounts of which are now common reading everywhere; but on the last voyage, he did not return home with the commander. After much persuasion and expostulation he got Amerigo's permission to be one of the twenty-four men who were left in a fort at the farthest point of the last voyage.[2] Being marooned in this way was altogether agreeable to him, as he was more anxious to pursue his travels than afraid of death. He would often say, 'The man who has no grave is covered by the sky,' and 'The road to heaven is equally short from all places.'[3] Yet this frame of mind would have cost him dear, if God had not been gracious to him. After Vespucci's departure, he traveled through many countries with five companions from the fort. At last, by strange good fortune, he got, via Ceylon, to Calicut,[4] where by good luck he found some Portuguese ships; and so, beyond anyone's expectation, he returned to his own country."

When Peter had told me this, I thanked him for his kindness in wishing to introduce me to a man whose conversation he hoped I would enjoy, and then I turned to Raphael. After greeting one another and exchanging the usual civilities of strangers upon their first meeting, we

8. The pilot of Aeneas slept over his steering oar, fell overboard, and perished: *Aeneid* 5.832 ff. Palinurus is a type of the careless traveler, Ulysses is a type of the man who learns from traveling, and Plato (who made trips to Sicily and Egypt) is a type of the man who travels to learn.

9. Raphael will not be known specifically as the "affable archangel" till Milton writes *Paradise Lost* a century and a half hence; still, he is already known as a comfortable, sociable archangel, as contrasted with Michael the warrior: witness his befriending of Tobias in the apocryphal Book of Tobit. The first root of "Hythloday" is surely Greek *huthlos*, meaning "nonsense"; the second part of the name may suggest *daien*, to distribute, i.e., a nonsense-peddler. A fantastic trilingual pun could make the whole name mean "God heals [Heb., *Raphael*] through the nonsense [Gr., *huthlos*] of God [Lat., *dei*]."

1. Amerigo Vespucci's last two voyages were made for the King of Portugal, so a Portuguese nationality was natural for Hythloday. By mak-

ing him a foreigner, More also disposed of him conveniently out of range of the curious. Vespucci, born in Florence, but employed by the monarchies of Spain and Portugal, claimed to have made four trips to America between 1497 and 1504. His account of these voyages (excerpted below, pp. 104–7) circulated widely through Europe after its publication in 1507, and did more to make him famous than the earlier and more substantial explorations of Columbus and Cabot.

2. Cape Frio, north of Rio de Janeiro in Brazil.

3. Both these dicta are from classical sources: Lucan, *Pharsalia* 7.819; and Cicero, *Tusculan Disputations* 1.104.

4. More covers in a prepositional phrase the distance from Eastern Brazil to Ceylon, a distance of about fifteen thousand miles. Somewhere in there is Utopia.

Calicut (from which we first received the cloth known as calico) is a district of India not far from Madras.

all went to my house. There in the garden we sat down on a bench covered with turf to talk together.

He told us that when Vespucci sailed away, he and his companions who had stayed behind in the fort often met with the people of the countryside, and by ingratiating speeches gradually won their friendship. Before long they came to dwell with them safely and even affectionately. The prince also gave them his favor (I have forgotten his name and that of his country), furnishing Raphael and his five companions not only with ample provisions, but with means for traveling—rafts when they went by water, wagons when they went by land. In addition, he sent with them a most trusty guide who was to introduce and recommend them to such other princes as they wanted to visit. After many days' journey, he said, they came to towns and cities, and to commonwealths that were both populous and not badly governed.

To be sure, under the equator and as far on both sides of the line as the sun moves, there lie vast empty deserts, scorched with perpetual heat. The whole region is desolate and squalid, grim and uncultivated, inhabited by wild beasts, serpents, and also by men no less wild and dangerous than the beasts themselves. But as they went on, conditions gradually grew milder. The heat was less fierce, the earth greener, men and even beasts less savage. At last they reached people, cities, and towns which not only traded among themselves and with their neighbors, but even carried on commerce by sea and land with remote countries. After that, he said, they were able to visit different lands in every direction, for he and his companions were welcome as passengers aboard any ship about to make a journey.

The first vessels they saw were flat-bottomed, he said, with sails made of papyrus-reeds and wicker, or occasionally of leather. Farther on, they found ships with pointed keels and canvas sails, very much like our own.[5] The seamen were skilled in managing wind and water; but they were most grateful to him, Raphael said, for showing them the use of the compass, of which they had been ignorant. For that reason, they had formerly sailed with great timidity, and only in summer. Now they have such trust in the compass that they no longer fear winter at all, and tend to be overconfident rather than cautious. There is some danger that through their imprudence, this discovery, which they thought would be so advantageous to them, may become the cause of much mischief.

It would take too long to repeat all that Raphael told us he had observed, nor would it make altogether for our present purpose. Perhaps in another place we shall tell more about the things that are most profitable, especially the wise and sensible institutions that he observed among the civ-

5. As a matter of fact, the native Americans, when they traveled by water, used canoes made of hollow logs. Likewise, they did not understand the use of the wheel, the casting of iron, or the forging of steel—all of which are common among the Utopians and their South American neighbors. But More was not interested in authenticity at that level.

ilized nations. We asked him many eager questions about such things, and he answered us willingly enough. We made no inquiries, however, about monsters, which are the routine of travelers' tales. Scyllas, ravenous Celaenos, man-eating Lestrygonians[6] and that sort of monstrosity you can hardly avoid, but governments solidly established and sensibly ruled are not so common. While he told us of many ill-considered usages in these new-found nations, he also described quite a few other customs from which our own cities, nations, races, and kingdoms might take example in order to correct their errors. These I shall discuss in another place, as I said. Now I intend to relate only what he told us about the manners and laws of Utopians, first explaining the occasion that led him to speak of that commonwealth. Raphael had been talking very wisely about the many errors and also the wise institutions found both in that hemisphere and this (as many of both sorts in one place as in the other), speaking as shrewdly about the manners and governments of each place he had visited briefly as though he had lived there all his life. Peter was amazed.

"My dear Raphael," he said, "I'm surprised that you don't enter some king's service; for I don't know of a single prince who wouldn't be eager to employ you. Your learning, and your knowledge of various countries and men would entertain him while your advice and your supply of examples would be very helpful in the counsel chamber. Thus you might advance your own interest and be useful at the same time to all your relatives and friends."

"I am not much concerned about my relatives and friends," he replied, "because I consider that I have already done my duty by them. While still young and healthy, I distributed among my relatives and friends the possessions that most men do not part with till they are old and sick (and then only reluctantly, because they can no longer keep them). I think they should be content with this gift of mine, and not expect that for their sake I should enslave myself to any king whatever."

"Well said," Peter replied; "but I do not mean that you should be in servitude to any king, only in his service."

"The difference is only a matter of one syllable," Raphael replied.[7]

"All right," said Peter, "but whatever you call it, I do not see any other way in which you can be so useful to your friends or to the general public, apart from making yourself happier."

"Happier indeed!" exclaimed Raphael. "Would a way of life so absolutely repellent to my spirit make my life happier? As it is now, I live as

---

6. Scyllas and Lestrygonians are Homeric bogeys, from *Odyssey* 12 and 10, a monster and a nation that eat men alive. Celaeno was the leader of the Harpies that so tormented Phineus (*Aeneid* 3.211 ff.). This is Professor Hexter's "curious paragraph," that marks the transition to the interpolated "dialogue of counsel," which was written and inserted after Book Two was completed. See *More's Utopia: the Biography of an Idea* (Princeton, 1952), Part 1, Sec. 3.

7. The play on words here rendered by "service" and "servitude" takes the form in Latin of *servias* and *inservias*.

I please, and I fancy very few courtiers, however splendid, can say that. As a matter of fact, there are so many men soliciting favors from the great that it will be no great loss if they have to do without me and a couple of others like me."

Then I said, "It is clear, my dear Raphael, that you want neither wealth nor power, and indeed I value and revere a man of such a disposition as much as I do the greatest persons in the world. Yet I think if you would devote your time and energy to public affairs, you would do a thing worthy of a generous and philosophical nature, even if you did not much like it. You could best perform such a service by joining the council of some great prince, whom you would incite to noble and just actions. I am sure you would do this if you held such an office, and your influence would be felt, because a people's welfare or misery flows in a stream from their prince, as from a never-failing spring. Your learning is so full, even if it weren't combined with experience, and your experience is so great, even without any learning, that you would be an extraordinary counsellor to any king in the world."

"You are twice mistaken, my dear More," he replied, "first in me and then in the situation itself. I don't have the capacity you ascribe to me, and if I had it in the highest degree, the public would not be any better off through the sacrifice of my peace. In the first place, most princes apply themselves to the arts of war, in which I have neither ability nor interest, instead of to the good arts of peace. They are generally more set on acquiring new kingdoms by hook or by crook than on governing well those that they already have. Moreover, the counsellors of kings are all so wise already that they need no other knowledge (or at least that's the way they see it). At the same time, they approve and even flatter the most absurd statements of favorites through whose influence they seek to stand well with the prince. It is only natural, of course, that each man should think his own opinions best: the old crow loves his fledglings, and the ape his cubs.[8] Now in a court composed of people who envy everyone else and admire only themselves, if a man should suggest something he had read of in other ages or seen in far places, the other counsellors would think their reputation for wisdom was endangered, and they would look like simpletons, unless they could find fault with his proposal. If all else failed, they would take refuge in some remark like this: 'The way we're doing it is the way we've always done it, this custom was good enough for our fathers, and I only hope we're as wise as they were.' And with this deep thought they would take their seats, as though they had said the last word on the subject—implying, forsooth, that it would be a very dangerous matter if a man were found to be wiser in any point than his forefathers were. As a matter of fact, we quietly

8. Another of Erasmus's *Adagia*, perhaps No. 115 or 3964.

neglect the best examples they have left us; but if something better is proposed, we seize the excuse of reverence for times past and cling to it desperately. Such proud, obstinate, ridiculous judgments I have encountered many times, and once even in England."

"What!" I asked. "Were you ever in England?"

"Yes," he answered, "I spent several months there. It was not long after the revolt of the Cornishmen against the king had been put down, with great slaughter of the poor folk involved in it.[9] At that time I was very deeply beholden to the reverend prelate John Cardinal Morton, Archbishop of Canterbury, and in addition at that time Lord Chancellor of England.[1] He was a man, my dear Peter (for More knows about him, and can tell what I'm going to say), as much respected for his wisdom and virtue as for his authority. He was of medium height, not bent over despite his years; his looks inspired respect rather than fear. In conversation, he was not forbidding though serious and grave. When suitors came to him on business, he liked to test their spirit and presence of mind by speaking to them sharply, though not rudely. He liked to uncover these qualities, which were those of his own nature, as long as they were not carried to the point of effrontery; and he thought such men were best qualified to carry on business. His speech was polished and pointed; his knowledge of the law was great, he had a vast understanding and a prodigious memory—for he had improved extraordinary natural abilities by constant study and practice. At the time when I was in England, the king depended greatly on his advice, and he seemed the chief support of the nation as a whole. He had left school for court when scarcely more than a boy, had devoted all his life to important business, and had acquired from many changes of fortune and at great cost a supply of wisdom, which is not soon lost when so purchased.

"One day when I was dining with him, there was present a layman,[2] learned in the laws of your country, who for some reason took occasion to praise the rigid execution of justice then being practiced upon thieves. They were being executed everywhere, he said, with as many as twenty at a time being hanged on a single gallows. And then he declared that he could not understand how so many thieves sprang up everywhere, when so few of them escaped hanging. I ventured to speak freely before the Cardinal, and said, 'There is no need to wonder: this way of punishing thieves goes beyond the call of justice, and is not, in any case, for the public good. The penalty is too harsh in itself, yet it isn't an effective

---

9. Angered by the greedy taxation of Henry VII, the men of Cornwall revolted in 1497 and marched on London but were defeated at Blackheath and savagely slaughtered.
1. Morton (1420–1500) was a distinguished prelate, statesman, and administrator. More's father, following the custom of the age, sent his son to serve as a page for two years (1490–92) in the cardinal's household; the seventy-year-old cardinal was so impressed with the twelve-year-old More that he arranged for his education at Oxford.
2. It was unusual at that time for a layman to have legal training; but More, who is going to attribute cruel and stupid opinions to this man, wants to dissociate him from the Church and the Cardinal.

deterrent. Simple theft[3] is not so great a crime that it ought to cost a man his head, yet no punishment however severe can withhold a man from robbery when he has no other way to eat. In this matter not only you in England but a good part of the world seem to imitate bad school-masters, who would rather whip their pupils than teach them. Severe and terrible punishments are enacted against theft, when it would be much better to enable every man to earn his own living, instead of being driven to the awful necessity of stealing and then dying for it.'

" 'Oh, we've taken care of that,' said the fellow. 'There are the trades and there is farming, by which men may make a living unless they choose deliberately to be rogues.'

" 'Oh no, you don't,' I said, 'you won't get out of it that way. We may disregard for the moment the cripples who come home from foreign and civil wars, as lately from the Cornish battle and before that from your wars with France.[4] These men, wounded in the service of king and country, are too badly crippled to follow their old trades, and too old to learn new ones. But since wars occur only from time to time, let us, I say, disregard these men, and consider what happens every day. There are a great many noblemen who live idly like drones, off the labors of others, their tenants whom they bleed white by constantly raising their rents.[5] (This is the only instance of their tight-fistedness, because they are prodigal in everything else, ready to spend their way to the poor-house.) These noblemen drag around with them a great train of idle servants,[6] who have never learned any trade by which they could earn a living. As soon as their master dies, or they themselves fall ill, they are promptly turned out of doors, for lords would rather support idlers than invalids, and the son is often unable to maintain as big a household as his father had, at least at first. Those who are turned off soon set about starving, unless they set about stealing. What else can they do? Then when a wandering life has left their health impaired and their clothes threadbare, when their faces look pinched and their garments tattered, men of rank will not want to engage them. And country people dare not do so, for they don't have to be told that one who has been raised softly to idle pleasures, who has been used to swaggering about with sword and buckler, is likely to look down on the whole neighborhood, and despise everybody as beneath him. Such a man can't be put to work with spade

3. Theft is simple when not accompanied by violence or intimidation; when so accompanied, it is robbery.
4. Though savage early in the fifteenth century, recent French wars had not amounted to much. In 1492, Henry VII briefly supported, or feigned to support, the independence of Brittany against Charles VIII, but the matter was quickly compromised (see below, p. 23, fn. 3).
5. In the endless argument between landlords

and tenants, both are likely to overlook conditions that are the fault of neither, such as inflation. Still, the consequences for tenants are generally worse than for landlords; the abuses at which More is pointing, through Hythloday, were real and getting worse.
6. The retainers against whom More inveighs were the last vestiges of the private armies by which, under feudalism, every lord had to be followed.

and mattock; he will not serve a poor man laboriously for scant wages and sparse diet.'

" 'We ought to encourage these men in particular,' said the lawyer. 'In case of war the strength of our army depends on them, because they have a bolder and nobler spirit than workmen and farmers have.'

" 'You may as well say that thieves should be encouraged on account of wars,' I answered, 'since you will never lack for thieves as long as you have men like these. Just as some thieves are not bad soldiers, some soldiers turn out to be pretty good robbers, so nearly are these two ways of life related. But the custom of keeping too many retainers is not peculiar to this nation, it is common to almost all of them. France suffers from an even more grievous plague.[7] Even in peacetime—if you can call it peace—the whole country is crowded with foreign mercenaries, hired on the same principle that you've given for your noblemen keeping idle servants. Wiseacres have a saying that the public safety depends on having ready a strong army, preferably of veteran soldiers. They think inexperienced men are not reliable, and they sometimes hunt out pretexts for war, just so they may have trained soldiers and experienced cutthroats—or, as Sallust neatly puts it, that "hand and spirit may not grow dull through lack of practice."[8] But France has learned to her cost how pernicious it is to feed such beasts. The examples of the Romans, the Carthaginians, the Syrians,[9] and many other peoples show the same thing; for not only their governments, but their fields and even their cities were ruined more than once by their own standing armies. Besides, this preparedness is unnecessary: not even the French soldiers, practiced in arms from their youth, can boast of having often got the best of your fresh levies.[1] I shall say no more on this point, lest I seem to flatter present company. At any rate, neither your town workmen nor your rough farm laborers seem to be much afraid of fighting the idle pensioners of gentlemen, as long as they're not weakened by some accident or cowed by extreme poverty. So you need not fear that retainers, once strong and vigorous (for that's the only sort gentlemen deign to corrupt), but now soft and flabby because of their idle, effeminate life, would be

---

7. Charles VII of France (Joan of Arc's "Dauphin") had tried during the early century to establish a national army; but his successor, Louis XI, reverted to mercenaries, mostly Swiss infantrymen.

8. The quotation is from *Catiline's War*, Chap. 16.

9. The Romans and Carthaginians both had to fight servile wars against gladiators and mercenaries; the "Syrians" may perhaps be the Turks and Egyptians, who employed alien soldiers under the titles of janizaries and mamelukes; or else the word may refer to much earlier Syrian empires, as described by Polybius 5. 31–87.

1. Past English victories over the French included Crécy (1346), Poitiers (1356), and Henry V's triumph at Agincourt (1415); Machiavelli treats it as a commonplace that raw English recruits will always beat French veterans, *Discorsi* 1.21. English chauvinism has always maintained that the stout English yeoman, nourished on beef and beer, can overcome ten meager Frenchmen, nourished on sour wine and black bread. (Since the French took up rugby football, less has been heard of this theory.)

weakened if they were taught practical crafts to earn their living, and trained to manly labor. Anyway, I cannot think it's in the public interest to maintain for the emergency of war such a vast multitude of people who trouble and disturb the peace. You never have war unless you choose it, and peace is always more to be considered than war. Yet this is not the only circumstance that makes thieving necessary. There is another one, peculiar (as I see it) to the English people alone.'

" 'What is that?' asked the Cardinal.

" 'Your sheep,'[2] I replied, 'that used to be so meek and eat so little. Now they are becoming so greedy and wild that they devour men themselves, as I hear. They devastate and pillage fields, houses, and towns. For in whatever parts of the land the sheep yield the softest and most expensive wool, there the nobility and gentry, yes, and even some abbots though otherwise holy men, are not content with the old rents that the land yielded to their predecessors. Living in idleness and luxury, without doing any good to society, no longer satisfies them; they have to do positive evil. For they leave no land free for the plow: they enclose every acre for pasture; they destroy houses and abolish towns, keeping only the churches, and those for sheep-barns. And as if enough of your land were not already wasted on woods and game-preserves, these worthy men turn all human habitations and cultivated fields back to wilderness. Thus one greedy, insatiable glutton, a frightful plague to his native country, may enclose many thousand acres of land within a single hedge. The tenants are dismissed and compelled, by trickery or brute force or constant harassment, to sell their belongings. By hook or by crook these miserable people—men, women, husbands, wives, orphans, widows, parents with little children, whole families (poor but numerous, since farming requires many hands)—are forced to move out. They leave the only homes familiar to them, and they can find no place to go. Since they cannot afford to wait for a buyer, they sell for a pittance all their household goods, which would not bring much in any case. When that little money is gone (and it's soon spent in wandering from place to place), what remains for them but to steal, and so be hanged—justly, you'd say!—or to wander and beg? And yet if they go tramping, they are jailed as sturdy beggars. They would be glad to work, but they can find no one who will hire them. There is no need for farm labor, in which they have been trained, when there is no land left to be plowed. One herdsman or shepherd can look

2. The wet climate of England provided ideal conditions for sheep-grazing, and her insular position kept her from being overrun by mass armies, whose first activity was always, everywhere, to slaughter stock for food. Thus the English wool trade was favored from the first. In a steadily inflating economy, wool, which could be sold on an international market for cash, had a special advantage over other crops, which had to be sold or even bartered locally. Finally, sheep required less manpower than tillage: a single shepherd with his dog replaced a hundred plowmen. Petitions, statutes, and pamphlets of the day provide copious evidence that More was not exaggerating.

after a flock of beasts large enough to stock an area that would require many hands if it were plowed and harvested.

" 'This enclosing has had the effect of raising the price of grain in many places. In addition, the price of raw wool has risen so much that poor people who used to make cloth are no longer able to buy it, and so great numbers are forced from work to idleness. One reason is that after the enlarging of the pasture-land, rot killed a great number of sheep—as though God were punishing greed by sending upon the animals a murrain, which in justice should have fallen on the owners! But even if the number of sheep should increase greatly, their price will not fall a penny. The reason is that the wool trade, though it can't be called a monopoly because it isn't in the hands of one single person, is concentrated in few hands (an oligopoly, you might say) and these so rich, that the owners are never pressed to sell until they have a mind to, and that is only when they can get their price.

" 'For the same reason other kinds of livestock also are priced exorbitantly, and this is all the easier because, with so many cottages being pulled down, and farming in a state of decay, there are not enough people to look after the breeding of cattle. These rich men will not breed calves as they do lambs, but buy them lean and cheap, fatten them in their own pastures, and then sell them at a high price. I don't think the full impact of this bad system has yet been felt. We know these dealers raise prices where the fattened cattle are sold. But when, over a period of time, they keep buying beasts from other localities faster than they can be bred, then as the supply gradually diminishes where they are purchased, a widespread shortage is bound to ensue. So your island, which seemed especially fortunate in this matter, will be ruined by the crass avarice of a few. For the high price of grain causes rich men to dismiss as many retainers as they can from their households; and what, I ask, can these men do, but rob or beg? And a man of courage is more likely to steal than to cringe.

" 'To make this hideous poverty worse, it exists side by side with wanton luxury.[3] Not only the servants of noblemen, but tradespeople, farmers, and people of every social rank are given to ostentatious dress and gluttonous greed. Look at the eating houses, the bawdy houses, and those other places just as bad, the taverns, wine-shops, and alehouses. Look at all the crooked games of chance like dice, cards, backgammon, tennis, bowling, and quoits, in which money slips away so fast. Don't all these lead their habitués straight to robbery? Banish these blights, make those who have ruined farms and villages restore them, or rent them to someone who will rebuild. Restrict the right of the rich to buy

<hr>

3. In fact, the court of Henry VII and the style of life in the period 1497–1500, when Hythloday is supposed to be addressing Cardinal Morton, were notably modest and restrained. More is projecting onto the earlier period, perhaps unconsciously, a kind of extravagant display that began in 1509 with the accession of Henry VIII, and was current when he wrote.

up anything and everything, and then to exercise a kind of monopoly. Let fewer people be brought up in idleness. Let agriculture be restored and the wool manufacture revived, so there will be useful work for the whole crowd of those now idle—whether those whom poverty has already made into thieves, or those whom vagabondage and habits of lazy service are converting, just as surely, into the robbers of the future.

" 'If you do not find a cure for these evils, it is futile to boast of your severity in punishing theft. Your policy may look superficially like justice, but in reality it is neither just nor practical. If you allow young folk to be abominably brought up and their characters corrupted, little by little, from childhood; and if then you punish them as grownups for committing crime to which their early training has inclined them, what else is this, I ask, but first making them thieves and then punishing them for it?'

"As I was speaking thus, the lawyer had made ready his answer, choosing the solemn, formal style of disputants who are better at summing up than at replying, and who like to show off their memory. So he said to me, 'You have talked very well for a stranger, but you have heard about more things than you have been able to understand correctly. I will make the matter clear to you in a few words. First, I will repeat in order what you have said; then I will show how you have been misled by ignorance of our customs; finally, I will demolish all your arguments and reduce them to rubble. And so to begin where I promised, on four points you seemed to me————'

" 'Hold your tongue,' said the Cardinal, 'for you won't be finished in a few words, if this is the way you start. We will spare you the trouble of answering now, and reserve the pleasure of your reply till our next meeting, which will be tomorrow, if your affairs and Raphael's permit it. Meanwhile, my dear Raphael, I am eager to hear why you think theft should not be punished with death, or what other punishment you think would be more in the public interest. For I'm sure even you don't think it should go unpunished entirely. Even as it is, the fear of death does not restrain evildoers; once they were sure of their lives, as you propose, what force or fear could restrain them? They would look on a lighter penalty as an open invitation to commit more crimes—it would be like offering them a reward.'

" 'It seems to me, most kind and reverend father,' I said, 'that it's altogether unjust to take away a man's life for the loss of someone's money. Nothing in the world that fortune can bestow is equal in value to a man's life. If they say the thief suffers not for the money, but for violation of justice and transgression of laws, then this extreme justice should really be called extreme injury. We ought not to approve of these fierce Manlian laws[4] that invoke the sword for the smallest violations.

---

4. Manlian laws (like those imposed by Titus Manlius in the fourth century B.C.) are very strict. Manlius executed his own son for dis-obeying one of them: Livy 8.7.1–22 and Machiavelli, *Discorsi* 3.22.

Neither should we accept the Stoic view that considers all crimes equal,[5] as if there were no difference between killing a man and taking a coin from him. If equity means anything, there is no proportion or relation at all between these two crimes. God has said, "Thou shalt not kill"; shall we kill so readily for the theft of a bit of small change? Perhaps it will be argued that God's law against killing does not apply where human laws allow it. But then what prevents men from making other laws in the same way—perhaps even laws legalizing rape, adultery, and perjury? God has taken from each person the right not only to kill another, but even to kill himself. If mutual consent to human laws on manslaughter entitles men freely to exempt their agents from divine law and allows them to kill where he has given no example, what is this but preferring the law of man to the law of God? The result will be that in every situation men will decide for themselves how far it suits them to observe the laws of God. The law of Moses is harsh and severe, as for an enslaved and stubborn people, but it punishes theft with a fine, not death.[6] Let us not think that in his new law of mercy, where he treats us with the tenderness of a father, God has given us greater license to be cruel to one another.

" 'These are the reasons why I think it is wrong to put thieves to death. But everybody knows how absurd and even harmful to the public welfare it is to punish theft and murder alike. If theft carries the same penalty as murder, the thief will be encouraged to kill the victim whom otherwise he would only have robbed. When the punishment is the same, murder is safer, since one conceals both crimes by killing the witness. Thus while we try to terrify thieves with extreme cruelty, we really invite them to kill innocent men.

" 'Now since you ask what better punishment can be found, in my judgment, it would be much easier to find a better one than a worse. Why should we question the value of the punishments long used by the Romans, who were most expert in the arts of government? They condemned those convicted of heinous crimes to work, shackled, for life, in stone quarries and mines. But of all the alternatives, I prefer the method which I observed in my Persian travels among the people commonly called the Polylerites.[7] They are a sizable nation, not badly governed, free and subject only to their own laws, except that they pay annual tribute to the Persian Shah. Living far from the sea, they are nearly surrounded by mountains. Being contented with the products of their own land, which is by no means unfruitful, they have little to do with any other nation, nor are they much visited. According to their ancient

---

5. That all crimes were equal was maintained by some Stoics and ridiculed by Horace, *Satires* 1.3.94 ff.
6. The Mosaic law is that spelled out in the first verses of Exodus 22. It provides various penalties for theft over and above restitution,

but nowhere death. This is contrasted with the "new law" of Christ, under which England is supposed to be operating.
7. The name comes from the Greek words *polus* and *leiros*, meaning "much nonsense." The people are of course imaginary.

customs, they do not try to enlarge their boundaries, and easily protect themselves behind their mountains by paying tribute to their overlord. Thus they have no wars and live in a comfortable rather than a glorious manner, more contented than ambitious or famous. Indeed, I think they are hardly known by name to anyone but their next-door neighbors.

" 'In their land, whoever is found guilty of theft must make restitution to the owner, not (as elsewhere) to the prince; they think the prince has no more right to the stolen goods than the thief. If the stolen property has disappeared, the value of the thief's property is estimated, and restitution is made from it. All the rest is handed over to the thief's wife and children, while the thief himself is sentenced to hard labor.

" 'Unless their crimes were compounded with atrocities, thieves are neither imprisoned nor shackled, but go freely and unguarded about their work on public projects. If they shirk and do their jobs slackly, they are not chained, but they are whipped. If they work hard, they are treated without any insults, except that at night after roll call they are locked up in their dormitories. Apart from constant work, they undergo no discomfort in living. As they work for the state, they are decently fed out of the public stores, though arrangements vary from place to place. In some districts they are supported by alms. Unreliable as this support may seem, the Polylerites are so charitable that no way is found more rewarding. In other places, public revenues are set aside for their support, or a special tax is levied; and sometimes they do not do public work, but anyone in need of workmen can go to the market and hire a convict by the day at a set rate, a little less than that for free men. If they are lazy, it is lawful to whip them. Thus they never lack for work, and each one of them brings a little profit into the public treasury beyond the cost of his keep.

" 'They are all dressed in clothes of the same distinctive color. Their hair is not shaved but trimmed close about the ears, and the tip of one ear is cut off. Their friends are allowed to give them food, drink, or clothing, as long as it is of the proper color; but to give them money is death, both to the giver and to the taker. It is just as serious a crime for any free man to take money from them for any reason whatever; and it is also a capital crime for any of these slaves (as the condemned are called) to carry weapons. In each district of the country they are required to wear a special badge. It is a capital crime to throw away the badge, to go beyond one's own district, or to talk with a slave of another district. Plotting escape is no more secure than escape itself: it is death for any other slave to know of a plot to escape, and slavery for a free man. On the other hand, there are rewards for informers—money for a free man, freedom for a slave, and for both of them pardon and amnesty. Thus it can never be safer for them to persist in a plan of escape than to renounce it.

" 'Thus I've described their policies in this matter. It is clear how mild and practical they are, for the aim of the punishment is to destroy vices and save men. The criminals are treated so that they see the necessity of being honest, and for the rest of their lives they atone for the wrong they have done before. There is so little danger of relapse that travelers going from one part of the country to another think slaves the most reliable guides, changing them at the boundary of each district. The slaves have no means of committing robbery since they are unarmed, and any money in their possession is evidence of a crime. If caught, they would be instantly punished, and there is no hope of escape anywhere. Since every bit of a slave's clothing is unlike the usual clothing of the country, how could a slave escape, unless he fled naked? Even then his cropped ear would give him away at once. Might not the slaves form a conspiracy against the government? Perhaps. But the slaves of one district could hardly expect to succeed unless they first involved in their plot the slave-gangs of many other districts. And that is impossible, since they are not allowed to meet or talk together or even to greet one another. No one would risk a plot when they all know joining is so dangerous to the participant and betrayal so profitable to the informer. Besides, no one is quite without hope of gaining his freedom eventually if he accepts his punishment in the spirit of obedience and patience, and gives promise of future good conduct. Indeed, every year some are pardoned as a reward for their submissive behavior.'

"When I had finished this account, I added that I saw no reason why this system could not be adopted, even in England, and with much greater advantage than the 'justice' which my legal antagonist had praised so highly. But the lawyer replied that such a system could never be adopted in England without putting the whole nation in serious peril. And so saying, he shook his head, made a wry face, and fell silent. All the company signified their agreement in his opinion.

"Then the Cardinal remarked, 'It is not easy to guess whether this scheme would work well or not, since nobody has yet tried it out. But perhaps when the death sentence has been passed on a thief, the king might reprieve him for a time without right of sanctuary,[8] and thus see how the plan worked. If it turned out well, then he might establish it by law; if not, he could execute immediate punishment on the man formerly condemned. This would be no more inconvenient or unjust than if the condemned man had been put to death before, yet the experiment would involve no risk. I think vagabonds too might be treated this way, for though we have passed many laws against them, they have had no real effect as yet.'

"When the Cardinal had concluded, they all began praising enthusiastically ideas which they had received with contempt when I suggested

---

8. In earlier days almost any criminal could take sanctuary in any church and be safe from the law. By More's time, this privilege had been much abridged, but it still applied here and there, and More was hostile to it as adding an element of lottery to the administration of justice.

them; and they particularly liked the idea about vagabonds because it was the Cardinal's addition.

"I don't know whether it is worthwhile telling what followed, because it was silly, but I'll tell it anyhow, for it's not a bad story and it bears on our subject. There was a hanger-on standing around, who was so good at playing the fool that you could hardly tell him from the real thing. He was constantly making jokes, but so awkwardly that we laughed more at him than at them; yet sometimes a rather clever thing came out, confirming the old proverb that a man who throws the dice often will sooner or later make a lucky cast.[9] One of the company happened to say, 'Well, Raphael has taken care of the thieves, and the Cardinal has taken care of the vagabonds, so now all we have to do is take care of the poor whom sickness or old age has kept from earning a living.'

" 'Leave that to me,' said the fool, 'and I'll set it right at once. These are people I'm eager to get out of my sight, having been so often vexed with them and their woeful complaints. No matter how pitifully they beg for money, they've never whined a single penny out of my pocket. Either I don't want to give them anything, or I haven't anything to give them—it's one of the two. Now they're getting wise; they know me so well, they don't waste their breath, but let me pass without a word or a hope—no more, by heaven, than if I were a priest. But I would make a law sending all these beggars to Benedictine monasteries,[1] where the men could become lay brothers, as they're called, and the women could be nuns.'

"The Cardinal smiled and passed it off as a joke; the rest took it seriously. But a certain friar, graduate in divinity, took such pleasure in this jest at the expense of secular priests and monks that he too began to make merry, though generally he was grave to the point of sourness. 'You will not get rid of the beggars,' he began, 'unless you take care of us friars[2] too.'

" 'You have been taken care of already,' retorted the fool. 'The Cardinal provided for you splendidly when he said vagabonds should be arrested and put to work, for you friars are the greatest vagabonds of all.'

"When the company, watching the Cardinal closely, saw that he admitted this jest like the other, they all took it up with vigor—except for the friar. He, as you can easily imagine, was stung by the vinegar,[3] and flew into such a rage that he could not keep from abusing the fool. He called him a knave, a slanderer, a ribald, and a 'son of perdition,'

9. Erasmus, *Adagia*, No. 113, perhaps. The parallel is not quite exact.

1. The Benedictine order was one of the largest, and also one of the strictest; a lay brother within it would get his full share of work, mostly menial, but would not be admitted even to minor orders. He would be working strictly for the love of God.

2. Specifically, a friar is a member of a mendicant (begging) order, as opposed to a monk who lives, and labors, in a cloister.

3. More's locution reminds the knowing reader of a phrase in Horace's *Satires* 1.7.32–33: *italo perfusus aceto*, "soaked in Italian vinegar."

quoting in the meanwhile terrible denunciations from Holy Writ. Now
the joker began to jest in earnest, for he was clearly on his own ground.

" 'Don't get angry, good friar,' he said, 'for it is written, "In your
patience, possess ye your souls." ' "[4]

"In reply, the friar said, and I quote his very words: 'I am not angry,
you gallows-bird, or at least I do not sin, for the psalmist says, "Be ye
angry, and sin not." ' "[5]

"At this point the Cardinal gently cautioned the friar to calm down,
but he answered: 'No, my lord, I speak only from great zeal, as I ought
to. For holy men have had great zeal. That is why Scripture says, "The
zeal of Thy house has eaten me up,"[6] and we sing in church, "those
who mocked Elisha for being bald, as he went up to the house of God,
felt the effects of his zeal."[7] Just so this mocker, this rascal, this ribald
fellow may very well feel it.'

" 'Perhaps you mean well,' said the Cardinal, 'but you would act in a
more holy, and certainly in a wiser way, if you didn't set your wit against
a fool's wit and try to spar with a professional jester.'

" 'No, my lord,' he replied, 'I would not act more wisely. For Solomon himself, the wisest of men, said, "Answer a fool according to his
folly,"[8] and that's what I'm doing now. I am showing him the pit into
which he will fall if he does not take care. For if the many mockers of
Elisha, who was only one bald man, felt the effects of his zeal, how
much more effect shall be felt by a single mocker of many friars, who
include a great many bald-heads! And besides, we have a papal bull, by
which all who mock us are excommunicated.'

"When the Cardinal saw there was no end to the matter, he nodded
to the fool to leave, and turned the conversation to another related subject. Soon after, he rose from table, and, going to hear petitioners, dismissed us.

"Look, my dear More, what a long story I have inflicted on you. I
would be quite ashamed, if you had not yourself asked for it, and seemed
to listen as if you did not want to miss any of it. Though I might have
shortened my account somewhat, I have told it in full, so you might see
how those who rejected what I said at first approved of it immediately
afterward, when they saw the Cardinal did not disapprove. In fact they
went so far in their flattery that they applauded in good earnest ideas that
he tolerated only as the jesting of a fool. From this episode you can see
how little courtiers would value me or my advice."

4. Luke 21.19.
5. Psalms 4.4.
6. Psalms 69.9.
7. Some children mocked Elisha, son of Eli-
jah the prophet, for his baldness; but he called
numerous bears out of the woods, and they ate
up the bad children: 2 Kings 2.23. There is a
hymn based on this cautionary tale, by Adam
of Saint Victor. In the course of his diatribe the
furious friar makes a mistake in his Latin syntax, which a marginal note (by Peter Giles or
Erasmus himself) points out; but it is too
recondite to be worth translating.
8. Proverbs 26.5. Compare also the previous
verse: "Answer not a fool according to his folly,
lest thou also be like unto him."

To this I answered, "You have given me great pleasure, my dear Raphael, for everything you've said has been both wise and witty. As you spoke, I seemed to be a child and in my own native land once more, through the pleasant recollection of that Cardinal in whose court I was brought up as a lad. Dear as you are to me on other accounts, you cannot imagine how much dearer you are because you honor his memory so highly. Still, I don't give up my former opinion: I think if you could overcome your aversion to court life, your advice to a prince would be of the greatest advantage to mankind. This, after all, is the chief duty of every good man, including you. Your friend Plato thinks that commonwealths will become happy only when philosophers become kings or kings become philosophers.[9] No wonder we are so far from happiness when philosophers do not condescend to assist even kings with their counsels."

"They are not so ill disposed," Raphael replied, "but that they would gladly do it; in fact, they have already done it in a great many published books, if the rulers would only read their good advice. But doubtless Plato was right in foreseeing that unless kings became philosophical themselves, they would never take the advice of real philosophers, drenched as they are and infected with false values from boyhood on. Plato certainly had this experience with Dionysius of Syracuse.[1] If I proposed wise laws to some king, and tried to root out of his soul the seeds of evil and corruption, don't you suppose I would be either banished forthwith, or treated with scorn?

"Imagine, if you will, that I am at the court of the king of France.[2] Suppose I were sitting in his royal council, meeting in secret session, with the king himself presiding, and all the cleverest counsellors were hard at work devising a set of crafty machinations by which the king might keep hold of Milan, recover Naples, which has proved so slippery; then overthrow the Venetians and subdue all Italy; next add Flanders, Brabant, and the whole of Burgundy to his realm, besides some other nations he had in mind to invade.[3] One man urges him to make an alliance with the Venetians for just as long as the king finds it convenient—perhaps to develop a common strategy with them, and even allow them some of the loot, which can be recovered later when things work

9. Plato, *Republic* 5.473.

1. Plato was imported into Syracuse to improve Dionysius the Younger, who had become tyrant by the death of his father in 367 B.C. The anticipated improvement did not come about, and Plato shortly left in disgust.

2. Either Charles VIII, who died in 1498; Louis XII, who died in 1515; or Francis I may have been in More's mind; they were all would-be imperialists who bogged down in the intricacies of Italian political intrigue.

3. The French house of Anjou had various dynastic claims to the rule of Milan and Naples, but after much maneuvering and warfare was driven out of both states by 1513. The enormous program of the French monarchy for unifying its own kingdom (including Brittany and Burgundy, parts of Flanders, but not ultimately Brabant) had preoccupied most French kings of the fifteenth century.

out according to plan. His neighbor recommends hiring German *Land-sknechte* and paying the Swiss to stay neutral.[4] A third voice suggests soothing the Emperor's wounded pride with a lavish and agreeable lotion of gold.[5] Still another, who is of a different mind, thinks a settlement should be made with the king of Aragon, and that, to cement the peace, he should be allowed to take Navarre from its proper ruler.[6] Finally someone suggests snaring the prince of Castille into a marriage alliance—a first step would be to buy up some nobles of his court with secret pensions.[7]

"The hardest problem of all is what to do about England. They all agree that the alliance, which is weak at best, should be strengthened as much as possible; but while the English are being treated as friends, they should also be suspected as enemies. And so the Scots must be kept in constant readiness, poised to attack the English in case they stir ever so little.[8] Also a banished nobleman with some pretensions to the English throne must be secretly encouraged (there are treaties against doing it openly), and in this way pressure can be brought to bear on the English king, and a ruler kept in check who can't really be trusted.

"Now in a meeting like this one, where so much is at stake, where so many brilliant men are competing to think up intricate strategies of war, what if an insignificant fellow like myself were to get up and advise going on another tack entirely? Suppose I said the king should leave Italy alone and stay at home,[9] because the single kingdom of France all by itself is almost too much for one man to govern, and the king should not dream of adding others to it. Then imagine I told about the decrees of the Achorians[1] who live off the island of Utopia toward the southeast. Long ago, these people went to war to gain another realm for their king, who

4. Many German mercenaries took service in Italy, either as individuals or in companies, during the incessant warfare that began in 1494; as foot soldiers, they were second in Europe only to the Swiss, whose talents were such that they frequently didn't have to fight to get paid: they collected for staying neutral.

5. Maximilian of Austria, Holy Roman Emperor, whom Machiavelli sketches sharply in Chap. 23 of *The Prince*, had grandiose schemes (he even dreamed of being Pope) but little money. He was always accessible to a bribe.

6. Machiavelli characterizes the tricky Ferdinand of Aragon in Chap. 21 of *The Prince*. Navarre was a small independent enclave astride the Pyrenees, long disputed between Spain and France. In 1512 Ferdinand took one piece of it from Jean III d'Albret; in 1598 Henri IV snapped up the remainder for France.

7. Already in his teens, Charles V was a great matrimonial and diplomatic catch. (Before he was twenty, he had been engaged ten different times.) The question of a French marriage that would unite the two greatest Continental and

Catholic powers was continually in the air throughout the century. On the use of international bribery as an everyday tactic of European "statecraft," see J. W. Thompson and S. K. Padover, *Secret Diplomacy* (New York, 1965), Chap. 4.

8. The Scots, as traditional enemies of England, were traditional allies of France. Though the pretender Richard de la Pole has been suggested, nobody is really sure of who the "banished nobleman" of the next sentence could be. But the point of the passage is the devious intricacy of the counsellors' thoughts; if there were no banished nobleman, they would find or invent one.

9. One of history's great unanswered problems is why three successive French kings (Charles VIII, Louis XII, and Francis I) felt they had to conquer Italy, when they had more trouble than they could manage simply in governing France properly.

1. The name arises from the Greek *a* ("without") and *chora* ("place"): people from nowhere.

had inherited an ancient claim to it through marriage. When they had conquered it, they soon saw that keeping it was going to be as hard as getting it had been. Their new subjects were continually rebelling or being attacked by foreign invaders, the Achorians had to be constantly at war for them or against them, and they saw no hope of ever being able to disband their army. In the meantime, they were being heavily taxed, money flowed out of their kingdom, their blood was being shed for the advantage of others, and peace was no closer than it ever was. The war corrupted their own citizens by encouraging lust for robbery and murder; and the laws fell into contempt because their king, distracted with the cares of two kingdoms, could give neither one his proper attention.

"When they saw that the list of these evils was endless, the Achorians took counsel together and very courteously offered their king his choice of keeping whichever of the two kingdoms he preferred, because he couldn't rule them both. They were too numerous a people, they said, to be ruled by half a king; and they added that a man would not even hire a muledriver, if he had to divide his services with somebody else. The worthy king was thus obliged to be content with his own realm and give his new one to a friend, who before long was driven out.

"Finally, suppose I told the French king's council that all this warmongering, by which so many different nations were kept in social turmoil as a result of one man's connivings, would certainly exhaust his treasury and demoralize his people, and yet very probably in the end come to nothing through some mishap or other. And therefore I would advise the French king to look after his ancestral kingdom, improve it as much as he could, cultivate it in every conceivable way. He should love his people and be loved by them; he should live among them, govern them kindly, and let other kingdoms alone, since his own is big enough, if not too big for him. How do you think, my dear More, the other counsellors would take this speech of mine?"

"Not very well, I'm sure," said I.

"Well, let's go on," he said. "Suppose the counsellors of some other king are discussing various schemes for raising money to fill his treasury. One man recommends increasing the value of money when the king pays his debts and devaluing it when he collects his revenues.[2] Thus he can discharge a huge debt with a small payment, and collect a large sum when only a small one is due him. Another suggests a make-believe war, so that money can be raised under pretext of carrying it on; then, when the money is in, he can conclude a ceremonious peace treaty—which simple-minded people will attribute to the piety of their prince and his

2. Edward IV, Henry VII, and (after *Utopia* was written) Henry VIII all fiddled with the English currency in ways like those suggested here.

careful compassion for the lives of his subjects.[3] Another counsellor calls to mind some old motheaten law, antiquated by long disuse, which no one remembers being made and consequently everyone has transgressed. By imposing fines for breaking these laws, the king will get great sums of money, as well as credit for upholding law and order since the whole procedure can be made to look like justice.[4] Another recommendation is that he forbid under particularly heavy fines a lot of practices that are contrary to the public interest; afterward, he can dispense with his own rules for large sums of money. Thus he pleases the people and makes a double profit, one from the heavy fines imposed on law-breakers, and the other from selling licenses. Meanwhile he seems careful of his people's welfare, since it is plain he will not allow private citizens to do anything contrary to the public interest except for a huge price.[5]

"Another counsellor proposes that he gain influence with the judges, so that they will decide every case in favor of the king. They should be summoned to court often, and invited to debate his affairs in the royal presence. However unjust his claims, one or another of the judges, whether from love of contradiction, or desire to seem original, or simply to serve his own interest, will be bound to find some way of twisting the law in the king's favor. If the judges can be brought to differ, then the clearest matter in the world will be obscured, and the truth itself brought into question. The king is given leverage to interpret the law as he will, and everyone else will acquiesce from shame or fear. The judges will have no hesitations about supporting the royal interest, for there are always plenty of pretexts for giving judgment in favor of the king. Either equity is on his side, or the letter of the law happens to make for him, or the words of the law can be twisted into obscurity—or, if all else fails, he can appeal above the law to the royal prerogative, which is a never-failing argument with judges who know their 'duty.'[6]

"Thus all the counsellors agree with the famous maxim of Crassus: a king who wants to maintain an army can never have too much gold.[7] Further, that a king, even if he wants to, can do no wrong, for all property belongs to the king, and so do his subjects themselves; a man owns nothing but what the king, in his goodness, sees fit to leave him. The

3. Something like this happened in 1492, when King Henry VII not only pretended war with France on behalf of Brittany and levied taxes for the war (which was hardly fought), but collected a bribe from Charles VIII for not fighting it.
4. This had been common practice under Henry VII, whose ministers Empson and Dudley scratched up a great many forgotten laws for strictly mercenary purposes.
5. For a Christian saint, More has a terrible practical insight into the ways of government hypocrisy, which we sometimes call, indulgently, public relations.

6. "Prerogative" was a catchall phrase, used in those days to justify verbally what couldn't be justified logically, much like "executive privilege" or "the national interest" in our own times.
7. Quoted by Cicero, De Officiis 1.8.25. Crassus was a rich Roman (his name means "fat") who joined with Pompey and Caesar to form the First Triumvirate. A vindictive Parthian is said to have disproved his maxim by pouring molten gold down his throat (Florus 3.11).

king should in fact leave his subjects as little as possible, because his own safety depends on keeping them from growing insolent with wealth and freedom. For riches and liberty make men less patient to endure harsh and unjust commands, whereas meager poverty blunts their spirits, makes them patient, and grinds out of the oppressed the lofty spirit of rebellion.

"Now at this point, suppose I were to get up again and declare that all these counsels are both dishonorable and ruinous to the king? Suppose I said his honor and his safety alike rest on the people's resources, rather than his own? Suppose I said that men choose a king for their own sake, not for his, so that by his efforts and troubles, they may live in comfort and safety?[8] This is why, I would say, it is the king's duty to take more care of his people's welfare than of his own, just as it is the duty of a shepherd who cares about his job to feed his sheep rather than himself.[9]

"They are absolutely wrong when they say that the people's poverty safeguards public peace—experience shows the contrary. Where will you find more squabbling than among beggars? Who is more eager for revolution than the man who is most discontented with his present position? Who is more reckless about creating disorders than the man who knows he has nothing to lose and thinks he may have something to gain? If a king is so hated or despised by his subjects that he can rule them only by mistreatment, plundering, confiscation, and pauperization of his people, then he'd do much better to abdicate his throne—for under these circumstances, though he keeps the name of authority, he loses all the majesty of a king. A king has no dignity when he exercises authority over beggars, only when he rules over prosperous and happy subjects. This was certainly what that noble and lofty spirit Fabricius meant when he said he would rather be a ruler of rich men than be rich himself.[1]

"A solitary ruler who enjoys a life of pleasure and self-indulgence while all about him are grieving and groaning is acting like a jailer, not a king. Just as an incompetent doctor can cure his patient of one disease only by throwing him into another, so it's an incompetent king who can rule his people only by depriving them of all life's pleasures. Such a king openly confesses that he does not know how to rule free men.

"A king of this stamp should correct his own sloth or arrogance, because these are the vices that cause people to hate or despise him. Let him live on his own income without wronging others, and limit his spending to his income. Let him curb crime, and by wise training of his subjects

---

8. Though phrased as the hypothetical speech of an imaginary person, this liberal doctrine was a deep element of More's constant thought. One of his little Latin poems contains a couplet that could be translated, "There's no way a ruler should rule longer than his subjects want him to." *Epigrams*, No. 103.
9. This metaphor is one of the great common-

places. Ezekiel 34.2 reads: "Woe be to the shepherds of Israel that do feed themselves: should not the shepherds feed the flocks?"
1. Gaius Fabricius Luscinus, who took part in the wars against Pyrrhus, King of Epirus (281–275 B.C.); the saying attributed to him here was actually coined by his colleague M. Curius Dentatus, but it is quite in his spirit.

keep them from misbehavior instead of letting it breed and then punishing it. Let him not suddenly revive antiquated laws, especially if they have been long forgotten and never missed. And let him never take money as a fine when a judge would regard an ordinary subject as a low fraud for claiming it.

"But suppose I should then describe for them the law of the Macarians,[2] a people who also live not far from Utopia? On the day that their king first assumes office, he must take an oath confirmed by solemn ceremonies that he will never have in his treasury at any one time more than a thousand pounds of gold, or its equivalent in silver. They say this law was made by an excellent king, who cared more for his country's prosperity than for his own wealth; he established it as a barrier against any king heaping up so much money as to impoverish his people.[3] He thought this sum would enable the king to put down rebellions or repel hostile invasions, but would not tempt him into aggressive adventures. His law was aimed chiefly at keeping the king in check, but he also wanted to ensure an ample supply of money for the daily business transactions of the citizens. Besides, a king who has to distribute all his excess money to the people will not be much disposed to oppress them. Such a king will be both a terror to evil-doers and beloved by the good.— Summing up the whole thing, don't you suppose if I set ideas like these before men strongly inclined to the contrary, they would turn deaf ears to me?"

"Stone deaf, indeed, there's no doubt about it," I said, "and no wonder! To tell you the truth, I don't think you should offer advice or thrust on people ideas of this sort that you know will not be listened to. What good will it do? When your listeners are already prepossessed against you and firmly convinced of opposite opinions, what good can you do with your rhapsody of new-fangled ideas? This academic philosophy is quite agreeable in the private conversation of close friends, but in the councils of kings, where grave matters are being authoritatively decided, there is no place for it."

"That is just what I was saying," Raphael replied. "There is no place for philosophy in the councils of kings."

"Yes, there is," I said, "but not for this scholastic philosophy which supposes that every topic is suitable for every occasion. There is another philosophy that is better suited for political action, that takes its cue, adapts itself to the drama in hand, and acts its part neatly and well. This is the philosophy for you to use. When a comedy of Plautus is being played, and the household slaves are cracking trivial jokes together, you

2. From the Greek *makarios*, "happy," "fortunate."
3. Once again More glances at the previous monarch, Henry VII, who died the richest prince in Christendom and probably the most hated. He combined unscrupulous greed with skinflint stinginess.

propose to come on stage in the garb of a philosopher, and repeat Seneca's speech to Nero from the *Octavia*.[4] Wouldn't it be better to take a silent role than to say something wholly inappropriate, and thus turn the play into a tragicomedy? You pervert and ruin a play when you add irrelevant speeches, even if they are better than the original. So go through with the drama in hand as best you can, and don't spoil it all simply because you happen to think another one would be better.

"That's how things go in the commonwealth, and in the councils of princes. If you cannot pluck up bad ideas by the root, if you cannot cure long-standing evils as completely as you would like, you must not therefore abandon the commonwealth. Don't give up the ship in a storm because you cannot direct the winds. And don't arrogantly force strange ideas on people who you know have set their minds on a different course from yours. You must strive to influence policy indirectly, handle the situation tactfully, and thus what you cannot turn to good, you may at least—to the extent of your powers—make less bad. For it is impossible to make all institutions good unless you make all men good, and that I don't expect to see for a long time to come."

"The only result of this," he answered, "will be that while I try to cure others of madness, I'll be raving along with them myself. If I am to speak the truth, I will simply have to talk in the way I have described. For all I know, it may be the business of a philosopher to recite lies, but it isn't mine. Though my advice may be repugnant to the king's counsellors, I don't see why they should consider it eccentric to the point of folly. What if I told them the kind of thing that Plato advocates in his *Republic*, or which the Utopians actually practice in theirs? However superior those institutions might be (and as a matter of fact they are), yet here they would seem inappropriate because private property is the rule here, and there all things are held in common.

"People who have made up their minds to rush headlong down the opposite road are never pleased with the man who calls them back and tells them they are on the wrong course. But, apart from that, what did I say that could not and should not be said anywhere and everywhere? If we dismiss as out of the question and absurd everything which the

---

4. Most of the plays of Plautus involve low intrigue: needy young men, expensive prostitutes, senile moneybags, and clever slaves, in predictable combinations. *Octavia*, a tragedy like those of Seneca, involving Seneca as a personage, but not by Seneca (though long supposed to be so), is full of high seriousness. In a letter written by Pico to Andrew Corneus and dated 15 October 1492 (More included it with his translation of a tiny *Life of Pico della Mirandola*, published 1510) there occurs this answer to a suggestion that Pico take service with a prince: "but I see well that as yet you have not known that opinion that philosophers have of

themselves, who (as Horace says) repute themselves kings of kings: they love liberty: they cannot bear the proud manners of estate [nobility]: they cannot serve. They dwell with themselves and are content with the tranquillity of their own minds; they suffice themselves and more; they seek nothing outside of themselves" (English much modernized by the editor of this volume).

There is a Latin idiom, "scenae servire," which means to go through with the demands of a public performance: Cicero, *Ad Brutum*, 1.9.2. It may have suggested More's metaphor.

perverse customs of men have made to seem unusual, we shall have to set aside most of the commandments of Christ even in a community of Christians. Yet he forbade us to dissemble them, and even ordered that what he had whispered to his disciples should be preached openly from the housetops.[5] Most of his teachings differ more radically from the common customs of mankind than my discourse did. But preachers, like the crafty fellows they are, have found that men would rather not change their lives to conform to Christ's rule, and so, just as you suggest, they have accommodated his teaching to the way men live, as if it were a leaden yardstick.[6] At least in that way they can get the two things to correspond on one level or another. The only real thing they accomplish that I can see is to make men feel a little more secure in their consciences about doing evil.

"And this is all that I could accomplish in a prince's court. For either I would have different ideas from the others, and that would come to the same thing as having no ideas at all, or else I would agree with them, and that, as Mitio says in Terence, would merely confirm them in their madness.[7] When you say I should 'influence policy indirectly,' I simply don't know what you mean; remember, you said I should try hard to handle the situation tactfully, and what can't be made good I should try to make as little bad as possible. In a council, there is no way to dissemble, no way to shut your eyes to things. You must openly approve the worst proposals, and consent to the most vicious decisions. A man who went along only halfheartedly even with the worst decisions would immediately get himself a name as a spy and perhaps a traitor. How can one individual do any good when he is surrounded by colleagues who would sooner corrupt the best of men than do any reforming of themselves? Either they will seduce you, or, if you keep yourself honest and innocent, you will be made a screen for the knavery and madness of others. Influencing policy indirectly! You wouldn't have a chance.

"This is why Plato in a very fine comparison declares that wise men are right in keeping clear of government matters.[8] They see the people swarming through the streets and getting soaked with rain, and they cannot persuade them to go indoors and get out of the wet. They know if they go out themselves, they can do no good but only get drenched with the rest. So they stay indoors and are content to keep themselves dry, since they cannot remedy the folly of everyone else.

---

5. A reminiscence of Luke 12.3: "that which ye have spoken in the ear in closets shall be proclaimed upon the housetops." *Cf.* also Matthew 10.27, to the same effect.
6. A flexible yardstick made of lead was particularly useful in the sort of ancient building style, known as the "Lesbian" mode, because of the great number of curved mouldings. Aristotle in *Ethics* 5.10.7 uses it as a metaphor for adaptable moral standards.

7. The slave Mitio, speaking of his master, says: "If I provoke or even listen to his madness, I shall be as crazy as he is" (*Adelphi* 1.2.66–67).
8. Plato *Republic* 6.496. This attitude that the wise man should avoid not only politics but public service and even marriage was characteristic of many early humanists. Hans Baron traces in *The Crisis of the Early Italian Renaissance* (Princeton, 1966) the process by which "civic humanism" took its place.

"But as a matter of fact, my dear More, to tell you what I really think, as long as you have private property, and as long as cash money is the measure of all things, it is really not possible for a nation to be governed justly or happily. For justice cannot exist where all the best things in life are held by the worst citizens; nor can anyone be happy where property is limited to a few, since those few are always uneasy and the many are utterly wretched.

"So I reflect on the wonderfully wise and sacred institutions of the Utopians who are so well governed with so few laws. Among them virtue has its reward, yet everything is shared equally, and all men live in plenty. I contrast them with the many other nations which are constantly passing new ordinances and yet can never order their affairs satisfactorily. In these other nations, whatever a man can get he calls his own private property; but all the mass of laws old and new don't enable him to secure his own, or defend it, or even distinguish it from someone else's property. Different men lay claim, successively or all at once, to the same property; and thus arise innumerable and interminable lawsuits—fresh ones every day. When I consider all these things, I become more sympathetic to Plato and do not wonder that he declined to make laws for any people who refused to share their goods equally.[9] Wisest of men, he easily perceived that the one and only road to the welfare of all lies through the absolute equality of goods. I doubt whether such equality can ever be achieved where property belongs to individual men. However abundant goods may be, when every man tries to get as much as he can for his own exclusive use, a handful of men end up sharing the whole thing, and the rest are left in poverty. The result generally is two sorts of people whose fortunes ought to be interchanged: the rich are rapacious, wicked, and useless, while the poor are unassuming, modest men who work hard, more for the benefit of the public than of themselves.

"Thus I am wholly convinced that unless private property is entirely done away with, there can be no fair or just distribution of goods, nor can mankind be happily governed. As long as private property remains, by far the largest and the best part of mankind will be oppressed by a heavy and inescapable burden of cares and anxieties. This load, I admit, may be lightened a little bit under the present system, but I maintain it cannot be entirely removed. Laws might be made that no one should own more than a certain amount of land or receive more than a certain income.[1] Or laws might be passed to prevent the prince from becoming

---

9. The Arcadians and Thebans united to build a great city, we are told, and asked Plato to be its legislator. He made communism a condition of his going there, and when the inhabitants would not consent, declined the offer. Diogenes Laertius, *The Lives of the Eminent Philosophers* 3.17.

1. From time to time Rome, and many Italian city-states, had passed sumptuary laws regulating finery in dress, number of servants, and quantity of display; agrarian laws limiting land ownership were also often attempted.

too powerful and the populace too unruly. It might be made unlawful for public offices to be solicited, or put up for sale, or made burdensome for the officeholder by great expense. Otherwise, officeholders are tempted to get their money back by fraud or extortion, and only rich men can afford to seek positions which ought to be held by wise men. Laws of this sort, I agree, may have as much effect as good and careful nursing has on men who are chronically or even incurably sick.[2] The social evils I mentioned may be alleviated and their effects mitigated for a while, but so long as private property remains, there is no hope at all of effecting a cure and restoring society to good health. While you try to cure one part, you aggravate the disease in other parts. Suppressing one symptom causes another to break out, since you cannot give something to one man without taking it away from someone else."

"But I don't see it that way," I replied. "It seems to me that men cannot possibly live well where all things are in common.[3] How can there be plenty of commodities where every man stops working? The hope of gain will not spur him on; he will rely on others, and become lazy. If a man is driven by want of something to produce it, and yet cannot legally protect what he has gained, what can follow but continual bloodshed and turmoil, especially when respect for magistrates and their authority has been lost? I for one cannot conceive of authority existing among men who are equal to one another in every respect."

"I'm not surprised," said Raphael, "that you think of it in this way, since you have no idea, or only a false idea, of such a state. But you should have been with me in Utopia, and seen with your own eyes their manners and customs as I did—for I lived there more than five years, and would never have left, if it had not been to make that new world known to others. If you had seen them, you would frankly confess that you had never seen a people so well governed as they are."

"You will have a hard time persuading me," said Peter Giles, "that people in that new land are better governed than in the world we know. Our minds are not inferior to theirs, and our governments, I believe, are older. Long experience has helped us develop many conveniences of life, and by good luck we have discovered many other things which human ingenuity could never hit on."

"As for the relative ages of the governments," Raphael replied, "you might judge more accurately if you had read their histories. If we believe these records, they had cities before there were even human inhabitants here. What ingenuity has discovered or chance hit upon could have turned up just as well in one place as the other. As a matter of fact, I

2 A problem with social reform throughout the ages is that the patient tends to dictate to the doctor what his diagnosis shall be.

3. These preliminary objections are chiefly founded on those of the hard-headed Aristotle,

Politics 2.1–3. Most of them reduce to the prediction (painfully verified in several "egalitarian" societies of our own day) that if you are to make the donkey go without carrots, you will have to hit him often and hard with a stick.

believe we surpass them in natural intelligence, but they leave us far behind in their diligence and zeal to learn.[4]

"According to their chronicles, they had heard nothing of men-from-beyond-the-equator (that's their name for us) until we arrived, except that once, some twelve hundred years ago, a ship which a storm had blown toward Utopia was wrecked on their island.[5] Some Romans and Egyptians were cast ashore, and never departed. Now note how the Utopians profited, through their diligence, from this one chance event. They learned every single useful art of the Roman civilization either directly from their guests, or indirectly from hints and surmises on which they based their own investigations. What benefits from the mere fact that on a single occasion some Europeans landed there! If a similar accident has hitherto brought any men here from their land, the incident has been completely forgotten, as it will be forgotten in time to come that I was ever in their country. From one such accident they made themselves masters of all our useful inventions, but I suspect it will be a long time before we accept any of their institutions which are better than ours. This willingness to learn, I think, is the really important reason for their being better governed and living more happily than we do, though we are not inferior to them in brains or resources."

"Then let me implore you, my dear Raphael," said I, "to describe that island to us. Do not try to be brief, but explain in order everything relating to their land, their rivers, towns, people, manners, institutions, laws—everything, in short, that you think we would like to know. And you can take it for granted that we want to know everything that we don't know yet."

"There's nothing I'd rather do," he replied, "for these things are fresh in my mind. But it will take quite some time."

"In that case," I said, "let's first go to lunch. Afterward, we shall have all the time we want."

"Agreed," he said. So we went in and had lunch. Then we came back to the same spot, and sat down on the bench. I ordered my servants to take care that no one should interrupt us. Peter Giles and I urged Raphael to keep his promise. When he saw that we were eager to hear him, he sat silent and thoughtful a moment, and then began as follows:

The End of Book One

*   *   *   *   *

4. Precisely the opposite judgment was reached by early English explorers among the Indians of Virginia. In native ingenuity, they said, the Indians were often superior, but the larger difference lay in European technology. See Thomas Hariot's *Brief and true report of . . . Virginia*, included in Hakluyt's *Principal Navigations*, 1600.
5. In A.D. 315 (about 1200 years before *Uto-* pia was written), Europeans would have had little to teach the Utopians in the way of technology or social organization; and, as appears later, these early arrivals knew nothing of Christianity. More is trying to indicate that the two cultures started about even, on the path of their development, with the Roman and Egyptian rudiments.

BOOK TWO

The Geography of Utopia

The island of the Utopians is two hundred miles across in the middle part where it is widest, and is nowhere much narrower than this except toward the two ends. These ends, drawn toward one another as if in a five-hundred-mile circle, make the island crescent-shaped like a new moon.[6] Between the horns of the crescent, which are about eleven miles apart, the sea enters and spreads into a broad bay. Being sheltered from the wind by the surrounding land, the bay is never rough, but quiet and smooth instead, like a big lake. Thus, nearly the whole inner coast is one great harbor, across which ships pass in every direction, to the great advantage of the people. What with shallows on one side, and rocks on the other, the entrance into the bay is very dangerous. Near the middle of the channel, there is one rock that rises above the water, and so presents no dangers in itself; on top of it a tower has been built, and there a garrison is kept. Since the other rocks lie under water, they are very dangerous to navigation. The channels are known only to the Utopians, so hardly any strangers enter the bay without one of their pilots; and even they themselves could not enter safely if they did not direct themselves by some landmarks on the coast. If they should shift these landmarks about, they could lure to destruction an enemy fleet coming against them, however big it was.

On the outer side of the island there are likewise occasional harbors; but the coast is rugged by nature, and so well fortified that a few defenders could beat off the attack of a strong force. They say (and the appearance of the place confirms this) that their land was not always an island. But Utopus, who conquered the country and gave it his name (it had previously been called Abraxa),[7] brought its rude and uncouth inhabitants to such a high level of culture and humanity that they now excel in that regard almost every other people. After subduing them at his first landing, he cut a channel fifteen miles wide where their land joined the continent, and caused the sea to flow around the country.[8] He put not only the natives to work at this task, but all his own soldiers too, so that the vanquished would not think the labor a disgrace. With the work

---

6. The island is about the size of England; it is the shape of an atoll or (for the Freudian-minded) of a womb. See the woodcut "map" or drawing, from the edition of 1518, p. 2.

7. The name "Abraxa" connotes mystical antiquity; it was engraved on various stones by the followers of Basilides the Gnostic (second century A.D.), and nobody knows precisely what it means. For what it's worth, the Greek letters

making it up have numerical equivalents that add up to 365.

8. There is a story that Xerxes did something like this at Mt. Athos—not, however, to make an island, but to get his ships across an isthmus; see Herodotus, 7.22–24. The parallel might be insignificant, but More does emphasize later the connections between the Utopians and the Persians, see below, pp. 57, 72, fn. 8.

divided among so many hands, the project was finished quickly, and the neighboring peoples, who at first had laughed at his folly, were struck with wonder and terror at his success.

There are fifty-four cities on the island, all spacious and magnificent, identical in language, customs, institutions, and laws. So far as the location permits, all of them are built on the same plan, and have the same appearance. The nearest are at least twenty-four miles apart, and the farthest are not so remote that a man cannot go on foot from one to the other in a day.[9]

Once a year each city sends three of its old and experienced citizens to Amaurot[1] to consider affairs of common interest to the island. Amaurot is the chief city, lies near the omphalos[2] of the land, so to speak, and convenient to every other district, so it acts as a capital. Every city has enough ground assigned to it so that at least twelve miles of farm land are available in every direction, though where the cities are farther apart, they have much more land. No city wants to enlarge its boundaries, for the inhabitants consider themselves good tenants rather than landlords. At proper intervals all over the countryside they have built houses and furnished them with farm equipment. These houses are inhabited by citizens who come to the country by turns to occupy them. No rural house has fewer than forty men and women in it, besides two slaves. A master and mistress, serious and mature persons, are in charge of each household. Over every thirty households is placed a single phylarch.[3] Each year twenty persons from each rural household move back to the city, after completing a two-year stint in the country. In their place, twenty others are sent out from town, to learn farm work from those who have already been in the country for a year, and who are better skilled in farming. They, in turn, will teach those who come the following year.[4] If all were equally unskilled in farm work, and new to it, they might harm the crops out of ignorance. This custom of alternating farm workers is solemnly established so that no one will have to do such hard work against his will for more than two years; but many of them who take a natural pleasure in farm life ask to stay longer.

The farm workers till the soil, raise cattle, hew wood, and take it to the city by land or water, as is most convenient. They breed an enor-

9. A conscious absurdity, no doubt—since only an exceptional athlete, walking as fast as he can, will cover much more than twenty-four miles from dawn to dusk. Maxima and minima are about the same.
1. From the Greek, implying "dark city." It is probably only a coincidence that a major medieval heretic, whose teachings were responsible for several communist sects of the Free Spirit among the cloth traders of Flanders, was Amaury of Bène (died 1206 or 1207), whose followers were called "Amaurians."

2. Navel, umbilicus; an ancient word for the spiritual as well as the physical center of a nation.
3. From the Greek, meaning head (arché) of a tribe (phylon).
4. We learn later that everyone studies agriculture in school and gets practical experience of it on field trips; in addition, a man who spent half his adult life on the farm would, by the age of forty, have had at least ten and probably fifteen years of experience.

mous number of chickens by a marvelous method. Men, not hens, hatch the eggs by keeping them in a warm place at an even temperature. As soon as they come out of the shell, the chicks recognize the men, follow them around, and are devoted to them instead of to their real mothers.

They raise very few horses, and these full of mettle, which they keep only to exercise the young men in the art of horsemanship.[5] For the heavy work of plowing and hauling they use oxen, which they agree are inferior to horses over the short haul, but which can hold out longer under heavy burdens, are less subject to disease (as they suppose), and so can be kept with less cost and trouble. Moreover, when oxen are too old for work, they can be used for meat.

Grain they use only to make bread. They drink wine, apple or pear cider, or simple water, which they sometimes mix with honey or licorice, of which they have an abundance.[6] Although they know very well, down to the last detail, how much grain each city and its surrounding district will consume, they produce much more grain and cattle than they need for themselves, and share the surplus with their neighbors. Whatever goods the folk in the country need which cannot be produced there, they request of the town magistrates, and since there is nothing to be paid or exchanged, they get what they want at once, without any haggling. They generally go to town once a month in any case, to observe the holy days. When harvest time approaches, the phylarchs in the country notify the town-magistrates how many hands will be needed. Crews of harvesters come just when they're wanted, and in one day of good weather they can usually get in the whole crop.

Their Cities, Especially Amaurot

If you know one of their cities, you know them all, for they're exactly alike, except where geography itself makes a difference. So I'll describe one of them, and no matter which. But what one rather than Amaurot the most worthy of all?—since its eminence is acknowledged by the other cities which send representatives to the annual meeting there; besides which, I know it best because I lived there for five full years.

Well, then, Amaurot lies up against a gently sloping hill; the town is almost square in shape. From a little below the crest of the hill, it runs down about two miles to the river Anyder,[7] and then spreads out along

---

5. Horses did not exist in the New World till Europeans imported them. More is not meticulous about such details.

6. Beer and ale are rather strikingly omitted from the list of Utopian drinks. Perhaps More considered them an undue temptation, as being easier to make than wine and more agreeable to the taste of the English workingman. Utopia's drinking habits are more middle class than

a plowman accustomed to beer would consider Utopian.

7. From the Greek, meaning "waterless." Many of the details of Amaurot (its situation on a tidal river, its stone bridge, though not the location of that bridge) are reminiscent of London. Even the second little stream, which provides Amaurot's water-supply, suggests the brook known as the Fleet.

the river bank for a somewhat greater distance. The Anyder rises from a small spring about eighty miles above Amaurot, but other streams flow into it, two of them being pretty big, so that, as it runs past Amaurot, the river has grown to a width of half a mile. It continues to grow even larger until at last, sixty miles farther along, it is lost in the ocean. In all this stretch between the sea and the city, and also for some miles above the city, the river is tidal, ebbing and flowing every six hours with a swift current. When the tide comes in, it fills the whole Anyder with salt water for about thirty miles, driving the fresh water back. Even above that for several miles farther, the water is brackish; but a little higher up, as it runs past the city, the water is always fresh, and when the tide ebbs, the water runs clean and sweet all the way to the sea.

The two banks of the river at Amaurot are linked by a bridge, built not on wooden piles but on many solid arches of stone. It is placed at the upper end of the city, farthest removed from the sea, so that ships can sail along the entire length of the city quays without obstruction. There is also another stream, not particularly large, but very gentle and pleasant, which rises out of the hill, flows down through the center of town, and into the Anyder. The inhabitants have walled around the source of this river, which takes its rise a little outside the town, and joined it to the town proper so that if they should be attacked, the enemy would not be able to cut off the stream or divert or poison it. Water from the stream is carried by tile piping into various sections of the lower town. Where the terrain makes this impractical, they collect rain water in cisterns, which serve just as well.

The town is surrounded by a thick, high wall, with many towers and bastions. On three sides it is also surrounded by a dry ditch, broad and deep and filled with thorn hedges; on its fourth side the river itself serves as a moat. The streets are conveniently laid out for use by vehicles and for protection from the wind. Their buildings are by no means paltry; the unbroken rows of houses facing each other across the streets through the different wards make a fine sight. The streets are twenty feet wide.[8] Behind each row of houses at the center of every block and extending the full length of the street, there are large gardens.

Every house has a door to the street and another to the garden. The doors, which are made with two leaves, open easily and swing shut automatically, letting anyone enter who wants to—and so there is no private property. Every ten years, they change houses by lot.[9] The Utopians are

---

8. For a city on an island with no tradition of civil strife and no record of foreign invasion, Amaurot is heavily fortified—as were almost all the towns of which More had personal knowledge. The twenty feet that he assigns as the width of streets seem to us absurdly inadequate; but for a medieval town they were lavish.

9. Redistributing housing by lottery every decade seems likely to create as many problems as it solves, especially when combined with the shorter cycle of two years in the city and two years in the country. An average stay in any particular house of just five years must make for a nomadic existence at best. The purpose is, of course, to keep people from getting attached to things. For a striking similarity of custom, founded on a wholly different reason, see Vespucci's account of the American aborigines he saw, below, p. 104.

very fond of these gardens of theirs. They raise vines, fruits, herbs, and flowers, so thrifty and flourishing that I have never seen any gardens more productive or elegant than theirs. They keep interested in gardening, partly because they delight in it, and also because of the competition between different streets which challenge one another to produce the best gardens.[1] Certainly you will find nothing else in the whole city more useful or more pleasant to the citizens. And this gives reason to think that the founder of the city paid particular attention to the siting of these gardens.

They say that in the beginning the whole city was planned by King Utopus himself, but that he left to posterity matters of adornment and improvement, such as could not be perfected in one man's lifetime. Their records begin 1,760 years ago with the conquest of the island, and are carefully preserved in writing. From these records it appears that the first houses were low, like cabins or peasant huts, built out of any sort of timber, with mud-plastered walls and steep roofs, ridged and thatched with straw. But now their houses are all three stories high and handsomely constructed; the fronts are faced with stone, stucco, or brick, over rubble construction. The roofs are flat, and are covered with a kind of plaster that is cheap but fireproof, and more weather-resistant even than lead. Glass is very generally used in windows to keep out the weather;[2] and they also use thin linen cloth treated with oil or gum so that it lets in more light and keeps out more wind.

Once a year, every group of thirty households elects an official, formerly called the syphogrant,[3] but now called the phylarch. Over every group of ten syphogrants with their households there is another official, once called the tranibor but now known as the head phylarch. All the syphogrants, two hundred in number, are brought together to elect the prince. They take an oath to choose the man they think best qualified; and then by secret ballot they elect the prince from among four men nominated by the people of the four sections of the city. The prince holds office for life, unless he is suspected of aiming at a tyranny.[4] Though the tranibors are elected annually, they are not changed for light or casual reasons. All their other officials hold office for a single year only.

The tranibors meet to consult with the prince every other day, and more often if necessary: they discuss affairs of state, and settle the occasional disputes between private parties (if there are any and they are in any case very few), acting as quickly as possible. The tranibors always

---

1. How one can have competition between gardeners when anyone is free at any time to pick any fruits or flowers he wants is a practical problem into which More does not enter.
2. During More's day in England window glass was not common; oiled cloth was more frequent.
3. Neither *syphogrant* nor *tranibor* has any distinct meaning or etymological insinuation,

nor is there any explanation of why Hythloday consistently uses what he describes as the "older" form of the title.
4. Since the prince normally holds office for life, and his relation to the tranibors is strangely undefined (they meet together regularly, but whether or when he must follow their advice is never stated), it's not clear what "aiming at a tyranny" would involve.

invite two syphogrants to the senate chamber, different ones every day. There is a rule that no decision can be made on a matter of public business unless it has been discussed in the senate on three separate days. It is a capital offense to consult together on public business outside of the senate or the popular assembly.[5] The purpose of these rules, they say, is to prevent the prince and the tranibors from conspiring together to alter the government and enslave the people. Therefore all matters which are considered important are first laid before the popular assembly of the syphogrants. They talk the matter over with the households they represent, debate it with one another, then report their recommendation to the senate. Sometimes the question is brought before the general council of the whole island.

The senate has a standing rule never to discuss a matter on the same day when it was first introduced; all new business is deferred to the next meeting. They do this so that a man will not blurt out the first thought that occurs to him, and then devote all his energies to defending those foolish impulses, instead of considering impartially the public good. They know that some men would rather jeopardize the welfare of the state than admit to having been heedless and shortsighted—so perverse and preposterous is their sense of pride. They should have had enough foresight at the beginning to speak with prudence rather than haste.

Their Work-Habits

Agriculture is the one occupation at which everyone works, men and women alike, with no exceptions. They are trained in it from childhood, partly in the schools where they learn theory, and partly through field trips to nearby farms, which make something like a game of practical instruction. On these trips they not only watch the work being done, but frequently pitch in and get a workout by doing the jobs themselves.

Besides farm work (which, as I said, everybody performs), each person is taught a particular trade of his own, such as wool-working, linen-making, masonry, metal-work, or carpentry. There is no other craft that is practiced by any considerable number of them.[6] Throughout the island people wear, and down through the centuries they have always worn, ℘ the same style of clothing, except for the distinction between the sexes,

5. The crucial term here is "consult together" (*inire consilia*); it could mean "hold an informal discussion," or "organize a subversive plot," or anything in between. More does not indicate what he has in mind. The next sentence suggests that the prince and the tranibors are the prime suspects. But why such a fierce law, limiting the liberties of all, to prevent a conspiracy by a mere handful of officials?

6. Among the objects in Utopia that nobody seems to make are glassware, ceramics, books, statuary, horseshoes and harness, wheels, candles, armor, arrows, ships, and musical as well as astronomical instruments. Among the "unexplained" professions, which people practice but for which they are never trained, are sailors, judges, doctors, nurses, teachers, miners, musicians, plumbers, bakers, and stewards.

and between married and unmarried persons. Their clothing is attractive, does not hamper bodily movement, and serves for warm as well as cold weather; what is more, each household can make its own.

Every person (and this includes women as well as men) learns a second trade, besides agriculture. As the weaker sex, women practice the lighter crafts, such as working in wool or linen; the heavier jobs are assigned to the men. As a rule, the son is trained to his father's craft, for which most feel a natural inclination. But if anyone is attracted to another occupation, he is transferred by adoption into a family practicing the trade he prefers. When anyone makes such a change, both his father and the authorities make sure that he is assigned to a grave and responsible householder. After a man has learned one trade, if he wants to learn another, he gets the same permission. When he has learned both, he pursues whichever he likes better, unless the city needs one more than the other.

The chief and almost the only business of the syphogrants is to manage matters so that no one sits around in idleness, and assure that everyone works hard at his trade. But no one has to exhaust himself with endless toil from early morning to late at night, as if he were a beast of burden. Such wretchedness, really worse than slavery, is the common lot of workmen in all countries, except Utopia. Of the day's twenty-four hours, the Utopians devote only six to work. They work three hours before noon, when they go to lunch. After lunch they rest for a couple of hours, then go to work for another three hours. Then they have supper, and at eight o'clock (counting the first hour after noon as one), they go to bed and sleep eight hours.[7]

The other hours of the day, when they are not working, eating, or sleeping, are left to each man's individual discretion, provided he does not waste them in roistering or sloth, but uses them busily in some occupation that pleases him. Generally these periods are devoted to intellectual activity. For they have an established custom of giving public lectures before daybreak;[8] attendance at these lectures is required only of those who have been specially chosen to devote themselves to learning, but a great many other people, both men and women, choose voluntarily to attend. Depending on their interests, some go to one lecture, some to another. But if anyone would rather devote his spare time to his trade, as many do who don't care for the intellectual life, this is not discouraged; in fact, such persons are commended as especially useful to the commonwealth.

---

7. Another way of calculating is that if the Utopians work six hours a day and sleep eight, they have ten hours a day free for eating and leisure. But More has done something to mitigate the dangers of this leisure by allocating most of it to the early morning hours. If they go to bed at eight, as he says, and sleep eight hours, the Utopians will rise at four A.M. Work does not start till nine. There may be problems with this timetable, but boredom is only one of them.

8. Renaissance universities got under way at inhumanly early hours; first lecture was between five and seven A.M.

After supper, they devote an hour to recreation, in their gardens when the weather is fine, or during winter weather in the common halls where they have their meals. There they either play music or amuse themselves with conversation. They know nothing about gambling with dice, or other such foolish and ruinous games. They do play two games not unlike our own chess. One is a battle of numbers, in which one number captures another. The other is a game in which the vices fight a battle against the virtues. The game is set up to show how the vices oppose one another, yet readily combine against the virtues; then, what vices oppose what virtues, how they try to assault them openly or undermine them insidiously; how the virtues can break the strength of the vices or turn their purposes to good; and finally, by what means one side or the other gains the victory.[9]

But in all this, you may get a wrong impression, if we don't go back and consider one point more carefully. Because they allot only six hours to work, you might think the necessities of life would be in scant supply. This is far from the case. Their working hours are ample to provide not only enough but more than enough of the necessities and even the conveniences of life. You will easily appreciate this if you consider how large a part of the population in other countries exists without doing any work at all. In the first place, hardly any of the women, who are a full half of the population, work;[1] or, if they do, then as a rule their husbands lie snoring in bed. Then there is a great lazy gang of priests and so-called religious men. Add to them all the rich, especially the landlords, who are commonly called gentlemen and nobility. Include with them their retainers, that mob of swaggering bullies. Finally, reckon in with these the sturdy and lusty beggars, who go about feigning some disease as an excuse for their idleness. You will certainly find that the things which satisfy our needs are produced by far fewer hands than you had supposed.

And now consider how few of those who do work are doing really essential things. For where money is the standard of everything, many vain, superfluous trades are bound to be carried on simply to satisfy luxury and licentiousness. Suppose the multitude of those who now work were limited to a few trades, and set to producing just those conveniences and commodities that nature really requires. They would be bound to produce so much that the prices would drop, and the workmen would be unable to gain a living. But suppose again that all the workers

9. Moral games of this general character were popular with Renaissance educators. Jacques Lefèvre d'Etaples invented one of the first sort, and Sir Thomas Elyot (in *The Governor*) mentions one of the second sort. But he may have picked up the idea for it from this passage.

1. More is rather less than generous to women, who, in addition to selecting, preparing, and cooking the family food, doing the family laundry, making the family clothes, cleaning the house, and doing a thousand other routine tasks of domestic drudgery, were responsible for taking care of the children. This seems to be the contemplated routine, both in More's England and in Utopia (where, in addition, the women are blessed with a full-time trade); if it doesn't constitute "work," that word must have a very special meaning.

in useless trades were put to useful ones, and that all the idlers (who now guzzle twice as much as the workingmen who make what they consume) were assigned to productive tasks—well, you can easily see how little time each man would have to spend working, in order to produce all the goods that human needs and conveniences require—yes, and human pleasure too, as long as it's true and natural pleasure.

The experience of Utopia makes this perfectly apparent. In each city and its surrounding countryside barely five hundred of those men and women whose age and strength make them fit for work are exempted from it.[2] Among these are the syphogrants, who by law are free not to work; yet they don't take advantage of the privilege, preferring to set a good example to their fellow-citizens. Some others are permanently exempted from work so that they may devote themselves to study, but only on the recommendation of the priests and through a secret vote of the syphogrants. If any of these scholars disappoints their hopes, he becomes a workman again. On the other hand, it happens from time to time that a craftsman devotes his leisure so earnestly to study, and makes such progress as a result, that he is relieved of manual labor, and promoted to the class of learned men. From this class of scholars are chosen ambassadors, priests, tranibors, and the prince himself,[3] who used to be called Barzanes, but in their modern tongue is known as Ademus.[4] Since all the rest of the population is neither idle nor occupied in useless trades, it is easy to see why they produce so much in so short a working day.

Apart from all this, in several of the necessary crafts their way of life requires less total labor than does that of people elsewhere. In other countries, building and repairing houses requires the constant work of many men, because what a father has built, his thriftless heir lets fall into ruin; and then his successor has to repair, at great expense, what could easily have been maintained at a very small charge. Further, even when a man has built a splendid house at vast cost, someone else may think he has finer taste, let the first house fall to ruin, and then build another one somewhere else for just as much money. But among the Utopians, where everything has been established according to plan, and the commonwealth is carefully regulated, building a brand-new home on a new site is a rate event. They are not only quick to repair damage, but foresighted in preventing it. The result is that their buildings last for

2. Figuring six thousand families per city, thirteen adults per family, and three of those too old or feeble for work, we have sixty thousand working adults per city and the same number in the surrounding countryside. So the rate of those exempted from work is under half a percent.

3. The apparent democracy of Utopia is sharply limited by this provision; in fact, what we have here is an incipient managerial class, as in the USSR or, more proximately, in that Brahmin caste that Calvinism tended to breed, for example, in Geneva, Edinburgh, and Boston.

4. Barzanes, "Son of Zeus" in Greek; Ademus, "Without People." In Lucian's dialogue "Menippus," which More translated, there is a wise and wonderful Chaldean named "Mithrobarzanes," Lucian, *Works*, tr. H. W. Fowler and F. G. Fowler (Oxford, 1965), 1, 159.

a very long time with minimal repairs; and the carpenters and masons sometimes have so little to do, that they are set to hewing timber and cutting stone in case some future need for it should arise.

Consider, too, how little labor their clothing requires. Their work clothes are loose garments made of leather which last as long as seven years. When they go out in public, they cover these rough working-clothes with a cloak. Throughout the entire island, everyone wears the same colored cloak, which is the color of natural wool.[5] As a result, they not only need less wool than people in other countries, but what they do need is less expensive. They use linen cloth most, because it requires least labor. They like linen cloth to be white and wool cloth to be clean; but they put no price on fineness of texture. Elsewhere a man is not satisfied with four or five woolen cloaks of different colors and as many silk shirts, or if he's a clothes-horse, even ten of each are not enough. But a Utopian is content with a single cloak, and generally wears it for two seasons. There is no reason at all why he should want any others, for if he had them, he would not be better protected against the cold, nor would he appear in any way better dressed.

When there is an abundance of everything, as a result of everyone working at useful trades, and nobody consuming to excess, then great numbers of the people often go out to work on the roads, if any of them need repairing. And when there is no need even for this sort of public work, then the officials very often proclaim a shorter work day, since they never force their citizens to perform useless labor. The chief aim of their constitution is that, whenever public needs permit, all citizens should be free, so far as possible, to withdraw their time and energy from the service of the body, and devote themselves to the freedom and culture of the mind. For that, they think, is the real happiness of life.

Social and Business Relations

Now I must explain the social relations of these folk, the way the citizens behave toward one another, and how they distribute their goods within the society.

Each city, then, consists of households, the households consisting generally of blood-relations. When the women grow up and are married, they move into their husbands' households. On the other hand, male children and after them grandchildren remain in the family, and are subject to the oldest parent, unless his mind has started to fail, in which case, the next oldest takes his place. To keep the city from becoming too large or too small, they have decreed that there shall be no more than six thousand households in it (exclusive of the surrounding coun-

5. Furs and feathers evidently exist on the island, but are not used for clothing lay people, perhaps because they would raise awkward issues of unequal distribution.

tryside), each family containing between ten and sixteen adults.[6] They do not, of course, try to regulate the number of minor children in a family. The limit on adults is easily observed by transferring individuals from a household with too many into a household with not enough. Likewise if a city has too many people, the extra persons serve to make up a shortage of population in other cities. And if the population throughout the entire island exceeds the quota,[7] then they enroll citizens out of every city and plant a colony under their own laws on the mainland near them, wherever the natives have plenty of unoccupied and uncultivated land. Those natives who want to live with the Utopian settlers are taken in. When such a merger occurs, the two peoples gradually and easily blend together, sharing the same way of life and customs, much to the advantage of both. For by their policies the Utopians make the land yield an abundance for all, which had previously seemed too barren and paltry even to support the natives. But if the natives will not join in living under their laws, the Utopians drive them out of the land they claim for themselves, and if they resist make war on them. The Utopians say it's perfectly justifiable to make war on people who leave their land idle and waste, yet forbid the use of it to others who, by the law of nature, ought to be supported from it.[8]

If for any reason, one of their cities shrinks so sharply in population that it cannot be made up from other cities without bringing them too under proper strength, then the population is restored by bringing people back from the colonies. This has happened only twice, they say, in their whole history, both times as a result of a frightful plague. They would rather that their colonies dwindled away than that any of the cities on their island should get too small.

But to return to their manner of living. The oldest of every household, as I said, is the ruler. Wives are subject to their husbands, children to their parents, and generally the younger to their elders. Every city is divided into four equal districts, and in the middle of each district is a market for all kinds of commodities. Whatever each household produces is brought here, and stored in warehouses, each kind of goods in its own place. Here the head of each household looks for what he or his family

6. When houses are exchanged by lottery every ten years, the difference between ten and sixteen adults may be very considerable—not to speak of the further difference in the potential number of children. Either all Utopian houses have thirty bedrooms, or there is a lot of squeezing and cramping every ten years.

7. The population of Utopia works out, by crude arithmetic (six thousand families of thirteen adults, times fifty-four cities, with a healthy allowance for country dwellers and children), to at least ten million inhabitants, not counting slaves.

8. Every imperialism in the world's history has

proceeded on the assumption that the "natives" don't know what to do with the land that Providence has unfairly bestowed on them, and that superior races are therefore entitled to take over. Shortly after the First World War, and probably under its inflammatory influence, a group of German scholars began polemicizing aginst the *Utopia* as a blueprint or even an *apologia* for British imperialism. They were so thoroughly demolished by H. W. Donner, *Introduction to Utopia* (London, 1945) as to render not only the thesis but its refutation largely obsolete.

needs, and carries off what he wants without any sort of payment or compensation. Why should anything be refused him? There is plenty of everything, and no reason to fear that anyone will claim more than he needs. Why would anyone be suspected of asking for more than is needed, when everyone knows there will never be any shortage? Fear of want, no doubt, makes every living creature greedy and avaricious—and, in addition, man develops these qualities out of pride, pride which glories in putting down others by a superfluous display of possessions. But this kind of vice has no place whatever in the Utopian way of life.

Next to the marketplace of which I just spoke are the food markets, where people bring all sorts of vegetables, fruit, and bread. Fish, meat, and poultry are also brought there from designated places outside the city, where running water can carry away all the blood and refuse. Slaves do the slaughtering and cleaning in these places: citizens are not allowed to do such work. The Utopians feel that slaughtering our fellow-creatures gradually destroys the sense of compassion, which is the finest sentiment of which our human nature is capable. Besides, they don't allow anything dirty or filthy to be brought into the city lest the air become tainted by putrefaction and thus infectious.[9]

Each ward has its own spacious halls, equally distant from one another, and each known by a special name. In these halls live the syphogrants. Thirty families are assigned to each hall, to take their meals in common—fifteen live on one side of the hall, fifteen on the other. The stewards of each hall meet at a fixed time in the market and get food according to the number of persons for whom each is responsible.

In distributing food, first consideration goes to the sick, who are cared for in public hospitals. Every city has four of these, built at the city limits, slightly outside the walls, and spacious enough to appear like little towns. The hospitals are large for two reasons: so that the sick, however numerous they may be, will not be packed closely and uncomfortably together, and also so that those who have a contagious disease, such as might pass from one to the other, may be isolated. The hospitals are well ordered and supplied with everything needed to cure the patients, who are nursed with tender and watchful care. Highly skilled physicians are in constant attendance. Consequently, though nobody is sent there against his will, there is hardly anyone in the city who would not rather be treated for an illness at the hospital than at home.

When the hospital steward has received the food prescribed for the sick by their doctors, the rest is fairly divided among the halls according to the number in each, except that special regard is paid to the prince, the high priest, and the tranibors, as well as to ambassadors and foreign-

---

9. In cramped medieval cities, this rule was necessary; even in modern towns, slaughterhouses are still generally located in the outskirts.

ers, if there are any. In fact, foreigners are very few; but when they do come, they have certain furnished houses assigned to them.

At the hours of lunch and supper, a brazen trumpet summons the entire syphogranty to assemble in their hall, except for those who are bedridden in the hospitals or at home. After the halls have been served with their quotas of food, nothing prevents an individual from taking food home from the marketplace. They realize that no one would do this without good reason. For while it is not forbidden to eat at home, no man does it willingly, because it is not thought proper; and besides, a man would be stupid to take the trouble of preparing a worse meal at home when he had a sumptuous one near at hand in the hall.

In the syphogrant's hall, slaves do all the particularly dirty and heavy work. But planning the meal, as well as preparing and cooking the food, is carried out by the women alone, with each family taking its turn.[1] Depending on their number, they sit down at three or more tables. The men sit with their backs to the wall, the women on the outside, so that if a woman has a sudden qualm or pain, such as occasionally happens during pregnancy, she may get up without disturbing the others, and go off to the nurses. A separate dining room is assigned to the nurses and infants, with a plentiful supply of cradles, clean water, and a warm fire. Thus the nurses may lay the infants down, change them, dress them, and let them play before the fire. Each child is nursed by its own mother, unless death or illness prevents. When that happens, the wife of the syphogrant quickly finds a suitable nurse. The problem is not difficult. Any woman who can gladly volunteers for the job, since all the Utopians applaud her kindness, and the child itself regards its new nurse as its natural mother.

Children under the age of five sit together in the nursery. All other minors, both boys and girls up to the age of marriage, either wait on table, or if not old and strong enough for that, stand by in absolute silence. They eat whatever is handed to them by those sitting at the table, and have no other time set for their meals.

The syphogrant with his wife sits in the middle of the first table, at the highest part of the dining hall. This is the place of greatest honor, and from this table, which is placed crosswise of the hall, the whole gathering can be seen. Two of the eldest sit with them, for they always sit in groups of four; if there is a church in the district, the priest and his wife sit with the syphogrant, and preside with him. On both sides of them sit younger people, next to them older people again, and so through the hall; those of about the same age sit together, yet are mingled with

---

1. Every meal is thus cooked for a minimum of 390 persons (thirty families averaging thirteen adults). But we must also add the children (males under twenty-two, females under eighteen) and the slaves required to help with these mammoth meals and clean up afterward, since they have to eat too. The total of those eating in each syphogranty can hardly be short of 700 persons per meal.

others of a different age. The reason for this, as they explained it, is that the dignity of the aged, and the respect due them, may restrain the younger people from improper freedom of words and gestures, since nothing said or done at table can pass unnoticed by the old, who are present on every side.

Dishes of food are not served down the tables in order from top to bottom, but all the old persons, who are seated in conspicuous places, are served with the best food; and then equal shares are given to the rest. The old people, as they feel inclined, give their neighbors a share of those delicacies which are not plentiful enough to be served to everyone. Thus, due respect is paid to seniority, yet the principle of equality is preserved.

They begin every lunch and supper with some reading on a moral topic,[2] but keep it brief lest it become a bore. Taking that as an occasion, the elders introduce topics of conversation, which they try not to make gloomy or dull. They never monopolize the conversation with long monologues, but are ready to hear what the young men say. In fact, they deliberately draw them out in order to discover the natural temper and quality of each one's mind, as revealed in the freedom of mealtime talk.

Their lunches are light, their suppers rather more elaborate, because lunch is followed by work, supper by rest and a night's sleep, which they think particularly helpful to good digestion. Never a meal passes without music, and the dessert course is never scanted; during the meal, they burn incense and scatter perfume, omitting nothing which will make the occasion festive. For they are much inclined to think that no kind of pleasure is forbidden, provided harm does not come of it.

This is the ordinary pattern of life in the city; but in the country, where they are farther removed from neighbors, they all eat in their own homes. No family lacks for food, since, after all, whatever the city-dwellers eat comes originally from those in the country.

Travel and Trade in Utopia

Anyone who wants to visit friends in another city, or simply to see the country, can easily obtain permission from his syphogrant and tranibor, unless for some special occasion he is needed at home. They travel together in groups, taking a letter from the prince granting leave to travel and fixing a day of return. They are given a wagon and a public slave to drive the oxen and look after them, but unless women are in the company, they usually dispense with the wagon as an unnecessary bother. Wher-

2. Humanists were fond of this social custom, the origins of which were part monastic, part classical.

ever they go, though they take nothing with them, they never lack for anything, because they are at home everywhere. If they stay more than a day in one place, each man practices his trade there in the shop of the local artisans, by whom he is gladly received.

Anyone who takes upon himself to leave his district without permission, and is caught without the prince's letter, is treated with contempt, brought back as a runaway, and severely punished. If he is bold enough to try it a second time, he is made a slave. Anyone who wants to stroll about and explore the extent of his own district is not prevented, provided he first obtains his father's permission and his wife's consent. But wherever he goes in the countryside, he gets no food until he has completed either a morning's or an afternoon's stint of work. On these terms, he may go where he pleases within his own district, yet be just as useful to the community as if he were at home.

So you see there is no chance to loaf or kill time, no pretext for evading work; no taverns, or alehouses, or brothels; no chances for corruption; no hiding places, no spots for secret meetings. Because they live in the full view of all, they are bound to be either working at their usual trades, or enjoying their leisure in a respectable way. Such a life style must necessarily result in plenty of life's good things, and since they share everything equally, it follows that no one can ever be reduced to poverty or forced to beg.

In the annual gathering at Amaurot (to which, as I said before, three representatives come from each city), they survey the island to find out where there are shortages and surpluses, and promptly satisfy one district's shortage with another's surplus. These are outright gifts; those who give receive nothing in return from those to whom they give. Though they give freely to one city, they get freely from another to which they gave nothing; and thus the whole island is like a single family.

After they have accumulated enough for themselves—and this they consider to be a full two-years' store, because next year's crop is always uncertain—then they export their surpluses to other countries. They sell abroad great quantities of grain, honey, wool, flax, timber, scarlet and purple dye-stuffs, hides, wax, tallow, and leather, as well as livestock. One-seventh of their cargo they give freely to the poor of the importing country, and the rest they sell at moderate prices. In exchange they receive not only such goods as they lack at home (in fact, the one important thing they lack is iron) but immense quantities of silver and gold. They have been carrying on trade for a long time now, and have accumulated a greater supply of the precious metals than you would believe possible. As a result, they now care very little whether they sell for cash or credit, and most payments to them actually take the form of promissory notes. However, in all such transactions, they never trust individuals but insist that the foreign city become officially responsible. When the day of payment comes, the city collects the money due from private

debtors, puts it into the treasury, and enjoys the use[3] of it till the Utopians claim payment. Most of it, in fact, is never claimed. The Utopians
think it hardly right to take what they don't need away from people who
do need it. But if they want to lend the money to some other nation,
then they call it in—as they do also when they must wage war. This is
the only reason that they keep such an immense treasure at home, as a
protection against extreme peril or sudden emergency. They use it above
all to hire, at extravagant rates of pay, foreign mercenaries, whom they
would much rather risk in battle than their own citizens. They know
very well that for large enough sums of money the enemy's soldiers can
themselves be bought, or set at odds with one another, either secretly or
openly.

Their Gold and Silver

For these reasons, therefore, they have accumulated a vast treasure,
but they do not keep it like a treasure. I'm really quite ashamed to tell
you how they do keep it, because you probably won't believe me. I
would not have believed it myself if someone had just told me about it;
but I was there, and saw it with my own eyes. It is a general rule that
the more different anything is from what people are used to, the harder
it is to accept. But, considering that all their other customs are so unlike
ours, a sensible man will not be surprised that they use gold and silver
quite differently than we do. After all, they never do use money among
themselves, but keep it only for a contingency which may or may not
actually arise. So in the meanwhile they take care that no one shall
overvalue gold and silver, of which money is made, beyond what the
metals themselves deserve. Anyone can see, for example, that iron is far
superior to either; men could not live without iron, by heaven, any more
than without fire or water. But gold and silver have, by nature, no function that we cannot easily dispense with. Human folly has made them
precious because they are rare. Like a most wise and generous mother,
nature has placed the best things everywhere and in the open, like air,
water, and the earth itself; but she has hidden away in remote places all
vain and unprofitable things.

If in Utopia gold and silver were kept locked up in some tower, foolish
heads among the common people might well concoct a story that the
prince and the senate were out to cheat ordinary folk and get some
advantage for themselves. They might indeed put the gold and silver
into beautiful plate-ware and rich handiwork, but then in case of necessity the people would not want to give up such articles, on which they
had begun to fix their hearts, only to melt them down for soldiers' pay.

---

3. The Latin word, here translated "use," is "usure"—the way to use money in More's world is
to put it out at interest.

To avoid all these inconveniences, they thought of a plan which conforms with their institutions as clearly as it contrasts with our own. Unless we've actually seen it working, their plan may seem ridiculous to us, because we prize gold so highly and are so careful about protecting it. With them it's just the other way. While they eat from pottery dishes and drink from glass cups, well made but inexpensive, their chamber pots and stools—all their humblest vessels, for use in the common halls and private homes—are made of gold and silver. The chains and heavy fetters of slaves are also made of these metals. Finally, criminals who are to bear through life the mark of some disgraceful act are forced to wear golden rings on their ears, golden bands on their fingers, golden chains around their necks, and even golden crowns on their heads. Thus they hold gold and silver up to scorn in every conceivable way. As a result, when they have to part with these metals, which other nations give up with as much agony as if they were being disemboweled, the Utopians feel it no more than the loss of a penny.

They find pearls by the seashore, diamonds and rubies in certain cliffs, but never go out of set purpose to look for them. If they happen to find some, they polish them, and give them to the children who, when they are small, feel proud and pleased with such gaudy decorations. But after, when they grow a bit older, and notice that only babies like such toys, they lay them aside. Their parents don't have to say anything, they simply put these trifles away out of a shamefaced sense that they're no longer suitable, just as our children when they grow up put away their rattles, marbles, and dolls.

Different customs, different feelings: I never saw the adage better illustrated than in the case of the Anemolian[4] ambassadors, who came to Amaurot while I was there. Because they came to discuss important business, the senate had assembled ahead of time, three citizens from each city. But the ambassadors from nearby nations, who had visited Utopia before and knew something of their customs, realized that fine clothing was not much respected in that land, silk was despised, and gold was a badge of contempt; and therefore they came in the very plainest of their clothes. But the Anemolians, who lived farther off and had had fewer dealings with the Utopians, had heard only that they all dressed alike, and very simply; so they took for granted that their hosts had nothing to wear that they didn't put on. Being themselves rather more proud than wise, they decided to dress as resplendently as the very gods and dazzle the eyes of the poor Utopians by the glitter of their garb.

Consequently the three ambassadors made a grand entry with a suite of a hundred attendants, all in clothing of many colors, and most in silk. Being noblemen at home, the ambassadors were arrayed in cloth of gold,

4. "Windy People" in Greek. The story of the absurd Anemolian ambassadors may owe something to a dialogue of Lucian, in which a rich Roman makes a fool of himself by stalking around Athens in a purple robe: "Nigrinus," in Lucian, *Works*, tr. Fowler and Fowler, 1, 16.

with heavy gold chains on their necks, gold rings on their ears and fingers, and sparkling strings of pearls and gems on their caps. In fact, they were decked out in all the articles which in Utopia are used to punish slaves, shame wrongdoers, or pacify infants. It was a sight to see how they strutted when they compared their finery with the dress of the Utopians who had poured out into the street to see them pass. But it was just as funny to see how wide they fell of the mark, and how far they were from getting the consideration they wanted and expected. Except for a very few Utopians who for some special reason had visited foreign countries, all the onlookers considered this pomp and splendor a mark of disgrace. They therefore bowed to the humblest servants as lords, and took the ambassadors to be slaves because they were wearing golden chains, passing them by without any reverence at all. You might have seen children, who had themselves thrown away their pearls and gems, nudge their mothers when they saw the ambassadors' jeweled caps, and say:

"Look at that big lummox, mother, who's still wearing pearls and jewels as if he were a little kid!"

But the mother, in all seriousness, would answer:

"Hush, my boy, I think he is one of the ambassador's fools."

Others found fault with the golden chains as useless, because they were so flimsy any slave could beak them, and so loose that he could easily shake them off and run away whenever he wanted. But after the ambassadors had spent a couple of days among the Utopians, they learned of the immense amounts of gold which were as thoroughly despised there as they were prized at home. They saw too that more gold and silver went into making the chains and fetters of a single runaway slave than into costuming all three of them. Somewhat crestfallen, then, they put away all the finery in which they had strutted so arrogantly; but they saw the wisdom of doing so after they had talked with the Utopians enough to learn their customs and opinions.

Their Moral Philosophy

The Utopians marvel that any mortal can take pleasure in the weak sparkle of a little gem or bright pebble when he has a star, or the sun itself, to look at. They are amazed at the foolishness of any man who considers himself a nobler fellow because he wears clothing of specially fine wool. No matter how delicate the thread, they say, a sheep wore it once, and still was nothing but a sheep. They are surprised that gold, a useless commodity in itself, is everywhere valued so highly that man himself, who for his own purposes conferred this value on it, is far less valuable. They do not understand why a dunderhead with no more brains than a post, and who is about as depraved as he is foolish, should command a great many wise and good people, simply because he happens to have a great pile of gold. Yet if this booby should lose his money to the lowest rascal in his household (as can happen by chance, or through some legal trick—for the law can produce reversals as violent as luck itself), he would promptly become one of the fellow's scullions, as if he were personally attached to the coin, and a mere appendage to it. Even more than this, the Utopians are appalled at those people who practically worship a rich man, though they neither owe him anything, nor are obligated to him in any way. What impresses them is simply that the man is rich. Yet all the while they know he is so mean and grasping that as long as he lives not a single penny out of that great mound of money will ever come their way.

These and the like attitudes the Utopians have picked up partly from their upbringing, since the institutions of their society are completely opposed to such folly, and partly from instruction and their reading of good books. For though not many people in each city are excused from labor and assigned to scholarship full time (these are persons who from childhood have given evidence of unusual intelligence and devotion to learning), every child gets an introduction to good literature, and throughout their lives a large part of the people, men and women alike, spend their leisure time in reading.

They can study all the branches of learning in their native tongue, which is not deficient in terminology or unpleasant in sound, and adapts itself fluently to the expression of thought. Just about the same language is spoken throughout that entire area of the world, though elsewhere it is somewhat more corrupt, depending on the district.

Before we came there, the Utopians had never so much as heard about a single one of those philosophers whose names are so celebrated in our part of the world. Yet in music, dialectic, arithmetic, and geometry they have found out just about the same things as our great men of the past. But while they equal the ancients in almost all other subjects, they are far from matching the inventions of our modern logicians.[5] In fact they have not discovered even one of those elaborate rules about restrictions, amplifications, and suppositions which our own schoolboys study in the *Small Logicals*.[6] They are so far from being able to speculate on "second intentions," that not one of them was able to conceive of "man-in-general,"[7] though I pointed straight at him with my finger, and he is, as you well know, bigger than any giant, maybe even a colossus. On the other hand, they have learned to plot expertly the courses of the stars and the movements of the heavenly bodies. They have devised a number of different instruments by which they compute with the greatest exactness the course of the sun, the moon, and the other stars that

5. The scholastic philosophers, traditional enemies of the humanists.
6. A textbook of logic by Peter of Spain (Petrus Spanheym), later Pope John XXI (died 1277).

7. More is using this entire passage, in the name of that common sense on which the humanists prided themselves, to ridicule logical abstractions.

are visible in their area of the sky. As for the friendly and hostile influences of the planets, and that whole deceitful business of divination by the stars, they have never so much as dreamed of it. From long experience in observation, they are able to forecast rains, winds, and other changes in the weather. But as to the causes of the weather, of the flow of the sea and its saltiness, and the origins and nature of the heavens and the universe, they have various opinions. Generally they treat of these matters as did our ancient philosophers, but they also disagree with one another, as the ancients did, and are unable to come up with any generally accepted theories of their own.

In matters of moral philosophy, they carry on much the same arguments as we do. They inquire into the nature of the good, distinguishing goods of the body from goods of the mind and external gifts. They ask whether the name of "good" may be applied to all three, or applies simply to goods of the mind. They discuss virtue and pleasure, but their chief concern is human happiness, and whether it consists of one thing or many. They seem overly inclined to the view of those who think that all or most human happiness consists of pleasure. And what is more surprising, they seek support for this hedonistic philosophy from their religion, which is serious and strict, indeed, almost stern and forbidding. For they never discuss happiness without joining to their philosophic rationalism the principles of religion. Without these religious principles, they think that philosophy is bound to prove weak and defective in its effort to investigate true happiness.

Their religious principles are of this nature: that the soul of man is immortal, and by God's goodness it is born for happiness; that after this life, rewards are appointed for our virtues and good deeds, punishments for our sins. Though these are indeed religious beliefs, they think that reason leads men to believe and accept them. And they add unhesitatingly that if these beliefs were rejected, no man would be so stupid as not to realize that he should seek pleasure regardless of right and wrong. His only care would be to keep a lesser pleasure from standing in the way of a greater one, and to avoid pleasures that are inevitably followed by pain. Without religious principles, a man would have to be actually crazy to pursue harsh and painful virtue, give up the pleasures of life, and suffer pain from which he can expect no advantage. For if there is no reward after death, a man has no hope of compensation for having passed his entire existence without pleasure, that is, miserably.

In fact, the Utopians believe that happiness is found, not in every kind of pleasure, but only in good and honest pleasure.[8] Virtue itself,

8. Though they are somewhat idealized Epicureans, the Utopians are not so deeply infused with Christian grace as some of their "defenders" have claimed. For despite his vulgar reputation as a besotted sensualist, Epicurus in his own right really meant by "pleasure" a discriminating intellectual virtue that could easily be exalted into a spiritual and then into a religious principle.

they say, draws our nature to this kind of pleasure, as to the supreme good. There is an opposed school which declares that virtue is itself happiness.

They define virtue as living according to nature; and God, they say, created us to that end. When a man obeys the dictates of reason in choosing one thing and avoiding another, he is following nature. Now the first rule of reason is to love and venerate the Divine Majesty to whom men owe their own existence and every happiness of which they are capable. The second rule of nature is to lead a life as free of anxiety and as full of joy as possible, and to help all one's fellow men toward that end. The most hard-faced eulogist of virtue and the grimmest enemy of pleasure, while they invite us to toil and sleepless nights and self-laceration, still admonish us to relieve the poverty and misfortune of others, as best we can. It is especially praiseworthy, they tell us, when we provide for our fellow-creature's comfort and welfare. Nothing is more humane (and humanity is the virtue most proper to human beings) than to relieve the misery of others, assuage their griefs, and by removing all sadness from their life, to restore them to enjoyment, that is, plea-sure. Well, if this is the case, why doesn't nature equally invite us to do the same thing for ourselves? Either a joyful life (that is, one of pleasure) is a good thing or it isn't. If it isn't, then you should not help anyone to it— indeed, you ought to take it away from everyone you can, as harmful and deadly to them. But if such a life is good, and if we are supposed, indeed obliged, to help others to it, why shouldn't we first of all seek it for ourselves, to whom we owe no less charity than to anyone else? When nature prompts us to be kind to our neighbors, she does not mean that we should be cruel and merciless to ourselves. Thus they say that nature herself prescribes for us a joyous life, in other words, pleasure, as the goal of our actions; and living according to her prescriptions is to be defined as virtue. And as nature bids men to make one another's lives merrier, to the extent they they can, so she warns us constantly not to seek our own advantages so avidly that we cause misfortune to our fel-lows. And the reason for this is an excellent one; for no man is placed so highly above the rest, that he is nature's sole concern, she cherishes alike all those living beings to whom she has granted the same form.

Consequently, the Utopians maintain that men should not only abide by their private agreements, but also obey all those public laws which control the distribution of vital goods, such as are the very substance of pleasure. Any such laws, provided they have been properly promulgated by a good king, or ratified by a people free of force and fraud, should be observed; and as long as they are observed, any man is free to pursue his own interests as prudence prompts him. If, in addition to his own inter-ests, he concerns himself with the public interest, that is an act of piety; but if, to secure his own pleasure, he deprives others of theirs, that is injustice. On the other hand, deliberately to decrease one's own pleasure in order to augment that of others is a work of humanity and benevolence which never fails to benefit the doer more even than he benefits others. he may be repaid for his kindness; and in any case, he is conscious of having done a good deed. His mind draws more joy from recalling the gratitude and good will of those whom he has benefited than his body would have drawn pleasure from the things he gave away.[9] Finally they believe (as religion easily persuades a well-disposed mind to believe) that God will recompense us for surrendering a brief and transitory pleasure, with immense, and neverending joy. And so they conclude, after carefully considering and weighing the matter, that all our actions and the virtues exercised within them look toward pleasure and happiness as their ultimate end.

By pleasure they understand every state or movement of body or mind in which man naturally finds delight. They are right in considering man's appetites natural. By simply following his senses and his right reason a man may discover what is pleasant by nature—it is a delight that does not injure others, that does not preclude a greater pleasure, and that is not followed by pain. But a pleasure which is against nature, and which men call "delightful" only by the emptiest of fictions (as if one could change the real nature of things just by changing their names), does not really make for happiness; in fact they say, it destroys happiness. And the reason is that men whose minds are filled with false ideas of pleasure have no room left for true and genuine delight. As a matter of fact, there are a great many things which have no sweetness in them, but are mainly or entirely bitter—yet which through the perverse enticements of evil lusts are considered very great pleasures, and even the supreme goals of life.

Among the devotees of this false pleasure the Utopians include those whom I mentioned before, the people who think themselves finer fellows because they wear finer clothes. These people are twice mistaken: first in thinking their clothes better than anyone else's, and then in thinking themselves better because of their clothes. As far as a coat's usefulness goes, what does it matter if it was woven of thin thread or thick? Yet they act as if they were set apart by nature herself, rather than their own fantasies; they strut about, and put on airs. Because they have a fancy suit, they think themselves entitled to honors they would never have expected if they were dressed in homespun, and they get very angry if someone passes them by without showing special respect.

---

9. Not for its literary merits, but for its thematic relation to this passage, we reproduce here a bit of More's verse paraphrase of the "XII Rules of John Pico della Mirandola" involving the virtuous life:

Any good work if thou with labor do,
The labor goeth, the goodness doth remain;

If thou do evil, with pleasure joined thereto,
The pleasure which thine evil work doth contain
Glideth away, thou mayst him not restrain.
The evil then in thy breast cleaveth behind
With grudge of heart and heaviness of mind.

It is the same kind of absurdity to be pleased by empty, ceremonial honors. What true and natural pleasure can you get from someone's bent knee or bared head? Will the creaks in your own knees be eased thereby, or the madness in your head? The phantom of false pleasure is illustrated by other men who run mad with delight over their own blue blood,[1] plume themselves on their nobility, and applaud themselves for all their rich ancestors (the only ancestors that count nowadays), and all their ancient family estates. Even if they don't have the shred of an estate themselves, or if they've squandered every penny of their inheritance, they don't consider themselves a bit less noble.

In the same class the Utopians put those people I described before, who are mad for jewelry and gems, and think themselves divinely happy if they find a good specimen, especially of the sort that happens to be fashionable in their country at the time—for stones vary in value from one market to another. The collector will not make an offer for the stone till it's taken out of its setting, and even then he will not buy unless the dealer guarantees and gives security that it is a true and genuine stone. What he fears is that his eyes will be deceived by a counterfeit. But if you consider the matter, why should a counterfeit give any less pleasure when your eyes cannot distinguish it from a real gem? Both should be of equal value to you, as they would be, in fact, to a blind man.[2]

Speaking of false pleasure, what about those who pile up money, not because they want to do anything with the heap, but so they can sit and look at it? Is that true pleasure they experience, or aren't they simply cheated by a show of pleasure? Or what of those with the opposite vice, the men who hide away money they will never use and perhaps never even see again? In their anxiety to hold onto their money, they actually lose it. For what else happens when you deprive yourself, and perhaps other people too, of a chance to use money, by burying it in the ground? And yet when the miser has hidden his treasure, he exults over it as if his mind were now free to rejoice. Suppose someone stole it, and the miser died ten years later, knowing nothing of the theft. During all those ten years, what did it matter whether the money was stolen or not? In either case, it was equally useless to the owner.

To these false and foolish pleasures they add gambling, which they have heard about, though they've never tried it, as well as hunting and hawking. What pleasure can there be, they wonder, in throwing dice on a table? If there were any pleasure in the action, wouldn't doing it over and over again quickly make one tired of it? What pleasure can there be

---

1. In the *Life of Pico della Mirandola*, which More translated, pride of ancestry is much ridiculed. If the ancestor has no honor himself, there's no point in recollecting him; and even if he did have honor, he could never leave it to his descendants as an inheritance.

2. Erasmus tells a story about More that he gave his wife a false gem and then teased her (rather meanly) at being disappointed when its falsity was pointed out to her (*Praise of Folly and Other Writings* [Norton, 1989], p. 47).

in listening to the barking and yelping of dogs—isn't that rather a disgusting noise? Is there any more real pleasure when a dog chases a rabbit than there is when a dog chases a dog? If what you like is fast running, there's plenty of that in both cases; they're just about the same. But if what you really want is slaughter, if you want to see a living creature torn apart under your eyes, then the whole thing is wrong. You ought to feel nothing but pity when you see the hare fleeing from the hound, the weak creature tormented by the stronger, the fearful and timid beast brutalized by the savage one, the harmless hare killed by the cruel dog. The Utopians, who regard this whole activity of hunting as unworthy of free men, have assigned it, accordingly, to their butchers, who as I said before, are all slaves. In their eyes, hunting is the lowest thing even butchers can do. In the slaughterhouse, their work is more useful and honest—since there they kill animals only from necessity; but hunters seek merely their own pleasure from the killing and mutilating of some poor little creature. Taking such relish in the sight of death, even if it's only beasts, reveals, in the opinion of the Utopians, a cruel disposition. Or if he isn't cruel to start with, the hunter quickly becomes so through the constant practice of such brutal pleasures.

Most men consider these activities, and countless others like them, to be pleasures; but the Utopians say flatly they have nothing at all to do with real pleasure since there's nothing naturally pleasant about them. They often please the senses, and in this they are like pleasure, but that does not alter their basic nature. The enjoyment doesn't arise from the experience itself, but only from the perverse mind of the individual, as a result of which he mistakes the bitter for the sweet, just as pregnant women, whose taste has been turned awry, sometimes think pitch and tallow taste sweeter than honey. A man's taste may be similarly depraved, by disease or by custom, but that does not change the nature of pleasure, or of anything else.[3]

They distinguish several different classes of true pleasure, some being pleasures of the mind and others pleasures of the body. Those of the mind are knowledge and the delight which rises from contemplating the truth, also the gratification of looking back on a well-spent life and the unquestioning hope of happiness to come.

Pleasures of the body they also divide into two classes. The first is that which fills the senses with immediate delight. Sometimes this happens when organs that have been weakened by natural heat are restored with food and drink; sometimes it happens when we eliminate some excess in the body, as when we move our bowels, generate children, or relieve an itch somewhere by rubbing or scratching it. Now and then pleasure rises, not from restoring a deficiency or discharging an excess, but from

---

3. Seneca provides a relevant analogue: "Natural desires are limited, but those which spring from false opinion can have no stopping point." *Moral Epistles* 16.

something that excites our senses with a hidden but unmistakable force, and attracts them to itself. Such is the power of music.

The second kind of bodily pleasure they describe as nothing but the calm and harmonious state of the body, its state of health when undisturbed by any disorder. Health itself, when undisturbed by pain, gives pleasure, without any external excitement at all. Even though it appeals less directly to the senses than the gross gratifications of eating and drinking, many consider this to be the greatest pleasure of all. Most of the Utopians regard this as the foundation of all the other pleasures, since by itself alone it can make life peaceful and desirable, whereas without it there is no possibility of any other pleasure. Mere absence of pain, without positive health, they regard as insensibility, not pleasure.

They rejected long ago the opinion of those who doubted whether a stable and tranquil state of health was really a pleasure, on the grounds that pleasure made itself felt only when aroused from without. (They have arguments of this sort, just as we do.) But now they mostly agree that health is the greatest of bodily pleasures. Since pain is inherent in disease, they argue, and pain is the bitter enemy of pleasure, while disease is the enemy of health, then pleasure must be inherent in quiet good health. You may say pain is not the disease itself, simply an accompanying effect; but they argue that that makes no difference. For whether health is itself a pleasure or is merely the cause of pleasure (as fire is the cause of heat), the fact remains that those who have permanent health must also have pleasure.

When we eat, they say, what happens is that health, which was starting to fade, takes food as its ally in the fight against hunger. While our health gains strength, the simple process of returning vigor gives us pleasure and refreshment. If our health feels delight in the struggle, will it not rejoice when the victory has been won? When at last it is restored to its original strength, which was its aim all through the conflict, will it at once become insensible, and fail to recognize and embrace its own good? The idea that health cannot be felt they consider completely wrong. Every man who's awake, they say, feels that he's in good health—unless he isn't. Is any man so torpid and dull that he won't admit health is delightfully agreeable to him? And what is delight except pleasure under another name?

Of all the different pleasures, they seek mostly those of the mind, and prize them most highly, because most of them arise from the practice of the virtues and the consciousness of a good life. Among the pleasures of the body, they give the first place to health. As for eating and drinking and other delights of the same sort, they consider these bodily pleasures desirable but only for the sake of health. They are not pleasant in themselves, but only as ways to withstand the insidious attacks of sickness. A wise man would rather escape sickness altogether than have a good cure for it; he would rather prevent pain than find a palliative for it. And so it would be better not to need this kind of pleasure at all than to be comforted by it.

Anyone who thinks happiness consists of this sort of pleasure must confess that his ideal life would be one spent in an endless round of hunger, thirst, and itching, followed by eating, drinking, scratching, and rubbing. Who fails to see that such an existence is not only disgusting but miserable? These pleasures are certainly the lowest of all, as they are the most adulterate—for they never occur except in connection with the pains that are their contraries. Hunger, for example, is linked to the pleasure of eating, and far from equally, since the pain is sharper and lasts longer; it precedes the pleasure, and ends only when the pleasure ends with it. So the Utopians think pleasures of this sort should not be much valued, except as they are necessary to life. Yet they enjoy these pleasures too, and acknowledge gratefully the kindness of Mother Nature, who coaxes her children with allurements and cajolery to do what from hard necessity they must always do. How wretched life would be, if the daily diseases of hunger and thirst had to be overcome by bitter potions and drugs, like some other diseases that afflict us less often!

Beauty, strength, and agility, as special and pleasant gifts of nature, they joyfully accept. The pleasures of sound, sight, and smell they also accept as the special seasonings of life, recognizing that nature intended these delights to be the particular province of man. No other kind of animal contemplates the shape and loveliness of the universe, or enjoys odors, except in the way of searching for food, or distinguishes harmonious from dissonant sounds. But in all their pleasures, the Utopians observe this rule, that the lesser pleasure must not interfere with a greater, and that no pleasure shall carry pain with it as a consequence. If a pleasure is false, they think it will inevitably lead to pain.

Moreover, they think it is crazy for a man to despise beauty of form, to impair his own strength, to grind his energy down to lethargy, to exhaust his body with fasts, to ruin his health, and to scorn natural delights, unless by so doing he can better serve the welfare of others or the public good. Then indeed he may expect a greater reward from God. But otherwise, such a man does no one any good. He gains, perhaps, the empty and shadowy reputation of virtue; and no doubt he hardens himself against fantastic adversities which may never occur. But such a person the Utopians consider absolutely crazy—cruel to himself, as well as most ungrateful to nature—as if, to avoid being in her debt, he were to reject all of nature's gifts.

This is the way they think about virtue and pleasure. Human reason, they think, can attain to no surer conclusions than these, unless a revelation from heaven should inspire men with holier notions. In all this, I have no time now to consider whether they are right or wrong, and don't feel obliged to do so. I have undertaken only to describe their principles, not to defend them. But of this I am sure, that whatever you

think of their ideas, there is not a happier people or a better commonwealth anywhere in the whole world.

In body they are active and lively, and stronger than you would expect
from their stature, though they're by no means tiny. Their soil is not
very fertile, nor their climate of the best, but they protect themselves
against the weather by temperate living, and improve their soil by industry, so that nowhere do grain and cattle flourish more plentifully, nowhere
are men more vigorous and liable to fewer diseases. They do all the
things that farmers usually do to improve poor soil by hard work and
technical knowledge, but in addition they may even transplant a forest
from one place to another. They do this not so much for the sake of
better growth, but to make transportation easier, in order to have wood
closer to the sea, the rivers, or the cities themselves. For grain is easier
than wood to transport over a long distance, especially by land.

Their Delight in Learning

The people in general are easygoing, cheerful, clever, and fond of
leisure. When they must, they can stand heavy labor, but otherwise they
are not much given to it. In intellectual pursuits, they are tireless. When
they heard from us about the literature and learning of the Greeks (for
we thought there was nothing in Latin except the historians and poets
that they would enjoy), it was wonderful to behold how eagerly they
sought to be instructed in Greek. We therefore began to study a little of
it with them, at first more to avoid seeming lazy than out of any expectation that they would profit by it. But after a short trial, their diligence
convinced us that our efforts would not be wasted. They picked up the
forms of the letters so quickly, pronounced the language so aptly, mem-
orized it so quickly, and began to recite so accurately that it seemed like
a miracle. Most of our pupils were established scholars, of course, picked
for their unusual ability and mature minds; and they studied with us,
not just of their own free will, but at the command of the senate. Thus
in less than three years they had perfect control of the language, and
could read the best Greek authors fluently, unless the text was corrupt.
I suspect they picked up Greek more easily because it was somewhat
related to their own tongue. Though their language resembles the Persian in most respects, I suspect them of deriving from Greece because
their language retains quite a few vestiges of Greek in the names of cities
and in official titles.

Before leaving on the fourth voyage, I placed on board, instead of
merchandise, a good-sized packet of books; for I had resolved not to
return at all, rather than to come home soon. Thus they received from
me most of Plato's works and many of Aristotle's, as well as Theophrastus's book *On Plants*, though the latter, I'm sorry to say, was somewhat

mutilated.[4] During the voyage I left it lying around, a monkey got hold of it, and out of sheer mischief ripped a few pages here and there. Of the grammarians they have only Lascaris, for I did not take Theodorus with me, nor any dictionary except that of Hesychius; and they have Dioscorides.[5] They are very fond of Plutarch's writings, and delighted with the witty persiflage of Lucian. Among the poets they have Aristophanes, Homer, and Euripides, together with Sophocles in the small Aldine edition.[6] Of the historians they possess Thucydides and Herodotus, as well as Herodian.

As for medical books, a comrade of mine named Tricius Apinatus[7] brought with him some small treatises by Hippocrates, and that summary of Galen known as *Microtechne*.[8] They were delighted to have these books because they consider medicine one of the finest and most useful parts of knowledge, even though there's hardly a country in the world that needs doctors less. They think when they thus explore the secrets of nature, they are gratifying not only themselves but the Author and Maker of Nature. They suppose that, like other artists, he created this visible mechanism of the world to be admired—and by whom, if not by man, who is alone in being able to appreciate such an intricate object? Therefore he is bound to prefer a careful observer and sensitive admirer of his work before one who, like a brute beast, looks on the grand spectacle with a stupid and blockish mind.

Once stimulated by learning, the minds of the Utopians are wonderfully quick to seek out those various arts which make life more agreeable and convenient. Two inventions, to be sure, they owe to us: the art of printing and the manufacture of paper. At least they owe these arts partly to us, and partly to their own ingenuity. While we were showing them the Aldine editions of various books, we talked about paper-making and typecutting, though without giving a detailed explanation of either process, for none of us had had any practical experience. But with great sharpness of mind, they immediately grasped the basic principles. While

4. Aristotle is slighted by comparison with Plato; Theophrastus, Aristotle's pupil, was studied in the Renaissance not as a quaint curiosity but as the last word in botanical studies.

5. Constantine Lascaris and Theodore of Gaza wrote Renaissance dictionaries of Greek, much used when that language was first being studied in the West. Hesychius of Alexandria (fifth century A.D.) did a valuable book on Greek dialects and idioms; but Dioscorides Pedanius of Anazarba, who lived about the time of Nero, wrote on *materia medica*—a treatise on drugs and herbs, not properly a dictionary at all.

6. The first modern edition of Sophocles was that of Aldus Manutius in 1502. The house of Aldus, established in Venice toward the end of the fifteenth century, was not only the first establishment to print Greek texts in Greek type,

but was responsible for some of the best-designed books in the history of the art. Their editions are collectors' items.

7. In effect, "Mr. Silly Nonsense": cf. Martial 14.1.7: "Sunt apinae tricaeque, & si quid vilius istis" ("They're Apinas and Tricas, and what's lower than that, if anything is"). Trica and Apina were tiny townlets in Apulia, symbolizing ridiculous unimportance.

8. To Hippocrates of Cos (fifth century B.C.) and Galen of Pergamus (second century A.D.) were attributed, in addition to some writings admittedly theirs, dozens of other medical treatises, which were variously translated, expanded, summarized, and combined for use sometimes as medical encyclopedias or sometimes as handbooks of medical practice.

previously they had written only on vellum, bark, and papyrus, they now undertook to make paper and to print letters. Their first attempts were not altogether successful, but with practice they soon mastered both arts. If they had texts of the Greek authors, they would soon have no lack of volumes; but as they have no more than those I mentioned, they have contented themselves with reprinting each in thousands of copies.[9]

Any sightseer coming to their land who has some special intellectual gift, or who has traveled widely and seen many countries, is sure of a special welcome, for they love to hear what is happening throughout the world. This is why we were received so kindly. Few merchants, however, go there to trade. What could they import except iron—or else gold and silver, which everyone would rather bring home than send abroad? As for their own export trade, the Utopians prefer to do their own transportation, rather than invite strangers to do it. By carrying their own cargos they are able to learn more about their neighbors and keep up their skill in navigation.

Slaves[1]

The Utopians enslave prisoners of war only if they are captured in wars fought by the Utopians themselves. The children of slaves are not automatically enslaved, nor are nay men who were enslaved in a foreign country. Most of their slaves are either their own former citizens, enslaved for some heinous offense, or else men of other nations who were condemned to death in their own land. Most are of the latter sort. Sometimes the Utopians buy them at a very modest rate, more often they ask for them, get them for nothing, and bring them home in considerable numbers. Both kinds of slaves are kept constantly at work, and are always fettered. The Utopians deal with their own people more harshly than with others, feeling that their crimes are worse and deserve stricter punishment because, as it is argued, they had an excellent education and the best of moral training, yet still couldn't be restrained from wrongdoing. A third class of slaves consists of hardworking penniless drudges from other nations who voluntarily choose to become slaves in Utopia. Such people are treated well, almost as well as citizens, except that they are given a little extra work, on the score that they're used to it. If one of them wants to leave, which seldom happens, no obstacles are put in his way, nor is he sent off emptyhanded.

9. Apparently, the Utopians have little or no accumulated literature of their own.
1. Alongside "servus," meaning simply "slave," Latin has another word, "famulus," often translated "bondsman", and implying a lesser degree of unfreedom. A "famulatium" is a family of such bondsmen. The *Utopia* uses both such words. But the three classes of slaves listed below are all "servi."

Care of the Sick and Dying

As I said before, the sick are carefully tended, and nothing is neglected in the way of medicine or diet which might cure them. Everything is done to mitigate the pain of those who are suffering from incurable diseases; and visitors do their best to console them by sitting and talking with them. But if the disease is not only incurable, but excruciatingly and continually painful, then the priests and public officials come and urge the invalid not to endure such agony any longer. They remind him that he is now unfit for any of life's duties, a burden to himself and to others; he has really outlived his own death. They tell him he should not let the disease prey on him any longer, but now that life is simply torture and the world a mere prison cell, he should not hesitate to free himself, or to let others free him, from the rack of living. This would be a wise act, they say, since for him death puts an end, not to pleasure, but to agony. In addition, he would be obeying the advice of the priests, who are the interpreters of God's will; which ensures that it will be a holy and a pious act.[2]

Those who have been persuaded by these arguments either starve themselves to death or take a potion which puts them painlessly to sleep, and frees them from life without any sensation of dying. But they never force this step on a man against his will; nor, if he decides against it, do they lessen their care of him. Under these circumstances, when death is advised by the authorities, they consider self-destruction honorable. But the suicide, who takes his own life without the approval of priests and senate, they consider unworthy either of earth or fire, and throw his body, unburied and disgraced, into the nearest bog.

Marriage Customs

Women do not marry till they are eighteen, nor men till they are twenty-two. Premarital intercourse, if discovered and proved, brings severe punishment on both man and woman, and the guilty parties are forbidden to marry during their whole lives, unless the prince, by his pardon, alleviates the sentence. In addition both the father and mother of the household where the offense occurred suffer public disgrace for having been remiss in their duty. The reason they punish this offense so severely is that they suppose few people would join in married love—with confinement to a single partner, and all the petty annoyances that married

---

2. The Utopian view of suicide is clearly more Stoic than Christian, but different from both in the very strong emphasis placed on the social element of the decision. No other society (until, perhaps, our own) seems to have contemplated making the life or death of an individual a matter for decision by a committee.

life involves—unless they were strictly restrained from a life of promiscuity.[3]

In choosing marriage partners, they solemnly and seriously follow a custom which seemed to us foolish and absurd in the extreme. Whether she is a widow or a virgin, the bride-to-be is shown naked to the groom by a responsible and respectable matron; and, similarly, some respectable man presents the groom naked to his future bride. We laughed at this custom and called it absurd; but they were just as amazed at the folly of all other peoples. When men go to buy a colt, where they are risking only a little money, they are so suspicious that though the beast is almost bare they won't close the deal until the saddle and blanket have been taken off, lest there be a hidden sore underneath. Yet in the choice of a mate, which may cause either delight or disgust for the rest of their lives, people are completely careless. They leave all the rest of her body covered up with clothes and estimate the attractiveness of a woman from a mere handsbreadth of her person, the face, which is all they can see. And so they marry, running great risk of hating one another for the rest of their lives, if something in either's person should offend the other. Not all people are so wise as to concern themselves solely with character; even the wise appreciate physical beauty, as a supplement to a good disposition.[4] There's no question but that deformity may lurk under clothing, serious enough to make a man hate his wife when it's too late to be separated from her. When deformities are discovered after marriage, each person must bear his own fate, so the Utopians think everyone should be protected by law beforehand.

There is extra reason for them to be careful, because in that part of the world, they are the only people who practice monogamy. Their marriages are seldom terminated except by death, though they do allow divorce for adultery or for intolerably difficult behavior. A husband or wife who is an aggrieved party to such a divorce is granted permission by the senate to remarry, but the guilty party is considered disreputable and permanently forbidden to take another mate. They absolutely forbid a husband to put away his wife against her will because of some bodily misfortune; they think it cruel that a person should be abandoned when most in need of comfort; and they add that old age, since it not only entails disease but is actually a disease itself, needs more than a precarious fidelity.

---

3. Cf. Bernard Shaw, "Virtue is the trade unionism of the married" (*Man and Superman*, Act 3).
4. More wrote in his own person several epigrams on the topic of choosing a wife. His own performance in the matter (choosing the less favored older daughter to avoid hurting her feelings, though the younger one attracted him

more) was decorous to the point of seeming a little chilly. When he compares taking a wife to buying a colt (the Latin is "in equuleo comparando"), he can hardly have failed to recall that the maiden name of his first wife, Jane, was Jane Colt. See also Seneca, *Moral Epistle* 80: "When you buy a horse, you order its blanket to be removed."

It happens occasionally that a married couple cannot get along, and have both found other persons with whom they hope to live more harmoniously. After getting the approval of the senate, they may then separate by mutual consent and contract new marriages. But such divorces are allowed only after the senators and their wives have carefully investigated the case. They allow divorce only very reluctantly because they know that husbands and wives will find it hard to settle down together if each has in mind that another new relation is easily available.

They punish adulterers with the strictest form of slavery. If both parties were married, they are both divorced, and the injured parties may marry one another, if they want, or someone else. But if one of the injured parties continues to love such an undeserving spouse, the marriage may go on, providing the innocent person chooses to share in the labor to which every slave is condemned. And sometimes it happens that the repentance of the guilty, and the devotion of the innocent party, move the prince to pity, so that he restores both to freedom. But a second conviction of adultery is punished by death.

Punishments, Legal Procedures, and Customs

No other crimes carry fixed penalties; the senate sets specific penalties for each particular misdeed, as it is considered atrocious or venial.[5] Husbands chastise their wives and parents their children, unless the offense is so serious that public punishment seems to be in the public interest. Generally, the gravest crimes are punished by slavery, for they think this deters offenders just as much as instant capital punishment, and is more beneficial to the state. Slaves, moreover, are permanent and visible reminders that crime does not pay. If the slaves rebel against their condition, then, like savage beasts which neither bars nor chains can tame, they are put instantly to death. But if they are patient, they are not left altogether without hope. When subdued by long hardships, if they show by their behavior that they regret the crime more than the punishment, their slavery is lightened or remitted altogether, sometimes by the prince's pardon, sometimes by popular vote.

A man who tries to seduce a woman is subject to the same penalties as if he had actually done it. They think that a crime attempted is as bad as one committed, and that failure should not confer advantages on a criminal who did all he could to succeed.

---

5. In Utopia there are thus no legal precedents. The common law of England, in which More had his training, consists of nothing but precedents. Half the predictive value of law (emphasized below) thus vanishes, for no man can ever estimate (in the absence of precedents) the penalty for disobedience. All law is equity law, i.e., up to the individual judge's incalculable intuitions of right and wrong.

They are very fond of fools, and think it contemptible to insult them. There is no prohibition against enjoying their foolishness, and they even regard this as beneficial to the fools. If anyone is so serious and solemn that the foolish behavior and comic patter of a clown do not amuse him, they don't entrust him with the care of such a person, for fear that a man who gets no fun from a fool's only gift will not treat him kindly.

To mock a person for being deformed or crippled is considered disgraceful, not to the victim, but to the mocker, who stupidly reproaches the cripple for something he cannot help.

They think it a sign of a weak and sluggish character to neglect one's natural beauty, but they consider cosmetics a detestable affectation. From experience they have learned that no physical beauty recommends a wife to her husband so effectually as truthfulness and integrity. Though quite a few men are captured by beauty alone, none are held except by virtue and compliance.

As they deter men from crime by penalties, so they incite them to virtue by public honors. They set up in the marketplaces statues of distinguished men who have served their country well, thinking thereby to preserve the memory of their good deeds, and to spur on the citizens to emulate the glory of their ancestors.

In Utopia any man who campaigns too eagerly for a public office is sure to fail of that one, and of all others as well. As a rule, they live together harmoniously, and the public officials are never arrogant or unapproachable. Instead, they are called "fathers," and that is the way they behave. Because the officials never extort respect from the people against their will, the people respect them spontaneously, as they should. Not even the prince is distinguished from his fellow citizens by a robe or crown; he is known only by a sheaf of grain carried before him, just as the high priest is distinguished by a wax candle.[6]

They have very few laws, and their training is such that they need no more. The chief fault they find with other nations is that, even with infinite volumes of laws and interpretations, they cannot manage their affairs properly. They think it completely unjust to bind men by a set of laws that are too many to be read and too obscure for anyone to understand. As for lawyers, a class of men whose trade it is to manipulate cases and multiply quibbles, they have no use for them at all. They think it is better for each man to plead his own case, and say the same thing to the judge that he would tell his lawyer. This makes for less ambiguity, and readier access to the truth. A man speaks his mind without tricky instructions from a lawyer, and the judge examines each point carefully, taking pains to protect simple folk against the false accusations of the crafty. It is hard to find this kind of plain dealing in other countries, where they

6. The grain (prosperity) and the candle (vision) obviously symbolize the special function of each ruler.

have such a multitude of incomprehensibly intricate laws. But in Utopia everyone is a legal expert. For the laws are very few, as I said, and they consider the most obvious interpretation of any law to be the fairest. As they see things, all laws are promulgated for the single purpose of teaching every man his duty. Subtle interpretations teach very few, since hardly anybody is able to understand them, whereas the more simple and apparent sense of the law is open to everyone. If laws are not clear, they are useless; for simpleminded men (and most men are of this sort, and most men of this sort need to be told where their duty lies) there might as well be no laws at all, as laws which can be interpreted only by devious minds after endless disputes. The average, common man cannot understand this legal chicanery, and couldn't even if he devoted his whole life to studying it, since he has to earn a living in the meanwhile.

Foreign Relations

Some time ago the Utopians helped various of their neighbors to throw off the yoke of tyranny; and since then, these people (who have learned to admire Utopian virtue) have made a practice of asking for Utopians to rule over them. Some of these rulers serve one year, others five. When their service is over, they return with honor and praise to their own home, and others are sent in their place. These countries seem to have settled on an excellent scheme to safeguard their happiness and safety. Since the welfare or ruin of a commonwealth depends wholly on the character of the officials, where could they make a more prudent choice than among Utopians, who cannot be tempted by money? For money is useless to them when they go home, as they soon must, and they can have no partisan or factional feelings, since they are strangers to the affairs of the city over which they rule. Wherever they take root in men's minds, these two evils, greed and faction, are the destruction of all justice—and justice is the strongest bond of any society. The Utopians call these people who have borrowed governors from them their *allies*; others whom they have benefited they call simply *friends*.

While other nations are constantly making treaties, breaking them, and renewing them, the Utopians never make any treaties at all. If nature, they say, doesn't bind man adequately to his fellow man, will an alliance do so? If a man scorns nature herself, is there any reason to think he will care about mere words? They are confirmed in this view by the fact that in that part of the world, treaties and alliances between kings are not generally observed with much good faith.

In Europe, of course, the dignity of treaties is everywhere kept sacred and inviolable, especially in these regions where the Christian religion prevails. This is partly because the kings are all so just and virtuous, partly also because of the reverence and fear that everyone feels toward the ruling Popes.[7] Just as the Popes themselves never promise anything which they do not most conscientiously perform, so they command all other chiefs of state to abide by their promises in every way. If someone quibbles over it, they compel him to obey by means of pastoral censure and sharp reproof. The Popes rightly declare that it would be particularly disgraceful if people who are specifically called "the faithful" did not adhere faithfully to their solemn word.

But in that new world which is scarcely removed from ours by geography so far as it is by customs and life style, nobody trusts treaties. The greater the formalities, the more numerous and solemn the oaths, the sooner the treaty will be broken. The rulers will find some defect in the wording of it, which often enough they deliberately inserted themselves, so that they're never at a loss for a pretext. No treaty can be made so strong and explicit that a government will not be able to worm out of it, breaking in the process both the treaty and its own word. If such craft, deceit, and fraud were practiced in the contracts of businessmen, the righteous politicians would raise a great outcry against both parties, calling them sacrilegious and worthy of the gallows. Yet the very same politicians think themselves clever fellows when they give this sort of advice to kings. As a consequence, plain men are apt to think that justice is a humble, plebeian virtue, far beneath the majesty of kings. Or else they conclude that there are two kinds of justice, one which is only for the common herd, a lowly justice that creeps along the ground, encumbered with chains; and the other, which is the justice of princes, much more free and majestic, so that it can do anything it wants and nothing that it doesn't want.

This royal practice of keeping treaties badly is, I suppose, the reason the Utopians don't make any; doubtless if they lived here in Europe, they would change their minds. However, they think it a bad idea to make treaties at all, even if they are faithfully observed. The treaty implies that men who are separated by some natural obstacle as slight as a hill or a brook are joined by no bond of nature; it assumes that they are born rivals and enemies, and are right in aiming to destroy one another except insofar as the treaty restrains them. Moreover, they see that treaties do not really promote friendship; for both parties still retain the right to prey upon one another, unless extreme care has been used, in drawing up the treaty, to outlaw freebooting.[8] The Utopians think, on the other hand, that no man should be considered an enemy who has done you

---

7. The irony here lies thick to the point of sarcasm. Not to speak of English kings, all the crowned heads of Europe—Ferdinand of Spain, Maximilian of Austria, and three successive French kings—were ruthless and casual violators of treaties. But they were far outdone by the successive Popes of the day, Alexander VI and Julius II, who raised duplicity to a fine art.
8. More has in mind a kind of trade mixed with blackmail and occasional informal piracy, common enough in his day, but for which we have now no proper denomination.

no harm, that the fellowship of nature is as good as a treaty, and that men are united more firmly by good will than by pacts, by their hearts than by their words.

Warfare

→ They despise war as an activity fit only for beasts,[9] yet practiced more by man than by any other creature. Unlike almost every other people in the world, they think nothing so inglorious as the glory won in battle. Yet on certain fixed days, both men and women alike carry on vigorous military training, so they will be fit to fight should the need arise.[1] They go to war only for good reasons; among these are the protection of their own land, the protection of their friends from an invading army, and the liberation of an oppressed people from tyranny and servitude. Out of human sympathy, they not only protect their friends from present danger, but avenge previous injuries; they do this, however, only if they themselves have previously been consulted, have approved the cause, and have demanded restitution in vain. Then and only then they think themselves free to declare war. They take this final step not only when their friends have been plundered, but also when their friends' merchants have been subjected to extortion in another country, either through laws unfair in themselves or through the perversion of good laws.

This and no other was the cause of the war which the Utopians waged a little before our time on behalf of the Nephelogetes against the Alaopolitans.[2] Under pretext of right, a wrong, as they saw it, had been inflicted on some Nephelogete traders residing among the Alaopolitans. Whatever the rights and wrongs of the quarrel, it developed into a fierce war, into which the neighboring nations poured all their resources, thereby inflaming mutual hatreds. Some prosperous nations were ruined completely, others badly shaken. One trouble led to another, and in the end the Alaopolitans were crushed and reduced to slavery (since the Utopians weren't involved on their own account) by the Nephelogetes—a people who, before the war, had not been remotely comparable in power to their rivals.

So severely do the Utopians punish wrong done to their friends, even in matters of mere money; but they are not so strict in standing up for their own rights. When they are cheated in any way, so long as no bodily harm is done, their anger goes no further than cutting off trade relations with that nation till restitution is made. The reason is not that they care more for their allies' citizens than for their own, but simply this: when

---

9. A folk etymology, mistaken like most of them, derived *bellum* (war) from *belua* (beast). Erasmus used it in the *Adages*, "Dulce bellum inexpertis."

1. The citizen-soldier has been idealized since classical days and was the object of Machiavelli's fondest hopes (Chap. 13, *The Prince*).

2. "People born in the clouds" versus "people without a country."

the merchants of allies are cheated, it is their own property that is lost, but when the Utopians lose something, it comes from the common stock, and is bound to be in plentiful supply at home; otherwise they wouldn't have been exporting it. Hence no one individual has to stand the loss. So small a loss, which affects neither the life nor the livelihood of any of their own people, they consider it cruel to avenge by the death of many soldiers. On the other hand, if one of their own is killed or maimed anywhere, whether by a government or a private citizen, they first send envoys to look into the circumstances; then they demand that the guilty persons be surrendered; and if that demand is refused, they are not to be put off, but at once declare war. If the guilty persons are surrendered, their punishment is death or slavery.

The Utopians are not only troubled but ashamed when their forces gain a bloody victory, thinking it folly to pay too high a price even for good goods. But if they overcome the enemy by skill and cunning, they exult mightily, celebrate a public triumph, and raise a monument as for a mighty exploit. They think they have really acted with manly virtue when they have won a victory such as no animal except man could have won—a victory achieved by strength of understanding. Bears, lions, boars, wolves, dogs, and other wild beasts fight with their bodies, they say; and most of them are superior to us in strength and ferocity; but we outdo them all in shrewdness and rationality.

The only thing they aim at, in going to war, is to secure what would have prevented the declaration of war, if the enemy had conceded it beforehand. Or if they cannot get that, they try to take such bitter revenge on those who have injured them that they will be afraid ever to do it again. These are their chief concerns, which they go after energetically, yet in such a way as to avoid danger, rather than to win fame and glory.

As soon as war is declared, therefore, they have their secret agents set up overnight many placards, each marked with their official seal, in the most conspicuous places throughout the enemy territory. In these proclamations they promise immense rewards to anyone who will kill the enemy's king. They offer smaller but still very substantial sums for killing any of a list of other individuals whom they name. These are the persons whom they regard as most responsible, after the king, for plotting aggression against them. The reward for an assassin is doubled for anyone who succeeds in bringing in one of the proscribed men alive. The same reward, plus a guarantee of personal safety, is offered to any one of the proscribed men who turns against his comrades. As a result, the enemies of the Utopians quickly come to suspect everyone, particularly one another; and the many perils of their situation lead to panic. They know perfectly well that many of them, including their prince as well, have been betrayed by those in whom they placed complete trust—so effective are bribes as an incitement to crime. Knowing this, the Utopians are lavish in their promises of bounty. Being well aware of the risks their agents must run, they make sure that the payments are in proportion to the peril; thus they not only offer, but actually deliver, enormous sums of gold, as well as large landed estates in very secure locations on the territory of their friends.

Everywhere else in the world, this process of bidding for and buying the life of an enemy is condemned as the cruel villainy of a degenerate mind;[3] But the Utopians consider it good policy, both wise and merciful. In the first place, it enables them to win tremendous wars without fighting any actual battles; and in the second place it enables them, by the sacrifice of a few guilty men, to spare the lives of many innocent persons who would have died in battle, some on their side, some on the enemy's. They pity the mass of the enemy's soldiers almost as much as their own citizens, for they know common people do not go to war of their own accord, but are driven to it by the madness of their rulers.

If assassination does not work, they sow the seeds of dissension in enemy ranks by inciting the king's brother or some member of the nobility to scheme for the crown. If internal discord dies down, they try to rouse up the neighboring peoples against the enemy, by reviving forgotten claims to dominion, of which kings always have an ample supply.[4]

When they promise their resources to help in a war, they send money very freely, but commit their own citizens only sparingly. They hold their own people dear, and value them so highly that they would not exchange one of their citizens for an enemy's king. Since they keep their gold and silver for the purpose of war alone, they spend it without hesitation; after all, they will continue to live just as well even if they waste the whole sum. Besides the wealth they have at home, they have a vast treasure abroad since, as I described before, many nations owe them money. So they hire mercenary soldiers from all sides, especially the Zapoletes.[5]

These people live five hundred miles to the east of Utopia, and are rude, rough, and fierce. The forests and mountains where they are bred are the kind of country they like—tough and rugged. They are a hard race, capable of standing heat, cold, and drudgery, unacquainted with any luxuries, careless of what houses they live in or what they wear; they don't till the fields, but raise cattle instead. Most of them survive by hunting and stealing. These people are born for battle and are always eager for a fight; they seek it out at every opportunity. Leaving their own

3. This is not altogether ironic; regicide was considered ignoble and treacherous until the sixteenth-century wars of religion made it common practice and produced formal, learned justifications of it.

4. More seems to have forgotten that these devices, which he admires in the Utopians, were cited as examples of low craft in unscrupulous courtiers, and indignantly repudiated by Hythloday in Book 1; cf. above, pp. 20–26.

5. "Busy sellers"; the Swiss were the best known and ablest mercenaries of Europe (a remnant still survives as the Swiss Guard in the Vatican); they correspond in many ways with the Zapoletes. John Froben, printer of the third and fourth editions of *Utopia*, was Swiss himself, and had his shop in Basel; he prudently omitted from his editions a note making explicit the unflattering Swiss-Zapolete comparison.

country in great numbers, they offer themselves for cheap hire to anyone in need of warriors. The only art they know for earning a living is the art of taking life.

They fight with great courage and incorruptible loyalty for the people who pay them, but they will not bind themselves to serve for any fixed period of time. If someone, even the enemy, offers them more money tomorrow, they will take his side; and day after tomorrow, if a trifle more is offered to bring them back, they'll return to their first employers. Hardly a war is fought in which a good number of them are not engaged on both sides. It happens every day that men who are united by ties of blood and have served together in intimacy through long campaigns, but who are now separated into opposing armies, meet in battle. Forgetful of kinship and comradeship alike, they furiously run one another through, with no other motive than that they were hired for paltry pay by opposing kings. They care so much about money that they can easily be induced to change sides for an increase of only a penny a day. They have picked up the habit of avarice, and none of the profit; for what they earn by shedding blood, they quickly squander on debauchery of the most squalid sort.

Because the Utopians give higher pay than anyone else, these people are ready to serve them against any enemy whatever. And the Utopians, who seek out the best possible men for proper uses, hire these, the worst possible men, for improper uses. When the situation requires, they thrust the Zapoletes into the positions of greatest danger by offering them immense rewards. Most of these volunteers never come back to collect their pay, but the Utopians faithfully pay off those who do survive, to encourage them to try it again. As for how many Zapoletes get killed, the Utopians never worry about that, for they think they would deserve very well of all mankind if they could exterminate from the face of the earth that entire disgusting and vicious race.

Beside the Zapoletes, they employ as auxiliaries the soldiers of the people for whom they have taken up arms, and then squadrons of all their other friends. Last, they add their own citizens, including some man of known bravery to command the entire army. In addition, they appoint two substitutes for him, who hold no rank as long as he is safe. But if the commander is captured or killed, the first of these two substitutes becomes his successor, and in case of a mishap to him, the other. Thus, though the accidents of war cannot be foreseen, they make sure that the whole army will not be disorganized through the loss of their leader.

Only volunteers are sent to fight abroad; they are picked men from within each city. No one is forced to fight abroad against his will, because they think a man who is naturally a bit fearful will act weakly at best, and may even spread panic among his comrades. But if their own country is invaded, they call everyone to arms, posting the fearful (as long as they are physically fit) on shipboard among braver men, or here and there along fortifications, where there is no place to run away. Thus shame at failing their countrymen, desperation at the immediate presence of the enemy, and the impossibility of flight often combine to overcome their fear, and they turn brave out of sheer necessity.

Just as no man is forced into a foreign war against his will, so women are allowed to accompany their men on military service if they want to—not only not forbidden, but encouraged and praised for doing so. They place each woman alongside her husband in the line of battle; and in addition they place around him all of a man's children, kinsmen, and blood- or marriage-relations, so that those who by nature have most reason to help one another may be closest at hand for mutual aid. It is a matter of great reproach for either partner to come home without the other, or a son to return after losing his father. The result is, that as long as the enemy stands his ground, the hand-to-hand fighting is apt to be long and bitter, ending only when everyone is dead.

As I observed, they take every precaution to avoid fighting in person, so long as they can bring the war to an end with mercenaries. But when they are forced to take part in battle, they are as bold in the struggle as they were formerly prudent in avoiding it while they could. In the first charge they are not fierce, but gradually as the fighting goes on they grow more determined, putting up a steady, stubborn resistance. Their spirit is so strong that they will die rather than yield ground. They have no anxieties about making a living at home, nor any worry about the future of their families (and that sort of worry often daunts the boldest spirits); so their spirit is exalted and unconquerable. Knowing the job of warfare and knowing it well gives them extra confidence; also from childhood they have been trained by example and instruction in the first principles of patriotism; and that too adds to their courage. They don't hold life so cheap that they throw it away recklessly, nor so dear as to grasp it avidly at the price of shame, when duty bids them give it up.

At the height of the battle, a band of the bravest young men who have taken a special oath devote themselves to seeking out the opposing general. They attack him directly, they lay secret traps for him, they hit at him from near and far. A continuous supply of fresh men keep up the assault as the exhausted drop out. In the end, they rarely fail to kill or capture him, unless he takes to flight.

When they win a battle, it never ends in a massacre, for they would much rather take prisoners than cut throats. They never pursue fugitives without keeping one line of their army drawn up under the colors and ready to renew the fight. They are so careful of this that if they win the victory with this last reserve force (supposing the rest of their army has been beaten), they would rather let the enemy army escape than be tricked into pursuing fugitives with their own ranks in disorder. They remember what has happened more than once to themselves: that when the enemy seemed to have the best of the day, had routed the main Utopian force and scattered to pursue the fugitives, a few Utopians held in reserve and watching their opportunity have suddenly attacked the dispersed enemy at the very moment when he felt safe and had lowered his guard. Thereby they changed the fortune of the day, snatched a certain victory out of the enemy's hands, and, though conquered themselves, were able to overcome their conquerors.

It is not easy to say whether they are more crafty in laying ambushes or more cautious in avoiding those laid for them. Sometimes they seem to be on the point of breaking and running when that is the very last thing they have in mind; but when they really are ready to retreat, you would never guess it. If they are too few to attack, or if the terrain is unsuitable, they shift their ground silently by night and slip away from the enemy by some stratagem. Or if they have to withdraw by day, they do so gradually, and in such good order that they are as dangerous to attack then as if they were advancing. They fortify their camps very carefully with a deep, broad ditch all around them, the earth being thrown inward to make a wall; the work is done not by workmen but by the soldiers themselves with their own hands. The whole army pitches in, except for a guard which is posted around the workers to prevent a surprise attack. With so many hands at work, they complete great fortifications, enclosing wide areas with unbelievable speed.

The armor they wear is strong enough to protect them from blows, but does not prevent easy movement of the body; in fact, it doesn't interfere even with their swimming, and part of their military training consists of swimming in armor. For long-range fighting they use arrows, which they fire with great strength and accuracy, and from horseback as well as on the ground. At close quarters they use not swords but battle-axes, which, because of their sharp edge and great weight, are lethal weapons, whether used in slashing or thrusting. They are very skillful in inventing machines of war, but conceal them with the greatest care, since if they were made known before they were needed, the enemy might turn them to ridicule and lessen their effect. Their first consideration in designing them is to make them easy to carry and aim.[6]

When the Utopians make a truce with the enemy, they observe it religiously, and will not break it even if provoked. They do not ravage the enemy's territory or burn his crops; indeed, so far as possible, they avoid any trampling of the crops by men or horses, thinking they may

6. The military devices of the Utopians are a patchwork of different notions from the common knowledge of the day. The camps are fortified like Roman camps. English archers had won famous victories over the French at Crécy and Agincourt; and the Parthians, as well as the Scythians, were famous in antiquity for their ability to shoot arrows accurately from horseback. The "machines" are evidently like Roman ballistae, arietes, scorpiones (dart-hurlers, battering-rams, stone-throwers); but the emphasis on their portability probably reflects contemporary experience with cannon, which were terribly hard to drag over muddy medieval routes.

need the grain themselves later on. Unless he is a spy, they injure no unarmed man. When cities are surrendered to them, they keep them intact; even when they have stormed a place, they do not plunder it, but put to death the men who prevented surrender, enslave the other defenders, and do no harm to the civilians. If they find any of the inhabitants who recommended surrender, they give them a share in the property of the condemned, and present their auxiliaries with the rest, for the Utopians themselves never take any booty.

After a war is ended, they collect the cost of it, not from the allies for whose sake they undertook it, but from the conquered. They take as indemnity not only money which they set aside to finance future wars, but also landed estates from which they may enjoy forever a generous annual income. They now have property of this sort in many different countries, which over the years has increased little by little, and has been augmented in various ways, till it now amounts to over seven hundred thousand ducats a year.[7] As managers of these estates, they send abroad some of their own citizens, with the title of Financial Factors. Though they live on the properties in great style and conduct themselves like great personages, plenty of income is still left over, to be put in the public treasury, unless they choose to give the conquered nation credit. They often do the latter, until they happen to need the money, and even then it's rare for them to call in the entire debt. And of course some of the estates are given, as I've already described, to those who have risked great dangers in their behalf.

If any foreign prince takes up arms and prepares to invade their land, they immediately attack him in full force outside their own borders. They are most reluctant to wage war on their own soil, and no necessity could ever compel them to admit foreign auxiliaries onto their island.

Religions

There are different forms of religion throughout the island, and in each particular city as well. Some worship as a god the sun, others the moon, and still others one of the planets.[8] There are some who worship a man of past ages who was conspicuous either for virtue or glory; they consider him not only a god but the supreme god. Most of the Utopians,

---

7. These are doubtless Venetian ducats, a common medium of international exchange. The sum would translate into half as many English pounds of the time but would have to be multiplied by as much as fifty to get a rough modern equivalent in dollars. The point is simply that it's a whopping sum of money.

8. The various lights in the heavens are appro-priate objects of worship for a people influenced by Persian thought, which represented Mithra or Mazda, the spirit of light, as the supreme force of good in the universe. More could have learned a great deal about the ancient Persians from his reading of Pico della Mirandola.

however, and among these all the wisest, believe nothing of the sort: they believe in a single power, unknown, eternal, infinite, inexplicable, far beyond the grasp of the human mind, and diffused throughout the universe, not physically, but in influence. Him they call father, and to him alone they attribute the origin, increase, progress, change, and end of all visible things; they do not offer divine honors to any other.

Though the other sects of the Utopians differ from this main group in various particular doctrines, they all agree in this single head, that there is one supreme power, the maker and ruler of the universe, whom they all call in their native language Mithra. Different people define him differently, and each supposes the object of his worship is the special vessel of that great force which all people agree in worshipping. But gradually they are coming to forsake this mixture of superstitions, and to unite in that one religion which seems more reasonable than any of the others. And there is no doubt that the other religions would have disappeared long ago, except for various unlucky accidents that befell certain Utopians who were thinking about changing their religion. All the others immediately construed these events as a sign of heavenly anger, not chance, as if the deity who was being abandoned were avenging an insult against himself.[9]

But after they had heard from us the name of Christ, and learned of his teachings, his life, his miracles, and the no less marvelous devotion of the many martyrs who shed their blood to draw nations far and near into the Christian fellowship, you would not believe how they were impressed. Either through the mysterious inspiration of God, or because Christianity is very like the religion already prevailing among them, they were well disposed toward it from the start. But I think they were also much influenced by the fact that Christ had encouraged his disciples to practice community of goods, and that among the truest groups of Christians, the practice still prevails.[1] Whatever the reason, no small number of them chose to join our communion, and received the holy water of baptism. By that time, two of our group had died, and among us four survivors there was, I am sorry to say, no priest; so, though they received instruction in other matters, they still lack those sacraments which in our religion can be administered only by priests.[2] They do, however,

9. The ridicule is obviously pointed against superstitious interpretation of mere natural accidents. Yet the Utopians believe in miracles and are apparently commended for doing so: see below, p. 76 and note.
1. The communist practice of the disciples is described in Acts 2.44–45 and 4.32–35; see below, in the Backgrounds section, p. 92. Many monastic and ascetic orders made a practice of abolishing private property for their members.

The Latin word that More uses for "groups" is *conventus*, which means "gatherings" but has given rise to the English cognate *convents*.
2. Ordination, with its symbolic laying-on of hands, establishes a new priest in order of succession from Christ; baptism admits a new soul to the Christian community. The first is customarily performed by a bishop, the second by a priest; most of the other sacraments can, in case of need, be performed by a layman.

understand what they are and earnestly desire them. In fact, they dispute vigorously among themselves whether a man chosen from among themselves could legitimately assume the functions of a priest without a special mission from the Pope. Though they seemed on the point of selecting such a person, they had not yet done so when I left.

Those who have not accepted Christianity make no effort to restrain others from it, nor do they criticize new converts to it. While I was there, only one of the Christians got into trouble with the law. As soon as he was baptized, he took on himself to preach the Christian religion publicly, with more zeal than discretion. We warned him not to do so, but he soon worked himself up to a pitch where he not only preferred our religion, but condemned all others as profane in themselves, leading their impious and sacrilegious followers to the hell-flames they richly deserved. After he had been going on in this style for a long time, they arrested him. He was tried, on a charge not of despising their religion, but of creating a public disorder, convicted and sentenced to exile. For it is one of their oldest institutions that no man's religion, as such, shall be held against him.

Even before he came to the island, King Utopus had heard that the inhabitants were continually quarreling over religious matters. In fact, he found it was easy to conquer the country because the different sects were too busy fighting one another to oppose him. As soon as he had gained the victory, therefore, he decreed that every man might cultivate the religion of his choice, and might proselytize for it, provided he did so quietly, modestly, rationally, and without bitterness toward others. If persuasions failed, no man was allowed to resort to abuse or violence, under penalty of exile or enslavement.

Utopus laid down these rules, not simply for the sake of peace, which he saw was in danger of being destroyed by constant quarrels and implacable hatreds; but also for the sake of religion itself. In matters of religion, he was not at all quick to dogmatize, because he suspected that God perhaps likes various forms of worship and has therefore deliberately inspired different people with different views. On the other hand, he was quite sure that it was arrogant folly for anyone to enforce conformity with his own beliefs by means of threats or violence. He supposed that if one religion is really true and the rest false, that true one will prevail by its own natural strength, provided only that men consider the matter reasonably and moderately. But if they try to decide these matters by fighting and rioting, since the worst men are always the most headstrong, the best and holiest religion in the world will be crowded out by blind superstitions, like grain choked out of a field by thorns and briars. So he left the whole matter open, allowing each individual to choose what he would believe. The only exception he made was a positive and strict law against any person who should sink so far below the dignity of human nature as to think that the soul perishes with the body, or that the universe is ruled by mere chance, rather than divine providence.[3]

Thus the Utopians all believe that after this life vices are to be punished and virtue rewarded; and they consider that anyone who opposes this proposition is hardly a man, since he has degraded the sublimity of his own soul to the base level of a beast's wretched body. They will not even count him as one of their citizens, since he would undoubtedly betray all the laws and customs of society, if not prevented by fear. Who can doubt that a man who has nothing to fear but the law, and no hope of life beyond the grave, will do anything he can to evade his country's laws by craft or break them by violence, in order to gratify his own private greed? Therefore a man who holds such views is offered no honors, entrusted with no offices, and given no public responsibility; he is universally regarded as a low and sordid fellow. Yet they do not afflict him with punishments, because they are persuaded that no man can choose to believe by a mere act of the will.[4] They do not compel him by threats to dissemble his views, nor do they tolerate in the matter any deceit or lying, which they detest as next door to deliberate malice. The man may not argue with the common people in behalf of his opinion; but in the presence of the priests and other important persons, they not only permit but encourage it. For they are confident that in the end his madness will yield to reason.

There are some others, in fact no small number of them, who err in the opposite direction, in supposing that animals too have immortal souls,[5] though not comparable to ours in excellence, nor destined to equal felicity. These men are not thought to be evil, their opinion is not thought to be wholly unreasonable, and so they are not interfered with.

Almost all the Utopians are absolutely convinced that man's bliss after death will be enormous and eternal; thus they lament every man's sickness, but mourn over a death only if the man was torn from life despairingly and against his will.[6] Such behavior they take to be a very bad sign, as if the soul, being in anguish and conscious of guilt, dreaded death through a secret premonition of punishments to come. Besides, they suppose God can hardly be well pleased with the coming of one who, when he is summoned, does not come gladly, but is dragged off reluctantly and against his will. Such a death fills the onlookers with horror,

3. Like many Christians of More's day, the Utopians are rather dogmatic about a point (the immortality of the soul) that they themselves consider a matter of faith, not of demonstration. Among those holding that the world began as a chance concatenation of atoms. More might have had in mind Lucretius.

4. More, who in later years took part in the burning of obstinate heretics—i.e., Protestants—would have done well to remember these wiser words of his early middle age. His exact phrase here is "nullo afficiunt supplicio."

5. Pythagoreans, who believed in the transmigration of souls from form to form, were particularly likely to concede them to animals.
6. More's emphasis on cheerful dying is humanist in tone. When Pico was dying, we learn from the biography that More translated, "he lay always with a pleasant and merry countenance, and in the very twitches and pangs of death, he spake as though he beheld the heavens open."

and they carry away the corpse to the cemetery in melancholy silence. There, after begging God to have mercy on his spirit, and pardon his infirmities, they commit his body to the earth. But when a man dies blithely and full of good hope, they do not mourn for him, but carry the body cheerfully away, singing and commending the dead man's soul to God. They cremate him in a spirit more of reverence than of grief, and erect a tombstone on which the dead man's honors are inscribed. As they go home, they talk of his character and deeds, and no part of his life is mentioned more frequently or more gladly than his joyful death.

They think that recollecting the good qualities of a man helps the living to behave virtuously and is also the most acceptable form of honor to the dead. For they think that dead persons are actually present among us, and hear what we say about them, though through the dullness of human sight they are invisible to our eyes. Given their state of bliss, the dead must be able to travel freely where they please, and they are bound to want to revisit their friends, whom they loved and honored during their lives. Like all other good things, they think that after death freedom of motion is increased rather than decreased in all good men; and thus they believe the dead come frequently among the living, to observe their words and actions. Hence they go about their business the more confidently because of their trust in such protectors; and the belief that their forefathers are physically present keeps men from any secret dishonorable deed.

Fortune-telling and other vain forms of superstitious divination, such as other people take very seriously, they consider ridiculous and contemptible.[7] But they venerate miracles which occur without the help of nature, considering them direct and visible manifestations of the divine power. Indeed, they report that miracles have frequently occurred in their country. Sometimes in great and dangerous crises they pray publicly for a miracle, which they then anticipate with great confidence, and obtain.

They think that the careful contemplation of nature, and the sense of reverence arising from it, are acts of worship to God. There are some people, however, and quite a few of them, who for religious motives reject learning, pursue no studies, and refuse all leisure, but devote their full time to good works. Constant dedication to the offices of charity, these people think, will increase their chances of happiness after death; and so they are always busy. Some tend the sick; others repair roads; clean ditches; rebuild bridges, dig turf, gravel, or stones; fell trees and cut them up; and transport wood, grain, and other commodities into the cities by wagon. They work for private citizens, as well as the public,

7. Pico della Mirandola, whom More greatly admired, strongly condemned astrological divination. The opinion expressed below, that miracles can occur even in non-Christian countries, is standard Catholic doctrine.

and work even harder than slaves. They undertake with cheery good will any task that is so rough, hard, and dirty that most people refuse to tackle it because of the toil, boredom, and frustration involved. While constantly engaged in heavy labor themselves, they secure leisure for others, and yet they claim no credit for it.[8] They do not criticize the way other people live, nor do they boast of their own doings. The more they put themselves in the position of slaves, the more highly they are honored by everyone.

These people are of two opinions.[9] The first are celibates who abstain not only from sex, but also from eating meat, and some of them from any sort of animal food whatever. They reject all the pleasures of this life as harmful and look forward only to the joys of the life to come, which they hope to deserve by hard labor and all-night vigils. As they hope to attain it quickly, they are cheerful and active in the here and now. The other kind are just as fond of hard work, but prefer to marry. They don't despise the comforts of marriage, and they think as their duty to nature requires work, so their duty to their country draws them to beget children. They avoid no pleasure, unless it interferes with their labor, and gladly eat meat, precisely because they think it makes them stronger for any sort of heavy work. The Utopians regard the second sort as more sensible, but the first sort as the holier men. If anyone claimed to prefer celibacy to marriage, and a hard life to a comfortable one, on the grounds of reason alone, the Utopians would think him absurd. But since these men claim to be motivated by religion, the Utopians respect and revere them. There is no subject on which they are more careful of jumping to conclusions than this matter of religion. These then are the men whom in their own language they call Buthrescas, a term which may be translated as "especially religious men."

Their priests are men of great holiness, and therefore very few. In each city, there are no more than thirteen, one for each church.[1] In case of war, seven of them go out with the army, and seven substitutes are appointed to fill their places for the time being. When the regular priests come back, the substitutes return to their former posts—that is, they serve as assistants to the high priest, until one of the regular thirteen dies, and then one of them succeeds to his position. The high priest is, of course, in authority over all the others. Priests are elected, just like all

---

8. I.e., they are direct enemies of sloth, gluttony, avarice, pride, envy, and lust, and implicit enemies of anger, the seventh of the deadly sins. These ascetic Utopians are clearly congenial to More, in whom the strain of penitential, self-mortifying feeling ran very deep; their constant pursuit of disagreeable and painful activity contrasts with the laziness attributed to European monks in Book 1.

9. The Latin word for "opinions" is *haereses*—despite the sinister overtones of English "heresy," the Latin means simply "schools of thought."

1. As there are nearly 120,000 adults (plus children and slaves) in each city and its suburbs, the thirteen churches of each city must be able to accommodate, no doubt in several shifts, 10,000 worshippers apiece.

other officials, by secret popular vote, in order to avoid partisan feeling. [2] After election they are ordained by the college of priests.

Their chief functions are to preside over divine worship, decree religious rites, and act as censors of public morality. [3] For a man to be summoned before them, and scolded for not living an honorable life, is considered a great disgrace. As the duty of the priests is simply to counsel and advise, so correcting and punishing offenders is the duty of the prince and the other officials, though the priests may and do exclude from divine service persons whom they find to be extraordinarily wicked. Hardly any punishment is more dreaded than this; the man who is excommunicated incurs great disgrace and is tortured by the fear of damnation. Not even his body is safe for long, for unless he quickly convinces the priests of his repentance, he will be seized and punished by the senate for impiety.

The priests are entrusted with teaching the children and young people. [4] Instruction in good manners and pure morals is considered just as important as the accumulation of learning. From the very first they try to instill in the pupils' minds, while they are still young and tender, principles which will be useful to preserve the commonwealth. What is planted in the minds of children lives on in the minds of adults, and is of great value in strengthening the commonwealth: the decline of society can always be traced to vices which arise from wrong attitudes.

Women are not debarred from the priesthood, but only a widow of advanced years is ever chosen, and it doesn't happen often. [5] Except for women who are priests themselves, the wives of priests are the most important women in the whole country.

No official in Utopia is more honored than the priest. Even if one of them commits a crime, he is not brought into a court of law, but left to God and his own conscience. They think it is wrong to lay human hands on a man, however guilty, who has been specially consecrated to God as a holy offering, so to speak. This custom is the easier for them to observe, because their priests are very few and very carefully chosen. Besides, it rarely happens that a man selected for his goodness and raised to high dignities wholly because of his moral character will fall into corruption and vice. If such a thing should happen, human nature being as changeable as it is, no great harm is to be feared, because the priests are so few and have no power beyond that which derives from their good reputation. In fact, the reason for having so few priests is to prevent the

2. The election is popular and the ballot secret; but the slate is radically limited to the very small class of the professionally learned; see above, p. 39 and note.
3. Priests do not seem to hold secular office in Utopia, as, for example, Cardinal Morton and Cardinal Wolsey did in More's England. They hardly could, there being so few of them.
4. In view of their many other functions and small numbers (thirteen priests to supervise the

morals of 120,000 adults plus—let's say—half as many children), priests cannot be the only teachers. They evidently supervise the teaching program.
5. Among the early Christians, women frequently served in an ambiguous ecclesiastical office known as "deaconess"; whether they were actually priestesses is not wholly clear.

order, which the Utopians now esteem so highly, from being cheapened
by numbers. Besides, they think it would be hard to find many men
qualified for a dignity to which merely ordinary virtues could never raise
them.

Their priests are esteemed no less highly abroad than at home, which
can be seen from the following fact: Whenever their armies join in battle, the Utopian priests are to be found, a little removed from the fray
but not far, wearing their sacred vestments and down on their knees.
With hands raised to heaven, they pray first of all for peace, and then
for victory to their own side, but without much bloodshed on either
hand. Should their side be victorious, they rush among the combatants
and restrain the rage of their own men against the enemy. If any of the
enemy see these priests and call to them, it is enough to save their lives;
to touch the robe of a priest will save all their property from confiscation.
This custom has brought them such veneration among all peoples, and
given them such genuine authority, that they have saved the Utopians
from the rage of the enemy as often as they have protected the enemy
from their own men. Instances of this are well known. Sometimes when
the Utopian line has buckled, when the field was lost, and the enemy
was rushing in to kill and plunder, the priests have intervened, separated
the armies, and concluded an equitable peace. There was never anywhere a tribe so fierce, cruel, and barbarous as not to hold their persons
sacrosanct and inviolable.

The Utopians celebrate the first and last days of every month, and
likewise of each year, as holy days. They divide the year into months,
which they measure by the orbit of the moon, just as they measure the
year itself by the course of the sun. In their language the first days are
known as the Cynemern and the last days as the Trapemern, [6] which is
to say "First-feast" and "Last-feast." Their churches are beautifully constructed, finely adorned, and large enough to hold a great many people.
This is a necessity, since churches are so few. Their interiors are all
rather dark, not from architectural ignorance, but from deliberate policy;
for the priests think that in bright light the congregation's thoughts will
go wandering, whereas a dim light tends to concentrate the mind and
encourage devotion.

Though there are various religions in Utopia, as I've said, all of them,
even the most diverse, agree in the main point, which is worship of the
divine nature; they are like travelers going to one destination by different
roads. So nothing is seen or heard in the churches that does not square
with all the creeds. If any sect has a special rite of its own, that is celebrated in a private house; the public service is ordered by a ritual which
in no way derogates from any of the private services. Therefore in the

6. Cynemern really means, in Greek, "dog-day," Trapemern "turning-day."

churches no image of the gods is to be seen, so that each man may be free to form his own image of God after his heart's desire, in any shape he pleases. There is no special name for God, apart from the common word *Mithra*. Whatever the nature of the divine majesty may be, they agree to refer to it by that single word, and their prayers are so phrased as to accommodate the beliefs of all the different sects.

On the evening of the "Last-feast" they meet in their churches, and while still fasting they thank God for their prosperity during that month or year which is just ending. Next day, which is "First feast," they all flock to the churches in the morning, to pray for prosperity and happiness in the month or year which is just beginning. On the day of "Last-feast," in the home before they go to church, wives kneel before their husbands and children before their parents, to confess their various failures and negligences, and beg forgiveness for their offenses.[7] Thus if any cloud of anger and resentment has arisen in the family, it is dispersed, and they can attend divine services with clear and untroubled minds, for they consider it sacrilege to worship with a rankling conscience. If they are conscious of hatred or anger toward anyone, they do not take part in divine services till they have been reconciled and cleansed their hearts, for fear of some swift and terrible punishment.

As they enter the church, they separate, men going to the right side and women to the left. Then they take their seats so that the males of each household are placed in front of the head of that household, while the womenfolk are directly in front of the mother of the family. In this way they insure that everyone's behavior in public is supervised by the same person whose authority and discipline direct him at home. They take great care that the young are everywhere placed in the company of their elders. For if children were trusted to the care of the other children, they might spend in childish foolery the time they should devote to developing a religious fear of the gods, which is the greatest and almost the only incitement to virtue.

They do not slaughter animals in their sacrifices and do not think a merciful God, who gave life to all creatures, will be gratified with the shedding of blood. They light incense, scatter perfumes, and burn a great number of candles—not that they think these practices profit the divine nature in any way, any more than human prayers do; but they like this harmless kind of worship. They feel that sweet smells, lights, and rituals elevate the mind, and lift it with a livelier devotion toward the adoration of God.

When they go to church, the people all wear white. The priest wears a robe of many colors, wonderful for its workmanship and decoration, though not of materials as costly as one would suppose. It has no gold

---

7. It is not specific that the husbands have anything to confess or anywhere to confess it.

embroidery nor any precious stones, but is decorated with the feathers of different birds so skillfully woven together that the value of the handiwork far exceeds the cost of the most precious materials. They add that certain symbolic mysteries are hidden in the patterning of the feathers on the priest's robes, the meaning of which is carefully handed down among the priests. These messages serve to remind them of God's benefits toward them, and consequently of the gratitude they owe to God as well as of their duty to one another.

As the priest in his robes appears from the vestry, the people all fall to the ground in reverence. The stillness is so complete, that the scene strikes one with awe, as if a divinity were actually present. After remaining in this posture for some time, they rise at a word from the priest. Then they sing hymns to the accompaniment of musical instruments, quite different in shape from those in our part of the world. Many of them produce sweeter tones than ours, but others are not even comparable. In one respect, however, they are beyond doubt far ahead of us, because all their music, both vocal and instrumental, renders and expresses natural feelings, and perfectly matches the sound to the subject. Whether the words of the hymn are cheerful, supplicatory, troubled, mournful, or angry, the music represents the meaning through the melody so admirably that it penetrates and inspires the minds of the ardent hearers. Finally, the priest and the people together recite certain fixed forms of prayer, so composed that what they all repeat in unison each individual can apply to himself.

In these prayers, the worshippers acknowledge God to be the creator and ruler of the universe and the author of all good things. They thank God for benefits received, and particularly for the divine favor which placed them in the happiest of commonwealths and inspired them with religious ideas which they hope are the truest. If they are wrong in this, and if there is some sort of society or religion more acceptable to God than the present one, they pray that he will, in his goodness, reveal it to them, for they are ready to follow wherever he leads them. But if their form of society is the best and their religion the truest, then they pray that God will keep them steadfast, and bring other mortals to the same way of life and the same religious faith—unless, indeed, there is something in this variety of religions which delights his inscrutable will.

Then they pray that after an easy death God will receive each of them to himself, how soon or how late it is not for them to say. But, if God's divine majesty so please, they ask to be brought to him soon, even by the hardest possible death, rather than be kept away from him longer, even by the most prosperous of earthly careers. When this prayer has been said, they prostrate themselves on the ground again; then after a little while they rise and go home to dinner. The rest of the day they pass in games and military training.

Now I have described to you as accurately as I could the structure of that commonwealth which I consider not only the best but the only one that can rightfully claim that name. In other places men talk very liberally of the common wealth, but what they mean is simply their own wealth; in Utopia, where there is no private business, every man zealously pursues the public business. And in both places, men are right to act as they do. For among us, even thought the state may flourish, each man knows that unless he makes separate provision for himself, he may perfectly well die of hunger. Bitter necessity, then, forces men to look out for themselves rather than for others, that is, for the people. But in Utopia, where everything belongs to everybody, no man need fear that, so long as the public warehouses are filled, he will ever lack for anything he needs. Distribution is simply not one of their problems; in Utopia no men are poor, no men are beggars. Though no man owns anything, everyone is rich.

For what can be greater riches than for a man to live joyfully and peacefully, free from all anxieties, and without worries about making a living? No man is bothered by his wife's querulous complaints about money, no man fears poverty for his son, or struggles to scrape up a dowry for his daughter. Each man can feel secure of his own livelihood and happiness and of his whole family's as well: wife, sons, grandsons, great-grandsons, great-great-grandsons, and that whole long line of descendants that gentlefolk are so fond of contemplating. Indeed, even those who once worked but can do so no longer are cared for just as well as if they were still productive.

Now here I'd like to see anyone try to compare this justice of the Utopians with the so-called justice that prevails among other peoples—among whom let me perish if I can discover the slightest scrap of justice or fairness. What kind of justice is it when a nobleman or a goldsmith or a moneylender, or someone else who makes his living by doing either nothing at all or something completely useless to the public, gets to live a life of luxury and grandeur? In the meantime, a laborer, a carter, a carpenter, or a farmer works so hard and so constantly that even a beast of burden would perish under the load; and this work of theirs is so necessary that no commonwealth could survive a year without it. Yet they earn so meager a living and lead such miserable lives that a beast of burden would really be better off. Beasts do not have to work every minute, and their food is not much worse; in fact they like it better. And, besides, they do not have to worry about their future. But workingmen not only have to sweat and suffer without present reward, but agonize over the prospect of a penniless old age. Their daily wage is inadequate even for their present needs, so there is no possible chance of their saving toward the future.

Now isn't this an unjust and ungrateful commonwealth? It lavishes rich rewards on so-called gentry, bankers and goldsmiths and the rest of that crew, who don't work at all, are mere parasites, or purveyors of empty pleasures. And yet it makes no provision whatever for the welfare of farmers and colliers, laborers, carters, and carpenters, without whom the commonwealth would simply cease to exist. After the state has taken the labor of their best years, when they are worn out by age and sickness and utter destitution, then the thankless state, forgetting all their pains and services, throws them out to die a miserable death. What is worse, the rich constantly try to grind out of the poor part of their meager wages, not only by private swindling, but by public tax-laws. It is basically unjust that people who deserve most from the commonwealth should receive least. But now they have distorted and debased the right even further by giving their extortion the color of law; and thus they have palmed injustice off as "legal." When I run over in my mind the various commonwealths flourishing today, so help me God, I can see nothing in them but a conspiracy of the rich, who are fattening up their own interests under the name and title of the commonwealth.[8] They invent ways and means to hang onto whatever they have acquired by sharp practice, and then they scheme to oppress the poor by buying up their toil and labor as cheaply as possible. These devices become law as soon as the rich, speaking through the commonwealth—which, of course, includes the poor as well—say they must be observed.

And yet, when these insatiably greedy and evil men have divided among themselves goods which would have sufficed for the entire people, how far they remain from the happiness of the Utopians, who have abolished not only money but with it greed! What a mass of trouble was uprooted by that one step! What a multitude of crimes was pulled up by the roots! Everyone knows that if money were abolished, fraud, theft, robbery, quarrels, brawls, seditions, murders, treasons, poisonings, and a whole set of crimes which are avenged but not prevented by the hangman would at once die out. If money disappeared, so would fear, anxiety, worry, toil, and sleepless nights. Even poverty, which seems to need money more than anything else for its relief, would vanish if money were entirely done away with.

Consider if you will this example. Take a barren year of failed harvests, when many thousands of men have been carried off by hunger. If at the end of the famine the barns of the rich were searched, I dare say positively enough grain would be found in them to have saved the lives of all those who died from starvation and disease, if it had been divided equally among them. Nobody really need have suffered from a bad harvest at all. So easily might men get the necessities of life if that cursed money, which is supposed to provide access to them, were not in fact

---

8. In this famous, vehement assertion of his most radical position, More is in fact echoing the words of Saint Augustine, in *The City of* God, 4, 4: "Remota justita quid sunt regna nisi magna latrocinia?" ("Take away justice, and what are states but giant rip-offs?")

the chief barrier to our getting what we need to live. Even the rich, I'm sure, understand this. They must know that it's better to have enough of what we really need than an abundance of superfluities, much better to escape from our many present troubles than to be burdened with great masses of wealth. And in fact I have no doubt that every man's perception of where his true interest lies, along with the authority of Christ our Saviour (whose wisdom could not fail to recognize the best, and whose goodness would not fail to counsel it), would long ago have brought the whole world to adopt Utopian laws, if it were not for one single monster, the prime plague and begetter of all others—I mean Pride.

Pride measures her advantages not by what she has but by what other people lack. Pride would not condescend even to be made a goddess, if there were no wretches for her to sneer at and domineer over. Her good fortune is dazzling only by contrast with the miseries of others, her riches are valuable only as they torment and tantalize the poverty of others. Pride is a serpent from hell which twines itself around the hearts of men; and it acts like the suckfish[9] in holding them back from choosing a better way of life.

Pride is too deeply fixed in the hearts of men to be easily plucked out. So I am glad that the Utopians at least have been lucky enough to achieve this commonwealth, which I wish all mankind would imitate. The institutions they have adopted have made their community most happy, and as far as anyone can tell, capable of lasting forever. Now that they have rooted up the seeds of ambition and faction at home, along with most other vices, they are in no danger from internal strife, which alone has been the ruin of many other states that seemed secure. As long as they preserve harmony at home, and keep their institutions healthy, the Utopians can never be overcome or even shaken by their envious neighbors, who have often attempted their ruin, but always in vain.

When Raphael had finished his story, it seemed to me that not a few of the customs and laws he had described as existing among the Utopians were quite absurd. Their methods of waging war, their religious ceremonies, and their social customs were some of these, but my chief objection was to the basis of their whole system, that is, their communal living and their moneyless economy. This one thing alone takes away all the nobility, magnificence, splendor, and majesty which (in the popular view) are considered the true ornaments of any nation. But I saw Raphael was tired with talking, and I was not sure he could take contradiction in these matters, particularly when I remembered what he had

9. The relatively small remora (*Echeneis nau-crates*) has a suction plate atop its head, by which it attaches itself to the underbelly of larger fishes or the hulls of ships. Impressed by the tenacity of its grip, the ancients fabled that it could stop ships in their course. More is not above a pun here; the remora *remoratur*, i.e., "holds back."

said about certain counsellors who were afraid they might not appear wise unless they found out something to criticize in other men's ideas.

So with praise for the Utopian way of life and his account of it, I took him by the hand and led him in to supper. But first I said that we would find some other time for thinking of these matters more deeply, and for talking them over in more detail. And I still hope such an opportunity will present itself some day.

Meanwhile, though he is a man of unquestioned learning, and highly experienced in the ways of the world, I cannot agree with everything he said. Yet I confess there are many things in the Commonwealth of Utopia that I wish our own country would imitate—though I don't really expect it will.

End of Book Two
*   *   *   *   *

THE END OF THE AFTERNOON DISCOURSE OF
RAPHAEL HYTHLODAY ON THE LAWS AND
CUSTOMS OF THE ISLAND OF UTOPIA
HITHERTO KNOWN BUT TO FEW, AS
REPORTED BY THE MOST
DISTINGUISHED AND
MOST LEARNED MAN,
MR. THOMAS MORE,
CITIZEN AND SHERIFF OF LONDON

F I N I S
*   *   *   *

BACKGROUNDS

OVID

(First Century B.C.–First Century A.D.)

The myth of the Golden Age, from which man sprang and to which he may someday hope to return, is practically immemorial; as it has no point of origin, it has no fixed limits, significance, or precise definition. For example, Ovid, who under his slick, civilized Augustan surface had a deep feeling for the distant past, gave one memorable expression to the myth in the first book of his Metamorphoses. But, like other parts of that radiant poem, the tale of the Golden Age spread and had repercussions far beyond what Ovid himself could have visualized. Viewed from a Christian perspective, the Age of Gold transformed itself almost automatically into the Garden of Eden or the community of the saints. Long before Freud, psychological interpreters had no difficulty in reading it as nostalgia for the womb; and messianic revolutionaries, by simply transferring it to the other end of the historical time-scale, have easily converted it to the classless society or the New Jerusalem. Ovid himself would have been quite as amazed at these developments as at the notion that his poem had influenced Sir Thomas More's *Utopia*. But it did—not so much directly and specifically, as through a diffused and pervasive atmosphere of thought that identified a life of innocence, equality, and closeness to nature as the first and last state of man.

[The Golden Age] †

The age was formed of gold; in those first days
No law or force was needed; men did right
Freely; without duress they kept their word.
No punishment or fear of it; no threats
Inscribed on brazen tablets; no jostling crowds
Beseeching mercy from a lofty judge;
For without law or judge all men were safe.
High on its native hills the pine tree stood,
Unlopped as yet, nor yet compelled to cross
Ocean's wide waves, and help men leave their homes.
Towns had no moats; no horns of winding brass
Nor trumpets straight, nor swords nor shields existed.
The nations dozed through ages of soft time,
Safe without armies; while the earth herself,
Untouched by spade or plowshare, freely gave,
As of her own volition, all men needed:
And men were well content with what she gave
Unforced and uncompelled; they found the fruit
Of the arbutus bush, and cornel-cherries,

† Book 1, ll. 89–136.

Gathered wild berries from the mountain-sides,
Eating ripe fruit plucked from the thorny canes,
And acorns as they fell from Jove's wide oak.
Spring lasted all year long; the warm west wind
Played gently over flowers sprung from no seed:
Soon too the untilled earth brought forth profuse
Her crops of grain; and fields, uncultivated,
Whitened beneath their stalks of bearded wheat.
Streams flowed profuse, now milk, now nectar, and
The living oak poured streams of golden honey.

Later, with Saturn sent to gloomy Hell,
Jove ruled the world; the Age of Silver came,
Worse than the Age of Gold, though not so bad
As was to be the Age of yellow Brass.
Jove cut the old spring short and turned the year
To the four changing seasons, winter, spring
(Brief now), hot summer, and contrarious fall.
Then first the air burnt white with summer heat,
And icicles hung down, gripped by the winds:
Then men first sought out homes; they used to live
In caves, or else in thickets, where they wove
Together twigs and withes with strips of bark.
Then first the seeds of grain were set in rows,
And bullocks groaned, under the heavy yoke.

Third of the ages came the Age of Bronze,
Harder of mind, quicker to savage arms,
But not yet brutal. Last was the Age of Iron.
Evil at once broke forth; from such coarse stuff
Modesty, truth, and faith withdrew; their place
Was filled by tricks, deceitful plots, brute force,
Treachery, and the shameful lust for gain.

Sails now spread to the winds—at first, the sailors
Knew little of their use—while keels of wood
That long had stood on lofty mountain-tops,
Now leaped exultantly over strange waves.
And now the ground itself, which once had been
Common to all, like sunlight and the air,
Fell under the surveyor's drawn-out lines.   *   *   *

PLATO

(Fourth Century B.C.)

Though many stories are told of Plato's hostility to private property (More
alludes to one of them in the *Utopia*, above, p. 28), his ideal commonwealth is a mixed community that allows property to the inferior citizens,

but denies it to the caste of ruling "guardians." These are the philosopher-warrior-kings of the ideal state, with whose training Plato is primarily concerned: the subjects over whom they rule have little to do but obey.

Guardians are to be trained from youth on a deliberate lie or myth, the first element of which informs them that they are not children of particular fathers or mothers, but rather children of the land herself, to whom they owe absolute loyalty. They will also be told (by a peculiar socializing of the myth of the four ages of man) that they are the golden or at least the silver people—the lower castes over whom they rule are mere creatures of brass or iron. Partly as a way of fostering this myth, the guardians and their chosen women will consort strenuously and promiscuously together, and the children will be removed to crèches as soon as they are born. Thus no child will ever know its own mother or father, and no dynasty founded on wealth or kinship will ever be in danger of springing up. Far removed from these common temptations of ordinary humanity, the guardians—strenuous athletes of the ideal, shock-troops of the mind—will be able to bring perfect disinterested justice to the state over which they rule.

As usual, Socrates is the main speaker of this dialogue; his interlocutors (except for the furious Thrasymachus, who doesn't appear in this section) are even paler and more colorless than is customary. At the beginning of this excerpt, Socrates is expounding the myth on which he will have the guardians raised.

[The Guardians] †

Citizens, we shall say to them in our tale, you are brothers, yet God has framed you differently. Some of you have the power of command, and in the composition of these he has mingled gold, wherefore also they have the greatest honor; others he has made of silver, to be auxiliaries; others again who are to be husbandmen and craftsmen he has composed of brass and iron; and the species will generally be preserved in the children. But as all are of the same original stock, a golden parent will sometimes have a silver son, or a silver parent a golden son. And God proclaims as a first principle to rulers, and above all else, that there is nothing which they should so anxiously guard, or of which they are to be such good guardians, as of the purity of the race. They should observe what elements mingle in their offspring; for if the son of a golden or silver parent has an admixture of brass and iron, then nature orders a transposition of ranks, and the eye of the ruler must not be pitiful toward the child because he has to descend in the scale and become a husbandman or artisan, just as there may be sons of artisans who having an admixture of gold or silver in them are raised to honor, and become guardians or auxiliaries. For an oracle says that when a man of brass or

---

† From *The Republic*, Book 3, tr. Benjamin Jowett, 3, 3rd Edition (London: Oxford, 1892) 104–6.

iron guards the State, it will be destroyed. Such is the tale; is there any possibility of making our citizens believe in it?

Not in the present generation, he replied; there is no way of accomplishing this; but their sons may be made to believe in the tale, and their sons' sons, and posterity after them.   *   *   *

Then let us now consider what will be their way of life, if they are to realize our idea of them. In the first place, none of them should have any property of his own beyond what is absolutely necessary; neither should they have a private house or store closed against anyone who has a mind to enter; their provisions should be only such as are required by trained warriors, who are men of temperance and courage; they should agree to receive from the citizens a fixed rate of pay, enough to meet the expenses of the year and no more; and they will go to mess and live together like soldiers in a camp. Gold and silver we will tell them that they have from God; the diviner metal is within them, and they have therefore no need of the dross which is current among men, and ought not to pollute the divine by any such earthly admixture; for that commoner metal has been the source of many unholy deeds, but their own is undefiled. And they alone of all the citizens may not touch or handle silver or gold, or be under the same roof with them, or wear them, or drink from them. And this will be their salvation, and they will be the saviours of the state. But should they ever acquire homes or lands or moneys of their own, they will become good housekeepers and husbandmen instead of guardians, enemies and tyrants instead of allies of the other citizens; hating and being hated, plotting and being plotted against, they will pass their whole life in much greater terror of internal than of external enemies, and the hour of ruin, both to themselves and to the rest of the state, will be at hand. For all which reasons, may we not say that thus shall our state be ordered, and that these shall be the regulations appointed by us for our guardians concerning their houses and all other matters?

Yes, said Glaucon.

The Acts of the Apostles

(First Century A.D)

[The last verses of Chapter Four in the Acts of the Apostles describe in detail the life of the primitive, that is, the very early, Christians. The spirit of God was strongly on the little group—half a community, half a church—from which the entire body of Christian believers was to derive. In many matters where Jesus Christ left no explicit commandments, later ages assumed he meant the example set by these earliest Christians to prevail. Among their distinctive practices was community of material goods; none of them claimed anything as his own, but all things were held in common.]

(The Community of Love)

31. And when they had prayed, the place was shaken where they were assembled together; and they were all filled with the Holy Ghost, and they spake the word of God with boldness.

32. And the the multitudes of them that believed were of one heart and of one soul: neither said any of them that ought of the things which he possessed was his own; but they had all things common.

33. And with great power gave the apostles witness of the resurrection of the Lord Jesus: and great grace was upon them all.

34. Neither was there any among them that lacked: for as many as were possessors of lands or houses sold them, and brought the prices of the things that were sold,

35. And laid them down at the apostles' feet: and distribution was made unto every man according as he had need.

[But as the fervor of the first apostles cooled, while new converts entered the society, a stronger motive and a more dramatic story were required to motivate the practice of universal sharing. The story of Ananias and his wife, Sapphira, occupies the first eleven verses of Chapter Five in the Acts of the Apostles.]

(The Community of Fear)

But a certain man named Ananias, with Sàpphirà his wife, sold a possession,

2. And kept back *part* of the price, his wife also being privy *to it*, and brought a certain part, and laid *it* at the apostles' feet.

3. But Peter said, Ananias, why hath Satan filled thine heart to lie to the Holy Ghost, and to keep back *part* of the price of the land?

4. While it remained, was it not thine own? and after it was sold, was it not in thine own power? why hast thou conceived this thing in thine heart? thou has not lied unto men, but unto God.

5. And Ananias hearing these words fell down, and gave up the ghost: and great fear came on all of them that heard these things.

6. And the young men arose, wound him up, and carried *him* out, and buried *him*.

7. And it was about the space of three hours after, when his wife, not knowing what was done, came in.

8. And Peter answered unto her, Tell me whether ye sold the land for so much? And she said, Yea, for so much.

9. Then Peter said unto her, How is it that ye have agreed together to tempt the Spirit of the Lord? behold, the feet of them which have buried thy husband *are* at the door, and shall carry thee out.

10. Then fell she down straightway at his feet, and yielded up the ghost: and the young men came in, and found her dead, and carrying *her* forth, buried *her* by her husband.

11. And great fear came upon all the church, and upon as many as heard these things.

LUCIAN OF SAMOSATA

(Second Century A.D)

Lucian's "Saturnalian Letters" are address to Cronus or Saturn, the father and predecessor of Zeus, on the occasion of his particular festival, the Saturnalia. This was a seven-day festival falling just about the same time as Christmas, in the latter part of December. During the festival all schools were closed, no battles were fought, and no punishments were inflicted; distinctions of rank were abolished, slaves and servants sat at tables alongside their masters, and gifts were exchanged, particularly wax tapers and clay dolls. Behind all these observances lies the myth that Saturn's age was an Age of Gold, when life was simpler, men were better, and nature, as the common heritage of the human race, shared out its blessings equally to all.

Lucian, who was a cynical Syrian rhetorician, doesn't take any of this mythology very seriously. He writes to Saturn, asking that the abuses of his festival be corrected—that the rich be made truly generous and the ideals of the Age of Gold be brought somewhat closer to reality. But his letter suffers the usual fate of such communications in the modern world—Saturn says it doesn't come within the mandate of his department, and shuffles it off to Zeus, who will no doubt conveniently mislay it. Still, though it's only a joke, the occasion provides Lucian with a chance to revive that dream of the Golden Age in which nobody had too much and everybody had what he needed—when there wasn't very much, but everybody had as much as anybody else, and nobody needed more than he had.

[Saturn's Age] †

I to Cronus, Greeting:

* * *

Now the poets inform me that in the old days when you were king it was otherwise with men; earth bestowed her gifts upon them unsown

† From "Saturnalian Letters" 1 and 2 in the *Works of Lucian*, tr. H. W. Fowler and F. G. Fowler (London: Oxford UP, 1905), 4. 117–21.

and unploughed, every man's table was spread automatically, rivers ran wine and milk and honey. Most wonderful of all, the men themselves were gold, and poverty never came near them. As for us, we can hardly pass for lead; some yet meaner material must be found. In the sweat of our face the most of us eat bread. Poverty, distress, and helplessness, sighs and lamentations and pinings for what is not, such is the staple of man's life, the poor man's at least. All which, believe me, would be much less painful to us, if there were not the felicity of the rich to emphasize it. They have their chests of gold and silver, their stored wardrobes, their slaves and carriages and house property and farms, and, not content with keeping to themselves their superfluity in all these, they will scarce fling a glance to the generality of us.

Ah, Cronus, there is the sting that rankles beyond endurance— that one should loll on cloth of finest purple, overload his stomach with all delicacies, and keep perpetual feast with guests to wish him joy, while I and my like dream over the problematic acquisition of a sixpence to provide us a loaf white or brown, and send us to bed with a smack of cress or thyme or onion in our mouths. Now, good Cronus, either reform this altogether and feed us alike, or at the least induce the rich not to enjoy their good things alone; from their bushels of gold let them scatter a poor pint among us; the raiment that they would never feel the loss of though the moth were to consume it utterly, seeing that in any case it must perish by mere lapse of time, let them devote to covering our nakedness rather than to propagating mildew in their chests and drawers.

Further let them entertain us by fours and fives, and not as they now do, but more on principles of equality; let us all share alike. The way now is for one to gorge himself on some dainty, keeping the servant waiting about him till he is pleased to have done; but when it reaches us, as we are in the act of helping ourselves it is whisked off, and we have but that fleeting glimpse of the entrée or fag-end of a sweet. Or in comes a sucking-pig; half of it, including the head, falls to the host; the rest of us share the bones, slightly disguised. And pray charge the butlers not to make us call unto seven times, but bring us our wine when we ask for it first; and let it be a full-sized cup and a bumper, as it is for their masters. And the same wine, please, for every one at table; where is the legal authority for my host's growing mellow on the choicest bouquet while my stomach is turned with mere must?

These things if you correct and reform, you will have made life life, and your feast a feast. If not, we will leave the feasting to them, and just kneel down and pray that as they come from the bath the slave may knock down and spill their wine, the cook smoke their sauce and absent-mindedly pour the pea-soup over the caviare, the dog steal in while the scullions are busy and make away with the whole of the sausage and most of the pastry.

Cronus to his well-beloved me, Greeting:

My good man, why this absurdity of writing to me about the state of the world, and advising redistribution of property? It is none of my business; the present ruler must see to that. It is an odd thing you should be the only person unaware that I have long abdicated; my sons now administer various departments, of which the one that concerns you is mainly in the hands of Zeus; my own charge is confined to draughts and merry-making, song and good cheer, and that for one week only. As for the weightier matters you speak of, removal of inequalities and reducing of all men to one level of poverty or riches, Zeus must do your business for you.   *   *   *

ST. AMBROSE

(Fourth Century A.D)

Since Christianity began, many preachers have had occasion, or made it, to denounce the evildoing of the rich; few have been so unbridled in their invective as Saint Ambrose of Milan, the mentor and friend of Saint Augustine. From a set of sermons preached on the theme of "Naboth's Vineyard" and later assembled into a single consecutive discourse, A. O. Lovejoy has pieced together the following excerpts. The original source is that collection of writings of the "Church fathers" edited by Migne and known to scholars as "MPL" (Migne, *Patrilogia Latina*) 14. 767–72, 784. Lovejoy's essay, "The Communism of Saint Ambrose," may be found among *Essays in the History of Ideas*, by Arthur O. Lovejoy.

Naboth's Vineyard †

How far, ye rich, will you carry your insane cupidity?   *   *   * Why do you reject nature's partnership of goods, and claim possession of nature for yourselves? The earth was established to be in common for all, rich and poor; why do ye rich alone arrogate it to yourselves as your rightful property? Nature knows no rich, since she brings forth all men poor. For we are born without clothes and are brought forth without silver or gold. Naked she brings us to the light of day, and in want of food and covering and drink; and naked the earth receives back what she has brought forth, nor can she stretch men's tombs to cover their possessions. A narrow mound of turf is enough for rich and poor alike; and a bit of land

† From Arthur O. *Lovejoy, Essays in the History of Ideas*, (Baltimore: Johns Hopkins UP, 1948) 299–300. Copyright 1948 by The Johns Hopkins University Press. Reprinted by permission of the publisher.

of which the rich man when alive took no heed now takes in the whole of him. Nature makes no distinction among us at our birth, and none at our death. All alike she creates us, all alike she seals us in the tomb. Who can tell the dead apart? Open up the graves, and, if you can, tell which was a rich man.   *   *   *

But why do you think that, even while you live, you have abundance of all things? Rich man, you know not how poor you are, how destitute you would seem even to yourself, who call yourself wealthy. The more you have, the more you want; and whatever you may acquire, you nevertheless remain as needy as before. Avarice is inflamed by gain, not diminished by it.   *   *   *

You crave possessions not so much for their utility to yourself, as because you want to exclude others from them. You are more concerned with despoiling the poor than with your own advantage. You think yourself injured if a poor man possesses anything which you consider a suitable belonging for a rich man; whatever belongs to others you look upon as something of which you are deprived. Why do you delight in what to nature are losses? The world, which you few rich men try to keep for yourselves, was created for all men. For not alone the soil, but the very heaven, the air, the sea, are claimed for the use of the few rich. . . . Do the angels in heaven, think you, have their separate regions of space, as you divide up the earth by fixed boundaries?   *   *   *

How many men are killed to procure the means of your enjoyment! A deadly thing is your greed, and deadly your luxury. One man falls to death from a roof, in order that you may have your big granaries. Another tumbles from the top of a high tree while seeking for certain kinds of grapes, so that you may have the right sort of wine for your banquet. Another is drowned in the sea while making sure that fish or oysters shall not be lacking on your table. Another is frozen to death while tracking hares or trying to catch birds with traps. Another is beaten to death before your eyes, if he chances to have displeased you, and your very viands are bespattered with his blood.   *   *   *

Do you think your great halls (atria) exalt you—when they ought rather to cause you remorse because, though they are big enough to take in multitudes, they shut out the voice of the poor? Though, indeed, nothing is gained by your hearing their voice if, when you hear it, you do nothing about it. In fine, does not your very dwelling-place admonish you of your shame, in that in building it you wished to show that your riches surpass [those of others]—and yet you do not succeed? You cover walls, but you leave men bare. Naked they cry out before your house, and you heed them not: a naked man cries out, but you are busy considering what sort of marbles you will have to cover your floors. A poor man asks for money, and does not get it; a human being begs for bread, and your horse champs a golden bit. You gratify yourself with costly ornaments, while other men go without food. How great a judgment, O rich man, do you draw down upon yourself! The people go hungry, and you close your granaries; the people weep, and you turn your finger-ring about. Unhappy man, who have the power but not the will to save so many souls from death: the cost of the jewel in your ring would have sufficed to save the lives of a whole people.

ST. BENEDICT

Monastic Rules

(Sixth Century)

[The Utopians turned readily to Christianity because the early disciples set an example of communal living and because certain Christian communities continued to practice it. These were the monastic orders, of which the most famous and widespread was that of Saint Benedict. His famous Rule was developed for use by monks of the newly founded house of Monte Cassino. Though it has a reputation for strictness and austerity, the Rule was not in fact very severe; many different suborders of Benedictines (for example the Cistercians) split off from the main order in search of greater purity and stricter discipline. But on the question of personal property within the monastery, the Rule of Saint Benedict was, and remained, crisp and uncompromising. Chapters 33 and 34 present the core of the Rule's teaching on this point.]

Chapter 33
Whether Monks Should Have Anything of Their Own

This vice especially ought to be utterly rooted out of the monastery. Let no one presume to give or receive anything without the abbot's leave, or to have anything as his own, anything whatever, whether book or tablets or pen or whatever it may be; for monks should not have even their bodies and wills at their own disposal. But let them look to the father of the monastery for all that they require, and let it be unlawful to have anything which the abbot has not given or allowed. And, as the Scripture saith, *let all things be common to all*, nor let anyone say that *anything is his own*[1] or claim it for himself. But if anyone shall be found to indulge in this most wicked vice, let him be admonished once and a second time; if he do not amend, let him undergo punishment.

Chapter 34
Whether All Should Receive Necessaries in Like Measure

Let us follow the Scripture: *Distribution was made to every man according as he had need.*[2] By this we do not mean that there should be

---

1. Acts 4.32   2. Acts 4.35

respect of persons (God forbid), but consideration for infirmities. He that needeth less, let him thank God and not be discontented; he that needeth more, let him be humbled for his infirmity and not made proud by the mercy shown to him: so will all the members be at peace. Above all, let not the vice of murmuring show itself in any word or sign, for any reason whatever. But if a brother be found guilty of it, let him undergo strict punishment.

Cokayne

[In the medieval village, where the exhausting, monotonous routines of agriculture filled every moment of the turning year, the dreams of the drudges naturally turned toward an easier existence where food, drink, sex, and loafing were available to everyone all the time. Sometimes this dream-world took on the features of local institutions. Abbeys and monasteries, such as dotted the countryside, were supposed to be austere, ascetic retreats where holy monks and devout nuns devoted their lives to prayer and mortification of the flesh. So they may sometimes have been. But to the grumbling peasant in his endless round of toil, the monk often looked like a man with soft hands and round belly, who enjoyed free access to all the best women of the community—his own private flock of nuns. Jealous imaginings along these lines quickly brought the penitential monastery into line with the riotous fantasies of the ancient Land of Cokayne, where all the good things of life are available in unlimited quantities, and free for the asking.

The poem excerpted, and freely adapted, here is an anonymous twelfth-century satire, surviving in a single manuscript at Oxford. It illustrates the sort of popular fantasy that permeated peasant dreams of an ideal society. The pressure of these gluttonous, glorious fantasies surely influenced More to make his utopia the severe, disciplined, and rather disagreeable place that modern readers very often find it.]

> Far out to sea and west of Spain
> Lies a land known as Cokayne;
> There is no place beneath the sky
> Where men live more deliciously.
> Though Paradise is brisk and bright,
> Cokayne is a more glorious sight;
> For what has Paradise to show
> But plants and more plants row on row?
> Flowers are red there, grasses green,
> The moral atmosphere's serene,
> But though the bliss is absolute,
> The only thing to eat is fruit,
> And water's all you get to drink—
> Not much excitement there, I think.
> Society is pretty meager, too;
> After Elias and Enoch, I wonder who
> There is to talk to ? Fine men, no doubt,

But everyone else you have to do without.
   Cokayne o'erflows with meat and drink,
No need to sweat or strain or swink,
The meat is free, the drink flows clear,
Nothing to pay, nothing to fear,
Yours for the asking noon and night,
Everything for your delight

      *   *   *

   A noble abbey, proud in its array,
Crowded with monks both white and gray,
Raises its banners through the air;
Many bowers and halls are there;
The walls are made of pasty-pies,
Rising in turrets to the skies,
Stuffed all with fish and good red meat
The finest any man could eat;
The roofs of gingerbread, each and all,
Whether of church or cloister, tower or hall;
The postern-gates are fat pudding,
Fit for the feast of prince or king.
People may eat their fill, and stuff
Themselves enough and more than enough;
For all is common to young and old,
To stout and stern, to meek and bold.
   There the young monks every day
After dinner go out to play;
There is no hawk or quail so swift,
Half as nimble or as deft,
As these monks in joyous mood,
Their long sleeves flying and their hood
Floating on the evening air
As they dance across the lawn.
When the abbot sees them flee,
Who more joyous is than he?
Till he summons them along,
Crying, "Time for even-song!"
But feisty monks absorbed in play
Romp over the hills and far away.
When the abbot sees his crew
Frolic off, far from his view,
He picks a maiden from the flock
And gathers up her pretty smock,
And loudly sounds the recall drum
Upon the tabor of her bum.

      *   *   *

Another abbey is thereby,
Forsooth a great fine nunnery,
On a river of sweet milk
The countryside as soft as silk.
When a summer's day is hot,
The younger nuns take out a boat
And in the stream with active oar
Set boldly onward from the shore,
And having left their home behind
Strip to enjoy both wave and wind,
Then leaping boldly in the brim,
Dispose themselves to splash and swim.
The young monks, having them in sight,
Approach in haste, with great delight,
And coming to the nuns anon,
Each makes selection of his own,
And quickly leadeth back his prize
Out of the range of curious eyes,
Back to the abbey's private cot,
Where they may tie the true love's knot.
Each girl performs her act of true devotion
Contributing her own peculiar motion.
The monk who is reputed good,
And carries high aloft his hood,
He shall enjoy for his good cheer
At least a dozen wives a year,
By his own right and not through grace,
For his own pleasure and solace;
And for the monk whose eager zest
Keeps his lady all night from rest,
There is good grounds to hope he may
Himself be named abbot some day.

TASSO

Chorus from Act 2 of *Aminta* †

[Torquato Tasso (1544–95) was a courtier-poet, the son of a courtier-poet, and the most distinguished young man of his age. Handsome, accomplished, and witty, he was a universal favorite at the court of Urbino; and there, before he was out of his twenties, he completed the pastoral drama *Aminta*. This semi-dramatic piece, slight and artificial as it is, caught the rising tide of Italian music; it was sensual, plangent, melodious, and melancholy all at once—and immensely successful. The chorus at the end of

the first act is the most famous of its set-pieces. The characters who sing it
are partly shepherds who emphasize their humble simplicity, partly courtiers
who find themselves much inhibited by the restrictions of Honour; they are
also learned enough to know by heart Ovid's picture of the Golden Age, and
impudent enough to make fun of it. The communal society, which can be
severe enough to fit in a Benedictine monastery, here reduces itself to a
single point that on the main question girls can't ever say no.]

> O lovely age of gold,
> Lovely not just because each rill
> Ran white with milk and from each bough
> Pure drops of molten honey fell;
> Nor yet because, untouched by plough,
> Earth yielded up her choicest foison,
> While yet the silent snake could pass,
> Unhated, innocent of poison,
> Through the soft, compliant grass;—
> Not that the sun all year around
> Glowed down from cloudless skies
> To warm the grateful ground
> And urge the forms of spring to rise;
> Nor yet because no thought of war,
> No itch of conquest, and no greed of gain
> Had yet urged man to travel far
> Across the dangerous seas—
>
> No, for no reasons such as these,
> But just because that vain
> And empty idol, that disease
> Of hateful minds, and by them named
> "Honor" had not laid icy hands
> On our desires, not yet tied
> Our tender hearts in iron bands,
> Or crushed within her hateful maw
> The golden rule that nature's self decrees,
> Her sweet and universal law,
> "You are allowed to do whate'er you please."
>
> Amid wild flowers in a ring
> The tiny cupids used to settle down
> Without or torch or bow, content to sing
> Ditties for nymphs and shepherds, while around
> Gentle caresses and more gentle murmurs passed,
> With whispers and still sweeter kisses blent,
> Kisses drawn out, as if to last
> A lifetime of delight and pure content.
> The slender maiden, there reclined,

Opened her bosom to the vagrant air—
The rose that nowadays she does not dare
Release from underneath her heavy dress.
But then she freely slipped away to hide
Her unripe apples under rippling gleams
Of lucent water in the lakes and streams,
While with her joyous lover by her side
She frolicked in unfettered nakedness.

  You honor, you it was, who first
Poisoned the fountains of delight, denied
Refreshment to the lover's ardent thirst,
And forced those glorious eyes to hide
Behind the curtaining of downcast lashes;
You folded all those other sweets away
Like glowing coals beneath a pile of ashes;
You crushed beneath a net the bright array
Of freely floating hair; your turned to shame
The gentlest acts of dalliance, and poured blame
On lovers' playful toying; you encased
In rigid ice our native innocence.
Honor, the fault is yours, you who defaced
Love's fruitful field, and nature's gift of sense
Turned to the shape of theft and false pretense.

  These are the triumphs of your mighty war,
The griefs you have laid on us and the pains;
But, King of Love and Nature as you are,
Monarch of monarchs, what can be your gains
In overcoming us, a lowly folk
Who cannot understand your mighty schemes
Or recognize the grandeur of your yoke?
Off with you, then, and agitate the dreams
Of lofty rulers and aspiring minds;
Leave us, a lowly, unambitious crew,
To live our lives out by our own designs,
The way the ancient peoples used to do.
  We can then love and live our quiet hours
Making no sort of truce with passing years,
For only present time is truly ours.
Day being over, the sun disappears,
And when we lose its momentary light,
What's left for us but endless night?

AMERIGO VESPUCCI

The First Voyage †

[Vespucci's letter to Piero Soderini, describing his voyages to America, was the book about American exploration that we know More had read. It did have certain traceable influences on the Utopia; not so patent are the traditional European ideas about a golden age and a purely natural existence that the first explorers brought to their experience of America. Vespucci, for example, says nothing of the human sacrifices and cannibalistic practices that deeply impressed later (but not much later) explorers. Footnotes are the translator's unless credited.]

* * * We sailed with the north-west wind, thus running along the coast with the land ever in sight, continually in our course observing people along the shore: till after having navigated for two days, we found a place sufficiently secure for the ships, and anchored half a league from land, on which we saw a very great number of people: and this same day we put to land with the boats, and sprang on shore full 40 men in good trim: and still the land's people appeared shy of converse with us, and we were unable to encourage them so much as to make them come to speak with us: and this day we laboured so greatly in giving them of our wares, such as rattles and mirrors, beads, [1] *spalline*, and other trifles, that some of them took confidence and came to discourse with us: and after having made good friends with them, the night coming on, we took our leave of them and returned to the ships: and the next day when the dawn appeared we saw that there were infinite numbers of people upon the beach, and they had their women and children with them: we went ashore, and found that they were all laden with their wordly goods[2] which are suchlike as, in its [proper][3] place, shall be related: and before we reached the land, many of them jumped into the sea and came swimming to receive us at a bowshot's length [*from the shore*], for they are very great swimmers, with as much confidence as if they had for a long time been acquainted with us: and we were pleased with this their confidence. For so much as we learned of their manner of life and customs, it was that they go entirely naked, as well the men as the women, without covering any shameful part, not otherwise than when they issued

† From *The First Four Voyages of Amerigo Vespucci*, translated and annotated by "M. K." (London 1885), after the first edition written at Lisbon in 1504, printed at Florence in 1505, translated into French, retranslated into Latin, and in that form circulated throughout Europe, starting about 1507. Pp. 7–11, 45–46.

1. The word is *cente*, supposed to be a misprint for *conte*, an Italianised form of the Spanish *cuentas*. *Spalline* is a word not given in the dictionaries.. The Latin translator seems to have read the original as *certe cristalline*.
2. *Mantenimenti*. The word "all" (*tucte*) is feminine and probably refers only to the women.
3. Italicized and bracketed inserts are the work of the translator, to eke out Vespucci's crude Italian [*Editor*].

from their mother's womb. They are of medium stature, very well proportioned: their flesh is of a colour that verges into red like a lion's mane:
and I believe that if they went clothed, they would be as white as we:
they have not any hair upon the body, except the hair of the head which
is long and black, and especially in the women, whom it renders handsome: in aspect they are not very good-looking, because they have broad
faces, so that they would seem Tartar-like: they let no hair grow on their
eyebrows nor on their eyelids, nor elsewhere, except the hair of the head:
for they hold hairiness to be a filthy thing: they are very light-footed in
walking and in running, as well the men as the women: so that a woman
recks nothing of running a league or two, as many times we saw them
do: and herein they have a very great advantage over us Christians: they
swim [*with an expertness*] beyond all belief, and the women better than
the men: for we have many times found and seen them swimming two
leagues out at sea without any thing to rest upon. Their arms are bows
and arrows very well made, save that [*the arrows*] are not [*tipped*] with
iron nor any other kind of hard metal: and instead of iron they put
animals' or fishes' teeth, or a spike of tough wood, with the point hard-
ened by fire: they are sure marksmen, for they hit whatever they aim at:
and in some places the women use these bows: they have other weapons,
such as fire-hardened spears, and also clubs with knobs, beautifully carved.
Warfare is used amongst them, which they carry on against people not
of their own language, very cruelly, without granting life to any one,
except [*to reserve him*] for greater suffering. When they go to war, they
take their women with them, not that these may fight, but because they
carry behind them their worldly goods: for a woman carries on her back
for thirty or forty leagues a load which no man could bear: as we have
many times seen them do. They are not accustomed to have any Captain, nor do they go in any ordered array, for every one is lord of himself:
and the cause of their wars is not for lust of dominion, nor of extending
their frontiers, nor for inordinate covetousness, but for some ancient
enmity which in bygone times arose[4] amongst them: and when asked
why they made war, they knew not any other reason to give us than that
they did so to avenge the death of their ancestors, or of their parents:
these people have neither King, nor Lord, nor do they yield obedience
to any one, for they live in their own liberty: and how they be stirred up
to go to war is [*this*] that when the enemies have slain or captured any
of them, his oldest kinsman rises up and goes about the highways har-
anguing them to go with him and avenge the death of such his kinsman:
and so are they stirred up by fellow-feeling: they have no judicial system,
nor do they punish the ill-doer: nor does the father, nor the mother
chastise the children: and marvellously [*seldom*] or never did we see any

---

4. The expression in the original is *e suta*, an error for è surta.

dispute among them: in their conversation they appear simple, and they are very cunning and acute in that which concerns them:[5] they speak little and in a low tone: they use the same articulations as we, since they form their utterances either with the palate, or with the teeth, or on the lips:[6] except that they give different names to things. Many are the varieties of tongues: for in every 100 leagues we found a change of language, so that they are not understandable each to the other. The manner of their living is very barbarous, for they do not eat at certain hours, and as oftentimes as they will: and it is not much of a boon to them that the will may come more at midnight than by day, for they eat at all hours:[7] and they eat upon the ground without a table-cloth or any other cover, for they have their meats either in earthen basins which they make themselves, or in the halves of pumpkins: they sleep in certain very large nettings made of cotton,[8] suspended in the air: and although this their [fashion of] sleeping may seem uncomfortable, I say that it is sweet to sleep in those [nettings]: and we slept better in them than in the counterpanes. They are a people smooth and clean of body, because of so continually washing themselves as they do: when, saving your reverence, they evacuate the stomach they do their utmost not to be observed: and as much as in this they are cleanly and bashful, so much the more are they filthy and shameless in making water: since, while standing speaking to us, without turning round or shewing any shame, they let go their nastiness, for in this they have no shame: there is no custom of marriages amongst them: each man takes as many women as he lists: and when he desires to repudiate them, he repudiates them without any imputation of wrong-doing to him, or of disgrace to the woman: for in this the woman has as much liberty as the man: they are not very jealous and are immoderately libidinous, and the women much more so than the men, so that for decency I omit to tell you the artifice they practice to gratify[9] their inordinate lust: they are very prolific women, and do not shirk any work during their pregnancies: and their travails in childbed are so light that, a single day after parturition, they go abroad everywhere, and especially to wash themselves in the rivers, and are [then] as sound and healthy as fishes: they are so void of affection and cruel, that if they be angry with their husbands they immediately adopt an artificial method by which the embryo is destroyed in the womb, and procure abortion, and they slay an infinite number of creatures by that means: they are women of elegant persons very well proportioned, so that in their bodies there appears no ill-shaped part or limb: and although they

---

5. *Che loro cuple*. The Spanish word *complir*, with the sense of being important or suitable.

6. He means that they have no sounds in their language unknown to European organs of speech, all being either palatals or dentals or labials.

7. The words from "and it is not much" down to "at all hours" omitted in the Latin. I have translated "et non si da loro molto" as "it is not much of a boon to them," but it may be "it matters not much to them."

8. *Bambacia*.

9. In the original, *contar* for *contentar*.

go entirely naked, they are fleshy women, and, of their sexual organ, that portion which he who has never seen it may imagine, is not visible, for they conceal with their thighs everything except that part for which nature did not provide, which is, speaking modestly, the pectignone. [1] In fine, they have no shame of their shameful parts, any more than we have in displaying the nose and the mouth: it is marvellously [rare] that you shall see a woman's paps hang low, or her belly fallen in by too much childbearing, or other wrinkles, for they all appear as though they had never brought forth children: they shewed themselves very desirous of having connexion with us Christians. Amongst those people we did not learn that they had any law, nor can they be called Moors nor Jews, and [they are] worse than pagans: because we did not observe that they offered any sacrifice: nor even [2] had they a house of prayer: their manner of living I judge to be Epicurean: their dwellings are in common: and their houses [are] made in the style of huts, [3] but strongly made, and constructed with very large trees, and covered over with palm-leaves, secure against storms and winds: and in some places [they are] of so great breadth and length, that in one single house we found there were 600 souls: and we saw a village of only thirteen [4] houses where there were four thousand [5] souls: every eight or ten years [6] they change their habitations: and when asked why they did so: [they said it was] because of the soil [7] which, from its filthiness, was already unhealthy and corrupted, and that it bred aches in their bodies, which seemed to us a good reason: their riches consist of birds' plumes of many colours, or of rosaries [8] which they make from fishbones, or of white or green stones which they put in their cheeks and in their lips and ears, and of many other things which we in no wise value: they use no trade, they neither buy nor sell. In fine, they live and are contented with that which nature gives them. The wealth that we enjoy in this our Europe and elsewhere, such as gold, jewels, pearls, and other riches, they hold as nothing: and although they have them in their own lands, they do not labour to obtain them, nor do they value them.   *   *   *

1. Bigger bosom, *mons Veneris.*
2. *Nec etiam non.*
3. Waldseemüller has "bell-towers," having misread *campane* for *capanne,* huts or cabins. [Waldseemüller translated and reprinted Vespucci's letter as a supplement to his *Cosmographiae Introductio* (1507); Varnhagen (below, note 7) is a modern editor—*Editor.*]

4. Latin has *eight.*
5. Latin, *ten thousand.*
6. Latin has seven for ten.
7. *Suolo,* the ground or flooring, which Waldseemüller absurdly misread *sole,* the sun. Varnhagen, no less strangely, translates it "the atmosphere."
8. *Paternostrini,* necklaces.

The Humanist Circle: Letters

In his prefatory letter to Peter Giles, More mentions a certain churchman of his acquaintance who was trying to arrange with his ecclesiastical superiors to be sent as a missionary to the Utopians. Whether this story is serious or a joke (and if it is a joke, whoever cracked it), it certainly contains a truth: the verisimilitude of *Utopia* did impose on some readers, just as the verisimilitude of *Gulliver's Travels* was to do some two hundred years later. People took the story literally; they assumed that Utopia was a real place, and that Raphael Hythloday had visited it. Partly this was the result of More's straight-faced narrative technique; partly also it was the result of an informal, improvised conspiracy.

More was favored in imposing the *Utopia* on the general public as an actual story of a real place because the humanists of northern Europe formed such a tight and, on the whole, congenial network of personal acquaintances, with Erasmus at their center. More himself wrote a pair of prefatory letters to Peter Giles; under the urging of Erasmus, Peter Giles wrote a letter to the distinguished Jerome Busleiden, confirming More's story and adding a few "authentic"—or, at least, easily fabricated—particulars. Busleiden, a rather heavy-minded man, got the point, and carefully refrained, in his reply to More, from asking any difficult questions. Gerardus Noviomagus and Cornelius Graphaeus, Dutch humanists, wrote commendatory verses; Guillaume Budé wrote about the *Utopia* to Thomas Lupset; Erasmus wrote to the printer John Froben at Basle; and Joannes Paludanus of the University of Louvain wrote a letter to Peter Giles and a set of verses on the *Utopia*. Most of these letters and academic verses were reprinted with More's fantasy, in one edition or another; they formed a garland of humanist testimonials around the work. And while not all of them lent explicit support to the hoax, none of them was so crude as explicitly to question it. More's part in this bewildering epistolary roundabout was characteristically playful and evasive, his chief concern being to prevent the book from being taken too seriously by either naive or pedantic readers. Some contemporary criticism has called Hythloday's tale the real core of the book, viewing the "dialogue of counsel" as the first layer of protective coloration and camouflage and the ironic letters to Peter Giles as the second. More seems thus to be protecting himself from his own thought, as an oyster protects itself from an irritating grain of sand, with successive overlayers. Here, for better or worse, is at least one metaphor for the functioning of literature. Peter R. Allen has written for *Studies in the Renaissance 10* (1963): 91–107, an account of the prefatory letters and verses and their function.

Quite apart from this intricate epistolary interchange, we reprint a long excerpt from an even longer letter addressed by Erasmus to Ulrich von Hutten, a German humanist, in July 1519. Erasmus was simply trying to describe his friend More to a man who had never met him; the result is one of the warmest and most affectionate documents of the age.

Thomas More to Peter Giles †

My very dear Peter Giles, I am almost ashamed to be sending you after a full year's time this little book about the Utopian state which I'm sure you expected in less than six weeks. For, as you were well aware, I faced no problem in finding my materials, and had no reason to labor over the arrangement of them. All I had to do was repeat what you and I together heard Raphael describe. There was no occasion, either, for fine or far-fetched language, since what he said, being extempore and informal, couldn't be couched in fancy terms. And besides, as you know, he's a man better versed in Greek than in Latin; so that my language would be nearer the truth, the closer it approached to his casual simplicity. Truth in fact is the only quality at which I should have aimed, or did aim, in writing this book.

I confess, friend Peter, that having all these materials ready to hand made my own contribution so slight that there was hardly anything at all for me to do. Thinking up a topic like this from scratch and disposing it in proper order might have demanded a lot of time and work even if a man were gifted with talent and learning. And then if the matter had to be set forth with eloquence, not just bluntly and factually, there's no way I could have done that, however hard I worked, for however long a time. But now when I was relieved of all these problems, over which I could have sweated forever, there was nothing for me to do but simply write down what I had heard. Well, little as it was, that task was rendered almost impossible by my many other obligations. Most of my day is given to the law—listening to some cases, pleading others, compromising others, and deciding still others. I have to visit this man because of his official position and that man because of his lawsuit; and so almost the whole day is devoted to other people's business and what's left over to my own; and then for myself—that is, my studies—there's nothing left.

For when I get home, I have to talk with my wife, chatter with my children, and consult with the servants. All these matters I consider part of my business, since they have to be done unless a man wants to be a stranger in his own house. Besides, a man is bound to bear himself as

† Text from J. H. Lupton, ed., *Utopia* (Oxford: Oxford UP, 1895) 1–12 (translated by the editor of this volume).

agreeably as he can toward those whom nature or chance or his own choice has made the companions of his life. But of course he mustn't spoil them either with his familiarity, or by overindulgence turn the servants into his masters. And so, amid these concerns, the day, the month, and the year slip away.

What time do I find to write, then? especially since I still have taken no account of sleeping or even of eating, to which many people devote as much time as to sleep itself, which devours almost half of our lives. My own time is only what I steal from sleeping and eating. It isn't very much, but it's something, and so I've finally been able to finish our *Utopia*, even though belatedly, and I'm sending it to you now. I hope, my dear Peter, that you'll read it over and let me know if you find anything that I've overlooked. Though I'm not really afraid of having forgotten anything important—I wish my judgment and learning were up to my memory, which isn't half bad—still, I don't feel so sure of it that I would swear I've missed nothing.

For my servant John Clement has raised a great doubt in my mind. As you know, he was there with us, for I always want him to be present at conversations where there's profit to be gained. (And one of these days I expect we'll get a fine crop of learning from this young sprout, who's already made excellent progress in Greek as well as Latin.) Anyhow, as I recall matters, Hythloday said the bridge over the Anyder at Amaurot was five hundred paces long; but my John says that is two hundred paces too much—that in fact the river is barely three hundred paces wide there. So I beg you, consult your memory. If your recollection agrees with his, I'll yield to the two of you, and confess myself mistaken. But if you don't recall the point, I'll follow my own memory and keep my present figure. For, as I've taken particular pains to avoid untruths in the book, so I'd rather make an honest mistake than say what I don't believe. In short, I'd rather be truthful than correct.

But the whole matter can be cleared up if you'll ask Raphael about it—either directly, if he's still in your neighborhood, or else by letter. And I'm afraid you must do this anyway, because of another problem that has cropped up—whether through my fault, or yours, or Raphael's, I'm not sure. For it didn't occur to us to ask, nor to him to say, in what area of the New World Utopia is to be found. I wouldn't have missed hearing about this for a sizable sum of money, for I'm quite ashamed not to know even the name of the ocean where this island lies about which I've written so much. Besides, there are various people here, and one in particular, a devout man and a professor of theology, who very much wants to go to Utopia. His motive is not by any means idle curiosity, but rather a desire to foster and further the growth of our religion, which has made such a happy start there. To this end, he has decided to arrange to be sent there by the Pope, and even to be named Bishop to the Utopians. He feels no particular scruples about intriguing for this post, for he considers it a holy project, rising not from motives of glory or gain, but simply from religious zeal.

Therefore I beg you, my dear Peter, to get in touch with Hythloday—in person if you can, or by letters if he's gone—and make sure that my work contains nothing false and omits nothing true. It would probably be just as well to show him the book itself. If I've made a mistake, there's nobody better qualified to correct me; but even he cannot do it, unless he reads over my book. Besides, you will be able to discover in this way whether he's pleased or annoyed that I have written the book. If he has decided to write out his own story for himself, he may be displeased with me; and I should be sorry, too, if, in publicizing Utopia, I had robbed him and his story of the flower of novelty.

But to tell the truth, I'm still of two minds as to whether I should publish the book or not. For men's tastes are so various, the tempers of some are so severe, their minds so ungrateful, their tempers so cross, that there seems no point in publishing something, even if it's intended for their advantage, that they will receive only with contempt and ingratitude. Better simply to follow one's own natural inclinations, lead a merry, peaceful life, and ignore the vexing problems of publication. Most men know nothing of learning; many despise it. The clod rejects as too difficult whatever isn't cloddish. The pedant dismisses as mere trifling anything that isn't stuffed with obsolete words. Some readers approve only of ancient authors; most men like their own writing best of all. Here's a man so solemn he won't allow a shadow of levity, and there's one so insipid of taste that he can't endure the salt of a little wit. Some dullards dread satire as a man bitten by a hydrophobic dog dreads water; some are so changeable that they like one thing when they're seated and another when they're standing.

Those people lounge around the taverns, and as they swill their ale pass judgment on the intelligence of writers. With complete assurance they condemn every author by his writings, just as they think best, plucking each one, as it were, by the beard. But they themselves remain safely under cover and, as the proverb has it, out of harm's way. No use trying to lay hold of them; they're shaved so close, there's not so much as the hair of an honest man to catch them by.

Finally, some men are so ungrateful that even though they're delighted with a work, they don't like the author any better because of it. They are like rude, ungrateful guests who, after they have stuffed themselves with a splendid dinner, go off, carrying their full bellies homeward without a word of thanks to the host who invited them. A fine task, providing at your own expense a banquet for men of such finicky palates, such various tastes, and such rude, ungracious tempers.

At any rate, my dear Peter, will you take up with Hythloday the matter I spoke of? After I've heard from him, I'll take a fresh look at the whole matter. But since I've already taken the pains to write up the subject, it's too late to be wise. In the matter of publication, I hope we can have Hythloday's approval; after that, I'll follow the advice of my friends—and especially yours. Farewell, my dear Peter Giles. My regards to your excellent wife. Love me as you have always done; I remain more fond of you than ever.

Peter Giles to Jerome Busleiden †

[The obvious man to whom *Utopia* should have been dedicated was Erasmus. But Erasmus, who had already published the *Praise of Folly*, was too well known as a joker to sponsor the *Utopia*—it would have been giving away the spoof too cheaply. So Erasmus wrote to Peter Giles (on 17 October 1516), instructing him to send a copy of the manuscript to Jerome Busleiden, of whom more below. Giles, taking his cue from More's first letter to him, elaborated the hoax by inventing circumstances to explain the vagueness of Utopian geography, fabricating a special Utopian alphabet, and actually composing some limping verses in "Utopian."]

Most distinguished Busleiden, the other day Thomas More (who, as you very well know from your long acquaintance with him, is one of the great ornaments of our age) sent me his *Island of Utopia*. It is a place, known so far to only a few men, but which should be studied by many, as going far beyond Plato's Republic. It is particularly interesting because it has been so vividly described, so carefully discussed, and so acutely analyzed by a man of such great talents. As often as I read it, I seem to see even more than I heard from the actual mouth of Raphael Hythloday—for I was present at his discourse, along with More. As a matter of fact, Hythloday himself showed no mean rhetorical gifts in setting forth his topic; it was perfectly plain that he wasn't just repeating what he had heard from other people, but was describing exactly what he had seen with his own eyes and experienced in his own person, over a long period of time. I consider him a man with more knowledge of nations, peoples, and business than even the famous Ulysses. Such a man as this has not, I think, been born in the last eight hundred years; by comparison with him, Vespucci seems hardly to have seen anything. [1] Apart from the fact that we naturally describe what we have seen better than what we have just heard about, the man had a particular skill in explaining the details of a subject. And yet when I contemplate the same matters as sketched by More's pen, I am so affected by them that I sometimes seem to be living in Utopia itself. I can scarcely believe, by heaven, that Raphael saw as much in the five years he lived on the island as can be seen in More's description. That description contains, in every

---

† Text from Lupton, ed., *Utopia*, xcv–c (translated by the editor of this volume).

1. Amerigo Vespucci, Florentine explorer of America.

part of it, so many wonders that I don't know what to marvel at first or most. Perhaps it should be the accuracy of his memory, which could recite almost word for word so many different things that he had heard only once; or else perhaps his good judgment, which traced back to secret sources of which the common man is completely ignorant both the fortunate and unfortunate events that afflict a commonwealth. Or finally I might marvel at the nerve and fluency of his language, in which, while preserving a pure Latin style, he has expressed incisively and comprehensively a great many matters of important policy. This is all the more remarkable in a man distracted, as he is, by a mass of public business and private concerns. But of course none of these remarks will surprise you, most erudite Busleiden, since you have already learned from your intimate conversations with him to appreciate the more-than-human, the almost-divine genius of the man.

For the rest, I can add nothing to what he has written. There is, indeed, a little scrap of verse, written in the Utopian tongue, which Hythloday showed to me after More had gone away. I've prefixed to it an alphabet of the Utopian tongue, and added a few little notes in the margins.

As for More's difficulties about locating the island, Raphael did not try in any way to suppress that information, but he mentioned it only briefly and in passing, as if saving it for another occasion. And then an unlucky accident caused both of us to miss what he said. For while Raphael was speaking of it, one of More's servants came in to whisper something in his ear; and though I was listening, for that very reason, more intently than ever, one of the company, who I suppose had caught cold on shipboard, coughed so loudly that some of Raphael's words escaped me. But I will never rest till I have full information on this point, not just the general position of the island, but its exact latitude—provided only our friend Hythloday is safe and alive.

For we hear various stories about him, some people asserting that he died on the way home, others that he got home but didn't like the way things were going there, retained his old hankering for Utopia, and so made his way back to that part of the world.

It's true, of course, that the name of this island is not to be found among the old cosmographers, but Hythloday himself had a simple answer for that. For, he said, either the name that the ancients gave it has changed over the ages, or else they never discovered the island at all. Nowadays we find all sorts of lands turning up which the old geographers never mentioned. But what's the point of piling up these arguments authenticating the story, when we already have it on the word of More himself?

His uncertainty about having the book published, I attribute to his modesty, and very creditable it is. But on many scores, it seemed to me a work that should not be suppressed any longer; on the contrary, it

VTOPIENSIVM ALPHABETVM.   13

a b c d e f g h i k l m n o p q r s t u x y

TETRASTICHON VERNACVLA VTO-
PIENSIVM LINGVA.

Vtopos   ha   Boccas   peula   chama.

polta   chamaan

Bargol   he   maglomi   baccan

soma   gymnosophaon

Agrama   gymnosophon   labarem

bacha   bodamilomin

Voluala   barchin   heman   la

lauoluola   dramme   pagloni.

HORVM VERSVVM AD VERBVM HAEC
EST SENTENTIA.

Vtopus me dux ex non insula fecit insulam.
Vna ego terrarum omnium absq; philosophia,
Ciuitatem philosophicam expressi mortalibus.
Libenter impartio mea, non grauatim accipio meliora.

b 3

Me, once a peninsula, Utopus the king made an island.
Alone among all the nations, and without complex abstractions,
I set before men's eyes the philosophical city.
What I give is free: what is better I am not slow to take from others.

deserved to be sent forth into the hands of men, especially under the powerful protection of your name. Nobody knows More's good qualities better than you do, and no man is better suited than you to serve the commonwealth with good counsels. At this work you have labored for many years, earning the highest praise for wisdom as well as integrity. Farewell, then, you Maecenas[2] of learning, and ornament of our era.

Antwerp, 1 November 1516

Jerome Busleiden to Thomas More †

[Busleiden, to whom Giles addressed his letter of 1 November 1516, was an elderly man, well known in the world, wealthy and substantial. Among other offices, he was provost of Aire; treasurer of Saint Gudule's in Brussels; canon of Mechlin, Mons, and Liège; Archdeacon of Brussels and Cambray; Master of Requests; and Counsellor to Charles, Prince of Castille. During his embassy on the Continent, More had met Busleiden and had much admired his splendid house at Mechlin, as well as his impressive collection of antique coins. Poems on these topics are found among More's *Epigrams*. On the other hand, if we can judge from the few scraps of his remaining writing, Busleiden was more of a pompous rhetorician than a wit—an impressive figurehead, but perhaps also something of a stuffed shirt. The feature of *Utopia* that most impressed him was its communism; and he praised it as a pattern for all the nations in the world. The categorical assurance of this judgment strikes us as odd, given Busleiden's lordly way of life; and perhaps it worried More too—as we shall see.]

For you, my most distinguished friend More, it was not enough to devote all your care, labor, and energy to the interest and advantage of individuals: such is your goodness and liberality that you must bestow them on the public at large. You saw that this goodness of yours, however great it might be, would deserve more favor, achieve higher renown, and aim at greater glory, the more widely it was diffused, the more people shared in it and were benefited by it. This is what you've always tried to do on other occasions, and now by a singular stroke of luck you've attained it again—I mean by that "afternoon's discussion" which you've described and now published, about the right and proper constitution of the Utopian republic—a topic of which all people are now eager to hear.

It is a delightful description of a wonderful institution, replete with profound erudition and a consummate knowledge of human affairs. Both qualities meet in this work so equally and so congenially that neither yields to the other, but both contend on an even footing. You enjoy such a wide range of learning and such profound experience that what-

---

2. Maecenas was the patron of Virgil, Horace, and other Roman writers.

† Text from Lupton, 318–19 (tr. by the editor or this volume).

ever you write comes from full experience, and whatever decisions you take carry a full weight of learning. A rare and wonderful happiness! and all the more remarkable in that it withdraws itself from the multitude and imparts itself only to the few—to such, above all, as have the candor to wish, the erudition to understand, and the authority to judge in the common interest as honorably, accurately, and practically as you do now. For you clearly don't consider yourself born for yourself alone, but for the whole world and so by this splendid work, you have undertaken to place the whole world in your debt.

You could hardly have accomplished this end more effectually and correctly than by setting forth a pattern, a perfect formula for rational men, in the shape of an ideal commonwealth. And the world has never seen one more perfect than yours, more solidly established or more desirable. It far surpasses the many celebrated states of which so much has been said, those of Sparta, Athens, and Rome. Had they been founded under the same auspices as your commonwealth, with the same institutions, laws, regulations, and customs, certainly they would not now be lying flat, level with the ground, and extinguished—alas! beyond all hope of rebirth. On the contrary, they would now be intact, fortunate and prosperous, leading a happy existence—mistresses of the world, besides, and dividing a far-flung empire, by land and by sea.

Feeling pity for the wretched fate of these commonwealths, you feared lest others, which now hold supreme power, should undergo the same fate; so you drew the portrait of a perfect state, one which devoted its energies less to setting up perfect laws than to putting the very best men in charge of administering them. And in this they are absolutely right; for without good rulers, even the best laws (if we take Plato's word for it) would be nothing but dead letters. Such rulers as these serve above all as models of probity, specimens of good conduct, images of justice, and patterns of virtue for the guidance of any well-established commonwealth. What is needed is prudence in the rulers, courage in the military, temperance in the private citizenry, and justice among all men.

Since the state you praise so lavishly is clearly formed on these principles, no wonder if it seems not only a challenge to other nations but an object of reverence to all the peoples, and an achievement to be celebrated among future generations. Its great strength lies in the fact that all squabbles over private property are removed, and no one has anything of his own. Within the society all men have everything in common, and thus every action and each decision, whether public or private, trifling or important, is not directed by the greed of the many or the lusts of the few, but aims at upholding a single uniform rule of justice, equality, and community solidarity. All things being thus tightly bound to a single aim, there is bound to be a clean sweep of everything that might serve as torch, kindling, or fuel for the fires of ambition, luxury, injury, and wrong. These are vices into which even decent men are sometimes pushed against their will, and to their own incomparable loss, by private property or lust for gain or that most pitiful of emotions, ambition. From these sources rise quarrels, clashes, and wars worse than civil, which not only overthrow the flourishing state of supremely happy republics, but cause their previous glories, their splendid trophies, rich prizes, and proud spoils to be utterly defaced.

If my thoughts on this point should be less than absolutely convincing, only consider the swarm of perfectly reliable witnesses I can call to my support—I mean the many great cities destroyed, the states crushed, the republics beaten down, the towns burnt up. Not only have they disappeared without a trace—not even their names are preserved by any history, however far back it reaches.

Whatever our states may be now, in the future they will succeed in escaping these terrible downfalls, disasters, and devastations of war only if they adapt themselves to the good Utopian pattern and don't swerve from it, as people say, by a hair's breadth. If they act so, the result will fully convince them how much they have profited by the service you have done them; especially since, by your help, they will have learned to keep their republic healthy, unharmed, and victorious. Their debt to you will be no less than that owed to men who have saved not just one citizen of a state, but the entire state itself, from danger.

Farewell for now. May you continue to prosper, ever contriving, carrying out, and completing new plans which will bring long life to your country, and to yourself immortality. Farewell, most learned and humane More, supreme ornament of your Britain and of this world of ours. From my house at Mechlin, 1516.

Guillaume Budé to Thomas Lupset †

[In 1517, Thomas Lupset was no more then twenty-two years old. While studying in Paris, he had been acting as agent for his humanist friends, reading proof in a publishing house and, in the case of the second edition of *Utopia*, serving as publicity man. In this capacity, he evidently sent a copy of the book to Budé (or Budaeus, as he wrote it in Latin), who was a classical scholar of distinguished reputation. Like Busleiden, he was a man of considerable personal property; and like Busleiden, he turned out to be enchanted with the idea of communism. More, who had been uneasy from the beginning over the reception his book would find, must have been startled to find that the most radical feature of his ideal commonwealth was precisely what appealed most to these learned, conservative, and aristocratic men. Budé's letter to Lupset was printed with the second edition.]

The translation is that of J. H. Lupton in his edition of the *Utopia* (Oxford, 1895) lxxx–xcii but ͓h his footnotes replaced by those of the editor of this volume.

To His English Friend Thomas Lupset, Greeting:

I owe you many thanks, my learned young friend Lupset, for having sent me Thomas More's *Utopia*, and so drawn my attention to what is very pleasant, and likely to be very profitable, reading.

It is not long ago since you prevailed upon me (your entreaties seconding my own strong inclination) to read the six books of Galen *On the preservation of the Health*, to which that master of the Greek and Latin tongues, Dr. Thomas Linacre,[1] has lately rendered the service—or rather, paid the compliment—of translating them from the extant originals into Latin. So well has the task been performed, that if all that author's works (which I consider worth all other medical lore put together) be in time translated, the want of a knowledge of Greek is not likely to be seriously felt by our schools of medicine.

I have hastily skimmed over that work, as it stands in Linacre's papers (for the courteous loan of which, for so long a time, I am very greatly indebted to you) with the result that I deem myself much benefited by the perusal. But I promise myself still greater profit when the book itself, on the publication of which at the presses of this city you are now busily engaged, shall have appeared in print.

While I thought myself already under a sufficient obligation to you on this account, here you have presented to me More's *Utopia*, as an appendix or supplement to your former kindness. He is a man of the keenest discernment, of a pleasant disposition, well versed in knowledge of the world. I have had the book by me in the country, where my time was taken up with running about and giving directions to workpeople (for you know something, and have heard more, of my having been occupied for more than a twelvemonth on business connected with my country-house); and was so impressed by reading it, as I learnt and studied the manners and customs of the Utopians, that I well-nigh forgot, nay, even abandoned, the management of my family affairs. For I perceived that all the theory and practice of domestic economy, all care whatever for increasing one's income, was mere waste of time.

And yet, as all see and are aware, the whole race of mankind is goaded on by this very thing, as if some gadfly were bred within them to sting them. The result is that we must needs confess the object of nearly all legal and civil qualification and training to be this: that with jealous and watchful cunning, as each one has a neighbour with whom he is connected by ties of citizenship, or even at times of relationship, he should be ever conveying or abstracting something from him; should pare away, repudiate, squeeze, chouse, chisel, cozen, extort, pillage, purloin, thieve, filch, rob, and—partly with the connivance, partly with the sanction of the laws—be ever plundering and appropriating.

---

1. Thomas Linacre (1460–1524) was educated abroad, imbibed freely of the "new learning," and became the founder and first president of the Royal College of Physicians.

This goes on all the more in countries where the civil and canon law, as they are called, have greater authority in the two courts. For it is evident that their customs and institutions are pervaded by the principle, that those are to be deemed the high-priests of law and equity, who are skilled in *caveats*—or *capiats*, rather;[2] men who hawk at their unwary fellow-citizens; artists in formulas, that is, in gudgeon-traps; adepts in concocted law; getters up of cases; jurisconsults of a controverted, perverted, inverted *jus*.[3] These are the only fit persons to give opinions as to what is fair and good; nay, what is far more, to settle with plenary power what each one is to be allowed to have, and what not to have, and the extent and limit of his tenure. How deluded must public opinion be to have determined matters thus!

The truth is that most of us, blind with the thick rheum of ignorance in our eyes, suppose that each one's cause, as a rule, is *just*, in proportion to its accordance with the requirements of the *law*, or to the way in which he has based his claim on the *law*. Whereas, were we agreed to demand our rights in accordance with the rule of truth, and what the simple Gospel prescribes, the dullest would understand, and the most senseless admit, if we put it to them, that, in the decrees of the canonists, the divine law differs as much from the human; and, in our civil laws and royal enactments, true equity differs as much from law; as the principles laid down by Christ, the founder of human society, and the usages of His disciples, differ from the decrees and enactments of those who think the *summum bonum* and perfection of happiness to lie in the money-bags of a Croesus or a Midas.[4] So that, if you chose to define Justice now-a days, in the way that early writers liked to do, as the power who assigns to each his due, you would either find her nonexistent in public, or, if I may use such a comparison, you would have to admit that she was a kind of kitchen stewardess: and this, alike whether you regard the character of our present rulers, or the disposition of fellow-citizens and fellow-countrymen one towards another.

Perhaps indeed it may be argued, that the law I speak of has been derived from that inherent, world-old justice called *natural* law; which teaches that the stronger a man is, the more he should possess; and, the more he possesses, the more eminent among his countrymen he ought to be: with the result that now we see it an accepted principle in the law of nations, that persons who are unable to help their fellows by an art or practice worth mentioning, if only they are adepts in those complicated knots and stringent bonds, by which men's properties are tied up (things accounted a mixture of Gordian knots and charlatanry, with nothing very wonderful about them, by the ignorant multitude, and by scholars living, for the sake of recreation or of investigating the truth, at a dis-

---

2. *Caveats:* warnings; *capiats:* permissions to take.

3. *Jus:* law.

4. Proverbial rich men of antiquity.

tance from the courts),—that these persons, I say, should have an income equal to that of a thousand of their countrymen, nay, even of a whole state, and sometimes more than that; and that they should then be greeted with the honourable titles of wealthy men, thrifty men, makers of splendid fortunes. Such in truth is the age in which we live; such our manners and customs; such our national character. These have pronounced it lawful for a man's credit and influence to be high, in proportion to the way in which he has been the architect of his own fortunes and of those of his heirs: an influence, in fact, which goes on increasing, according as their descendants in turn, to the remotest generation, vie in heaping up with fine additions the property gained by their ancestors; which amounts to saying, according as they have ousted more and more extensively their connections, kindred, and even their blood relations.

But the founder and regulator of all property, Jesus Christ, left among His followers a Pythagorean communion and love; and ratified it by a plain example, when Ananias was condemned to death for breaking this law of communion.[5] By laying down this principle, Christ seems to me to have abolished, at any rate among his followers, all the voluminous quibbles of the civil law, and still more of the later canon law; which latter we see at the present day holding the highest position in jurisprudence, and controlling our destiny.

As for the island of Utopia, which I hear is also called *Udepotia*,[6] it is said (if we are to believe the story), by what must be owned a singular good fortune, to have adopted Christian usages both in public and in private; to have imbibed the wisdom thereto belonging; and to have kept it undefiled to this very day. The reason is, that it holds with firm grip to three divine institutions:—namely, the absolute equality, or, if you prefer to call it so, the civil communication, of all things good and bad among fellow-citizens; a settled and unwavering love of peace and quietness; and a contempt for gold and silver. Three things these, which overturn, one may say, all fraud, all imposture, cheating, roguery, and unprincipled deception. Would that Providence, on its own behalf, would cause these three principles of Utopian law to be fixed in the minds of all men by the rivets of a strong and settled conviction. We should soon see pride, covetousness, insane competition, and almost all other deadly weapons of our adversary the Devil, fall powerless; we should see the interminable array of law-books, the work of so many excellent and solid understandings, that occupy men till the very day of their death, consigned to bookworms, as mere hollow and empty things, or else given up to make wrapping-paper for shops.

---

5. Ananias sold a property and gave the Apostles only part of the price, instead of the whole gain, as he should have done. See Acts. 5.1–7 above, p. 93.

6. *Utopia* = "Noplace"; *Udepotia* = "Nev-

erplace." Playing a third change on the name, some of the commendatory verses written on More's book turned Utopia into *Eutopia* = "Goodplace."

Good heavens! what holiness of the Utopians has had the power of earning such a blessing from above, that greed and covetousness have for so many ages failed to enter, either by force or stealth, into that island alone? that they have failed to drive out from it, by wanton effrontery, justice and honour?

Would that great Heaven in its goodness had dealt so kindly with the countries which keep, and would not part with, the appellation they bear, derived from His most holy name! Of a truth, greed, which perverts and sinks down so many minds, otherwise noble and elevated, would be gone from hence once for all, and the golden age of Saturn would return. In Utopia one might verily suppose that there is a risk of Aratus and the early poets having been mistaken in their opinion, when they made Justice depart from earth, and placed her in the Zodiac.[7] For, if we are to believe Hythloday, she must needs have stayed behind in that island, and not yet made her way to heaven.

But in truth I have ascertained by full inquiry, that Utopia lies outside the bounds of the known world. It is in fact one of the Fortunate Isles, perhaps very close to the Elysian Fields; for More himself testifies that Hythloday has not yet stated its position definitely. It is itself divided into a number of cities, but all uniting or confederating into one state, named Hagnopolis;-[8] a state contented with its own customs, its own goods, blest with innocence, leading a kind of heavenly life, on a lower level indeed than heaven, but above the defilements of this world we know, which amid the endless pursuits of mankind, as empty and vain as they are keen and eager, is being hurried in a swollen and eddying tide to the cataract.

It is to Thomas More, then, that we owe our knowledge of this island. It is he who, in our generation, has made public this model of a happy life and rule for leading it, the discovery, as he tells us, of Hythloday: for he ascribes all to him. For while Hythloday has built the Utopians their state, and established for them their rites and customs; while, in so doing, he has borrowed from them and brought home for us the representation of a happy life; it is beyond question More, who has set off by his literary style the subject of that island and its customs. He it is who has perfected, as by rule and square, the City of the Hagnopolitans itself, adding all those touches by which grace and beauty and weight accrue to the noble work; even though in executing that work he has claimed for himself only a common mason's share. We see that it has been a matter of conscientious scruple with him, not to assume too important a part in the work, lest Hythloday should have just cause for complaint, on the ground of More having plucked the first flowers of that fame, which would have been left for him, if he had himself ever decided to

7. Aratus of Soli wrote a Greek poem on astronomy, *Phaenomena*; he lived in the third century B.C.

8. From the Greek, "City of the Saints."

give an account of his adventures to the world. "He was afraid, of course, that Hythloday, who was residing of his own choice in the island of Udepotia, might some day come in person upon the scene, and be vexed and aggrieved at this unkindness on his part, in leaving him the glory of this discovery with the best flowers plucked off. To be of this persuasion is the part of good men and wise."[9]

Now while More is one who of himself carries weight, and has great authority to rest upon, I am led to place unreserved confidence in him by the testimony of Peter Giles of Antwerp. Though I have never made his acquaintance in person—apart from recommendations of his learning and character that have reached me—I love him on account of his being the intimate friend of the illustrious Erasmus, who has deserved so well of letters of every kind, whether sacred or profane; with whom personally I have long corresponded and formed ties of friendship.

Farewell, my dear Lupset. Greet for me, at the first opportunity, either by word of mouth or by letter, Linacre, that pillar of the British name in all that concerns good learning; one who is now, as I hope, not more yours than ours. He is one of the few whose good opinion I should be very glad, if possible, to gain. When he was himself known to be staying here, he gained in the highest degree the good opinion of me and of Jehan Ruelle, my friend and the sharer in my studies.[1] And his singular learning and careful industry I should be the first to look up to and strive to copy.

Greet More also once and again for me, either by message, as I said before, or by word of mouth. As I think and often repeat, Minerva has long entered his name on her selectest album; and I love and revere him in the highest degree for what he has written about this isle of the New World, Utopia.

In his history our age and those which succeed it will have a nursery, so to speak, of polite and useful institutions; from which men may borrow customs, and introduce and adapt them each to his own state. Farewell.

From Paris, the 31st of July.[2]

Erasmus of Rotterdam to John Froben

[John Froben was a printer with a shop in Basle; he was also intimate with Erasmus, who got him to print the third and fourth editions of *Utopia* because the first two had been full of errors. Erasmus was "god-sib" to Froben because he had served as godfather to Froben's son, named (inevitably) Erasmus Froben.]

9. The passage within quotes is in Greek in the original.
1. Ruelle, like Linacre, was a scholar-physician.

2. The year, 1517, is understood. The second edition appeared sometime in the fall and winter of 1517–18.

His Beloved Gossip, Greeting:

While heretofore I have always thought extremely well of my friend More's writings, yet I rather mistrusted my own judgment because of the close friendship between us. But when I see all the learned subscribe to my opinion, and praise even more highly than I the divine wit of this man, not because they love him better but because they see more deeply into his merits, I must speak from a full heart, and no longer shrink from saying openly what I feel. How would his fortunate disposition have stood forth if his genius had been nurtured in Italy! if he had devoted his whole energy to the service of the Muses, maturing gradually, as it were, toward his own proper harvest! As a youth, he toyed with epigrams, many written when he was only a boy. He has never left Britain except a couple of times to serve his prince as an ambassador to Flanders.[1] Apart from the cares of a family man and the responsibilities of domesticity, apart from his official posts and floods of legal cases, he is distracted by so many and such important matters of state business, that you would marvel he finds any free time at all for books.

For this reason I am sending you his *Youthful Exercises* and his *Utopia*, so that, if you think proper, their appearance under your imprint may commend them to the world and to posterity. For the authority of your name is such that a book is sure of pleasing the learned as soon as it is known to issue from the house of Froben. Farewell to you, to your excellent father-in-law, your dear wife, and your delightful children. Make sure that Erasmus, the little son we share in common, and who was born to letters, continues to work at his studies.

Louvain, 25 August 1517

Thomas More to Peter Giles†

[The second letter of More to Peter Giles appeared only in the second edition of *Utopia* (Paris, 1517–18). Like the first, it deprecates (under the pretext of defending) the seriousness with which Hythloday's narration is to be taken. One may speculate that the persons who praised More too highly and too clumsily, may have been Busleiden or Budé, both of whom had been surprisingly emphatic in endorsing the idea of community property. More evidently preferred to retain some ironic reservations, or at least room for ironic maneuver; and his relief at finding a more critical reader (whoever he was) breathes through this second epistle.]

---

1. Erasmus exaggerates here; in 1508 More had visited the universities of Louvain and Paris. But since Erasmus wrote sometimes as many as forty letters a day, it's no wonder that he occasionally misspoke.

† Reprinted by permission of Yale University

Press from St. Thomas More, *Utopia*, edited by Edward Surtz, S.J., and J. H. Hexter (New Haven: Yale UP, 1965) 248–252. Copyright © 1965 by Yale University. Translated by the editor of this edition.

My dear Peter, I was absolutely delighted with the opinion of that very sharp man whom you know. He posed this dilemma about my *Utopia*: if the story is put forward as true, he said, then I see a number of absurdities in it; but if it's a fable, then it seems to me that in various respects More's usual good judgment is at fault. I suspect this fellow of being learned, and I see that he's a friend; but whoever he is, my dear Peter, I'm much obliged to him. By this frank opinion of his, he has pleased me more than anyone else since the book was published.

For in the first place, either out of devotion to me or interest in the subject itself, he seems to have borne up under the burden of reading the book all the way through—and that not perfunctorily or hastily, the way priests read the hours—those, at least, who read them at all.[1] No, he read slowly and attentively, noting all the particular points. Then, having singled out certain matters for criticism, and not very many, as a matter of fact, he gives careful and considered approval to the rest. And finally, in the very expressions he uses to criticize me, he implies higher praises than some of those who have put all their energies into compliment. It's easy to see what a high opinion he has of me when he expresses disappointment over reading something imperfect or inexact—whereas I don't expect, in treating so many different matters, to be able to say more than one or two things which aren't totally ridiculous.

Still, I'd like to be just as frank with him as he was with me; and in fact, I don't see why he should think himself so keen (so "spirituel," as the Greeks would say), just because he's discovered some absurdities in the institutions of Utopia, or caught me putting forth some half-baked ideas about the constitution of their state. Isn't there something absurd in the institutions of most other states elsewhere in the world? and haven't most of the philosophers who've written about the state, its ruler, and even the office of a private citizen, managed to say something that needs correcting?

But when he wonders whether *Utopia* is true or a fiction, then I find *his* judgment, in turn, sorely at fault. It's perfectly possible that if I'd decided to write about a republic, and a fable of this sort had occurred to me, I might have spread a little fiction, like so much honey, over the truth to make it more acceptable. But I would certainly have tempered the fiction so that, while it deceived the common folk, it also tipped the wink to the learned, who were capable of seeing through it. So, if I'd done nothing but give special names to the prince, the river, the city, and the island, which hinted to the learned that the island was nowhere, the city was a phantom, the river was waterless, and the prince had no people, that would not have been hard to do, and would have been a good deal more clever than what I actually did. Unless I had a historian's

---

1. Priests read assigned prayers on the hours, with varying degrees of enthusiasm, according to More.

devotion to fact, I am not so stupid as to have used those barbarous and senseless names of Utopia, Anyder, Amaurot, and Ademus.

Still, my dear Giles, I see some people are so suspicious that what we naive fellows have written down of Hythloday's account can hardly find any credence at all with these circumspect and sagacious persons. I'm afraid my personal reputation, as well as my authority as a historian, may be threatened by his skepticism; so it's a good thing that I can defend myself by saying, as Terence's Mysis says about Glycerium's boy, to confirm his legitimacy: "Praise be to God there were some free women present when I gave birth." [2] And so it was a good thing for me that Raphael told his story not just to you and me, but to a great many perfectly respectable and seriousminded men. Whether he told them more things, and more important things, than he told us, I don't know; but he certainly told them just as much as he did us.

Well, if these doubters won't believe such witnesses, let them consult Hythloday himself, for he is not yet dead. I heard only recently from some travelers coming out of Portugal that on the first of last March he was as healthy and vigorous a man as he ever was. Let them get the truth from him—dig it out of him with questions, if they want. I only want them to understand that I'm responsible for my own work, and my own work alone, not for somebody else's good faith.

Farewell, my dearest Peter, to you, your lovely wife, and your delightful little girl. My wife wishes them long life and the best of health.

Erasmus to Ulrich von Hutten †

[Three years after the first publication of *Utopia*, Ulrich von Hutten, author of the satirical *Letters of Obscure Men*, asked Erasmus about Thomas More, whom he admired but had never met. The sketch that Erasmus wrote in response to this request needs no further introduction.]

Most illustrious Hutten, your love, I had almost said your passion for the genius of Thomas More,—kindled as it is by his writings, which, as you truly say, are as learned and witty as anything can possibly be,—is, I assure you, shared by many others; and moreover the feeling in this case is mutual; since More is so delighted with what you have written, that I am myself almost jealous of you. It is an example of what Plato says of that sweetest wisdom, which excites much more ardent love among men than the most admirable beauty of form. It is not discerned by the eye of sense, but the mind has eyes of its own, so that even here the Greek saying holds true, that out of Looking grows Liking; and so it

2. Terence, *The Lady of Andros*, lines 771–72.

† From *Epistles of Erasmus*, tr. Francis M. Nichols (London: Longmans, Green, 1917) 3. 387–99. Footnotes are by the editor of this volume, unless credited to Nichols.

comes to pass that people are sometimes united in the warmest affection, who have never seen or spoken to each other. And, as it is a common experience, that for some unexplained reason different people are attracted by different kinds of beauty, so between one mind and another, there seems to be a sort of latent kindred, which causes us to be specially delighted with some minds, and not with others.

As to your asking me to paint you a full-length portrait of More, I only wish my power of satisfying your request were equal to your earnestness in pressing it. For to me too, it will be no unpleasant task to linger awhile in the contemplation of a friend, who is the most delightful character in the world. But, in the first place, it is not given to every man to be aware of all More's accomplishments; and in the next place, I know not whether he will himself like to have his portrait painted by any artist that chooses to do so. For indeed I do not think it more easy to make a likeness of More than of Alexander the Great, or of Achilles; neither were those heroes more worthy of immortality. The hand of an Apelles is required for such a subject, and I am afraid I am more like a Fulvius or a Rutuba than an Apelles.[1] Nevertheless I will try to draw you a sketch, rather than a portrait, of the entire man, so far as daily and domestic intercourse has enabled me to observe his likeness and retain it in my memory. But if some diplomatic employment should ever bring you together, you will find out, how poor an artist you have chosen for this commission; and I am afraid you will think me guilty of envy or of wilful blindness in taking note of so few out the many good points of his character.

To begin with that part of him which is least known to you,—in shape and stature More is not a tall man, but not remarkably short, all his limbs being so symmetrical, that no deficiency is observed in this respect. His complexion is fair, his face being rather blonde than pale, but with no approach to redness, except a very delicate flush, which lights up the whole. His hair is auburn inclining to black, or if you like it better, black inclining to auburn; his beard thin, his eyes a bluish grey with some sort of tinting upon them. This kind of eye is thought to be a sign of the happiest character, and is regarded with favour in England, whereas with us black eyes are rather preferred. It is said, that no kind of eye is so free from defects of sight. His countenance answers to his character, having an expression of kind and friendly cheerfulness with a little air of raillery. To speak candidly, it is a face more expressive of pleasantry than of gravity or dignity, though very far removed from folly or buffoonery. His right shoulder seems a little higher than his left, especially when he is walking, a peculiarity that is not innate, but the result of habit, like

---

1. In the passage of Horace here alluded to (Sat. 2. 7. 96), Fulvius and Rutuba are generally understood to be the names of gladiators, depicted in a popular handbill. But Erasmus appears to interpret them as the names of humble artists dealing with such commonplace subjects [Nichols's note].

many tricks of the kind. In the rest of his body there is nothing displeasing,—only his hands are a little coarse, or appear so, as compared with the rest of his figure. He has always from his boyhood been very negligent of his toilet, so as not to give much attention even to the things which, according to Ovid, are all that men need care about.[2] What a charm there was in his looks when young, may even now be inferred from what remains; although I knew him myself when he was not more than three and-twenty years old; for he has not yet passed much beyond his fortieth year. His health is sound rather than robust, but sufficient for any labours suitable to an honourable citizen; and we may fairly hope, that his life may be long, as he has a father living of a great age, but an age full of freshness and vigour.

I have never seen any person less fastidious in his choice of food. As a young man, he was by preference a water-drinker, a practice he derived from his father. But, not to give annoyance to others, he used at table to conceal this habit from his guests by drinking, out of a pewter vessel, either small beer almost as weak as water, or plain water. As to wine, it being the custom, where he was, for the company to invite each other to drink in turn out of the same cup, he used sometimes to sip a little of it, to avoid appearing to shrink from it altogether, and to habituate himself to the common practice. For his eating he has been accustomed to prefer beef and salt meats, and household bread thoroughly fermented, to those articles of diet which are commonly regarded as delicacies. But he does not shrink from things that impart an innocent pleasure, even of a bodily kind, and has always a good appetite for milk-puddings and for fruit, and eats a dish of eggs with the greatest relish.

His voice is neither loud nor excessively low, but of a penetrating tone. It has nothing in it melodious or soft, but is simply suitable for speech, as he does not seem to have any natural talent for singing, though he takes pleasure in music of every kind. His articulation is wonderfully distinct, being equally free from hurry and from hesitation.

He likes to be dressed simply, and does not wear silk, or purple, or gold chains, except when it is not allowable to dispense with them. He cares marvellously little for those formalities, which with ordinary people are the test of politeness; and as he does not exact these ceremonies from others, so he is not scrupulous in observing them himself, either on occasions of meeting or at entertainments, though he understands how to use them if he thinks proper to do so; but he holds it to be effeminate and unworthy of a man to waste much of his time on such trifles.

He was formerly rather disinclined to a court life and to any intimacy with princes, having always a special hatred of tyranny and a great fancy

2. Ovid, *de Arte Amandi*, lib. 1. 514, "recommends that the toga fit properly, have no holes in it, etc." [*Nichols's note*; quoted portion of note translated by the editor of this volume.]

for equality; whereas you will scarcely find any court so well-ordered, as not to have much bustle and ambition and pretence and luxury, or to be free from tyranny in some form or other. He could not even be tempted to Henry the Eighth's court without great trouble, although nothing could be desired more courteous or less exacting than this Prince. He is naturally fond of liberty and leisure; but as he enjoys a holiday when he has it, so whenever business requires it, no one is more vigilant or more patient.

He seems to be born and made for friendship, of which he is the sincerest and most persistent devotee. Neither is he afraid of that multiplicity of friends, of which Hesiod disapproves.[3] Accessible to every tender of intimacy, he is by no means fastidious in choosing his acquaintance, while he is most accommodating in keeping it on foot, and constant in retaining it. If he has fallen in with anyone whose faults he cannot cure, he finds some opportunity of parting with him, untying the knot of intimacy without tearing it; but when he has found any sincere friends, whose characters are suited to his own, he is so delighted with their society and conversation, that he seems to find in these the chief pleasure of life, having an absolute distaste for tennis and dice and cards, and the other games with which the mass of gentlemen beguile the tediousness of Time. It should be added that, while he is somewhat neglectful of his own interest, no one takes more pains in attending to the concerns of his friends. What more need I say? If anyone requires a perfect example of true friendship, it is in More that he will best find it.

In company his extraordinary kindness and sweetness of temper are such as to cheer the dullest spirit, and alleviate the annoyance of the most trying circumstances. From boyhood he was always so pleased with a joke, that it might seem that jesting was the main object of his life; but with all that, he did not go so far as buffoonery, nor had ever any inclination to bitterness. When quite a youth, he wrote farces and acted them. If a thing was facetiously said, even though it was aimed at himself, he was charmed with it, so much did he enjoy any witticism that had a flavour of subtlety or genius. This led to his amusing himself as a young man with epigrams, and taking great delight in Lucian. Indeed, it was he that suggested my writing the *Moria*, or Praise of Folly,[4] which was much the same thing as setting a camel to dance.

There is nothing that occurs in human life, from which he does not seek to extract some pleasure, although the matter may be serious in itself. If he has to do with the learned and intelligent, he is delighted with their cleverness, if with unlearned or stupid people, he finds amusement in their folly. He is not offended even by professed clowns, as he adapts himself with marvellous dexterity to the tastes of all; while

3. Hesiod, the father of Greek didactic poetry, flourished in the eighth century B.C.; his *Works and Days* is full of this sort of practical advice.

4. *Moria* is Greek for "folly"; Erasmus wrote the *Praise of Folly* in More's house (1509).

with ladies generally, and even with his wife, his conversation is made up of humour and playfulness. You would say it was a second Democritus, or rather that Pythagorean philosopher, who strolls in leisurely mood through the market-place, contemplating the turmoil of those who buy and sell. There is no one less guided by the opinion of the multitude, but on the other hand no one sticks more closely to common sense.

One of his amusements is in observing the forms, characters and instincts of different animals. Accordingly there is scarcely any kind of bird, that he does not keep about his residence, and the same of other animals not quite so common, as monkeys, foxes, ferrets, weasels and the like. Beside these, if he meets with any strange object, imported from abroad or otherwise remarkable, he is most eager to buy it, and has his house so well supplied with these objects, that there is something in every room which catches your eye, as you enter it; and his own pleasure is renewed every time that he sees others interested.

When of a sentimental age, he was not a stranger to the emotions of love, but without loss of character, having no inclination to press his advantage, and being more attracted by a mutual liking than by any licentious object.

He had drunk deep of good letters from his earliest years; and when a young man, he applied himself to the study of Greek and of philosophy; but his father was so far from encouraging him in this pursuit, that he withdrew his allowance and almost disowned him, because he thought he was deserting his hereditary study, being himself an expert professor of English law. For remote as that profession is from true learning, those who become masters of it have the highest rank and reputation among their countrymen; and it is difficult to find any readier way to acquire fortune and honour. Indeed a considerable part of the nobility of that island has had its origin in this profession, in which it is said that no one can be perfect, unless he has toiled at it for many years. It was natural that in his younger days our friend's genius, born for better things, should shrink from this study; nevertheless, after he had had a taste of the learning of the schools, he became so conversant with it, that there was no one more eagerly consulted by suitors; and the income that he made by it was not surpassed by any of those who did nothing else; such was the power and quickness of his intellect.

He also expended considerable labour in perusing the volumes of the orthodox fathers; and when scarcely more than a youth, he lectured publicly on the *De Civitate Dei* of Augustine [5] before a numerous audience, old men and priests not being ashamed to take a lesson in divinity from a young layman, and not at all sorry to have done so. Meantime he applied his whole mind to religion, having some thought of taking

5. Saint Augustine, *The City of God*.

orders, for which he prepared himself by watchings and fastings and prayers and such like exercises; wherein he showed much more wisdom than the generality of people, who rashly engage in so arduous a profession without testing themselves beforehand. And indeed there was no obstacle to his adopting this kind of life, except the fact, that he could not shake off his wish to marry. Accordingly he resolved to be a chaste husband rather than a licentious priest.

When he married, he chose a very young girl, a lady by birth, with her character still unformed, having been always kept in the country with her parents and sisters,—so that he was all the better able to fashion her according to his own habits. Under his direction she was instructed in learning and in every kind of music, and had almost completely become just such a person as would have been a delightful companion for his whole life, if an early death had not carried her away. She had however borne him several children, of whom three girls, Margaret, Alice and Cecily, and one boy, John, are still living.

More did not however long remain single, but contrary to his friends' advice, a few months after his wife's death, he married a widow, more for the sake of the management of his household, than to please his own fancy, as she is no great beauty, nor yet young, *nec bella admodum nec puella*, as he sometimes laughingly says, but a sharp and watchful housewife; with whom nevertheless he lives, on as sweet and pleasant terms as if she were as young and lovely as any one could desire; and scarcely any husband obtains from his wife by masterfulness and severity as much compliance as he does by blandishments and jests. Indeed, what more compliance could he have, when he has induced a woman who is already elderly, who is not naturally of a yielding character, and whose mind is occupied with business, to learn to play on the harp, the viol, the spinet and the flute, and to give up every day a prescribed time to practice? With similar kindness he rules his whole household, in which there are no tragic incidents, and no quarrels. If anything of the kind should be likely, he either calms it down, or applies a remedy at once. And in parting with any member of his household he has never acted in a hostile spirit, or treated him as an enemy. Indeed his house seems to have a sort of fatal felicity, no one having lived in it without being advanced to higher fortune, no inmate having ever had a stain upon his character.

It would be difficult to find any one living on such terms with a mother as he does with his step-mother. For his father had brought in one step-mother after another; and he has been as affectionate with each of them as with a mother. He has lately introduced a third, and More swears that he never saw anything better. His affection for his parents, children and sisters is such, that he neither wearies them with his love, nor ever fails in any kindly attention.

His character is entirely free from any touch of avarice. He has set aside out of his property what he thinks sufficient for his children, and spends the rest in a liberal fashion. When he was still dependent on his profession, he gave every client true and friendly counsel with an eye to their advantage rather than his own, generally advising them, that the cheapest thing they could do was to come to terms with their opponents. If he could not persuade them to do this, he pointed out how they might go to law at least expense; for there are some people whose character leads them to delight in litigation.

In the city of London, where he was born, he acted for some years as judge in civil causes. This office, which is by no means burdensome,— inasmuch as the Court sits only on Thursday before dinner,—is considered highly honorable; and no judge ever disposed of more suits, or conducted himself with more perfect integrity. In most cases he remitted the fees which are due from the litigants, the practice being for the plaintiff to deposit three groats before the hearing, and the defendant a like sum, and no more being allowed to be exacted. By such conduct he made himself extremely popular in the city.

He had made up his mind to be contented with this position, which was sufficiently dignified without being exposed to serious dangers. He has been thrust more than once into an embassy, in the conduct of which he has shown great ability; and King Henry in consequence would never rest until he dragged him into his court. 'Dragged him,' I say, and with reason; for no one was ever more ambitious of being admitted into a court, than he was anxious to escape it. But as this excellent monarch was resolved to pack his household with learned, serious, intelligent and honest men, he especially insisted upon having More among them,— with whom he is on such terms of intimacy that he cannot bear to let him go. If serious affairs are in hand, no one gives wiser counsel; if it pleases the King to relax his mind with agreeable conversation, no man is better company. Difficult questions are often arising, which require a grave and prudent judge; and these questions are resolved by More in such a way, that both sides are satisfied. And yet no one has ever induced him to accept a present. What a blessing it would be for the world, if magistrates like More were everywhere put in office by sovereigns!

Meantime there is no assumption of superiority. In the midst of so great a pressure of business he remembers his humble friends; and from time to time he returns to his beloved studies. Whatever authority he derives from his rank, and whatever influence he enjoys by the favour of a powerful sovereign, are employed in the service of the public, or in that of his friends. It has always been part of his character to be most obliging to every body, and marvellously ready with his sympathy; and this disposition is more conspicuous than ever, now that his power of doing good is greater. Some he relieves with money, some he protects by his authority, some he promotes by his recommendation, while those whom he cannot otherwise assist are benefited by his advice. No one is sent away in distress, and you might call him the general patron of all poor people. He counts it a great gain to himself, if he has relieved some oppressed person, made the path clear for one that was in difficulties, or brought back into favour one that was in disgrace. No man more readily confers a benefit, no man expects less in return. And successful as he is in so many ways,—while success is generally accompanied by self-conceit,—I have never seen any mortal being more free from this failing.

I now propose to turn to the subject of those studies which have been the chief means of bringing More and me together. In his first youth his principal literary exercises were in verse. He afterwards wrestled for a long time to make his prose more smooth; practising his pen in every kind of writing in order to form that style, the character of which there is no occasion for me to recall, especially to you, who have his books always in your hands. He took the greatest pleasure in declamations, choosing some disputable subject, as involving a keener exercise of mind. Hence, while still a youth, he attempted a dialogue, in which he carried the defense of Plato's community even to the matter of wives! He wrote ana answer to Lucian's *Tyrannicide*, in which argument it was his wish to have me for a rival, in order to test his own proficiency in this kind of writing.

He published his *Utopia* for the purpose of showing, what are the things that occasion mischief in commonwealths; having the English constitution especially in view, which he so thoroughly knows and understands. He had written the second book at his leisure, and afterwards, when he found it was required, added the first off-hand. Hence there is some inequality in the style.

It would be difficult to find any one more successful in speaking *ex tempore*, the happiest thoughts being attended by the happiest language; while a mind that catches and anticipates all that passes, and a ready memory, having everything as it were in stock, promptly supply whatever the time, or the occasion, demands. In disputations nothing can be imagined more acute, so that the most eminent theologians often find their match, when he meets them on their own ground. Hence John Colet, a man of keen and exact judgment, is wont to say in familiar conversation, that England has only one genius, whereas that island abounds in distinguished intellects.

However averse he may be from all superstition, he is a steady adherent of true piety; having regular hours for his prayers, which are not uttered by rote, but from the heart. He talks with his friends about a future life in such a way as to make you feel that he believes what he says, and does not speak without the best hope. Such is More, even at Court; and there are still people who think that Christians are only to be found in monasteries! Such are the persons, whom a wise King admits into his household, and into his chamber; and not only admits, but invites, nay, compels them to come in. These he has by him as the constant witnesses and judges of his life,—as his advisers and travelling companions. By these he rejoices to be accompanied, rather than by dissolute young men or by fops, or even by decorated grandees, or by crafty ministers, of whom one would lure him to silly amusements, another would incite him to tyranny, and a third would suggest some fresh schemes for plundering his people. If you have lived at this Court, you would, I am sure, give a new description of Court life, and cease to be *Misaulos*;[6] though you too live with such a prince, that you cannot wish for a better, and have some companions like Stromer and Copp, whose sympathies are on the right side. But what is that small number compared with such a swarm of distinguished men as Mountjoy, Linacre, Pace, Colet, Stokesley, Latimer, More, Tunstall, Clerk, and others like them, any one of whose names signifies at once a world of virtues and accomplishments? However, I have no mean hope, that Albert, who is at this time the one ornament of our Germany, will attach to his household a multitude of persons like himself, and set a notable example to other princes; so that they may exert themselves in their own circles to do the like.[7]

6. A hater of courts.
7. The letter trails off in gossip and compliments; the portrait of More is complete.

CRITICISM

R. W. CHAMBERS

The Meaning of *Utopia* †

An ex-Cabinet minister is still alive who dates his political career from the accidental purchase of a copy of *Utopia* at a second-hand bookstall. One of his colleagues in the Cabinet has written of *Utopia*, that no treatise is better calculated to nourish the heart of a Radical. *Utopia* has become a text-book of Socialist propaganda. It did more to make William Morris a Socialist than ever Karl Marx did.[1] All this testifies to its abiding power; yet we must never think of More as writing it for Nineteenth-Century Radicals or Twentieth-Century Socialists. Even he could not do that.

The first step to an appreciation of *Utopia* is to understand how it must have struck a scholar in the early Sixteenth Century. That is a difficult task, yet not an impossible one; and if we would understand More himself, it is a task which we must undertake.

We shall then find, I think, that few books have been more misunderstood than *Utopia*. It has given the English language a word 'Utopian' to signify something visionary and unpractical. Yet the remarkable thing about *Utopia* is the extent to which it adumbrates social and political reforms which have either been actually carried into practice, or which have come to be regarded as very practical politics. Utopia is depicted as a sternly righteous and puritanical State, where few of us would feel quite happy; yet we go on using the word 'Utopia' to signify an easy-going paradise, whose only fault is that it is too happy and ideal to be realized. *Utopia* is the first of a series which we have christened 'Ideal Commonwealths'. Some of these, for example William Morris' *News from Nowhere*, really *are* ideal. They are 'Utopian' in the current sense, that is to say, they are quite unpractical fancies of what this world might be like if the dreamer could shatter it to bits, and then remould it nearer to the heart's desire. For instance, in *News from Nowhere* we might be sure that the Divine Worship of the citizens would be Morris' ideal. If he gives them no Divine Worship, that also tells its tale. Now, More does not make his Utopians Christian. So modern scholars have argued; 'Utopia is an ideal commonwealth; *argal* More thought the vague deism of his Utopians more ideal than the popular religious beliefs of his time.'

† From *Thomas More* (London: Jonathan Cape, 1953) 125–32, 135–37, and 143–44. Reprinted by permission of Jonathan Cape Ltd. on behalf of the Estate of R. W. Chambers. References to the text of *Utopia* have been changed to reflect the paging of this edition. Chambers's notes are marked as his; others are by the editor of this volume.

1. William Morris (1834–96), among his many other diverse activities, was a socialist agitator. *News from Nowhere*, his brief tract, is Marxism with a thick overlay of nostalgia for the medieval.

Such argument might be reasonable if *Utopia* were a modern 'Ideal Commonwealth'. But we must never forget that More's education fell not in the Nineteenth but in the Fifteenth Century. To a man educated in that century, the distinction was obvious between the virtues which might be taught by human reason alone, and the further virtues taught by Catholic orthodoxy. It was part of the medieval system to divide the virtues into the Four Cardinal Virtues (to which the heathen might attain) and the Three Christian Virtues. The Four Cardinal Virtues—Wisdom, Fortitude, Temperance, and Justice—are the foundation of Plato's commonwealths, as outlined in the *Republic* and the *Laws*.[2] These virtues were taken into the medieval system—part of the immense debt it owes to Greek philosophy. The Three Christian Virtues—Faith, Hope, and Charity—come of course from St. Pauls' *First Epistle to the Corinthians*. Four and Three make Seven—the Perfect Number, which was extremely comforting. The perfect Christian character must comprise all seven. But the four heathen virtues were sufficient to ensure that a man or a State might be a model of conduct in secular matters. In Dante's *Divine Comedy* Virgil represents Philosophy, Reason, Human Wisdom. He is able to rescue Dante from the dark wood (although he was one of those who had not the three sacred virtues) because he knew and followed the four other virtues without fault. So Virgil can guide Dante till he meets Beatrice, but can go no further.

For a pattern of a State, Dante turns to Heathen Rome or to Heathen Greece. And it is not because of his deep learning that Dante does this. Our great English medieval poet, William Langland, the author of *Piers Plowman*, had but a commonplace education, but his system is similar. *Do Well* is the virtue of secular life, and the examples of it are the great non-Christian philosophers and rulers: Aristotle, Solomon, Socrates, Trajan. *Do Better* and *Do Best* represent forms of Christian virtues. And so More's friend, Busleiden, in his introductory letter to *Utopia*, tells us that the perfect commonwealth must unite 'Wisdom in the ruler, Fortitude in the soldiers, Temperance in private individuals, and Justice in all.'

In basing his *Utopia* upon these four heathen virtues, More is following medieval tradition; further, he is following his great examples, Plato's *Republic* and *Laws*; but, above all, he makes his satire upon contemporary European abuses more pointed. The virtues of Heathen Utopia show up by contrast the vices of Christian Europe. But the Four Cardinal Virtues are subsidiary to, not a substitute for, the Christian virtues. More has done his best to make this clear. It is not his fault if he has been misunderstood, as the following example will show.

---

2. *Republic*, Book IV; *Laws*, Book XII [*Chambers's note*].

Most of us would agree with Dame Alice in deploring More's extreme austerities.[3] We have seen that, years before *Utopia* was written, she had complained to More's confessor about that shirt of hair. It was no good. It may have been some ten years after *Utopia* was written that, as Roper tells us, More's daughter-in-law, young Anne Cresacre, noticed it:

> My sister More, in the summer as he sat at supper, singly in his doublet and hose, wearing thereupon a plain shirt, without ruff or collar, chancing to spy, began to laugh at it. My wife [Margaret Roper] not ignorant of his manner, perceiving the same, privily told him of it; and he, being sorry that she saw it, presently amended it. He used also sometimes to punish his body with whips, the cords knotted, which was known only to my wife, whom for her secrecy above all other he specially trusted, causing her, as need required, to wash the same shirt of hair.[4]

Now, despite all this, we are told that the Utopians condemn bodily austerities as 'a point of extreme madness, and a token of a man cruelly minded toward himself'.

More's biographers and commentators have been puzzled. Yet the very next sentence of *Utopia* explains the puzzle. The Utopians have only reason to guide them, and they believe that *by man's reason* nothing can be found truer than their view, *'unless any godlier be inspired into man from Heaven'*. The same point is made by More later. There *are* orders of ascetics in *Utopia*: if the ascetics grounded their action on reason the Utopians would mock them; but as they base it on religion, the Utopians honour them and regard them as holy.[5]

We find More, a dozen years later, urging against the Reformers this same doctrine which lies at the root of *Utopia:* 'That Reason is servant to Faith, not enemy.' More argues against the Lutherans that Reason, Philosophy, and even Poetry have their part to play: the Lutherans, who would cast away all learning except the Bible are, says More, 'in a mad mind', and he quotes St. Jerome to prove that pagan Philosophy and Poetry have their use for Christians. By 'Poetry' More of course means any work of the imagination: his Protestant critics deride *Utopia* as 'poetry', and More himself as a 'poet'. When a Sixteenth-Century Catholic depicts a pagan state founded on Reason and Philosophy, he is not depicting his ultimate ideal. Erasmus tells us that More's object was 'to show whence spring the evils of States, with special reference to the English State, with which he was most familiar'. The underlying thought of *Utopia* always is, *With nothing save Reason to guide them, the Utopians do this; and yet we Christian Englishmen, we Christian Europeans . . .!*

---

3. Dame Alice was More's second wife, who strongly objected to her husband's strict principles and ascetic practices.

4. Roper, *Life of More*, p. 49 [*Chambers's note*].
5. *Utopia*, above, pp. 50 and 77.

Just as More scored a point against the wickedness of Christian Europe, by making his philosophers heathen, so Jonathan Swift scored a point against the wickedness of mankind by representing *his* philosophers, the Houyhnhnms, as having the bodies of horses. Yet we do not call Swift inconsistent, because he did not live on a diet of oats, or, like poor Gulliver, fall into the voice and manner of horses in speaking. Swift did not mean that all horses are better than all men. He meant that some men are worse than horses. More did not mean that Heathendom is better than Christianity. He meant that some Christians are worse than heathen.

Dante and Langland and innumerable medieval writers had said the same before him. The conviction that life might be nobly lived on the basis of the four heathen cardinal virtues was one which the Catholic Middle Ages had inherited from Greek philosophy.

So, naturally, More is interested in the problem which for half a life-time tormented Dante and Langland; what will be the fate, in the next world, of the just heathen, who are an example to us in the affairs of this world? More's answer is tentative, but he quotes with approval the 'comfortable saying' of Master Nicholas de Lyra, the Franciscan, Dante's younger contemporary. Nicholas de Lyra argued that, though a much fuller faith is demanded from Christians, it suffices for the heathen to have believed 'that God is, and that He is the rewarder of them that seek Him'; these are, says de Lyra, 'two points such as every man may attain by natural reason, holpen forth with such grace as God keepeth from no man'.

And More quoted this,[6] not in his alleged 'emancipated' youth, but in his last book, the *Treatise upon the Passion*, written in the Tower, when he had dismissed all worldly affairs, and was awaiting martyrdom 'for the faith of the Catholic Church'.

What, then, is the attitude of *Utopia* as to these two articles, which represent, in More's view, the orthodoxy to which a heathen may attain? King Utopus tolerated all varieties of belief and disbelief, save on these two points; he forbade, 'ernestly and straitly' that any man should disbelieve in either (1) Divine Providence, or (2) a future life in which, as the Utopians believed, the just would be rewarded by God's presence.

So far was this simple creed from appearing lax to More's friends, that the marginal note (written either by Erasmus or by Peter Giles) contrasts the Utopian faith in immortality with the laxity and doubts of many Christians; *'The immortality of the soul, concerning which not a few, though Christians, to-day doubt or dispute.'* But in Utopia, the man who disbelieves either of these articles is not counted as a citizen, or even as a man; he is excluded from all office, and despised, as being necessarily of a base and vile nature. To suffer lifelong public contumely, in a land

6. *Works*, 1557, p. 1287–8 [*Chambers's note*].

where all life is lived in public, and where, save as a citizen, a man has and is nothing, is a punishment which many would feel to be worse than death. Yet the sceptic may not, publicly, argue in his own defence. Then comes the sentence which has been so often quoted, out of its context. In the old translation it runs, 'Howbeit they put him to no punishment'. Of course, More did not write such nonsense. What he really says is, "They do not put him to any bodily punishment'—so long, that is, as he humbly submits to the disgrace and to the silence which his heresies involve.[7] The charge against More of inconsistency rests upon refusing to notice his distinction between liberty to hold an opinion, and liberty to preach that opinion; between a man being in More's phrase 'a heretic alone by himself', and being 'a seditious heretic'.

Bishop Creighton,[8] to prove that More in later life 'put his principles aside,' quotes the passage which tells how King Utopus, when settling the Utopian constitution, found many religions prevalent in the land, and ordained that they should all be tolerated. Creighton then omits the passage about Utopus disgracing and muzzling those who held the opinions he thought pernicious. But this passage is vital; for, in the light of it, we find that Utopus did *not* tolerate the preaching of all views, but only of those which he, in his wisdom, thought tolerable. Then Creighton begins to quote again. Even those who held most noxious opinions 'were put to no punishment'. They are put to no bodily punishment, so long as they will submit to being disfranchised, despised, and silenced.

But, as the watchman says to Dogberry, 'How if they will not?'[9]

We can tell what would happen *then*, when we remember that, even in the discussion of such opinions as the State allows, any violent or seditious speech is punished in Utopia by banishment or bondage. And, in Utopia, if a man condemned to bondage jibs at his punishment, he is slain out of hand like a wild beast. Suppose that two sceptics, who did not believe the soul of man to be immortal, had discussed, in private, in Utopia, how they could get the law repealed which silenced and disenfranchised them. They would have incurred the penalty imposed on those who plot against the fundamental laws of Utopia. And, even for the highest magistrates, that penalty is death.

Still, within these narrow limits, the Utopian has liberty of conscience. He may not spread among the common people a belief which the State thinks harmful, nor may he discuss the most innocent opinions in a way likely to cause sedition and dissension. He may not, in private, discuss any affair of State. But, if he submits to these restrictions, he is left alone; he is not to be terrorized into saying that he believes what he does not believe.

7. See translation, p. 75 and note 4.
8. Bishop Mandell Creighton, nineteenth-century historian, wrote many books on the early Reformation period in England.

9. The allusion is to Shakespeare's *Much Ado About Nothing*, Act 3.

It may be a low ideal of liberty which allows, to a man who holds views disapproved by the authorities, freedom of thought only on condition that he does not claim freedom of speech. But that *is* the liberty Utopia allows. I shall try, later, to show how far More stuck to that ideal.

Utopia and the Problems of 1516

But we merely confuse the issues if we use our modern questionbegging terminology, and contrast More's alleged 'emancipated youth' with his orthodox old age. If we try to judge it in relation to the early Sixteenth Century, we shall find that *Utopia* is by no means 'emancipated'; it is rather a protest against undue 'emancipation'.

Utopia is, in part, a protest against the New Statesmanship: against the new idea of the autocratic prince to whom everything is allowed. I do not say that it is an impartial protest. The evil counsellors, who are represented in the First Book of *Utopia* egging the prince to despotism, might have replied that their ideal was not necessarily base or sycophantic. Patriots have sometimes seen in tyranny the only force strong enough to make their country great; reformers have sometimes seen in it the only force strong enough to carry through the reformation they desire. But *Utopia* is hostile to it.

Again, *Utopia* is, in part, a protest against the New Economics: the enclosures of the great landowners, breaking down old law and custom, destroying the old common-field agriculture. Here again, we must not suppose that *Utopia* gives us the full story. There was much more in the problem of enclosures than the greed of the great landlord, 'the very plague of his native country'.[1] The up-to-date farmer was also in favour of sweeping away all traces of the older communal husbandry. Thomas Tusser, a humble but practical agriculturist, says:

> Where all things in common do rest,
> Yet what doth it stand ye in stead?[2]

Now, in contrast to this changing world, More depicts a state where "all things in common do rest", and where there is no place for the grabbing superman. More's theoretical *Utopia*, looking back to Plato's *Republic* and to corporate life in the Middle Ages, probably seemed to some contemporaries the reverse of 'progressive'. Cardinal Pole has told of a conversation he had in his youth with Thomas Cromwell. Cromwell ridiculed the *Republic* of Plato, which, after so many centuries, has led to nothing. *He* had a book on statesmanship in manuscript, by a

---

1. See *Utopia*, above, p. 12
2. Thomas Tusser published in 1557 "A Hundredth Good Pointes of Husbandrie," describ-

ing in lame but quaint verse the way to make crops grow.

practical modern writer, based on experience. The book which Cromwell offered to lend to Pole, was *The Prince* of Nicholas Machiavelli.[3]

It is noteworthy that the two most potent books on the State written in the Sixteenth Century were written within so few years of each other. Parts of *Utopia* read like a commentary on parts of *The Prince*, as Johnson's *Rasselas* reads like a commentary on Voltaire's *Candide*, though we know that in neither case can the English writer have read his continental predecessor.[4] There is a reason for the coincidence; before *The Prince* was written, ideas used in *The Prince* had been gaining ground. They were the 'progressive' ideas, and we may regard *Utopia* as a 'reaction' against them.[5] Over and over again, in Book I of *Utopia*, Raphael Hythloday imagines himself as counseling a prince, telling him what he ought to do, against those who are telling him what he *can* do; and always Raphael admits that these ideas of justice which he has brought from Utopia are opposed to all that the most-up-to-date statesmen of Europe are thinking and doing.

And so, from the point of view of the new age of Machiavellian statesmanship and commercial exploitation, *Utopia* is old-fashioned. The King is to 'live of his own', in medieval wise, and to turn a deaf ear to the counsellors who would make him all powerful. The big landlords are to have mercy on their tenants, and not to allow them to be sacrificed to economic progress, and the law of supply and demand in the wool market.

* * *

Another leading problem of controversy was the immortality of the soul. Did philosophy and human reason, apart from revelation, teach such immortality? There were philosophers who said 'No'; and, three years before *Utopia* was published, this matter also had come before the Lateran Council.[6] Teachers of philosophy were enjoined to point out how Christian philosophy corrected the views of the heathen on immortality; they were to refute these heathen errors, and steps were taken to ensure that the student in *sacris ordinibus constitutus*[7] should not spend

---

3. *Epistolarum*, Pars I, BRESCIA, 17444, pp. 135–7. An attempt has been made to argue that Pole mistook the book, and that Cromwell really meant to lend him *The Courtier* of CASTIGLIONE. (VAN DYKE, *Renascence Portraits*, p. 401.) The argument is unconvincing [*Chambers's note*].

4. Dr. Johnson published *Rasselas* and Voltaire *Candide*, within a few weeks of each other in 1759; Machiavelli's *Prince* was written in 1513, two years before *Utopia*, though not published till much later.

5. I had written this before reading Hermann Oncken's lecture on the *Utopia* (1922), but I am glad to find that I have the support of his authority: *Sitzungsberichte der Heidelberger Akademie, Phil.-Hist. Klasse* (1922), 2, p. 12 [*Chambers's note*].

6. 19 Dec. 1513: *Concilium Lateranense* V, *Session viii*. See *Conciliorum Omnium tomus XXXIV*, Paris, 1644, pp. 333–5, 557 [*Chambers's note*]. [The Lateran Council, held in the Roman church of St. John Lateran, was the last of five going under that name. It was in session from 1512 to 1517.]

7. Students studying for holy orders, theology students.

more than five years upon philosophy and poetry, before diluting them with the safer studies of theology and pontifical law.

Now, let us try and look at *Utopia* from the point of view of 1516. Here is a heathen community, whose religion is founded on philosophy and natural reason. Yet, so far from doubting the immortality of the soul, they base their whole polity upon it. No disbeliever in immortality may be a citizen of Utopia. In life, and in death, every true Utopian has a firm trust in the communion of saints.

So that, in the eyes of More's friends, Erasmus or Peter Giles, *Utopia* is a striking defense of a vital tenet of the Christian faith. More will not tolerate the ambiguous formula: 'As an orthodox Catholic I believe in immortality; as a philosopher I doubt.' Reason and philosophy teach the Utopian to affirm that he is somehow in touch with the souls of the noble dead, mighty overseers whose presence encourages him to do his duty the more courageously.

Thus here we find More in *Utopia* opposing the scepticism of his age, precisely as we have seen him opposing its Machiavellian statecraft. And so thoroughly is *Utopia* a book of the hour, that here again More seems to be making a comment on a book which he had never seen. For it was in the very same November of 1516, in which Peter Giles was writing the dedicatory epistle of *Utopia*, that the professor of Philosophy at Bologna, Pomponazzi, published his famous treatise on the Immortality of the Soul. Pomponazzi submitted to the Church in all matters of faith, but, as a philosopher, he stubbornly upheld his doubt as to the doctrine of immortality.[8]

Therefore More's *Utopia*, among other things, is a contribution to this current controversy. More attacks the enemy in their philosophical camp, and makes his heathen Utopians into unexpected allies of the Catholic faith with regard to this great dogma—and, as we shall see later, with regard to other things as well.

But the imminent problem was monasticism. There was an incompatibility between the declining spirit of the monastic common life, and the rising commercialism of the grasping 'new rich'. Within a quarter of a century commercialism was to destroy monasticism in England. More stands, as it were, at the crossways, and asks, 'Why not destroy commercialism? Is not the spirit of the common life really better worth preserving?' It is significant that *the religious houses are the one European institution which the Utopians are said to approve*. And with reason, for in Utopia, though the rule of celibacy is necessarily absent, the monastic idea is at work. The Utopian State is as sumptuous as many a religious house was. But the Utopian, like the monk or friar, may possess nothing. Everyone in Utopia must wear the common habit (in a letter to Erasmus we shall find More calling it Franciscan).[9] There are four

8. The *Tractatus de immortalitate animae* is dated Bologna, 6 Nov. 1516; *Utopia* is dated Antwerp, 1 Nov. 1516 [*Chambers's note*].

9. P. S. Allen, ed., *Letters of Erasmus*, II, No. 499 [*Chambers's note*].

varieties, for men and women, married and unmarried. The cloaks of the Utopians are all of one colour, and that is the natural colour of the wool.' Their hours of work, of recreation, the very games they may play, are all regulated. There are no foolish and pernicious games like dice. Instead, the Utopians have two games, one of which is intended to teach mathematics, and the other to teach morals. The Utopians eat in refectories, beginning every dinner and supper by reading something pertaining to good manners and virtue. Talk at table is initiated and directed by the elders, who graciously encourage the younger married people to join in the discussion, by turning it into a kind of oral examination. As for the men below twenty-two and the girls below eighteen: they serve, or else stand by, in marvellous silence, watching their elders eat and talk.

In much of this, More is perhaps joking; it was his way to utter his jests with such a solemn face as to puzzle his own household.[1] But, underneath More's fun, was a creed as stern as that of Dante, just as, underneath his gold chain, was the shirt of hair. And, quite certainly, the ideal of *Utopia* is discipline, not liberty. It is influenced by some of the most severe disciplines the world has ever known. Through Plato's *Republic* it goes back to the barrack life of a Spartan warrior; through More's own experience to the life of a Charterhouse monk.[2] And the discipline of Utopia is enforced rigidly, even ferociously. If the Utopian attempts to break the laws of his native land, there is the penalty of bondage, and, if that fails, of death. We have seen that even to speak of State affairs, except at the licensed place and hour, is punishable in Utopia with death, lest permission to discuss politics might lead to revolution. Has any State, at any time, carried terrorism quite so far?

Many framers of ideal commonwealths have shirked the question of compulsion, by imagining their citizens to have all become moral overnight. More does not choose this easy way. He recognizes that there will be a minority, to whom higher motives do not appeal. For them, there is penal servitude; if that fails, death.

But no great State can be founded on terrorism. For the mass of its citizens, Utopia is founded on religious enthusiasm. Faith in God, and in the immortal destiny of the human soul, supplies the driving power which is to quench human passion and human greed.[3] Based on religion, Utopia is supported by a belief in the dignity of manual labour. Even rulers and magistrates, although legally exempt, share in this work as an example to others.[4] So a six-hour day suffices, and the rest of the time is free for those intellectual and artistic pursuits in which, to the Utopians, pleasure consists.[5] But religion is the basis of all.

1. Cresacre More, 1726, p. 179; cf. *Works*, 1557, p. 127 [*Chambers's note*]. Cresacre More was Sir Thomas's great grandson; he compiled a life of his distinguished forebear about the year 1627.

2. A Carthusian monk, one attached to an extremely strict order.
3. See *Utopia*, above, pp. 75–76.
4. *Ibid.*, p. 39.
5. *Ibid.*, esp. p. 40.

Now a monk of to-day, Dom Ursmer Berlière, of the Abbey of Maredsous, has pointed out how at the beginning of the Middle Ages, monasticism, as St. Benedict shaped it, gave a pattern to the State. St. Benedict's monastery 'was a little State, which could serve as a model for the new Christian society which was arising from the fusion of the conquered and conquering races—a little State which had for its basis, religion; for its support, the honour given to work; for its crown a new intellectual and artistic culture.' The writer was not thinking of *Utopia*. I do not know if he had ever read it. But, at the end of the Middle Ages, we find More depicting a State founded on just these things: the common life, based on religion; honour given to manual labour; intellectual and artistic culture. However far these things might sometimes be from monastic practice, the writer of *Utopia* could never have approved of the destruction of monasticism; he looked for its reform.

                                *   *   *

We can only understand *Utopia* if we remember the Europe for which it was written; at home John Rastell preaching exploration to the More household;[6] abroad the travels of Vespucci in every man's hands; Vespucci, who had found folk holding property in common, and not esteeming gold, pearls, or jewels. (It is important to remember that the Inca empire of Peru, which in more than one detail had a likeness to Utopia, was not known till some fourteen years later; Cortes had not yet conquered Mexico.)

The problem of poverty and unemployment (destined in England to be aggravated by the dissolution of the Monasteries) was already a European one. Ten years after *Utopia*, More's friend Vives wrote a tract on it.[7] At the root of More's interest in colonization lies his pity for the unemployed labourers:

> 'Poor silly[8] wretched souls; away they trudge out of their known and accustomed houses; all their household stuff, being suddenly thrust out, they be constrained to sell it for a thing of naught. And when they have, wandering about, soon spent that, what can they do but steal, and then be hanged, or else go about abegging. Whom no man will set awork, though they never so willingly offer themselves thereto.'

But the fact that *Utopia* belongs to its age does not mean that it is the less epoch-making. Some things which may now seem commonplaces to us were less so then. It may seem quite natural to us that in Utopia there should be no class distinctions. It was less obvious to a scholar of the Renaissance. Plato's Commonwealths had been based on class dis-

6. John Rastell was More's brother-in-law.
7. Juan Luis Vives, Spanish humanist, wrote prodigiously on a vast range of subjects.

8. Foolish. The translation of *Utopia* is Ralph Robynson's; cf. above, *Utopia*, p. 12.

tinction. In the *Laws* the citizens fall into four classes. In the *Republic*, also, there are classes, although so much attention is given to the warrior class, and their common life, that we almost forget the others. Plato is emphatic that every man should have one job only, and he does not waste words on his artisans, except to urge that they must be experts in their own business, and must stick to it. The Middle Ages inherited the same idea of the State: ploughmen and artisans to labour, clerks to pray and study, knights to fight. But the Utopian citizen does all three things; he labours with his hands, studies in his spare hours, and, though he hates warfare, is, at need, a soldier.

It is noteworthy that, despite his admiration for Greek life and thought, More did not build Utopia after the Hellenic pattern. His free citizens are not a privileged class dependent on slave labour, nor are his bond-men a distinct class. Bondage in Utopia is penal servitude—a humane substitute for the death penalty. The repentant bondman is restored to freedom, the incorrigible bondman is slain. But the citizens themselves are all workers.

Finally the outstanding feature of *Utopia* is implied in the great sentence with which Raphael ends his story:

> When I consider all these commonwealths which nowadays any-where do flourish, so God help me, I can perceive nothing but a conspiracy of rich men, procuring their own commodities under the name and title of the commonwealth.

The Middle Ages had often been charitable to the poor, and More's age had inherited vast charitable endowments. More altogether approved of these endowments, and, later, we shall find him defending them against the fanaticism of reformers who wished to hand them over to a conspiracy of rich men procuring their own commodities under the title of the commonwealth. But More's claim for *justice* goes far beyond medieval admonitions to charity. Its publication throughout Europe by the printing press marks an epoch.

J. H. HEXTER

The Roots of *Utopia* and All Evil†

We are better equipped to discover what those ends[1] are now that we know that bond labor, abolition of markets and money, and restriction

† From *More's Utopia: The Biography of an Idea* (Princeton: Reprinted by permission of the author. Princeton UP, 1952) 71–81 (Part 2, section 8). Footnotes are Hexter's except where credited to the editor of this volume. Refer- ences to the text of *Utopia* have been changed to reflect the paging of this edition. 1. Hexter has been discussing the ends of Uto-pian society, its objectives [*Editor.*]

of wants by enforced community of consumption are of a piece with the abolition of private property and profit and with the obligation to toil—indispensable motifs in the total pattern of More's best state of the commonwealth. A society where wants are tightly bound up and where the penal power of the state is made daily conspicuous by men in heavy gold chains—this is no ideal society of Modern Socialism. Altogether missing from *Utopia* is that happy anarchist last chapter of modern socialism intended to justify all the struggle, all the suffering, all the constraint that we must undergo in order to reach it. *Utopia* does not end in an eschatological dream.

More simply did not believe that all the evil men do can be ascribed to the economic arrangements of society, and that those evils and the very potentiality for evil will vanish when the economic arrangements are rectified and set on a proper footing. More believed no such thing because in his view of men and their affairs there was a strong and ineradicable streak of pessimism. More's pessimism was ineradicable because it was part and parcel of his Christian faith. He knew surely, as a profoundly Christian man he had to know, that the roots of evil run far too deep in men to be destroyed by a mere rearrangement of the economic organization of society. His residue of pessimism leads More to provide even "the best state of the commonwealth" with an elaborate complement of laws drastically limiting the scope given to individual human desires and to arm its government with extensive and permanent powers of coercion. Although he was convinced that the institutions of the society that he knew provided the occasions for the evils he saw, he did not—and as profoundly orthodox Christian he could not—believe that the evils were totally ascribable to the institutions. His probings led him to believe that the roots of the evils of sixteenth century Europe, though nourished in the rich black earth of an acquisitive society, were moistened by the inexhaustible stream of sin.

Underlying the whole catalogue of evils of his time he finds one or another of several sins. Luxury, gluttony, envy, vanity, vainglory, lust, hypocrisy, debauchery, sloth, bad faith and the rest all find an easy vent in the Christendom he knew, whose institutions seemed to him as if contrived to activate human wickedness and anesthetize human decency. Yet More does not give equal attention to all the kinds of sin; the realm of evil is not a republic of equals. The Deadly Sins themselves are not on an even footing in the Utopian Discourse. Gluttony and Anger get short shrift, Envy is there only as a counterfoil to a deadlier sin, and Lust, that whipping boy of our feeble latter-day Christianity, receives but a passing glance. The great triumvirate that rules the empire of evil, are Sloth, Greed, and Pride.

It is sloth that in More's day leads stout fellows able to work to enter into the idle bands of serving men; it is sloth that leads them to fill with drinking, gaming, and brawling the hours they ought to spend in honest toil.[2] It is sloth, the avoidance of labor, that the Utopians punish with bondage.[3] Yet although to More's mind idleness was among the most destructive cankers on the social body, although it preoccupied him as much as any other problem, he did not blame that idleness wholly on sloth. The lazy good-for-nothing scum that the great leave in their wake is conjured into being by the great men themselves, who provide their followers with the means of debauchery and vice. And it is not sloth but a greater sin that leads the great men to foster the infection of idleness in the body of the commonwealth.

Even above sloth in the hierarchy of sin lie greed and pride. In dealing with these two paramount sins More's Christian faith stood him in good stead. It provided him with a basic insight into the underlying pattern of evil, a pattern somewhat obscured by our modern climate of opinion. For he did not believe that greed and pride were on a parity with each other as sources of the social ills of his day, or that they offered equal obstacles to the establishment of the Good Society; but at this point it requires special care to read More's meaning right. The best known passage of *Utopia*, the attack on enclosure in the Dialogue section, is directed against the "inordinate and insatiable covetousness" of landlords and engrossers.[4] Much of the Discourse section, moreover, is taken up with variation after variation on a single theme; "The love of money is the root of all evil." Now the inordinate desire for riches is greed or avarice, and from this it would seem to follow almost as a syllogism that greed was what More discovered as a result of his social analysis to be the fount and origin of the sickness of his own society. Yet it is not so. Greed was a sin, revolting enough in More's eyes; but it is not a sufficiently attractive vice to stand alone. Men are impelled to it not by its charms, but, like other animals, by fear of want. "Why," Hythloday asks, "*should anyone consider seeking superfluities, when he is certain that he will never lack anything? Indeed in all kinds of living things it is . . . fear of want that creates greed and rapacity.*"[5] It is one of the perverse traits of the regime of private property, where each must make provision for and look after his own, that an amiable regard for his kin continually tempts man to the sin of avarice.[6]

But this sin, certain to beset a pecuniary society, is essentially, a parasite on the insecurity inherent in that kind of society and has no roots of its own. It is sustained rather by the institutional roots of the property system itself. Even the rich, More suggests, realize this, and are "not ignorant how much better it were to lack no necessary thing than to

---

2. See above, *Utopia*, pp. 10–12, 38.
3. See above, *Utopia*, p. 37.
4. See above, *Utopia*, p. 13.
5. "For why should it be thought that man would ask more than enough, which is sure never to lack? Certainly, in all kinds of living creatures, . . . fear of lack doth cause covetousness and ravine"; *Nam cur superaucua petiturus putetur is, qui certum habeat nihil sibi unquam defuturum? Nempe auidum ac rapacem . . . timor carendi facit, in omni animantum genere.* See above, *Utopia*, p. 42.
6. See above, *Utopia*, p. 82.

abound with overmuch superfluity, to be rid out of innumerable cares and troubles, than to be *bound down*[7] by great riches."[8] If avarice were the great danger to society the Utopian commonwealth could be instituted along lines far less rigorous and repressive than those More prescribes. But avarice is not all. Fear of want makes for greed in all living creatures, including man; in man alone greed has a second set of roots deeper in his nature even than fear. For men only of God's creatures are greedy out of "pride alone, which counts it a glorious thing to pass and excel others in the superfluous and vain ostentation of things."[9] Here, I think, lies the heart of the matter. Deep in the soul of the society of More's day, because it was deep in the soul of all men, was the monster Pride, distilling its terrible poison and dispatching it to all parts of the social body to corrupt, debilitate, and destroy them. Take but a single example: Why must the poor in Europe be "wearied from early in the morning to late in the evening with continual work like laboring and toiling beasts" leading a life "worse than the miserable and wretched condition of bondmen, which nevertheless is almost everywhere the life of workmen and artificers?"[1] Human beings are consigned to this outrageous slavery merely to support the enormous mass of the idle, and to perform the "vain and superfluous" work that serves "only for riotous superfluity and unhonest pleasure."[2] What feeds the unhonest pleasure that men derive from luxuries and vanities, or to use the phrase of a modern moralist, from conspicuous consumption and conspicuous waste? It is pride. Many men drudge out their lives making vain and needless things because other men "count themselves nobler for the smaller or finer thread of wool"[3] their garb is made of, because "they think the *value*[4] of their own persons is thereby greatly increased. And therefore the honor, which in a coarse gown they dare not have looked for, they require, as it were of duty, for their finer gowns' sake. And if they be passed by without reverence, they take it angrily and disdainfully."[5] The same sickness of soul shows itself in "pride in vain and unprofitable honors." "For what natural or true pleasure doest thou take of another man's bare head or bowed knees? Will this ease the pain of thy knees or remedy the frenzy of thy head? In this image of counterfeit pleasure they be of a marvelous madness *who flatter and applaud themselves with the notion of their own nobility.*"[6] It is to support this prideful and conceited burden to keep idlers in luxury. The great mass of wastrels bearing down on Christendom are maintained to minister to the pride and vainglory of the great. Such are "the flock of stout bragging rushbucklers,"[7] "the

7. "be besieged with"; *obsideri*
8. See above *Utopia*, p. 84.
9. See above, *Utopia*, p. 42.
1. See above, *Utopia*, p. 37.
2. See above, *Utopia*, p. 38.
3. See above, *Utopia*, p. 52.
4. "price"; *precii*

5. See above, *Utopia*, p. 52.
6. "which for the opinion of nobility rejoice much in their own conceit"; *ii qui nobilitatis opinione sibi blandiuntur ac plaudunt.* See above, *Utopia*, p. 53.
7. See above, *Utopia*, p. 38.

great . . . train of idle and loitering servingmen,"[8] that "rich men, especially all landed men, which commonly be called gentlemen and noblemen,"[9] themselves fainéants, "carry about with them at their tails."[1] Such too are the armies, maintained by those paragons of pride, the princes of Europe, out of the blood and sweat of their subjects, to sustain their schemes of megalomaniac self-glorification.[2] Thus seeking in outward, vain, and wicked things an earthly worship which neither their achievement nor their inner virtue warrants. Christians lure their fellow men into the sin of sloth, or subject them to endless labor, or destroy their substance, their bodies, and their souls too, in futile wars; and over the waste and the misery, over the physical ruin and the spiritual, broods the monster sin of pride.

The Utopian Discourse then is based on a diagnosis of the ills of sixteenth century Christendom; it ascribes those ills to sin, and primarily to pride, and it prescribes remedies for that last most disastrous infection of man's soul designed to inhibit if not to eradicate it. For our understanding of the Utopian Discourse it is of the utmost importance that we recognize this to be its theme. Unless we recognize it, we cannot rescue More from the ideologically motivated scholars of the Left and the Right, both as anxious to capture him for their own as if he were a key constituency in a close Parliamentary election. According to the Rightist scholars, who have allowed their nostalgia for an imaginary medieval unity to impede their critical perceptions, More was one of the last medieval men. He was the staunch defender of Catholic solidarism represented in medieval order and liberties, in a stable, agrarian subsistence economy, in guild brotherhood, monastic brotherhood, and Christian brotherhood against the inchoate growth of modern universal otherhood, already embodied, or shortly to be embodied in nascent capitalism, the New Monarchy, Protestantism, and Machiavellianism.[3] On the other hand, the most recent exponent of the *Utopia* as an exemplification of dialectical materialism has seen More as a fine early example of the Middle Class Man whose social views are one and all colored by his antipathy to late medieval feudalism as represented in the enfeebled but still exploitative Church and in the predatory and decadent dynastic warrior princes.[4]

Both of these formulations—that of the Left and that of the Right—are subject to a number of weaknesses. They are both based on conceptions of economic development and social stratification in the sixteenth century and earlier, more coherent than correct, and largely mythological in many respects. The Leftist scholars regarding More's age from

---

8. See above, *Utopia*, p. 10.
9. See above, *Utopia*, p. 38.
1. See above, *Utopia*, p. 10.
2. See above, *Utopia*, p. 11.
3. Chambers, passim; Campbell, passim. I

borrow the concept of modern "otherhood" from my friend Prof. Benjamin Nelson, *The Idea of Usury: From Tribal Brotherhood to Universal Otherhood*, The History of Ideas Series, 3.
4. Ames, passim.

a particular twentieth century perspective, the Rightists by regarding it from what they fondly imagine to be a medieval perspective deprive both More's opinions and his age of the measure of internal cohesion that both in truth possess. But to document these criticisms adequately would require an inordinate amount of space.[5] For the moment it must suffice to point out that from *Utopia* and from the events of More's life, scholarly ideologues both of the Left and the Right have been able to adduce a remarkable number of citations and facts to support their respective and totally irreconcilable views. Now this paradox is amenable to one of two possible explanations. The first would require us to assume that More's thought was so contradictory, disorderly, and illogical as to justify either of these interpretations or both, although in reason and common sense they are mutually contradictory. But the intellectual coherence and sureness of thought of the Utopian Discourse and the sense of clear purpose that it radiates seem to preclude this resolution of the paradox. The second possibility is that either point of view can be maintained only by an unconscious but unjustifiable underestimate of the weight of the citations and data offered in support of the opposite point of view, but that all the citations and data fall into a harmonious pattern if looked at in a third perspective.

The character of that third possible perspective I have tried to suggest: the Utopian Discourse is the production of a Christian humanist uniquely endowed with a statesman's eye and mind, a broad wordly experience, and a conscience of unusual sensitivity, who saw sin and especially the sin of pride as the cancer of the commonwealth. Now the social critic of any age is bound to direct his most vigorous attack at the centers of power in that age and reserve his sharpest shafts for the men possessing it. For however great the potentialities for evil may be in all men, real present social ills, the social critic's stock in trade, are immediately the consequence of the acts and decisions of the men actually in a position to inflict their wills on the social body. In a pecuniary society enjoying a reasonable measure of internal security and order but subject to great disparities of wealth, the social critic is bound to attack the very rich, because in such a society, where direct violence does not bear all the sway, riches become a most important source of power. This does not necessarily imply that pride is wholly confined to rich and powerful men, although by their possession of and preoccupation with money and power, the two goods most highly prized by the worldly, they are sure to be especially vulnerable to that sin. It is more to the point, however, that the pride of the powerful is, by virtue of their power, socially efficacious, since it is armed with the puissance of command. It can get what it

5. I have touched on two aspects of the general problem of sixteenth century society in two recent articles, "The Education of the Aristocracy in the Renaissance," *Journal of Modern History*, 22, 1950, pp. 1–20; and "The Myth of the Middle Class in Tudor England," *Explorations in Entrepreneurial History*, 2, 1949–1950, pp. 128–140.

wickedly wants. In More's Europe—the illicit violence of lordship almost everywhere having been suppressed by the new monarchs—it was the pride of the rich that did the real wicked work in the world, the work of fraud, oppression, debauchery, waste, rapine, and death. So More's shafts find their target in the rich and the powerful—in the bourgeois usurer, the engrosser, the court minion, the mighty lord of lands and men, the princes of the earth, in the encloser and depopulator whether that encloser was a parvenu grazier-butcher still reeking of the blood of the City shambles or a predacious noble of immaculate lineage or an ancient abbey rich in estates and poor in things of the spirit. These were his target not because together they form a homogeneous social class, for they do not, nor because they are all decadently medieval or all inchoately modern, for they are not all one or all the other, but because their riches and power sustained the empire of pride over the world that More knew and whose social ills he had traced to that center of evils.

Once we recognize that More's analysis of sixteenth century society led him to the conclusion that pride was the source of the greater part of its ills, the pattern of the Utopian commonwealth becomes clear, consistent, and intelligible. In its fundamental structure it is a great social instrument for the subjugation of pride. The pecuniary economy must be destroyed because money is the prime instrument through the use of which men seek to satisfy their yet insatiable pride. It is to keep pride down that all Utopians must eat in common messes, wear a common uniform habit, receive a common education, and rotate their dwelling places. In a society where no man is permitted to own the superfluities that are the marks of invidious distinction, no man will covet them. Above all idleness, the great emblem of pride in the society of More's time, a sure mark to elevate the aristocrat above the vulgar, is utterly destroyed by the common obligation of common daily toil. It is through no accident, through no backwardness of the Tudor economy, that More makes the Utopian commonwealth a land austere and rigorous beyond most of the imaginary societies elaborated by his later imitators. Had he cared only to consider man's material welfare, his creature comfort, it need not have been so. More was a logical man; he knew that to bind up pride on all sides it takes a strait prison, and he did not flinch from the consequences of his diagnosis. As he truly says this "kind of vice among the Utopians can have no place"[6]

Since More does not explicitly speak of pride very often in *Utopia*, my emphasis on its role in his social thought on both the critical and constructive side may seem exaggerated. Let anyone who thinks this is so consider the words with which More draws Hythloday's peroration and the whole Discourse of the best state of a commonwealth to its

6. See above, *Utopia*, p. 42.

conclusion: "I doubt not that the respect of every man's private commodity or else the authority of our Saviour Christ . . . would have brought all the world long ago into the laws of this weal public, if it were not that one only beast, the princess and mother of all mischief, Pride, doth withstand and let it. She measureth not wealth and prosperity by her own commodities but by the miseries and incommodities of others; she would not by her good will be made a goddess if there were no wretches left *over whom she might, like a scornful lady, rule and triumph*,[7] over whose miseries her felicity might shine, whose poverty she might vex, torment, and increase by gorgeously setting forth her riches. This hellhound creeps into men's hearts; and plucks them back from entering the right path of life, and is so deeply rooted in men's breasts that she cannot be plucked out."[8]

The disciplining of pride, then, is the foundation of the best state of the commonwealth. And more than that, it is pride itself that prevents actual realms from attaining to that best state.

ALISTAIR FOX

[An Intricate, Intimate Compromise] †

[A book like *Utopia*, which has been written about for hundreds of years, sometimes gives the impression of having been utterly exhausted. It is not that the problems have been solved, but that the positions have been laid out and worked over to the point that thinking or saying something new seems just about impossible. And then a new scholar comes along, who looks at the problems from a longer or wider perspective, with a new access of patience, or with a fresh mixture of sympathy and severe exactitude, which results in a new quality of vision. Professor Fox's study of More's thinking is not to be labeled as on this side or that of the long-running controversies that have sometimes seemed to divide the students of More into armed camps. The early years of More's life—those of his friendship with Erasmus and the writing of *Utopia*—are the most agreeable, as his last years of approaching martyrdom are the most imposing and heroic of his career. The middle years, which are filled with controversy and administrative business, have been neglected by contrast—and, from a literary point of view, deservedly so. But new translations and a lot of scholarly patience have made possible a broader and fuller view of More's whole career. Fox's book is not always easy reading, but the effect of studying it is to create a capacious and lucid view of a subject that had once seemed to be hopelessly fractured.

For the purposes of an elementary text, the present editor has eliminated most of Fox's Latin quotations and most of his footnotes. Notes that remain

7. "whom she might be lady over to mock and scorn"; *quibus imperare atque insultare possit.*
8. See above, *Utopia*, p. 84.

† From *Thomas More, History and Providence* (Yale UP, 1983) ch. 2, "The Morean Synthesis: Utopia."

have frequently been changed to accord with the pagination of this edition. For the entire argument in its meticulous detail, readers are referred to the original book, of which the excerpt chosen is but one introductory chapter.]

* * *

The circumstances were right for More to entertain his eutopian [1] fantasy when he sat down to write *Utopia* in 1515. His imagination had been excited by the discoveries of Cabot and Vespucci in the New World and the explorations of the Portuguese around the Cape of Good Hope to the East; his legal career in the City was advancing as well as he could wish; the momentum of Erasmian reform was approaching its height; and he had the stimulating company on the Flanders mission of Cuthbert Tunstal, Busleiden and Peter Giles, humanists with interests and ambitions similar to his own. The eutopian quality of the book can be seen in the extent to which More created the Utopians in his own image. They share his contempt for material ostentation, as attested by their simple monastic garb and their debasing use of gold for chamber pots and slaves' fetters, and of jewels for children's toys. They, too, believe that the secret of a happy life consists in the cultivation of the mind and achieve the same kind of communal domestic order for which More strove in his own household. Specifically, he projected into the eutopians his own fondness for gardens, his liking for music, his delight in fools, and his receptivity towards foreign guests. Even the monkey to be seen in Holbein's sketch of the family group finds his way into the action, having ripped up Hythlodaeus' copy of Theophrastus during the voyage.

Once the degree of whimsy in this self-projection is grasped, some of the book's thematic problems become more comprehensible, particularly those which arise from the Utopians' epicurean philosophy. This derives in part from Vespucci's description in *Mundus Novus* of people who 'live according to nature, and may be called Epicureans rather than Stoics', but also from More's own engagement with the problem that had interested him in Lucian's *Cynicus*: whether the enjoyment of temporal things is compatible with virtue, a thing indifferent, or repugnant, the ascetic way being better. Observing (like Menippus) the inconsistency in even the sternest ascetics who while imposing a life of labour, vigils and general discomfort on one nevertheless exhort that same person to relieve the privations of others, the Utopians focus the issue into a combined proposition-question:

> either a joyous life, that is, a pleasurable life, is evil, in which case not only ought you to help no one to it, but as far as you can, should take it away from everyone as being harmful and deadly, or

1. As Utopia means "no place," Eutopia means "the good place"; Fox uses "eutopian" to imply an optimistic view of the world.

else, if you not only are permitted but are obliged to win it for
others as being good, why should you not do so first of all for yourself, to whom you should show no less favour than to others?[2]

More then allows them a privilege he would never have allowed himself
in real life: to explore the implications of an assumption that virtue and
pleasure *are* compatible. After having Hythlodaeus utter a discreet disclaimer against it,[3] he gives a serious and coherent praise of pleasure.

Utopian hedonism is founded on much the same religious beliefs as
those More was still asserting as the basis of salvation at the end of his
career: 'those principles are as follows: that the soul is immortal and born
for happiness through the beneficence of God, and that our virtues and
good deeds are destined to be rewarded after this life, and our misdeeds
punished.' These beliefs make the Utopians Christians *de facto*, if not
in name, because, as More asserted later, pagans who accepted the end
of salvation implicitly professed Christ, who was the means.[4] One should
not, therefore, make too much of their paganism to explain away More's
excursus into theoretical hedonism. It cannot be seriously argued that
the Utopians' view embodies merely the findings of blind reason unil-
luminated by faith, for the Utopians themselves, acknowledging that
reason alone is inadequate for the investigation of happiness, realize that
the very legitimacy of their ethic depends upon religious principles ('ab
religione . . . sententiae'), and accept the necessary co-operation of reason and faith just as fervently as More did later in *A Dialogue Concerning Heresies*. As far as their morality was concerned, More allowed the
Utopians to live as he would have liked to have been able to live, but
could not. Nothing would have pleased him more than to have been
able to be a married priest, or to have gratified his five senses with the
harmless pleasures that grace, for example, Utopian meals; but although
desire inclined him towards them, other forces in his personality caused
him to withhold the assent of his will to them.

Much the same is true of the common ownership upon which Utopian polity rests. More could have it both ways: he could explore the
implications of a communal way of living without necessarily proposing
it, however much he may have felt emotionally or intellectually inclined
towards it, as one suspects he was. Hythlodaeus' summation of the general advantage of the Utopian way of life betrays the reason for its attractiveness to More; although no man owns anything, all are rich: 'For
what can be richer than to live with a happy and tranquil mind, free
from anxiety?'[5] In effect, the Utopians' repudiation of private property

---

2. See above, *Utopia*, p. 51.
3. See above, *Utopia*, p. 50.
4. *A Treatise on the Passion, Collected Works*,
3, p. 43.

5. See above, *Utopia*, p. 82.

is a remedy against the same Fortuna against whom More had railed in the *Verses for the Book of Fortune*. Once again, he allows them to live according to a synthesis he could only imagine: a fusion of the religious and secular lives. As Budé and Beatus Rhenanus recognized, and Giles indicated in his marginal glosses, the Utopians have adopted 'the customs and true wisdom of Christianity for public and private life', consisting of 1) the equality of all things among citizens, 2) love of peace and quiet, and 3) contempt for gold and silver. In short, they import all the virtues of monastic life into political and social affairs, and when More in a famous daydream indulged the fantasy that he was their king, it was in a 'Franciscan frock' that he saw himself, 'crowned with a diadem of wheat . . . carrying a handful of wheat as my sacred scepter'.[6] The complex collocation of associations in these images suggests that More enviously viewed the Utopians as successful Carthusian (Franciscan if you like) mercers, the governing of whom would allow him to bring the cloister into the court, where he already knew he might be headed.

A large part of book 2, then, describes the happy place of More's dream; but that reflects only one aspect of the titular paradox. As happy as eutopia is, it is also 'nusquama', nowhere, and 'udepotia', a land that will never be. To complicate the matter further, Utopia was conceived from the outset as being in an ambiguous relation with England: the more the two countries appear to be opposed, the more they turn out to be similar—the obvious differences paradoxically serve to underline the more significant parallels.

At one level, particularly with respect to geographical details, Utopia and England share a shadowy identity. Utopia is an island separated from the continent by a channel, Amaurotum, its capital city, together with the tidal river Anydrus, and the magnificently arched stone bridge across it, resemble London and the Thames, as the marginal glosses make clear, and the houses reflect those evolved in England in their disposition, their handsome flint facings, and their glass windows (even if their flat roofs and occasional oil-smeared linen window-screens are calculated to blur the image slightly). The stage is thus set up for the Utopian illusion to dissolve into the reality of England and Europe, as it does—at the very point where Hythlodaeus asserts the most extreme degree of contrast between the two.

This occurs in the description of the Utopians' mistrust of treaties, and of their military affairs. They never make treaties with any nation, Hythlodaeus says, 'because in those parts of the world treaties, and alliances between kings are not observed with much good faith.' He then

---

6. E. F. Rogers, *Selected Letters of Thomas More*, no. 11, p. 85.

draws a savagely satiric contrast with Europe, meaning the exact opposite of what he says:

> In Europe, however, and especially in those parts where the faith
> and religion of Christ prevails, the majesty of treaties is everywhere
> holy and inviolable, partly through the justice and goodness of kings,
> partly through the reverence and fear of the Sovereign Pontiffs.[7]

This ironic inversion is not simply rhetorical, but serves to focus the
reader's attention on the presence in the antipodean world of something
that makes the rationally ideal polity of the Utopians somewhat of a lie,
if not an irrelevancy—the ineradicable sinfulness of human nature.

Utopia gradually turns out to be no more and no less removed from
Europe in a social and moral sense than it is in a geographical one. As
an island it resembles England, but it also differs in at its tapering ends
give it the appearance of a 'renascent' moon. The emblem suggests at
one level that Utopia figures forth the renovated polity that an optimistic
humanist might envision for England in the context of the contemporary historical 'Renaissance'. But beneath the seductive appearance of
the Utopians' simplified, rationalized laws and mores is the human perversity that makes their existence necessary: the lust that wrecks their
ideal of the inviolability and permanence of marriage and leads them to
permit an extremely liberal policy of divorce, the recalcitrance of hard-
ened criminals which forces them to slaughter repeated offenders with a
savagery equal to that in Europe, and the anger which, in their warfare,
induces them to duplicate some of the most fiendish practices devised
by human nature: vengeful reprisals, rewards for assassination, the hiring of mercenaries, the fostering of treason, discord, and rival claims to
the throne of the enemy, and the surrounding of soldiers on the battle-
field by their wives and children. The Utopians even have their own
heretics, notably after the introduction of Christianity.

As well as being frustrated in their reformist idealism by the sinfulness
of human nature, the Utopians also experience a paradox in the nature
of things: that rational action can give rise to unreasonable consequences. Their most determined efforts to fulfill the most laudable of
intentions often meet with failure.

The most striking example of this is the war they fight on behalf of
the Nephelogetes against the Alaopolitans. Ironically, this grew out of
their willingness to fulfill what More would later describe as God's behest,
in which 'he byndeth euery man to the helpe and defence of his good
and harmless neyghbour / agaynst the malyce and cruelty of the wronge
doer', according to the text of Ecclesiastes 17. On these grounds, the
Utopians went to the assistance of the Nephelogetes, who claimed that

---

7. See above, *Utopia*, pp. 64–65.

they had suffered injustice at the hands of the Alaopolitans under the pretext of law. The outcome was catastrophically tragic:

> whether right or wrong, it was avenged by a fierce war. Into this war the neighboring nations brought their energies and resources to assist the power and to intensify the rancor of both sides. Most flourishing nations were either shaken to their foundations or griev- ously afflicted. The troubles upon troubles that arose were ended only by the enslavement and surrender of the Alaopolitans. Since the Utopians were not fighting in their own interest, they yielded them into the power of the Nephelogetes, a people who, when the Alaopolitans were prosperous, were not in the least comparable to them.[8]

More recognized, just as acutely as he had in the English poems, that what men experience is often very different from anything they intend, desire, seek or foresee.

Utopia is full of comparable instances of tragic paradox; for example, the suffocating constraints on individual liberty required to effectuate he Utopians' attempt to secure more liberty and leisure for all, or the moral injustice of the rational justice by which they regulate numbers in their families and colonies. Through imaginatively registering this vitiation of Utopian reformist aspirations, the reader is eventually brought to the same recognition that More had expressed in his earlier English poems: that in this temporal world men are always deprived of some portion of their will, however, rationally or virtuously they try to act. Utopia thus contains an inbuilt ambiguity; it represents to a large extent what More wished for, even while he saw that if it could be, which it never would, the human situation would remain essentially unchanged in its charac- ter and function.

Once More had finished describing his imaginary commonwealth, he could have left the work as it was—a self-contained speaking picture; instead, he chose to surround it with an elaborately developed dialogue concerning the question of whether or not a wise man should enter a king's service.

By late 1516 More was about to join Henry VIII's Court himself. Book I was contrived to dramatize the nature of the choice before him (or, possibly, already recently behind him) in terms that anticipate the frustration of Utopian eutopianism in book 2. Both books lead the reader into experiencing parallel cruces bearing closely upon what More might expect to achieve, or not achieve, in office, and what he was doing in accepting it. To gain this end, he created a dispute between two new

---

8. See above, Utopia, p. 66.

characters: Raphael Hythlodaeus, the embittered idealistic reformer, and Morus, a fictional version of himself.

The precise relation between Hythlodaeus and Morus to More has been the subject of much inconclusive scholarly debate. Opinions range from assumptions that More is Hythlodaeus, through Chambers' belief that More is Morus, to Hexter's gymnastic argument that More was Hythlodaeus when he wrote book 2, but Morus by the time he wrote book 1.[9] Viewing *Utopia* in the context of More's earlier works enables one to see that Hythlodaeus and Morus are both More, but in a far more complicated way than has been suggested of late.

There are, in fact, two Hythlodaeuses, who resemble the two Mores reflected in the English and Latin poems. The Hythlodaeus who enthusiastically extols the example of the Utopian commonwealth might have written the epigrams on the accession of Henry VIII; the Hythlodaeus who lacerates European perversity and declares his willingness to abandon it to its own satanic devices, in book 1, could easily have written the *Verses for the Book of Fortune*. Hythlodaeus' reformist impulse and his pessimism are both sides of the same Morean coin, and in him More contemplated the meaning of the conflict within his earlier self. Both impulses, he saw, were inadequate. Hythlodaeus' attitude towards reform is flawed because he believes in the necessity for absolute, radical change; he cannot comprehend the possibility of allowing to remain in existence a state that contains good and bad together; hence he is not satisfied merely with applying remedies that relieve symptoms of disease, but looks for the means of a complete cure. This attitude leads him wilfully to misread the meaning of his own exemplum by overestimating the extent to which Utopian communism has eliminated Pride. His peroration, which Hexter has convincingly argued was written at the same time as book 1, commits, metaphorically speaking, a form of euthanasia in the way it desperately frees Utopian polity from the human ills More had taken pains to depict in it—just as the Utopians themselves free their incurably sick from the ills of the body. His summation is full of images of deracination and pruning whose very forcefulness serves to beg the question:

> In Utopia all greed for money was entirely removed with the use of money. What a mass of troubles was then cut away! What a crop of crimes was then pulled up by the roots! Who does not know that fraud, theft, rapine, quarrels, disorders, brawls, seditions, murders, treasons, poisonings, which are avenged rather than restrained by daily executions, die out with the destruction of money? Who does not know that fear, anxiety, worries, toils, and sleepless nights will also perish at the same time as money?[1]

9. Hexter, *More's Utopia* (Princeton, 1952), pp. 99 ff.

1. See above, *Utopia*, p. 83.

Hythlodaeus cannot imagine that his questions are anything more than rhetorical, whereas the whole exemplum has served to emphasize that they are. He distorts the truth by reading into Utopia what he needs to be able to do in order to save himself from despair, but More has made it impossible for the reader to do likewise, even while inviting him to do so.

Just as Hythlodaeus' expectations are unrealistic, his reaction to their imagined frustration by European reality is out of all proportion in the degree of its pessimism. When Peter Giles suggests that his wide experience would make him an invaluable royal councillor if he were to enter some king's service, he denounced such a course of action as 'servitude'. The distinction Giles tries to draw between 'servitude' and 'service' has no meaning for him. In the same way that he wanted to see Utopian polity as more perfected than it really was, he wants to see European polity as more hopelessly vitiated than it really is. The most striking example of this occurs when he recounts his experience in the household of Cardinal Morton.

This inset story anticipates the mode and meaning of the larger Utopian exemplum by subverting the view it is ostensibly meant to illustrate. Hythlodaeus recounts the episode to prove his contention that people are so jealous of everyone else's ideas, so self-opinionated, and so full of proud, absurd and obstinate prejudices that he would not be listened to in a king's council if he were to suggest any wise policy. He was once sitting at Morton's table, he says, when an English lawyer's boasting over the stern measures taken to punish thieves provoked him into anatomizing the social and economic causes of thievery and proposing remedies for them. When Morton asked him to declare why he objected to capital punishment for theft, Hythlodaeus proposed as an alternative the example of the Polylerites, who punish crime more conveniently and humanely with slavery. He then describes the array of different reactions his proposal received: the lawyer patronizingly dismissed it out of hand; a jester treated it facetiously by using the occasion to propose a mock remedy for friars; and a friar aborts the whole proceeding by becoming indignantly outraged at the fool's affront to his vanity, eventually forcing the Cardinal to direct the conversation another way and then wind up the party. Hythlodaeus thinks the occasion justifies his determination to remain out of public service; however, he failed to appreciate the most important response he elicited—that of Morton himself.

Morton, significantly, is already *in* public office, and that the highest in the land under the king: Lord Chancellor of England. Without seeming to acknowledge that fact, Hythlodaeus praises him in the highest terms as 'a man who deserved respect as much for his prudence and virtue as for his authority' and as being 'greatly experienced in the law'. Morton has developed extraordinary natural gifts of remarkable intellect and a phenomenal memory further by 'learning and practice,' with the result that 'the king placed the greatest confidence in his advice, and the commonwealth seemed much to depend upon him'. Although Hythlodaeus conceals any recognition of it, Morton is thus an example of a man with his own kind of talents who has decided to follow the advice of Morus and Giles, and his reaction to Hythlodaeus will inevitably be more crucial to the ultimate significance of the exemplum than that of any of the other characters present.

Hythlodaeus was so paranoiacally indignant at the behaviour of the lawyer, jester and friar that he fails to see that Morton's response confutes him. Morton was genuinely interested in his anatomy of England's ills, and was keen to hear his objection to capital punishment for theft. When Hythlodaeus proposed the Polylerite system of penal servitude, far from dismissing it out of hand, Morton not only suggests an accommodation of the system to English circumstances, but contemplates its possible extension to cover vagrants as well. In short, he reacts with exactly the same kind of judicious receptivity that the Utopians themselves show towards any new possibility.

Not surprisingly, Morus sees a meaning in the exemplum directly opposite to that which Hythlodaeus intends, and urges his own viewpoint even more strongly:

> Even now, nevertheless, I cannot change my mind but must needs think that, if you could persuade yourself not to shun the courts of kings, you could do the greatest good to the common weal by your advice. The latter is the most important part of your duty as it is the duty of every good man.[2]

Such service is no longer described merely as being 'convenient', but as a positive responsibility; however, Morus' refusal to acclaim spontaneously the self-evident rightness of Hythlodaeus' conclusion drives the latter to deny even more vehemently any possible merit in the alternative course being suggested to him.

The most perturbing irony in book 1 is that however wrong Hythlodaeus is in some respects, he is nonetheless ultimately right. At the very moment More seems unequivocally to have destroyed Hythlodaeus' credibility of putting his objectivity in doubt, he permits Hythlodaeus' main point to challenge all that has been established against it. This occurs in the climactic clash of views after Hythlodaeus has imagined himself proposing the laws of the Achorians and Macarians in the French king's council. When he suggests that his advice would fall on deaf ears, Morus voices the objection that might occur to anyone moved by pragmatic common sense: ' "Deaf indeed, without doubt", I agreed, "and, by heaven, I am not surprised. Neither, to tell the truth, do I think that such ideas should be thrust on people, or such advice given, as you are

2. See above, *Utopia*, p. 20.

positive will never be listened to." Developing Menippus' sceptical conclusion in Lucian's *Necromantia*, More goes on to assert, with a blend
of idealistic cynicism, that there is another kind of practical philosophy,
which amounts to acting one's part in the play at hand, observing the
decorum of the piece so as not to turn it into a tragi-comedy. This saves
one from having to abandon the ship in a storm when one cannot control the winds, and allows that which cannot be turned to good to be
made as little bad as possible: ' "For it is impossible that all should be
well unless all men were good, a situation which I do not expect for a
great many years to come" '. Since More chose to act according to this
pragmatic philosophy for the next 16 years, it comes as a shock to find
that Hythlodaeus' repudiation of it is not refuted. If this advice were to
be followed, he replies, almost everything Christ himself taught would
need to be dissembled, when he forbad such dissembling ' "to the extent
that what He had whispered in the ears of His disciples He commanded
to be preached openly from the housetops" '. To do otherwise is to
accommodate Christ's teaching to men's morals like a rule of soft lead,
which is merely to allow men to be bad in greater comfort. All that the
indirect approach achieves, he continues, is to force one openly to 'approve
the worst counsels and subscribe to the most ruinous decrees' since at
Court one cannot keep one's opinion to oneself without being considered a traitor. The result is either a loss of personal integrity, or else a
willing connivance in the wickedness and folly of others. Although More
chose to follow Morus' advice for the time being, he foresaw the truth
of Hythlodaeus' claims as much as his own future experience would
tragically confirm them.

Book 1, by forcing the reader to recognize this moral crux, anticipates
the frustration of his idealism that he will experience in book 2, and thus
serves to make his sense of the absolute insolubility of the human dilemma
more complete; there is, More shows, no way of escaping the experience
of it. The problem is far larger than either Hythlodaeus or Morus thinks.
Hythlodaeus' response is inadequate because it renders him impotent in
a way that perverts the public responsibility that every man is enjoined
to fulfill. His insights are just, but his actions are not justified. To be
right he has to be wrong, and as his name implies, he is a faithless angel
whose pessimism amounts to an indictment of the human situation which
God, in his wisdom, has instituted. Morus' response, on the other hand,
is vitiated because it requires a man to compromise himself by winking
at tainted deeds.

Once the presence of this crux has been felt, the function of book 1
becomes clear. It has been constructed to force its readers into a state of
intellectual helplessness so as to make them all the more eager for Hythlodaeus to make good his claim that communal living can yet put all
things right. When the Utopian exemplum fails to justify the full extent
of Hythlodaeus' confidence in communal living as a radical cure-all,

the reader's perplexity is compounded because book 1 has made desperately necessary the proof of its success. The two books taken together
drive the reader into the same corner, from which he cannot move without either choosing some form of self-deception, or else acknowledging
his helplessness as a human being to determine the shape and condition
of his existence entirely according to his own wishes. But at the very
point where book 2 seems about to deprive the reader of any sure support, it presents evidence of a true remedy, of which Hythlodaeus' eutopian remedy turns out to have been a parody: the religious response of
the Utopians.

The essential feature of Utopian religion is that it is not definitive,
and resides in a responsive condition of mind rather than an elaborate
and arbitrary dogma. Its main principles were instituted by Utopus, the
founder of Utopia, who allowed for a range of beliefs and provided for
the possibility of wise doubting: 'On religion he did not venture rashly
to dogmatize. He was uncertain whether God did not desire a varied and
manifold worship, and therefore did not inspire different people with
different views. The Utopians must, however, accept two fundamental
tenets: that the world is governed by providence, not chance, and that
the soul is immortal and will receive rewards and punishments after this
life. To believe otherwise is to degenerate from the dignity of human
nature. In practice, they let their faith instruct their reason, so that they
are capable of modifying the rational rigour of their hedonistic philosophy to allow for the justified existence of their ascetic religious order as
well as that whose members prefer to marry and enjoy honest pleasures:

> The Utopians regard these men as the saner but the first-named as
> the holier. If the latter based upon arguments from reason their
> preference of celibacy to matrimony and of a hard life to a com-
> fortable one, they would laugh them to scorn. Now, however, since
> they say they are prompted by religion, they look up to and rever-
> ence them. For there is nothing about which they are more careful
> than not lightly to dogmatize on any point of religion.[3]

At the level of their religious response to life, as against their strictly
rational one, the Utopians are prepared, as here, to accept the experience of paradox. Correspondingly, they become far more flexible and
responsive to the leadings of the providence they believe in. Even more
crucially, in their common prayers, the account of which is strategically
placed by More at the climactic point of the whole work, they profess
willingness to contemplate the possibility that all their assumptions may,
after all, be false. After acknowledging God as the author of all blessings
and returning him thanks, particularly for having been placed in the

3. See above, *Utopia*, p. 77.

happiest commonwealth and given the truest form of religion, each individual reaffirms his readiness to follow wherever God might lead him:

> If he errs in these matters or if there is anything better and more approved by God than that commonwealth or that religion, he prays that He will, of His goodness, bring him to the knowledge of it, for he is ready to follow in whatever path He may lead him. But if this form of a commonwealth be the best and his religion the truest, he prays that then He may give him steadfastness and bring all other mortals to the same way of living and the same opinion of God— unless there be something in this variety of religions which delights His inscrutable will.[4]

Their prayers manifest immediate faith and hope arising out of mediate doubt, as reflected in the accumulation of conditional clauses and qualifications. In repudiating absolute certitude, the Utopians show themselves prepared to respond to the providence of each emergent occasion, without presuming to fix a form and limit to the purpose of the Almighty, and in so doing, they diverge from Hythlodaeus, whose inability to accept the providential nature of actual human experience amounts to a form of despair.

By choosing to opt for the political role of Morus, More must have believed he was affirming the same faith as the Utopians. His trust in providence was revealed in his readiness to commit himself to action, not in any confidence that his chosen course was definitively the best. On the contrary, he knew from the outset that his political career was fraught with moral dangers, but he knew equally that Hythlodaeus' way was even more perilous because it ended in a negation of human responsibility, both temporal and spiritual. More chose action because he realized that there was no solution in trying to escape from the continuous experience of the human dilemma: a frightened withdrawal from one peril could merely land one in another. But as he was later to declare in A *Dialogue of Comfort against Tribulation*, the danger of falling into a further peril should not prevent one from escaping from the immediate, Hythlodaean one:

> if the ship were in danger of falling into Scylla, the fear of falling into Charybdis on the other side shall never let any wise master thereof draw him from Scylla toward Charybdis first in all that ever he may (?as his first consideration?). But when he hath him once so far away from Scylla that he seeth him safe out of that danger, then wil he begin to take good heed to keep him well from the other.[5]

4. See above, *Utopia*, p. 81.   5. *Collected Works*, 12, p. 148.

More's career after *Utopia* shows his efforts to know when to avoid Hyth-lodaeus' Scylla, by being Morus, and to realize the time when, to save himself from falling into Morus' Charybdis, he had to choose to be Hythlodaeus. Rather than being the helpless victim of his contrary impulses, More, by 1516, had concluded that to avoid the dangers of either one, he needed to be prepared to enact both as the time required. He believed that one must be in a perpetual state of responsiveness, just as he had shown the Utopians ultimately prepared to be. As he advised John Batmanson in his *Letter to a Monk* of 1519–20, one should

> live in trembling, and though hopeful, still [be] very fearful not only of the possibility of falling in the future, according to the say-ing 'He who stands, let him take heed lest he fall,' but also of the possibility of having fallen in the past, yes, even at the very moment you thought you were advancing the most.[6]

Through the process of composing *Utopia*, More discovered the rudi-ments of his mature philosophy. Such a penetrating consideration of the meaning of things was bound to be tied inseparably to a sense of history; it is not surprising, therefore, to read in Stapleton's *Life of More* that 'he studied with avidity all the historical works he could find'. Few com-mentators have noticed that *Utopia* presents his first tentative conclu-sions concerning the process and pattern of history.

The Utopians preserve their historical records in annals ('diligenter et religiose perscriptos'), spanning 1,760 years from the original conquest of the peninsula by Utopus. He began the process whereby a rude and rustic rabble was eventually transformed into the most humane and cul-tured people in the world. Utopus did not attempt to institute a perfected state, but left Utopia in a condition to be embellished and developed through the course of future history, like the gardens of which he was so fond. The Utopians have always made the most of their open options by being willing to exploit historical 'accidents' and take the best from other races and civilizations, as when some Romans and Egyptians survived shipwreck on the Utopian coast in AD 315: 'Now mark what good advantage their industry took of this one opportunity. The Roman empire possessed no art capable of any use which they did not either learn from the shipwrecked strangers or discover for themselves after receiving the hints for investigation." Likewise, when Hythlodaeus tells them about Greek literature and philosophy, they reacted with the same eager responsiveness. They quickly mastered the language, and when shown some of Aldus' books, they shrewdly guessed how it was done: 'Though previously they wrote only on parchment, bark, and papyrus, from this time they tried to manufacture paper and print letters. Their first attempts were not very successful, but by frequent experiment they soon mastered

6. Rogers, *Selected Letters*, no. 26, p. 140.

both.' Thus, by remaining open to its possibilities, the Utopians discover that history becomes the medium of various kinds of revelation: both of the potentiality for scientific development and good use of nature's gifts, also of the nature of truth, which emerges, they believe, through the process of time by its own natural force. This is partly why they are so receptive to Christianity when it is preached to them, and why they allow for the possibility that further truths inherent in it may be revealed by its adaptation to their own situation, as when they fall into discussion concerning the necessity or otherwise of the apostolic succession.

Because of their responsiveness to it, the Utopians find in their history the known march of God's providence. Yet their annals also attest to another manifestation of that providence: the tribulations that prevent men from perfecting an earthly paradise at the same time as they induce in them the wish to attempt to do so. Violent epidemics of pestilence have ravaged the population at least twice in their history, requiring the Utopians to replenish their lost numbers by recalling citizens from their colonies. This in turn forces them into immoral and inequitable action, however rational: 'They would rather that the colonies should perish than that any of the cities of the island should be enfeebled'. As well, they have to confront a climate that is not particularly wholesome and a soil not naturally fertile.

The way that the Utopians respond to these deficiencies symbolically suggests the providential purpose behind them, and of tribulation at large. They improve the barrenness of their soil through art and industry, while they protect themselves against the atmosphere by a life of temperance. *Utopia* as a whole figures forth More's belief, which he was later to expound fully in the Tower works,[7] that the tribulatory imperfection of human nature itself similarly induces—or should induce—creative effort, social as well as individual, to mitigate its effects. Utopian history, particularly, shows what might be achieved, in the context of what cannot.

It is important to recognize the nature of More's embryonic sense of history, because it significantly foreshadows the view of the church he later argued in the controversial works, and helps explain the basis of some of the positions he assumed.

An analogy exists between the relation of Utopus to his posterity and that of Christ to his church. Both leave their followers fundamental beliefs whose implications will be worked out through the course of future history, and both establish institutions to be cultivated responsibly and developed. Even at the mundane level of their scientific advances, the Utopians learn the same truth about the nature of revelation that More would invoke against the reformers in arguing for the validity of the

---

7. The Tower works are those written by More while awaiting execution in the Tower: "A Treatise upon the Passion of Christ," "A Dialogue of Comfort against Tribulation," and "De Tristitia Christi."

unwritten traditions of the church: 'in dyuerse times there may be mo thinges farther and farther reveled, and other then were desclosed at the fyrst'. To try and bypass 1,000 years of the church's experience by returning to the scriptural fount was not only to misread the nature of that experience in the way Hythlodaeus misreads Utopia, but also faithlessly to deny the providence in it. In more ways than one, More, in *Utopia*, had learnt the foundations of all his future beliefs and actions.

Through retracing the steps of its composition, one has been able to see that *Utopia*, although begun as a rather whimsical hypothesis, soon turned into much more: the instrument for More's resolved understanding of the world and himself. A fascinating sequence of letters at this time suggests that the final product elicited a characteristically ambivalent response from him; on one hand he was so excited by it (and satisfied with it) that he ardently desired to have it published, on the other he felt a strong inclination to keep it cloistered unto himself. The letters show him swinging violently from first one attitude to the other. In a letter of 3 September 1516, presumably soon after he had completed book 1, he wrote to Erasmus to inform him that he was sending his 'Nusquamam' and to express confidence in Erasmus' ability to pay proper attention to 'everything else'; on 20 September he wrote again to impress upon Erasmus that he was anxious to have it published soon, and also that 'it be handsomely set off with the highest of recommendations, if possible, from . . . both intellectuals and distinguished statesmen';[8] on 31 October he was still very 'anxious' that *Utopia* should gain the approval of Tunstal, Busleiden and John le Sauvage, but feared that it might not, 'since they are so fortunate as to be top-ranking officials in their own governments'; on 4 December he described to Erasmus the expansive vision in which he imagined himself to be the Utopians' chosen leader; and on 15 December he was eagerly awaiting the arrival of his *Utopia* 'with the feelings of a mother waiting for her son to return from abroad'. Suddenly, soon after the time when he must have received some copies of the printed book, there is an abrupt change. In a letter of January 1517 to William Warham, former Archbishop of Canterbury, More, begging Warham to accept a copy, now protests that Peter Giles 'allowed his affection to outweigh his judgement, thought it worthy of publication, and without my knowledge had it printed'. He reiterates this notion in another letter of January 1517, to an unnamed member of Court, asserting that, without his knowledge Giles had ravished *Utopia* of the first flower of her maidenhead. There are various possible explanations for this about-face: More could have been being disingenuously modest, or he might have been annoyed that the text had been printed before he had had a chance of seeing any editorial emendations, or he may have been embarrassed by the printer's errors and the general shoddiness of

8. All these hesitations over the fate of *Utopia* are recorded in Rogers, *Selected Letters*.

the 1516 volume. Another letter of the same month, however, suggests a far deeper reason. It is written to Antonio (?Bonvisi), and in it More declares that Bonvisi's esteem for him is the result of love's having spread darkness over his thinking, as witnessed by his approval of *Utopia*, 'a book which I think clearly deserves to hide itself away forever in its own island.'[9] This sentiment implies far more than mere dissatisfaction at defects in the book's presentation; it suggests that More had had second thoughts about the wisdom of publishing it at all. He perhaps came nearest to revealing the real truth of the matter in his choice of the profoundly suggestive metaphors of another statement in his letter to the unnamed courtier; More wonders whether he should have kept *Utopia* with him 'ever unwed', or perhaps have consecrated her to Vesta and initiated her into Vesta's sacred fires.[1] These images invoke one of the forms of sanctity More most revered: chastity; they also associatively recall his yearning for the spiritual devotion of the cloister. *Utopia* is associated with both, which attests to the real importance that the book had for him, and also the deeply private and personal nature of its meaning. More must have realized, as he certainly did later, that few readers were likely to derive the same meaning from *Utopia* that he had, let alone want to. (History proves that indeed they have not!) For that reason, More regretted having published *Utopia* as soon as its publication was irrevocable—a familiar and understandable human reaction.

Utopia was the last occasion on which More succumbed to the temptation of airing the innermost complexities of his private thought in public. This book was the culmination of a strategy that had begun with the tacit contextual ironies of the earlier works, but which, after *Utopia*, was exhausted in its possibilities, dangerous for the misconceptions it could arouse, and unnecessary in any case. Thenceforth, More's works were cast in a different mould, being unambiguous, heuristic, and, with the exception of *De Tristitia Christi*, written primarily for others. More could afford to let them be so, because after *Utopia* he no longer had to struggle to find out what he understood about life and himself.

EDWARD L. SURTZ

Humanism and Communism †

[The communism of *Utopia* is the fulfilment of an ancient and many-faceted tradition, pagan as well as Christian, political as well as religious, heretical as well as orthodox, jocose as well as severely ascetic. In one respect alone, Raphael Hythloday, as he appears in the *Utopia*, seems exceptional;

---

9. Rogers, *Selected Letters*, no. 15, p. 90.
1. Rogers, *Selected Letters*, no. 14, p. 90.
† Reprinted by permission of the publishers from *The Praise of Pleasure* by Edward L. Surtz, Cambridge, Mass.: Harvard University Press.

that is, in the vehemence with which he insists that community of goods is not merely a virtuous but also a practical and efficient plan for distributing the world's good things. In studying the various backgrounds of More's communism, it is a good idea to consider not only the opinions expressed but whether they are expressed in a spirit of play, of fantasy, of anger over injustice. More, perhaps, than most books, *Utopia*, with its glittering, duplicitous surfaces, has a way of reflecting back—and in depth—the images of those who discuss it.]

* * *

The predilection of many humanists for Plato must have encouraged a reexamination of the accepted concepts of private property and communism. The communism of the guardians in the *Republic*, for whom Plato had prescribed that "none must possess any private property save the indispensable," is too well known to need description. Its foundation is the principle: "That city . . . is best ordered in which the greatest number use the expression 'mine' and 'not mine' of the same things in the same way." In the *Laws*, it is necessary to remember, Plato retains the completely communistic state as an ideal, but reluctantly abandons it in a more sober moment, since "such a course is beyond the capacity of people with the birth, rearing and training we assume." In *Politics*, Aristotle objects that Plato's attempt to produce uniformity is destructive of the state, which depends upon diversity of occupation, rank, etc. Common ownership, moreover, produces not harmony, but discord, for it generally leads to quarrels and litigations. It reduces the individual's interest in what is common, and waters down the force of family affection. This pithy summary of objections based on common sense and knowledge of normal human nature is to reappear in various form and phraseology throughout future centuries.[1]

To understand the relations of the Platonic and Aristotelian doctrine on communism to the Christian concept through the ages—and especially to the attitude of the Christian humanists at the time of the composition of the *Utopia*—it is essential to grasp clearly the practice of Christ and the early Christians. There can be no doubt that Christ Himself imposed upon His chosen band of apostles and disciples a strict and obligatory poverty and communism (Matt. x. 9–10; Mark vi. 8–9, x. 21; Luke ix. 57–58, x. 4, xiv. 33; John xii. 6, xiii. 29). But this common poverty was wholly voluntary, since a certain rich youth could refuse His gracious request to join this restricted group (Matt. xix. 22; Mark x. 22; Luke xviii. 23), and was directed solely to the perfect fulfillment of an apostolic life of teaching and preaching. "It was not an attempt at a social revolution for the benefit of the 'proletarians' of Palestine." In a

1. Plato, *Republic*, I, 311, 471; *Laws*, I, 365; W. L. Newman, *Aristotle's Politics* (Oxford, 1887), I, 158–168. Shorey's comment is pertinent: "Plato's communism is primarily a device to secure disinterestedness in the ruling class, though he sometimes treats it as a counsel of perfection for all men and states" (*Republic*, I, 310, note a).

word, the invitation to a life of communal poverty was *not* a *command-ment*, but a *counsel*.[2]

In spite of frequent misinterpretation of the pertinent texts in the Acts (ii. 44–45, iv. 32–35), the Christians in the church of Jerusalem did not practice a strict community of goods; they were free to retain their property or to sell it in order to give the proceeds to the poor. As for the Fathers of the Church, they in their genuine writings praise the voluntary communism among the monks, but condemn the heretics wishing to make it compulsory and universal; they assert the right of the individual to private property, but oblige the rich to the alleviation of the needs of the poor.[3]

Of special importance are the texts on the common life in Gratian's *Decretum*. Gratian gives as an example of the natural law "the common possession of all things," and later reiterates that "by the natural law all things are common." The right of private property arises from custom or positive human enactment. As St. Augustine maintains in his commentary on St. John, even the Church holds its goods, not by divine right, but by human right. The spurious epistle of Clement is quoted in its entirety in the *Decretum*. This epistle gives six reasons, ranging from the natural law and Plato's authority to texts in the *Acts*, to prove that all things ought to be common to all men, and explains that it was "through iniquity" that private ownership entered the world. The glosses on the assertions on communism in the *Decretum* are extremely interesting for their sense of the purely theoretical nature of the discussion and for their defense of the existing system of private property. There was agreement among the Scholastics, however, that if Adam had not sinned, things would have remained common. There was also agreement on salient points in regard to the justice of private property.[4]

The doctrine of Aquinas in its baldest form is the following. Private ownership is not against the natural law, for it is a necessary addition made to the natural law by human reason. As a right, it belongs, not strictly to positive human law, but to the *ius gentium* (Law of Nations), which, in the words of Drostan Maclaren, "lies as an intermediary between

2. M.-B. Schwalm, "Communisme," *Dict. de théol. cath.*, III, 578. The distinction between a counsel and a commandment was taken for granted among Christians in the Middle Ages and the Renaissance. Even the Wife of Bath says of St. Paul's advice on virginity: "conseillyng is no comandement" (*Prol.*, line 67).
3. R. B. Taylor, "Communism," *Encycl. of Rel. and Ethics*, III, 777: "The assumption is that the Jerusalem Church was communistic. Of this there is no proof." Consult the exhaustive note in C. Lattey, *The Acts of the Apostles* (London, 1936), pp. 141–142. For numerous and representative quotations from the Fathers, see Schwalm, *art. cit.*, III, 579–586, and for

the legitimacy of the right of property in the Fathers, see E. Dublanchy, "Morale," *Dict. de théol. cath.*, X, 2440. Consult also John A. Ryan, *Alleged Socialism of the Church Fathers* (St. Louis, 1913).
4. *Decretum Gratiani cum Glossis Joannis Theutonici, etc.*. (Venetiis, 1514), foll. ii, viii, cccxii (preface by Erasmus' friend, Beatus Rhenanus); W. J. McDonald, "Communism in Eden?" *The New Scholasticism*, XX (1946), 124. See Bede Jarrett, *Mediaeval Socialism* (London 1935), pp. 41–55, and *Social Theories of the Middle Ages, 1200–1500* (Boston, 1926), pp. 122–149.

natural law and human positive law" and which "consists of precepts
derived from the primary precepts of the natural law in the same way as
conclusions are derived from their premises; without the *ius gentium* it
would be impossible for man to live peacefully in society." Private property is best because man takes more care of his own than of the community's possessions, less confusion results, and greater order is effected
since altercations are fewer. Goods, however, remain common at least
in respect to *use*, insofar as the owner must be ready to share his goods
with others in time of need. Aquinas views the common life of the early
church in Jerusalem as only a temporary expedient for a particular church.
The Utopians, of course, claim that communism begets greater care of
common property, perfect order, and no lawsuits.[5]

Following the lead of earlier Scholastics, Duns Scotus tries to reconcile the texts of Gratian, Augustine, and Clement by developing the
theory that in the state of innocence all things would have been common by a precept of the law of nature or of God, but in the state of fallen
nature private property is a just right which is founded, not on the natural law (since it had determined human nature to common ownership),
nor on divine positive law, but on human positive law. The natural or
divine precept of community of possessions was revoked after the fall for
the sake of greater peace and order and for the protection of the weaker
members of society. Private property is natural, therefore, in the sense
that it rests upon the general principle that a community or a commonwealth must have peace. This aspect is true of almost all positive laws.
Scotus explains that there is always some principle which serves as the
basis for establishing other (or positive) laws or rights. The latter, however, do not follow simply and absolutely from that principle but declare
or explain that principle in regard to definite, particular circumstances.
These explanations, of course, are in close accord with the general natural principle. Thus, private property, according to Scotus, is not a simple and absolute necessity; but, in view of the weakness and acquisitiveness
of most men, the system is most suitable for peaceful existence. From
such statements it is clear that, except for a different approach and terminology, Scotus is in substantial agreement with Aquinas for all *practical* purposes—and so is almost every Scholastic.[6]

5. *Utopia*, pp. 105, 106, 304; Budé's and Bus-
leyden's letters, *ibid*,. pp. lxxxvii, 317 [see pp.
115–122, this volume]; Aquinas, *Summa
Theologica*, I–II, q. 94, a. 5; II–II, q. 66, a 2;
Com. in Arist. Polit., lib. 2, lect. 2 & 4; Dros-
tan Maclaren, *Privatè Property and the Natu-
ral Law* (Oxford, 1948), pp. 12–13. See
William J. McDonald, *The Social Value of
Property According to St. Thomas Aquinas*
(Washington, 1939), *passim*, and B. W.
Dempsey, "Property Rights," in *Summa Theo-
logica*, tr. Fathers of the English Dominican
Province (New York, 1948), III, 3357–3365.

6. Scotus, *In Lib. IV Sent.*, dist. 15, q. 2,
Opera (Paris, 1891–1895), XVIII, 255–270,
translated in Jarrett, *Social Theories*, p. 124; *Ox.*
1 3, dist. 37, q. un., quoted in Minges, *Scoti
Doctrina*, I, 409 (cf. 433–434); Antoninus,
Summa, III, 55 (cf. Bede Jarrett, S. *Antonino
and Medieval Economics* [London, 1914], p.
76); Richard Schlatter, *Private Property: The
History of an Idea* (New Brunswick, N.J., 1951),
p. 55, n. 1. For Suarez's criticism of Scotus'
"precept," see *Opera* (Paris, 1856–1878), V,
140.

In summary, one may say that the Schoolmen were ardent defenders of the theoretical right of private property. Strict communism on an extensive popular level, according to both Thomists and Scotists, was impracticable in existing conditions, whatever might have been the rule before the fall of man. Hence they rejected the social errors of the Apostolics who defended obligatory communism, the Manichaeans who viewed all matter as evil, the Albigensians who reprobated any attachment to material things and hence to property, the Waldensians who extolled landless poverty, the Spiritual Franciscans or Fraticelli who declared poverty to be of universal obligation, Wyclif and his followers who upheld the Dominion of Grace, John Ball who was one of the leaders in the Peasant Revolt of 1381, and the Beguines and Beghards who defended and practiced poverty and communism in the Netherlands.[7]

This rapid survey of the medieval background would hardly be complete without a word on another group in the Netherlands, the Brethren of the Common Life, the educators and inspirers of many northern humanists, including Erasmus. During their first days, the Brethren were attacked for presuming to lead the common life without religious vows taken in an order or congregation. In reply to these enemies, Gerard Zerbolt of Zutphen (1367–1398) wrote a treatise on the common life, entitled *The Manner of Life for a Society of Devout Men (De Modo Vivendi Devotorum Hominum Simul Commorancium)*, in which he collected all the pertinent arguments: Christ's advice to the rich young man (Matt. xix), the apostolic church in Jerusalem (Acts ii, iv), the recommendation of Fathers and Doctors of the Church, communism in the state of original innocence, the authority of pagan philosophers like Pythagoras and Seneca, the nature of men as social and mutually helpful animals, etc. Erasmus may have formed some of his ideas from the reading of Zerbolt's treatise or from conversation with the Brethren about the common life.[8]

English literature before *Utopia* offers interesting side lights on the whole question of communism. In the second half of the fourteenth century, the author of *Piers Plowman* denounces the friars for teaching communism to the people in spite of God's command not to covet one's neighbor's goods. Reginald Pecock in the middle of the fifteenth century tries to prove to the Lollards that the practice of the common life in the church of Jerusalem was a matter of counsel, not of precept. Early in the sixteenth century, Alexander Barclay, following Locher, speaks of

7. See McDonald, *Social Value*, pp. 73–79; Jarrett, *Social Theories*, pp. 145–146; and esp. Jarret, *Mediaeval Socialism*, pp. 29–41.
8. De Modo Vivendi," quoted in Latin in Hyma, *Christian Renaissance*, p. 372, n. 150 (cf. excellent summary of whole treatise on pp. 67–79); "Consuetudines Domus Nostrae," quoted in Latin in Jacobus Traiecti, alias de Voecht, *Narratio de Inchoatione Domus Cler-*

icorum in Zwollis, met Akten en Bescheiden betreffende dit Fraterhuis, ed. M. Schoengen (Amsterdam, 1908), pp. 266–267; Josse Bade, "Vita Thomae Malleoli," tr. in Thomas à Kempis, *Meditation on the Incarnation of Christ*, ed. D. V. Scully, pp. xxvii–xxviii, quoted in Hyma, *Christian Renaissance*, pp. 61–62.

the original golden age in which all things were common. A petition in the middle of the sixteenth century gives as a reason for putting an end to the original communism of the Church the fact that the idle and slothful need an incentive to work, namely, private ownership and profit.[9]

What are the views of More's humanistic friends and acquaintances in respect to communism and private property? The views of John Colet, who exerted great influence on Erasmus and More, should prove interesting and revealing. Before the coming of Christ, the majority of fallen mankind lived, not according to revelation, but according to *"the law of nature:*—not the law of simple, holy, and inviolate nature (for that state of innocence was in paradise alone), but of a defiled and corrupted nature." It was this law, under the aspect of the law of nations, which "brought in ideas of *meum* and *tuum*—of property, that is to say, and deprivation; ideas clean contrary to a good and unsophisticated nature: for that would have a community in all things." Colet, therefore, seems to hold that man's real nature is man's nature in the state of original justice, which inclined him toward common possession of all things. This natural inclination to communism remains, even though private property is now best in view of the weaknesses or evil propensities which afflict human nature at present. If Colet in the quotation given above really means to identify the natural law (even though it now is the "law of a corrupter nature") with the law of nations (which is "resorted to by nations all over the world")—the two are usually distinguished—he disagrees with Scotus in making the natural law, and not positive human enactment, the source of rights of property. But he does concur with Scotus in emphasizing communism for the state of original justice.[1]

The question is: does Colet advocate Christian communism? It is impossible to give a categorical reply. One must use the distinction between three states: the first, original justice *(status iustitiae originalis)*, the second, fallen nature *(status naturae lapsae)*, and the third, nature fallen and restored *(status naturae lapsae et reparatae)*. The last is that of the regenerated Christian in the state of grace. Needless to say, Colet holds communism to be the best system for the state of original justice. For the state of fallen nature, private ownership is the inevitable order. As for the state of nature fallen and restored (but not restored to the complete simplicity and integrity of the state of original justice, since mortality and concupiscence remain in the regenerated man), Colet would

9. *The Vision of William Concerning Piers the Plowman*, ed. W. W. Skeat (Oxford, 1886), I, 595 (cf. II, 283 n.); Pecock, *The Repressor of Over Much Blaming of the Clergy*, ed. C. Babington (London, 1860), II 316–317; Barclay, *Ship of Fools*, II, 103; Brant-Locher, *Stultifera Navis*, fol. xciir; A *Supplication of the Poore Commons*, ed. J. M. Cooper (London, 1871), pp. 71–72. See also Locher's "Epiodion: De Morte Plutonis & Reliquorū Demonum," *Poematia* (Augustae, 1513), sig a ivr, which describes the golden age of communism ensuing on the death of Pluto, e.g., "En natura parens rerum cōmunia fecit Omnia constituit omnibus atque modum."

1. Colet, "Exposition of Epistle to Romans," *Opuscula Quaedam Theologica*, tr. J. H. Lupton (London, 1876), p. 134.

probably say that for perfect followers of Christ communism is the ideal but that practically private property, animated by a spirit of generosity and self-sacrifice toward the poor and needy, is best for this state; for, though a redeemed nature is restored to justice, it remains, in certain respects, a fallen nature, and therefore a nature subject to weakness and defect. For this reason, Lupton can rightly maintain that the *Utopia* echoes the teaching of Colet who "expressed approval, though briefly and guardedly, of a Christian communism."[2]

Another English humanist, Thomas Elyot, believes that in the beginning the people "had all things in common, and equality in degree and condition," but that now "the best and most sure governance is by one king or prince, which ruleth only for the weal of his people to him subject." He apparently can conceive of a communistic state only as a "communalty" without order and without distinction of superior and inferior. He insists that *respublica* should be translated *public weal*, not *common weal*. The persons who think that it is called the *common weal* because "every thing should be to all men in common, without discrepance of any estate or condition," are led to this opinion "more by sensuality than by any good reason or inclination to humanity." Elyot has no more than these few words to say on communism.[3]

As one turns back a few years from England to the continent, one finds interesting views in the writings of Ficino. In his summary of the fourth book of the *Republic*, which had exerted influence on the *Utopia*, Ficino tells how Plato descends by degrees to "his mystery." This "mystery" is nothing else than the common possession of all things, so that some do not have more property with consequent luxury, pride, and indolence, and so that others do not have less with resultant envy, lying, and thievery. Even more significant of his attitude is the passage in a letter to Angelo Poliziano:

> God wished the water to be common to all aquatic creatures and the earth to be common to all terrestrial beings. Man alone, unhappy soul, separated what God had joined together. He contracted to a narrow compass his overlordship which by nature was spread far and wide. He introduced into the world *mine* and *thine*, the beginning of all dissension and wickedness., Therefore, not without justice did Pythagoras decree that all things are common among friends; and Plato, among fellow citizens. . . . [T]hey are just and happy, who, established in immense wealth, consider themselves to be the servants of God, the guardians of the poor, and the dispensers of great sums of money.

Basic to Ficino's conception of property and wealth is the notion that God originally wished all things to be common. Man thwarted that plan.

2. Lupton, *Colet*, pp. 74–75.   3. *Gouernour*, I, 2–11, II, 27.

The best that the wealthy—who, after all, receive their wealth ultimately from God—can do practically is not to get rid of their riches and establish a communistic society, but to behave as the stewards of God and protectors of the poor. They are to regard their property not as absolute owners but as Christian administrators. Ficino, therefore, is something of an eclectic philosopher. With Scotus he lays stress on communism as the proper order in the state of innocence; with Aquinas he believes in the communism of use, not of ownership, i.e., he advocates that in the present condition of mankind the rich view themselves as the dispensers of God's common bounty, especially in time of need.[4]

The opinion of Guillaume Budé, if one is to judge from his letter to Thomas Lupset first prefixed to the Paris edition (1517) of *Utopia*, is less conservative. The island of Utopia, according to Budé, "is said, . . . by what must be owned to be a singular good fortune, to have adopted Christian usages both in public and in private; to have imbibed the wisdom thereto belonging; and to have kept it undefiled to this very day" (*Vtopia vero insula . . . mirifica utique sorte . . . Christianos vero ritus ac germanam ipsam sapientiam publice priuatimque hausisse perhibetur, intemeratamque ad hunc usque diem seuruasse*). There is a certain ambiguity about this statement. In Budé's view, did the Utopians have Christian rites and wisdom only after the coming of Christianity? Certainly the phrase "to have have kept it undefiled to this very day" has little significance if it applies merely to the slightly more than a decade which has elapsed since Hythloday's arrival in Utopia. The phrase must apply rather to the rites and wisdom of the Utopians, curiously similar to those of the Christians, prevalent before the missionary endeavors of Hythloday. Later on, Budé marvels that avarice and covetousness have failed to penetrate Utopia "for so many ages" (*tot seculis*), a phrase which indicates that the Utopians had Christian practices and wisdom before the introduction of Christianity. Budé's comparison thus gains immensely in strength: pagan Utopia, unlike the Christian West, has clung tenaciously to "three divine institutions": (1) "the absolute equality, or . . . the civil communication of all things good and bad among fellow-citizens"; (2) "a settled and unwavering love of peace and quietness"; and (3) "a contempt for gold and silver." One may well speculate whether Budé designedly used the term *divine* instead of *Christian*. If he did, it would mean that such were God's plans for man from the very creation and that the Utopians have recaptured and preserved these three ideals independently of the preaching of Christ's gospel, which, of course, reëstablishes and perfects God's original designs. The three institutions are directed against crying evils of contemporary Europe: the first, against the great inequality of rich and poor, nobles and commons, among Christian peoples; the second, against the uninterrupted wars of Chris-

4. *Opera*, I, 642, II, 1402.

tian princes; and the third, against the greed for wealth which was cor-
rupting Christian countries. If Europeans had as firm convictions on
these points as the Utopians, there would be an end to all fraud, deception, avarice, pride, and litigation. Hence, Budé cries out: "Would that
great Heaven in its goodness had dealt so kindly with the countries which
keep, and would not part with, the appellation [i.e., Christian] they
bear, derived from His most holy name!"[5]

Christ, Budé writes, was the founder and dispenser of all possessions
(Matt. xxviii. 18; I Cor. xv. 24–27, etc.). What disposition did He make
of property? As far as His followers were concerned, He established among
them "a Pythagorean communion and love" (*Pythagoricam communi-
onem et charitatem*), a reference to the early Christians in Jerusalem
where they held "all things in common" (Acts ii. 44, iv. 32). Budé seems
to believe that these Christians not merely shared all their goods but
actually practised a loving communism such as prevailed among the
Utopians. For Christ showed what a heavy sanction He laid on His law
by making an impressive example of the case of Ananias, whom He
condemned to death for violation of the law of communion (*ob temer-
atam communionis legem*). Evidently Budé holds that Ananias was not
punished for telling a serious falsehood (as exegetes generally hold), but
for violation of the communism of the church in Jerusalem. Nevertheless, he does not make even an academic plea for the adoption of communism, but draws out of Christ's law a more immediate and practical
lesson for Christians: the abolition of the thousand and one unedifying
litigations about property in both the civil and the ecclesiastical courts.
Instead of making the noble law of love and communion, enunciated
by Pythagoras and proclaimed by Christ, the guiding principle of their
lives, Christians have lowered themselves to the ignoble norms and
increasing tyranny of the civil and canon laws.[6]

In summary of Budé's view, one may say that theoretically he sees a
mutual sharing of all things, if not strict communism itself, as the ideal
state for contemporary Europeans as it was for the earliest Christians and
as it is now for the Utopians, who are Christian in all but name. Practically, he descends to a concrete and particular application of the law
of love and communion: he wants the simple precepts of Christ set forth
in the gospel to displace the intricate and specious laws of church and
state on property and possession.

Christ and Pythagoras and Plato are often linked together as religious
teachers in the minds and works of many humanists, just as they are in
Budé's letter. In the introduction to his *Adages*, Erasmus declares that,
if one examines thoroughly the saying of Pythagoras on the community
of all things among friends, one will find therein the whole of human

5. *Utopia*, p. 121.
6. *Utopia*, p. 121, Taylor, "Communism," *Encycl. of Rel. and Ethics*, III, 777.

happiness in a nutshell. Plato did nothing else than advocate this community and friendship among the founders of his republic. If he had been successful in his plea, war, envy, and fraud would have departed forthwith from the city; and, to be brief, the whole mass of human plagues would have left once for all. Erasmus continues: "What else than this did Christ, the head of our religion, do? In fact, He gave to the world only a single commandment, that of charity, teaching that the whole of the law and the prophets depended upon it. Or what else does charity urge upon men but that all things must be common to all men?" Erasmus then reinforces his point with an appeal to the doctrine of the mystical body of Christ.[7]

This espousal of Christian communism by Erasmus is continued in this commentary on the very first of his *Adages:* "Friends have all things in common" *(Amicorum communia omnia).* He points out the use of this proverb by Aristotle and Plato. Plato, for example, realizes that the citizens of the best and happiest commonwealth, like friends, must have all things in common and must not utter the word *mine* and *not mine.* Yet it is wonderful to mark what displeasure Christians show toward this communism in Plato, in fact, what violent criticism they launch against it, although nothing has ever been said by a pagan philosopher more in accordance with the mind of Christ. Even Aristotle, who moderates Plato's communistic thought by assigning ownership and goods to definite private persons, wishes all things to be in common under the aspect of free and unhampered *use.* Gellius is Erasmus' authority for the statement that Pythagoras not only was the author of the saying on the community of all things among friends, but also introduced among his followers a communism of life and resources, "such as Christ wished to exist among all Christians." Whoever had been initiated into the company of Pythagoras' disciples, put into the common stock whatever he possessed in the way of money and household. In the second of his *Adages,* however, Erasmus observes that communism is not to be carried to the extent of giving things equally to old and young, learned and ignorant, stupid and wise, but goods are to be distributed in accordance with everyone's office, dignity, etc.[8]

The *Praise of Folly* even makes humorous use of this famous axiom of Pythagoras. Folly singles out "certain Pythagoreans, in whose eyes all things are common—to such a degree, in fact, that whatever they light upon that is lying around loose they carry off with a tranquil spirit, as if it passed to them by inheritance." Lister in a note explains that the joke is about thieves who take things from all as from their freinds, for "among friends all things are common."[9]

7. *Adagia,* Introd., p. 11.
8. *Adagia,* No. 1 *(Amicorum communia omnia),* col. 20; No. 2 *(Amicitia aequalitas, amicus alter ipse),* col. 21.

9. "Moria," *Opera,* IV, 456, and note; tr. Hudson, *Praise of Folly,* p. 69.

Erasmus thus seems to have had a settled conviction that Christ had wished communism—not merely the communism of use or alms, but the communism of joint ownership—to be the proper state for His followers. Here is yet another point of conflict between the humanistic Erasmus and the Aristotelian Schoolmen. The author of the *Adages* does not spare the latter in his denunciation of their amalgamation of the doctrines of Aristotle and Christ, which to him are as incompatible as fire and water. Here are his indignant words:

> We have reached such a point that the whole of Aristotle is accepted in the heart of Christian theology, in fact, accepted to such an extent that his authority is almost more sacred than that of Christ. For, if he says anything that is little in keeping with our Christian life, it is permissible to twist its meaning by a clever interpretation; but the man who dares even slightly oppose his oracular utterances, is downed [and silenced] on the spot. From Aristotle we have learned that the happiness of man is imperfect without the addition of goods of body and fortune. From Aristotle we have learned that the commonwealth in which all things are common cannot flourish. We keep trying to amalgamate the principles of Aristotle with the doctrine of Christ, that is, to mix water and fire.[1]

The whole implication of this passage is that for the Christian philosopher Aristotle's criticism of Plato's communism should be invalid. Christians should follow, not Aristotle's condemnation of joint ownership and his defense of private property, but Christ's doctrine which enjoins communism for the entire Christian community, not merely for monks and friars. In spite of his strong words in the *Adages*, however, Erasmus strangely has little to say on the practices of the early church in Jerusalem in his notes on the crucial texts in the Acts of the Apostles, either in his New Testament or in his paraphrase of the Acts.

In the preceding citations, Christ's law of love and community is linked to that of Pythagoras and Plato. On another occasion Erasmus found a bond between Christ and the Spartan Lycurgus. In his *Apophthegms* Erasmus writes:

> It was customary [among the Lacedaemonians] to use the slaves of neighbors, if anyone had need, as one's own. The same held for dogs and horses, unless their master had occasion to use them. What is more, in the country, if anyone needed anything, he opened the doors and took away from its possessor what was necessary for his present task; he merely marked the place from which he had taken anything and then went his way. In the midst of customs of this kind, where could insatiable avarice find a place? where the

---

1. *Adagia*, No. 3001 (*Dulce bellum inexpertis*), col. 1071.

rapacity of men who appropriate other people's property as their own? where the arrogance springing from riches? where the cruelty of robbers who cut the throat of an unknown and innocent traveler for a few pennies? Would you not say that this was a genuinely Christian custom if they had obtained Christ, instead of Lycurgus, as a maker of laws?[2]

Here, it is true, is found a communism of use, rather than of ownership, a concept which is more in the Aristotelian tradition, but it is a use carried so far that it amounts, for all practical purposes, to a communism of ownership.

Erasmus' whole concept of the strict communism which should prevail in Christendom must have received a severe jolt in the early years of the Reformation. Except on a purely theoretical basis, he seems hardly to have conceived of Christian communism on a large scale. If it had come peacefully and gradually, Erasmus would have welcomed the transformation and change. The violent espousal of total communism, as on the part of some Anabaptists, was quite another matter. Erasmus admits that for some time in the apostolic period at the origins of the early Church a community of all goods prevailed, but not even at that time among all Christians. For, with the spread of the gospel far and wide, communism could not be preserved, for the reason that it would have ended in revolt. He seems to be referring to distressing disagreements and conflicts, from which even the primitive church in Jerusalem had suffered in a small way: "Now in those days, as the number of the disciples was increasing, there arose a murmuring among the Hellenists against the Hebrews that their widows were being neglected in the daily ministration" (Acts vi. 1). His final decision is expressed thus: "More in accord with harmony is the following policy: the ownership of goods and the right of administration should be in the hands of lawful proprietors, but the use of these goods should be made common by charity." Face to face with hard reality, even the scholarly idealist has to admit that the same judgment of Aristotle and Aquinas, after all is said and done, is the best: private ownership with common use inspired by Christian love.[3]

The author of *Utopia*, too, in the heat of conflict indirectly asserts against the Anabaptists the right of private property. One of the worst charges he can launch against Tyndale is that the latter has added to his own heresies those of the Anabaptists, who say "that there ought to be no rulers at all in Christendom, neither spiritual nor temporal, and that no man should have anything proper of his own, but that all lands and all goods ought by God's law to be all men's in common, and that all

2. "Prisca Lacedaemoniorum Instituta," in "Apophthegmata," *Opera*, IV, 146.
3. "De Amabili Ecclesiae Concordia," *Opera*, V, 505. On the conservative aspect of Erasmus' political ideas, see, e.g., Ferdinand Geldner, *Die Staatsauffassung und Fürstenlehre des Erasmus von Rotterdam*, Historische Studien, Heft 191 (Berlin, 1930), pp. 115, 155, n. 3.

women ought to be common of all men."[4] Did More, in a way similar to Erasmus, suffer a change of opinion in regard to Christ's view of communism?

ROBERT C. ELLIOTT

The Shape of *Utopia* †

More's Utopians are a peace-loving people, but their land was born to controversy. Many claim it: Catholics and Protestants, medievalists and moderns, socialists and communists; and a well-known historian has recently turned it over to the Nazis. Methods of legitimating claims vary widely, although most are necessarily based upon ideological interpretation of More's book. Over the past generation, however, in all the welter of claim and counter-claim, one single interpretation has emerged to dominate the field. H. W. Donner calls it "the Roman Catholic interpretation" of *Utopia*.[1] Its most trenchant, certainly most influential, statement is by R. W. Chambers; the interpretation, in brief, amounts to this: "When a Sixteenth-Century Catholic depicts a pagan state founded on Reason and Philosophy, he is not depicting his ultimate ideal. . . . The underlying thought of *Utopia* always is, *With nothing save Reason to guide them, the Utopians do this; yet we Christian Englishmen, we Christian Europeans . . . !*"[2] This statement cuts cleanly through murky tangles of critical debate. It is founded upon awareness of the relation between reason and revelation in Catholic doctrine, and the importance of that relation in making judgments about *Utopia*; it is consonant with everything we know of More and his life. Most recently this interpretation has received powerful support from Edward L. Surtz, S.J., in a number of articles and in his two books on *Utopia*, *The Praise of Pleasure* (Cambridge, Mass., 1957) and *The Praise of Wisdom* (Chicago, 1957). Father Surtz begins and ends both books with versions of the Chambers thesis, which he too calls "the Catholic interpretation of *Utopia*."[3]

The interpretation itself seems to me unassailable, the way of labeling it open to grave question. How far, one is bound to ask, does acceptance

---

4. "Confutation of Tyndale," *Works*, p. 656.
† *English Literary History* 30 (December 1963) 4: 317–34. Copyright © 1963 by The Johns Hopkins University Press. Reprinted by permission of the publisher. Notes are Elliott's unless credited to the editor of this volume; references to *Utopia* have been changed to reflect the paging of this edition.

1. *Introduction to Utopia* (London, 1945), p. 81.
2. Raymond W. Chambers, *Thomas More* (London, 1935), p. 128. See above, p. 137.
3. "Interpretations of *Utopia*," *Catholic Historical Review*, XXXVIII (1952), 168 and note 52.

of this "Catholic" reading entail the acceptance of other Catholic interpretations which may seem corollary? The problem arises as one reads
the work of Father Surtz. In *The Praise of Wisdom*, Father Surtz
announced that his intention was to "produce additonal evidence, throw
more light, modify present interpretations, and draw new conclusions
on intriguing but vexing problems" (p. viii). The book and its companion volume fulfill splendidly this aim. But it is also true that in both
books Father Surtz arrives at Catholic interpretations of various issues in
the *Utopia* which seem to me—and, I would assume, to a good many
others—quite unacceptable. One admires the frankness with which he
admits the perplexities, even the irritations, he has encountered in dealing with prickly religious and moral sentiments expressed in *Utopia*, but
one cannot accept—even as satisfactory explanation—the way he has
dealt with some of them.

To be specific: the Utopians notoriously recommend euthanasia for
the incurably ill. There is no equivocation on this point in the text. As
Raphael Hythloday reports matters, the Utopians believe that a man whose
life has become torture to himself will be—and should be—glad to die;
in these extreme cases the priests and magistrates exhort the patient to
take his own life.[4] Responding to this passage, Father Surtz deals roundly
with the Utopians: they "need to be set straight by Christian revelation
on this point" (*Praise of Wisdom*, p. 91). Similarly, some Utopians "err,"
he writes "in the maintenance of an extreme view of immortality," for
they think the souls of even brute animals are immortal (pp. 77–78).
Because divorce is allowed in Utopia, Father Surtz scolds the inhabitants for violating the natural law "which is obligatory on all men, Christian and non-Christian, including the Utopians" (p. 247). Mistakes like
these would have become evident to the Utopians had they "been fortunate enough to possess supernatural revelation" (p. 11).

This way of dealing with religious questions in Utopia is not only to
number Lady Macbeth's children but to spank them as well.[5] Perhaps it
is a tribute to More's creative powers that Father Surtz should treat the
Utopians as though they were subject to judgments of the same order as
persons who actually live. "In his heart," he writes of Raphael Hythloday and his attitude toward Utopian communism, "he realizes that, given
the general run of Christians, his commonwealth, like the republic of
Plato, will never exist in the Christian West" (*Praise of Pleasure*, p. 181).
But Hythloday has no heart, and it is no good looking behind his words
to concealed or unacknowledged meanings: Hythloday *is* only the words
that the words of Thomas More say he speaks. Father Surtz's argument
against Hythloday on Utopian communism is undobutedly cogent from

4. See above, *Utopia*, p. 60.
5. The allusion is to a celebrated article by L
C. Knights, challenging the tendency to discuss literary characters as if they existed in the
real world [editor].

a doctrinal point of view, but it has little to do with the literary work in which the ideas on communism exist.

The major problem is one of method. Father Surtz seeks to discover More's "real intent and thought." In the last chapter of *The Praise of Pleasure* he writes that his method is "to study each problem by itself in the light of all his letters and writings and against the background of antecedent and contemporary literature and philosophy." In the Preface to *The Praise of Wisdom* he says that he examines the "pertinent sections in the *Utopia* point by point . . . to determine the relation of each point to fifteenth-century and sixteenth-century formulations of Catholic teaching." The result of the method is that we are given an admirable historical, philosophical, and religious context for the many vexed issues that arise in *Utopia*. Three chapters on communism in *The Praise of Pleasure*, for example, provide a comprehensive account of classical, scriptural, patristic, and humanist attitudes toward the matter. All the major issues of *Utopia* are thus "placed." We are given no sense, however, that these questions exist, not as abstract political, religious, or philosophical propositions, but as constitutive elements in a work of art. What is wanted instead of the Catholic interpretation of communism is an interpretation of *Utopia* that will show us how the question of communism is incorporated into the total structure of the work. Father Surtz is aware of a problem of literary interpretation; he recognizes the ironic structure of *Utopia*—in fact, he deplores it. "Unfortunately," he writes, "for purposes of satire or irony, he [More] has introduced into his 'philosophical city' institutions which impart an air of realism but which he himself terms silly or even absurd. Correct interpretation becomes troublesome and elusive" (*Praise of Pleasure*, p. 193). The *Utopia*, by virtue of what it *is*, becomes an obstacle to Father Surtz's purpose. Something is radically wrong.

Clearly we need, not the Catholic or the Marxist or the city-planner interpretation of *Utopia*, so much as we need an interpretation that will tell us what *Utopia* is, that will place it with respect to the literary conventions which give it form and control its meaning. In one sense, of course, *Utopia* made its own conventions: it is the beginning, it creates its own genre. More was like Adam in the Garden of Eden: his use of the name was constitutive; he named the thing and that is what it was.

But in another sense the Adamic form was hardly new at all. Its structure, its use of characters, its rhetorical techniques, its purpose, its subject, its tone—all these accord with the conventions of a literary genre firmly, if ambiguously, fixed in literary history. *Utopia* has the shape and the feel—the form—of satire. It is useful to think of it as a prose version with variations of the formal verse satire composed by Horace, Persius, and Juvenal. If we approach it in this way, we shall be able to adjust our expectations and our ways of interpreting and evaluating to conform to the laws of the country to which *Utopia* belongs.

We can establish the general shape of *Utopia* by putting together two comments of More's contemporaries. "If you have not read More's Uto-pia," writes Erasmus to his friend William Cop, "do look out for it, whenever you wish to be amused, or rather I should say, if you ever want to see the sources from which almost all the ills of the body politic arise."[6] The second comment is from Jerome Busleiden's letter to More, published with the *Utopia*: You have done the whole world inestimable service, he writes, "by delineating . . . an ideal commonwealth, a pat-tern and finished model of conduct, than which there has never been seen in the world one more wholesome in its institution, or more per-fect, or to be thought more desirable" (above, p. 116). Here are the two sides of *Utopia*: the negative, which exposes in a humorous way the evils affecting the body politic; the positive, which provides a normative model to be imitated. "O holy commonwealth, which Christian ought to emu-late" (*O sanctam rempublicam, et uel Christianis imitandam*), reads a marginal comment on the text by either Erasmus or Peter Giles (Lupton ed., p. 169). This general negative-positive structure is of course com-mon enough in many forms of discourse. St. Augustine very consciously organized *The City of God* this way: the first ten books attacking erro-neous beliefs, the last twelve establishing his own position, with destruc-tive and constructive elements working through both parts. Sermons are often put together on this principle, as are literary-moral forms like the beast fable in which the greedy fox comes to a bad and instructive end. But for our purposes it is significant that this too is the characteristic skeletal shape of the formal verse satire as it was written by Horace, Persius, and Juvenal. The Roman satire divides readily into two dispro-portionate elements: Part A (as Mary Claire Randolph has called it) in which some aspect of man's foolish or vicious behavior is singled out for exposure and dissection, and Part B, which consists (whether explicitly or implicitly) of an admonition to virtue and rational behavior.[7] It estab-lishes the standard, the "positive," against which vice and folly are judged.

Utopia and Roman satire have this general structural outline in com-mon, but many other canonical elements as well. So true is this that one must read the *Utopia* with an eye—and an ear—to complexities of the kind one finds in Horace and Alexander Pope, testing the voices of the speakers against the norms of the work, weighing each shift of tone for possible moral implication. The meaning of the work as a whole is a

6. Epistle 519 in *The Epistles of Erasmus*, trans. Francis M. Nichols (New York, 1962), II, 503.
7. "The Structural Design of the Formal Verse Satire," *Philological Quarterly*, XXI (1942), 368–74 Cf. A. Cartault: "Les satires morales d'Horace contiennent une partie de destruc-tion et une partie de construction; en d'autres termes une partie satirique at une partie proprement morale. Ce sont deux faces de la même oeuvre, mais elles sont étroitement sou-dées entre elles; on peut les distinguer, non les séparer." *Etude sur les Satires d'Horace* (Paris, 1899), p. 347. ["The moral satires of Horace contain one destructive and one constructive part; in other words, one part is satiric and one is, properly speaking, moral. They are two aspects of the same work, but intimately con-nected with one another; though you can dis-tinguish them, you cannot separate them."—tr. *Editor*.

function of the way those voices work with and against each other: a function of the pattern they form.

More knew ancient satire well. Lucian was one of his favorite authors: "If . . . there was ever anyone who fulfilled the Horatian precept and combined delight with instruction, I think Lucian certainly stood *primus inter pares* ["first among equals"] in this respect," he wrote in the dedicatory epistle prefacing the translation into Latin of some of Lucian's dialogues that he and Erasmus collaborated on.[8] The Latin satirists were part of the literary ambiance in which More moved most freely; he often quotes from them, and it is clear that he had given a good deal of thought to certain problems having to do with satire as a form. When the Louvain theologian Martin Dorp attacked Erasmus's *Praise of Folly*, More replied in a long letter in which he defends the *Folly* with arguments drawn from the *apologiae* of the Roman satirists and from St. Jerome's justification of his own satire. More's letter, together with the dedicatory essay to him in the *Praise of Folly* and Erasmus' own epistolary *apologia* written to the same Martin Dorp (who in real life played the conventional role of the *adversarius* in satire), form an elaborate compendium of arguments satirists have always used to justify their ambiguous art.[9]

The *Utopia*, like many formal verse satires, is "framed" by an encounter between a satirist and an adversary. Just as "Horace" gets entangled in talk with his intolerable bore, or engages in dialogue with his learned friend Trebatius, or "Juvenal" joins Umbricius on the way out of Rome,[1] so "More" encounters Raphael Hythloday who is to carry the burden of the long conversation in the garden in Antwerp. "More's" role is that of interlocutor and adversary; the satirist-narrator is Raphael Hythloday whose tale is prose but nonetheless Roman in purpose and in form.

This is particularly apparent in the first book. At one point a query by "More" leads Hythloday into reminiscence about his stay years before with Cardinal Morton in England. He recalls a foolish argument that developed at table one day between a jesting scoffer who was accustomed to play the fool and an irascible friar. The fool, says Hythloday, having delivered himself of some sharp gibes at the venality of monks, and finding his railing well received, made an equally sharp thrust at the friar, to the delight of the assembled company. The friar, "being thus touched

8. Translation by C. R. Thompson in his *The Translations of Lucian by Erasmus and St. Thomas More* (Ithaca, 1940), pp. 24–25.

9. For a study of the conventional *apologia*, see Lucius R. Shero, "The Satirist's *Apologia*," *Classical Studies*, Series No. 15 (Madison, 1922), pp. 148–67. More's letter is in *St. Thomas More: Selected Lelttters*, trans. Elizabeth F. Rogers (New Haven, 1961), pp. 40, 42, 55–61. Erasmus' letter in Epistle 337 in *Opus Epistolarum Des. Erasmi Roterodami*, ed. P. S. Allen and others (1906–58), II, 90–

114. For St. Jerome, see *Select Letters*, trans. F. A. Wright (Cambridge, 1954), Letters XXII, 32; XL; LII, 17. Good discussions of Jerome as satirist are in John Peter, *Complaint and Satire in Early English Literature* (Oxford, 1956), pp. 15 ff.; David S. Wiesen, "St. Jerome as a Satirist," (Harvard University diss., 1961).

1. The reference is to Horace, *Satires*, 1.9, and 2.1; and to Juvenal, Satire 3. These are the two great models of Roman satire. Names in quotation marks imply that the reference is not to an actual person but to a literary mask or representation of him *[Editor]*.

on the quick, and hit on the gall *(italo perfusus aceto)* so fret, and fumed, and chafed at it, and was in such a rage, that he could not refrain himself from chiding, scolding, railing, and reviling. He called the fellow ribald, villain, javel, back-biter, and the child of perdition, citing therewith terrible threatenings out of Holy Scripture. Then the jesting scoffer began to play the scoffer indeed, and verily he was good at that . . ." (above, pp. 18–19). The climax of the row came when the friar threatened to invoke the curse of Elisha against the fool and to excommunicate him. With that, Cardinal Morton intervened, says Hythloday, to end the grotesque little episode.

Hythloday apologizes twice for telling this story; and although it has some slight relevance to Hythloday's major theme and a burlesque-show quality of humor about it, it is not immediately apparent why More includes it. Certain elements in the scene, however—the spiraling invective, the character of contest and performance, of flyting, the threat of a fatal curse—are of the primitive stuff from which formal satire developed: the underwood of satire, Dryden called it.[2] But in addition to genetic sanctions, More had excellent literary precedent for the scene. It is modeled on Horace's *Satires*, I, 7, which consists largely of a contest in scurrility between a witty half-Greek trader and a "foul and venomous" Roman. (It is also very like the wit-contest in *Satires*, I, 5 ["The Journey to Brundisium"], between Sarmentus the jester and the buffoon Messius Cicirrus, which so delighted "Horace," "Maecenas," and "Virgil.") A marginal note to the Latin text of *Utopia* calls attention to More's use of the phrase *perfusus aceto* ["sprinkled with vinegar"] from Horace's satire, thus making explicit the relation between the two scenes. Horace's poem ends with a pun, More's episode with the discomfiture of the foolish friar. His satire is the sharper.

Immediately before this scene Hythloday had been engaged (he tells "More" and "Giles") in a more serious contest with a lawyer at Cardinal Morton's table. The lawyer praised the rigors of English justice which loads twenty thieves at a time on one gallows. Hythloday, radically disagreeing, attacked the severity of the punishment and the social conditions which drive men to theft. A single passage from this dialogue-within-a-dialogue is enough to establish Hythloday's superb talent as satirist. He speaks:

> There is another [necessary cause of stealing], which, as I suppose, is proper and peculiar to you Englishmen alone.
> What is that? quoth the cardinal.
> Forsooth, my lord, quoth I, your sheep that were wont to be so meek and tame and so small eaters, now, as I hear say, be become

2. Essay on Satire," *Works*, ed. Scott, Saintsbury (Edinburgh, 1887), XIII, 47. For discussion of the primitive materials out of which literary satire grew, see Robert C. Elliott, *The Power of Satire: Magic, Ritual, Art* (Princeton, 1960), Chaps. I, II, and pp. 158–59.

so great devourers and so wild, that they eat up and swallow down
the very men themselves. They consume, destroy, and devour whole
fields, houses, and cities. For look in what parts of the realm doth
grow the finest and therefore dearest wool, there noblemen and
gentlemen, yea certain abbots, holy men no doubt, not con-
tenting themselves with the yearly revenues and profits that were
wont to grow to their forefathers and predecessors of their lands,
nor being content that they live in rest and pleasure nothing prof-
iting, yea, much annoying the weal-public, leave no ground for
tillage. They enclose all into pastures; they throw down houses;
they pluck down towns, and leave nothing standing but only the
church to be made a sheep-house.

Here are characteristic devices of the satirist, dazzlingly exploited: the
beast fable compressed into the grotesque metaphor of the voracious
sheep;[3] the reality-destroying language which metamorphoses gentlemen and abbots into earthquakes, and a church into a sheep barn; the
irony coldly encompassing the passion of the scene. Few satirists of any
time could improve on this.

Hythloday is expert in his role, which means, of course, that More is
expert in his. It does not mean that More's satire and his values are
identical with those of the character he created. The interesting and
delicate critical question throughout *Utopia* is to determine where possible the relation between the two. To what degree does Thomas More
share in the negative criticism of Raphael Hythloday and in the standards of excellence (Part B of Hythloday's satire) which he voices from
time to time? The problem would seem to be simplified by the fact that
More is himself a character—a real character in a real garden—in the
dialogue; he argues with Hythloday, agrees with many things he says,
disagrees with others, and in general conducts himself in such a way
that we inevitably tend to identify "More" with More, the sentiments
uttered by "More" in the dialogue in the garden with those actually held
by the emissary from London. "For, when, in any dialogue," writes R.
W. Chambers, "More speaks in his own person, he means what he says.
Although he gives the other side a fair innings, he leaves us in no doubt
as to his own mind" (*More*, p. 155). A great many critics have agreed
with Chambers.

It is a dangerous assumption. More dealt habitually in irony: Beatus
Rhenanus once characterized him as "every inch pure jest,"[4] and no
one in life knew quite how to take him. "But ye use . . . to loke so

3. Marx quoted the passage in *Capital*; see the
translation of the 4th. ed. by Eden and Cedar
Paul (London, 1928), p. 797, note.
4. Thomas More, *Latin Epigrams*, trans.
Leicester Bradner and Charles A. Lynch (Chicago, 1953), p. 126. More suppressed this
characterization (which appears in the letter
prefacing the Epigrams) in the 3rd ed. of 1520;
see *Epigrams*, p. xvi. ["Beatus Rhenanus" was
the Latin pen-name of a Dutch humanist well
known to Erasmus and More—*Editor.*]

sadly when ye mene merely," More has a friend say in a dialogue, "that many times men doubte whyther ye speke in sporte, when ye mene good ernest."[5] It is unreasonable to assume that he could not be similarly mercurial in *Utopia*. Lucian and Horace, appearing as characters in their own dialogues, sometimes come croppers themselves, end up as butts of their own satire. More's capacities are similar. I see no way of resolving the cruxes in *Utopia* which have caused so much controversy except by avoiding a priori judgments and listening to the voices as they speak.

In the governing fiction of *Utopia* "More" is much taken with his new friend whose eloquence is remarkably persuasive; but on two major matters they disagree, and in Book I they argue their respective positions. The points at issue are, first, "More's" conviction that it is the duty of a philosopher like Hythloday to take service in a prince's court so that his wise counsel may benefit the commonwealth; and, second, Hythloday's contention that "where possessions be private, where money beareth all the stroke, it is hard and almost impossible that there the weal-public may justly be governed and prosperously flourish" (above, *Utopia*, p. 28)—in short, his argument for communism. Neither argument is conclusive in Book I, but for different reasons.

The Dialogue of Counsel (as J. H. Hexter calls it) is inconclusive because opponents, arguments, and rhetoric are evenly matched.[6] In many formal satires the interlocutor is a mere mechanism, set up to launch opinions for the satirist to shoot down. Not so here. "More" invokes Platonic doctrine as he urges upon Hythloday his duty to join the court of a king. Hythloday responds by creating hypothetical examples showing the folly of a moral man's attempting to influence the immoral counsels which prevail at European courts. But, says "More," a sense of decorum is necessary: counsel tempered to the possibilities available, the ability to take a part in the play actually; in hand. "You must not forsake the ship in a tempest because you cannot rule and keep down the winds . . . you must with a crafty wile and subtle train study and endeavour yourself, as much as in you lieth, to handle the matter wittily and handsomely for the purpose; and that which you cannot turn to good, so to order it that it be not very bad. For it is not possible for all things to be well unless all men were good, which I think will not be yet this good many years" (above, *Utopia*, p. 26).[7]

Both arguments are coherent, eloquent, persuasive; they meet head-on, as they were to meet 150 yeas later in the confrontation of Alceste and Philinte in Molière's *Misanthrope*; as they have met many times in

5. "A Dialogue Concernynge Heresyes," *Works*, ed. William Rastell (London, 1557), p. 127.
6. *More's Utopia* (Princeton, 1952), pp. 96–138.

7. Cf. Horace, *Satires*, II, 1, l. 59; Persius, *Satires*, I, l. 120; Juvenal, *Satires*, I, ll. 30, 79.

life and literature, with inconclusive results. From the text of *Utopia* itself it is impossible to say who "wins" in the Dialogue of Counsel. Not long after it was written, More was in the service of Henry VIII; and it is even possible that this dialogue was composed as a move in a complex political game; or perhaps it is better to think of it, with David Beving-ton, as a dialogue of More's mind with itself.[8] In any case, More's action in life has no necessary bearing on the debate conducted so brilliantly in the hypothetical realm of his book.

The argument over communism is inconclusive in Book I for a dif-ferent reason. Hythloday claims the authority of Plato when he says that only if all things are held in common can there be established a justly governed and prosperous commonwealth. "More" disagrees and in four bare sentences advances the classical objections to communism: it destroys initiative, encourages dependence on others and hence sloth, is condu-cive to sedition, bloodshed, and the destruction of authority. But, responds Hythloday (in the perennially effective gambit of utopian fiction), you have not seen Utopia! If you had lived there for five years as I did, "you would grant that you never saw people well ordered but there" (above, *Utopia*, p. 29). A good deal of Book II is, in effect, an answer to "More's" objections; and in this sense the dialogue continues, to be concluded only at the end of the tale.

Throughout Book I Raphael Hythloday's concentration is on those things which, in Erasmus' words, cause commonwealths to be less well off than they should be; this is consistent with his role as satirist. He exposes evil, bares the sources of corruption, as in his Juvenalian out-burst against "that one covetous and insatiable cormorant and very plague of its native country," who may enclose thousands of acres of land, forc-ing the husbandmen and their families out onto the road, into beggary, theft, thence to the gallows (above, *Utopia*, p. 12). Hythloday lays about him fiercely, but as he opens up one social problem after another he suggests remedies, balancing off the negative criticism with positive sug-gestion. On the enclosure question he exhorts to action: "Cast out these pernicious abominations; make a law that they which plucked down farms and towns of husbandry shall re-edify them. . . . Suffer not these rich men to buy up all to engross and forestall, and with their monopoly to keep the market alone as please them. Let . . . husbandry and tillage be restored . . ." (above, *Utopia*, p. 14). In the argument with the law-yer over the treatment of thieves ("What can they then else do but steal, and then justly pardy be hanged?"), he recommends for England the ways of the Polylerites, which he describes in detail. Within one frame of reference these are the positives—the standards—of Hythloday the satirist; and as they seem convincing to "Cardinal Morton," there is good reason to believe that Thomas More approves.

8. "The Dialogue in Utopia," *Studies in Philology*, LVIII (1961), 496–509.

Hythloday realizes, however, that these positives, important as they may be in the circumstances of the moment, are mere palliatives. In his view, as long as private property exists it will be impossible to remove from "among the most and best part of men the heavy and inevitable burden of poverty and wretchedness" (above, *Utopia*, p. 28). To be sure, mitigating laws can be passed, and he lists a number of possibilities; but this would be only to "botch up for a time" a desperately sick body; no cure is possible "whiles every man is master of his own to himself" (above, *Utopia*, p. 29). Hythloday is no man for half measures; his true positive, the standard to which he is passionately committed, is that of full cure. The necessary condition of cure in his view is community of property. "More," we know, flatly disagrees, and the burden of proof is left to Hythloday. Book II is the statement of his case.

The statement is largely expository and, until the very end, notably undramatic (an unhappy characteristic of most comparable statements, obligatory in subsequent literary utopias). Book II is still satiric, as we shall see, but it is as though the normal proportions of satire were here reversed, with Part B—the positives—in preponderance. Hythloday makes some pretense of being objective in his discussion of the institutions of Utopia ("we have taken upon us to shew and declare their laws and ordinances, and not to defend them" [above, *Utopia*, p. 56]), but his enthusiasm overwhelms objectivity. Only occasionally does he express any reservation, as when he remarks that the Utopians seem almost too much inclined to the opinion of those who place the felicity of man in pleasure (but then "pleasure" is scrupulously and favorably defined [above, *Utopia*, p. 52ff.]), or as when he and his fellows laugh at the custom according to which a Utopian wooer and his lady see each other naked before marriage. Although Hythloday finds this a "fond and foolish" practice, the arguments advanced by the Utopians (as reported by Hythloday) are most persuasive, so that the thrust of the rhetoric in the passage favors the custom, while Hythloday condemns it. This is a clear point at which the norms of the work itself are not in accord with Hythloday's standards. His disclaimer works as a double ironic shield for Thomas More: "I am not Hythloday, and besides, he is against it; he says so," Still, *Utopia* argues for the practice.[9]

Except for this, however, Hythloday's tale is of a realm that he finds ideal, where laws, customs, and institutions are designed to foster the good, and to suppress the wickedness, in man. Utopians are not perfect

---

9. The *Utopia* is a textbook on the use of irony as protective device. "Utopia" ("nowhere"), "Hythloday" ("purveyor of nonsense"), many of the place names bearing comparable significance act as formal disclaimers encompassing the harsh truths told in the work. In "A Dialogue Concernynge Heresyes," More mocks some of these devices while elaborately using them: "More" is discussing problems of heresy with the messenger from a friend. The messenger insists that what he says is not his opinion but what he has heard others say. But "More" forgets: "And first where ye saie. Nay quod he where thei say. Well quod I, so be it, where they say. For here euer my tong trippeth." *Works*, ed. Rastell, p. 124.

people, but their commonwealth is rationally conducted so that in nearly every point the Utopian achievement is a reproach to the nations of Europe. Chambers' comment is worth repeating: "The underlying thought of *Utopia* always is, *With nothing save Reason to guide them, the Utopians do this; and yet we Christian Englishmen, we Christian Europeans . . . !*" In this sense the very presentation of Utopian life has a satiric function in so far as it points up the discrepancy between what is and what ought to be.

Hythloday has a great deal of explanation to get through in Book II, and perhaps it is inevitable that the expository tone dominates his discourse. Still, that preoccupation does not force him to abandon his role as overt satirist. At times, while discussing the way of life of the Utopians he thinks of Europe and becomes hortatory, as though preaching to an audience rather than addressing "More" or "Giles." What shall I say, he asks, of misers who hide their gold? "And whiles they take care lest they shall lose it, do lose it indeed. For what is it else, when they hide it in the ground, taking it both from their own use and perchance from all other men's also? And yet thou, when thou hast hid thy treasure, as one out of all care hoppest for joy" (above, *Utopia*, p. 53). (*et tu tamen abstruso thesauro, urelut animi iam securus, laetitia gestis.* [Lupton ed., p. 198].) We are not to think here of "More" of "Giles" dancing in delight after digging his gold into the ground; the shift in person is to the indefinite "thou" *(tu)* of an audience "out there." Passages like these have the feel of medieval complaint, although in the sudden shift of person and the moralistic utterance they are completely in character with many Roman satires: some of Persius,' for example, or Horace's *Satires,* II, 3, 11. 122ff. which is on exactly the same theme.

Another variation of the satirist's tone is sounded when Hythloday speaks of the extraordinary learning of the Utopians who, without having heard of the Greeks, knew all that the Greeks knew of music, logic, and mathematics. "But," he adds, "as they in all things be almost equal to our old ancient clerks, so our new logicians in subtle inventions have far passed and gone beyond them. For they have not devised one of all those rules of restrictions, amplifications, and suppositions, very wittily invented in the small logicals which here our children in every place do learn" (above, *Utopia*, p. 49). The voice is suddenly that of the ingénu, of Gulliver speaking 200 years before his time, but with this difference: Gulliver would believe what he said, whereas Hythloday is ironic.

He can use the technique lightly, as above, or with a bitter, driving, daring intensity. He is explaining that the Utopians do not enter into treaties with their neighbors because treaties are often broken in their part of the world. It is not so in Europe, says Hythloday: "especially in these parts where the faith and religion of Christ reigneth, the majesty of leagues is everywhere esteemed holy and inviolable, partly through the justice and goodness of princes, and partly at the reverence and motion of the head bishops. Which, like as they make no promise themselves but they do very religiously perform the same, so they exhort all princes in any wise to abide by their promises, and them that refuse . . . they compel thereto. And surely they think well that it might seem a very reproachful thing if, in the leagues of them which by a peculiar name be called faithful, faith should have no place" (above, *Utopia*, p. 65). Again, the echoes set up in one's ears are from a later traveler to Utopia, whose praise of things European withered what it touched. His predecessor Hythloday, is using with exemplary skill the ancient rhetorical trick of blame-by-praise. As Alexander Pope puts it: "A vile encomium doubly ridicules."

This is superb; but the account of Utopia is enlivened only intermittently by such flashes—or by sudden bits of internal dialogue, so characteristic of Roman satire, like that between the mother and child on the sumptuous dress of the visiting Anemolians (above, *Utopia*, p. 48). The Utopians seem to be a fairly sober lot, although they are delighted with the works of Lucian that Hythloday has brought with him, and (like More) they take much pleasure in fools. Their sense of the satiric is more likely to be expressed in concrete than in verbal ways: they fetter their bondsmen with chains of gold, creating thus an image of the world.

At the end of his discourse, Hythloday summons his forces for summary and justification. Pulling together the major themes, he turns to "More" with a powerful and eloquent defense of the Utopian commonwealth ("which alone of good right may take upon it the name") and of communism ("though no man have anything, yet every man is rich"). From this he moves into outraged criticism of the ways of the world in Europe: the pampering of useless gentlemen, "as they call them," in savage contrast to the inhuman treatment of "plowmen, colliers, labourers, carters, ironsmiths, and carpenters, without whom no commonwalth can continue" (above, *Utopia*, p. 82); the codification of injustice into law which is used to mulct the poor. "Therefore, when I consider and weigh in my mind all these commonwealths which nowadays anywhere do flourish, so God help me, I can perceive nothing but a certain conspiracy of rich men procuring their own commodities under the name and title of the commonwealth. They invent and devise all means and crafts, first how to keep safely, without fear of losing, that they have unjustly gathered together, and next how to hire and abuse the work and labour of the poor for as little money as may be" (above, *Utopia*, p. 83). Christ counseled that all things be held in common, and the whole world would have come long ago to the laws of the Utopians were it not for that "one only beast, the princess and mother of all mischief, Pride" (above, *Utopia*, p. 84).

Hythloday's tone at the end of his tale is that of prophet or hero—his final variation on the scale of tones available to the satirist. It would be idle to look for a source; many satirists and many writers of complaint have sounded the same trumpet: Juvenal, St. Jerome, Piers Plowman, great medieval preachers like the Dominican John Bromyard, of whom G. R. Owst writes.[1]

But the heroic note is not the last note sounded. A final paragraph remains, bracketing Hythloday's peroration, winding up the debate on communism, reasserting by its very form the relation of *Utopia* to Roman satire—and, indeed, to a whole body of literature which distinguishes between exoteric and esoteric teaching. Nothing could be more deft than the way "More" excuses himself to the reader for not having voiced his objections to some of the Utopian laws: Hythloday was tired after his long discourse, and, besides, it was not certain he could abide opposition. "More" contents himself, before leading his friend into supper, with praising the Utopian institutions and Hythloday's account of them; and in enigmatic comment he admits that while he can not agree with all that has been said, there are many things "in the Utopian weal-public which in our cities I may rather wish for than hope for."

"More" leaves with us, however, a statement of the reservations which he withheld from Hythloday—reservations about certain laws and institutions of Utopia founded, in his view, "of no good reason" (the Latin *perquam absurde* ["quite absurd"] is considerably stronger). Among these are their methods of waging war and their religious customs, but chiefly in his mind is "the principal foundation of all their ordinances," the "community of their life and living without any occupying of money," "More" makes clear his objection: by doing away with money, "the true ornaments and honours, as the common opinion is, of a commonwealth, utterly be overthrown and destroyed." What, in this view, are the true ornaments and honours of a commonwealth? They are "nobility, magnificence, worship *(splendor)*, honour, and majesty." Of course we smile: this cannot be Thomas More speaking, whose heretical opinions about magnificence are well known. This is "More," a *persona* he has created for complex purposes of his own—a *persona* who suddenly adopts the values held dear by "common opinion": nobility, magnificence, and the rest are the true ornaments of a commonwealth. But, as Father Surtz admirably says, "the whole purpose of *Utopia* has been to prove that those are *not* the qualities which should distinguish a commonwealth."[2] Unless the whole satiric thrust of *Utopia* has failed for us (as the thrust of Hythloday's discourse has apparently failed for "More"), we must recognize that at this point "More" becomes a gull.

The formal situation here is like that sometimes found in Roman satire. "More" is precisely in the case of "Horace" (*Satires*, II, 3), who, after listening in silence to Damasippus' long Stoic discourse on the theme. Everyone save the wise man is mad, loses his temper at the end, thus neatly placing himself outside the category of the sane, "Horace," like "More," is undercut by his creator.[3]

The effect of this in *Utopia* is complex. In Book I "More" advanced cogent reasons for opposing the principle of communism advocated by Hythloday. Book II, while it covers a good deal of ground, is fundamentally an answer to "More's" objections: Hythloday's peroration points this up. "More" remains unconvinced, but the reasons he gives, *perquam absurde*, make no sense. His disclaimer is in effect nullified by the comically ineffective way he misses the point.[4] Where does this leave us? It leaves Hythloday riding high, his arguments unanswered, his eloquence ringing in our ears. Perhaps we have been deafened a bit—or frightened. Jerome Busleiden wrote that the commonwealth of Utopia was not only an object of reverence to all nations and "one for all generations to tell of," but also "an object of fear to many" (see above, p. 116).

And what of Thomas More, that man whose imagination pushed at the limits of the licit, and who wore a hair shirt? I think it very doubtful that we can ever know what he, in his many conflicting roles of philosopher, moralist, religious polemicist, man of great affairs—what this man "really" believed about communism.[5] Of Thomas More, author of *Utopia*, we can speak with confidence. The idea attracted him strongly. If by nothing else, he makes this plain in the way that, at the climactic point of the dialogue, he disclaims the attraction: by deliberately and unmistakably undercutting "More." The best evidence, of course, is in what he gives to Raphael Hythloday: the powerful criticism rooted in the realities of England; then the moral fervor and the compelling force of his eloquence as he argues for the institutions which make Utopia the best of all commonwealths. In a technical sense, "More's" early objections to communism are never met—how could they be? Hythloday simply points to Utopia and says, Look, it works! But we quickly forget the flimsiness of this "proof," if we have ever noticed it, as we are swept along by the passion of a man who has seen a vision and come back to

---

3. Cf. Horace, *Satires*, II, 7. More would have known the same technique in Lucian. He translated *The Cynic*, for example, in which "Lycinus" (a transparent cover name for Lucian) ridicules a Cynic and ends up badly worsted in debate. (The point is not affected by the fact that Lucian's authorship of *The Cynic* is in question).

4. Marie Delcourt, in her ed. of *L'Utopie* (Paris, 1936), p. 207, note, says that as a precaution, "More désavoue sa propre création," although "on ne sent . . . aucune conviction réelle."

["More disavows his own creation, though one feels no real conviction."] A plain disavowal would have been simple; as it is, it turns back on itself. It should be added that, technically, "More's" doubts remain about the Utopians' methods of warfare, religious practices, and other laws; his disclaimer is absurd, that is, only in its application to communism.

5. For a discussion of his relevant expressions of opinion outside the *Utopia*, see Surtz, *Praise of Pleasure*, pp. 184–90.

tell of it. *Utopia* argues for the ideal of communism by the best test available: More has given to Raphael Hythloday all the good lines.[6]

Thus the shape of *Utopia* is finished off, enigmatically but firmly, in the terms Hythloday provides. This reading of the work of course conflicts with the readings of Chambers, Father Surtz, and others in certain important respects; but it need not conflict with that fundamental interpretation of theirs cited at the beginning of this essay: "When a Sixteenth-Century Catholic depicts a pagan state founded on Reason and Philosophy, he is not depicting his ultimate ideal." It depends on the focus of interest. If we are interested in Thomas More as a man, his beliefs, his values, rather more than we are interested in *Utopia* as a thing in itself, then we must unquestionably posit a third standard, a third norm—one barely hinted at in the work. Two standards can be derived from within *Utopia* itself. The first is on the level of reform within existing institutions: laws to enforce the rebuilding of devastated farms and towns, the restriction of monopoly, provision of work for the idle, limitations on the power of the rich and the wealth of the king, etc. The second and higher standard is the ideal of the work itself, so to speak: Utopia, the model commonwealth, the only one worthy of the name. But if we go outside the *Utopia* to think of Thomas More's ideal, we must think of one far higher yet. Father Surtz cites the appropriate passage. For More, the ultimate ideal would be "the holy city, New Jerusalem, coming down out of heaven from God" (Revelation, XXI, 2).

G. R. ELTON

The Real Thomas More? †

How well do we really know Thomas More? Directed to one of the most familiar figures of the sixteenth century, the question must appear absurd. Even without the aid of stage and screen, surely everyone has a clear idea of England's leading humanist, great wit, friend of Erasmus and other Continental humanists, author of *Utopia*, family man, man of convictions, ultimately martyr. The familiar Holbein portrait seems to sum it all up, as does at greater length the much admired biography of R. W. Chambers. Chambers, in fact, completed the picture when,

---

6. Cf. Russell A. Ames, *Citizen Thomas More and His Utopia* (Princeton, 1949), who says that it should be no more necessary to prove that Hythloday speaks for More than to prove that the King of Brobdingnag speaks for Swift. "In general, it should be obvious that no sati-

rist will persuasively present at length major views with which he disagrees" (p. 56).
† Reprinted from *Reformation Principle and Practice, Essays in Honour of* A. G. *Dickens*, ed. Peter Newman Brooks (London: Scolar Press, 1980).

to his own satisfaction and that of others, he disposed of 'inconsistencies' discerned by earlier observers between the cheerful reformer and 'liberal' of 1516 on the one hand, and the fierce opponent of Lutheran reform and savage polemicist of 1528–33 on the other. No man's personality in that age, not even King Henry's, seems more fully explored and more generally agreed than More's.

If nevertheless I cannot accept that we yet can be sure of knowing Thomas More it is in part because of the way in which his portrait has been created. All modern assessments start axiomatically from an image constructed out of two sorts of evidence and brought to perfection in those famous last scenes—imprisonment, trial and death. More's life has in effect become a preliminary to his end and is written with that end in view. The evidence mentioned consist of Roper's *Life* and the descriptions left by More's friends, good sources indeed but like even the best sources in need of critical inspection. Roper's book—which permeates all the early lives and indeed still dominates in tone and structure even Chambers's book—was written with two motives in mind: filial affection, and a desire to prove his great father-in-law worthy of canonization. The words of Erasmus or Vives, all of them incidentally about the early More, the More of the Erasmian heyday, tell us why they were More's good friends and assuredly present a truth about the man, but again they do not form dispassionate or rounded appraisals. And even when the other massive evidence is employed—the evidence especially of More's own writings and deeds—it is always, no doubt unconsciously, adjusted to the figure first created out of Roper and those letters. Chambers in particular, while seeming to weigh judiciously the difficulties posed by some of More's books, really works hard at bringing them within the limits defined by the stereotype of the great and good Sir Thomas. Of course, I acknowledge that More so appeared to many who knew him, though even among his acquaintance other opinions could at times be found, and I know that the traditional More existed; but is he the whole, the real, More?

My difficulty in accepting that he might be can be stated simply. I do not find More inconsistent, or hard to understand on given occasions, or improbably described by those who knew him. I find him consistently ambiguous: at all sorts of points, his mind, his views, his actions, his person seem to me to tend in more than one direction, withdrawing from observation into consecutive layers of indeterminacy. Like any adept user of the ironical front, he hides his self behind vaguely transparent curtains; as the light flickers over him, so his face changes, subtly and strangely. His wit, which so enchanted his friends, nearly always had a sharp edge to it: he often, and knowingly, wounded his targets. We are told that his temper was exceptionally equable and his manner ever courteous; yet through nearly all his life he displayed restlessly combative moods and in his controversies lost his temper, dealing ruthless and often unfair blows. His famous merry tales pose some manifest psychological problems. Is it not strange that when this man, who created such a happy family life, wished to amuse he constantly resorted to strikingly antifeminist tales? I can recall no single story that shows a woman in a favourable light; that world of parables is peopled by shrews and much-oppressed males—almost the world of James Thurber's cartoons, and certainly the world of one well-established medieval tradition, but also a world presented by More with manifest enjoyment. His attitude to his second wife, Dame Alice, leaves me bewildered. He is supposed to have treated her with affection; yet the conviction that she was foolish and tiresome rests in great part on the sly allusions to female deficiencies scattered through his works which, as family tradition knew, were directed at her. More in office—flexible, diplomatic, at times accommodating—differs visibly from More the scholar and More at home. Some of his public attitudes can be called lawyer-like, in the pejorative sense of that term. The persecutor of heretics cannot really be buried in the sophistical arguments deployed by Chambers: he did in practice deny those forms of toleration which he had incorporated in *Utopia*. His part in the parliamentary opposition to Henry VIII's proceedings and his contacts with the Imperial ambassador's intrigues were not straightforward; his refusal to accept a friendly letter from Charles V, on the grounds that without it he could be of better use to their common cause, must be called ambiguous. And what did he really think of the papacy? He never properly explained his position, and the hints tend more than one way; I can well understand why Rome hesitated for four hundred years before bestowing the saint's halo.

I once spent half an hour before that splendid fireplace in the Frick Museum in New York above which Thomas Cromwell and Thomas More for ever stare past one another, with St Jerome in the middle keeping the peace. In the end I thought that I understood the plain, solid, straightforward man on the right, but the other man, with that subtle Machiavellian smile, whose looks and look kept altering before one's eyes, left a sense of unplumbable ambiguity. And I then did not even know what an X-ray investigation has since discovered: that the famous portrait is painted over an earlier attempt which reveals a much less refined, less humanist, Thomas More. Why, even the man's year of birth is uncertain because his father in recording it contrived to puzzle posterity: the year date first put down was rendered dubious by the addition of a weekday which does not fit the year. Ambiguity, wherever one touches him, in matters weighty and indifferent.

In one sense, of course, the ambiguity of Thomas More does not matter; his ability to present a kaleidoscope of aspects even helps to make him more interesting and attractive, especially as those variations quite clearly inhere in the man and are not merely reflections of the observer. They are of his essence and of his choosing. Yet anyone concerned to understand the early sixteenth century, the age of the Reformation, and the character of a powerful intellectual movement with far-reaching influences upon later generations, needs to come to terms with Thomas More. Once one ceases to be satisfied with the plaster saint created by the worshippers, one is cast loose upon an uncharted ocean where there lurk too many rocks and whirlpools to permit complacency. If More was not simply the finest, kindest, wisest of men foully done to death by wicked enemies who could not bear his saintliness, many things about that age need reconsidering. If he was not really that steadfast figure of tradition, we would want to know what exactly he died for—though that is a question I shall not pursue here. His ambiguity, if he was ambiguous, also makes his own actions harder to understand: why, for instance, did this man, who all his life had avoided the simplicities of a total and unmistakable public commitment, suddenly harden his conscience on an issue which on the face of it was itself ambiguous enough? I feel convinced that we need to understand Thomas More, or at least to make every effort to do so, even though in the end he may well escape us. Especially for someone who sees him so characterized by ambiguity as I do, the ambition to penetrate to his inner core may well be foolish, but it is worth the attempt. Where is the real Thomas More?

The best way to go about this search would seem to lie in ignoring what others said about him and in trying to grasp More's relation to mankind from what he himself said to those among whom he lived, from his books. I propose to look at three of his works which at first sight seem to have little enough in common, in order to see whether they can nonetheless reveal that common element which must be there if there is a real Thomas More to be fetched forth from the veils in which he hid himself. *Utopia*, not without reason always his most famous work, appears as an exciting intellectual exercise, a critique of the world of his day, a dream of better things, lively and sunny in manner, the product of true wit. *The Confutation of Tyndale's Answer*, endless, nearly always tedious, passionate, devoid of humour and markedly obsessive, was, of course, written in very different circumstances and for a very different purpose, but it was still written by the same man. *The Dialogue of Comfort*, too, in which passion is left behind and serenity deals sovereignly with some of the most frightful of human problems, breathes an air which is quite different again—but air from the same pair of lungs. Who is this Thomas More who held three such diverse manifestoes together in one single mind, however capacious?

The essence of *Utopia* is nowadays usually sought in More's condemnatory analysis of the political and social structure which he wished to reform, but that seems to me the wrong approach. Surely the ideal commonwealth of his devising can tell us more about him. His description is detailed enough to give us a very vivid sense of life in the island of Nowhere—ordered and orderly, hierarchically structured through a system of interlocked authorities, permanent and apparently not only incapable of change but not interested in any. Life in *Utopia* was comfortable and worthy enough, so long as no one resented its lack of diversity, lack of colour, indeed lack of anything dynamic. This is, as no one has ever doubted, a very restrictive commonwealth, subduing the individual to the common purpose and setting each man's life in predetermined, unalterable grooves. Whether More really thought such a commonwealth to be feasible, or whether he was perhaps hinting that the only good polity was also one unattainable on earth, is not the issue here, though the likelihood that the second alternative more correctly defines his intent bears on the object of our search. The fundamental question is this: why did More think it necessary to erect so rigid and oppressive a system for the sake of preserving his supreme good—peace and justice? And the answer lies in his identification of the wrong at the heart of all existing human communities. This wrong is the nature of man, fallen man, whom he regarded as incurably tainted with the sin of covetousness. Greed, he argued, underlay everything that troubled mankind. Wealth, and the search for it, ruined the human existence and all possibility of human contentment; the only cure that could work must remove all opportunity of acquiring wealth by prohibiting all private property and allowing to each man his sufficient subsistence at the hands of an all-wise, and despotic, ruling order. To judge from *Utopia*, that 'sunny' book written by a man in the fullness of his powers and before his world collapsed in a welter of contending ideologies, More from the first held a deeply pessimistic view of mankind whose natural instincts were, he maintained, totally selfish, anarchic and sinful.

By the time he came to do battle with Tyndale he had, of course, reason to think that the sinfulness of man had found a new and vastly more dangerous area of operations. The *Confutation* is really a distressing book to read—an interminable, high-pitched scream of rage and disgust which at times borders on hysteria. Even allowing for the conventions of sixteenth-century polemics, it is hard to feel that More had retained any sort of balance when confronted with the consequences of Luther's rebellion. Even among the opponents of Lutheran heresy More stands out for the violence of his explosion, as Erasmus was to note in his last remarks on his old friend, by then dead. The helpless fury of the *Confutation* is not convention; it is the very personal reaction of a very specific man. Yet this is the man who had always impressed his circle by the evenness of his temper, the man of whom William Roper alleged that in fourteen years of close acquaintance he had never known him to be in a fume.

Why did More lose all sense of proportion when faced with the new heresies, to the point of making his book vastly less effective than it might have been? The very passion of his involvement diminished the success of his assault. Surely we are once again in the presence of More's fundamental conviction about human nature. If man was by his nature so incapable of living the good life, it followed that only the outward restraints imposed by organized and institutional structures saved his world from falling into chaos; only obedience to the order decreed by God preserved the chance of salvation. If the Utopians, with all their advantages, could maintain their orderly commonwealth only by submitting to exceptional restraints, how much more necessary was it for real people, ever driven on by the pressures of sinful desires, to adhere to the established order? Because he thought that he understood the dark heart of man, More, it would seem, was exceptionally conscious of the thinness of the crust upon which civilization rests, a conclusion which our age has no cause to doubt. In consequence he held that in attacking the Church the Lutheran heretics had pierced that crust. There is no need to suppose that he wished to withdraw any of the criticisms of the Church that he had so freely uttered in earlier days; even when, in the *Dialogue of Comfort*, he regretted that he and Erasmus had in their time published critical views of what now stood in mortal danger, he wished only that they had not made those views public, not that they had never held them. More's defence of the Church arose not from a change of mind but from the same ultimate convictions which had earlier led him to attack it. It, too, was a human institution and therefore inexorably tainted with original sin, but it was also the instrument chosen by God to restrain and guide men towards their only hope, salvation through faith in Christ. Just because the Protestants made that hope the centre of their message, while destroying and denouncing the chosen instrument, More had to defend the Church with such immoderate commitment, such furious rage.

Thus whether he was planning the good commonwealth of humanist devising, or fighting off the threat to the divine order on earth in his war with the Lutherans, More rested all his argument on an inexorably pessimistic view of fallen man. In the extent of his Augustinianism he seems to me to have had only one equal among the major figures of the day—Martin Luther himself—however different the conclusions were that these two prophets drew from their identical premise. More (unlike Luther) was evidently of an essentially conservative temperament, concerned to preserve existing institutions because—man being what he is—all change is at the very least risky, while such revolutionary change as he discerned in the heretics' demands must certainly lead to the dissolution of all good order. Man simply could not be trusted to command his own fate, and a beneficent deity had recognized this fact when he provided institutional means for channelling the anarchic instinct into the restraints of enforced obedience. And those institutional instruments must therefore be allowed to preserve themselves at all costs, which meant enforcing the law with prison and the stake. The alternative was certain chaos here and now, and all hope gone for salvation in the hereafter. Sitting as he was on an eggshell beneath which raged the fires of hell, man could be permitted to dream and talk about how nice it would be to paint that shell in splendid colours, so long as he kept his feet still. But when he started dancing upon his fragile earthly habitation he must at once be stopped by the most drastic means available. The danger was simply too overwhelming to be tolerated.

If it is objected that the More I am describing—the deep pessimist about man and his nature—cannot be reconciled with the More we have heard so much about (a man full of human kindness and friendship), I reply that on the contrary this supposed contradiction supports my interpretation. Anyone so deeply conscious of the unhappy state of mankind in the mass is always likely to do what he can for particular specimens of it. Believing that man has cast away grace does not necessarily make the believer into a misanthrope; and in his courteous and considerate behaviour towards all and sundry More was only testifying to the compassion of his conservative instincts. Genuine conservatives despair of humanity but cherish individuals, even as true radicals, believing in man's capacity to better himself unaided, love mankind and express that love in hatred of particular individuals. To avoid any rash inferences touching the author of these remarks, I had better add that most of us oscillate between those extremes most of the time. More was more consistent.

The *Dialogue of Comfort* does not breathe quite so pervasive an air of despair about the human condition, for the interesting reason (in part at least) that it confronted genuine and real tribulations instead of the intellectual challenge of *Utopia* or the wild apprehensions of the *Confutation*. This is not the place to discuss it at length, though it matters that its chief purpose was not, I should assert, to discover a way in which man can overcome the miseries of his life, but rather to offer instructed guidance to this end. More was not seeking comfort but giving it, having himself long since found it in his meditations on the Passion. In consequence, the keynote of the work is a kind of hortatory and pedagogic serenity—that address to the individual human being who must be cherished, rather than to the whole of fallen mankind who must be despaired of, which was so noticeably absent from the other two works considered. However, the *Dialogue* also provides one specific clue helpful in the present search. Concerned with imminent death, More needs to attend to the problem of hell and does so several times, in the process making his views very plain. Hell to him was a physical place—'the very pit and dungeon of the devil of hell' sited at 'the centre of the earth'—where the souls of sinners suffered 'torment world without end'. Not for More those modern evasions. Hell was to him not other people, or eternal ice, or eternal loneliness, or a state of mind, or any of the devices for expressing merely human despair. It was yet another of the creator's chosen instruments for the control of his creation, with a real location, where real

devils inflicted real pain on real souls. Hell was there to take care of the
consequences of the Fall for those who refused to admit those consequences and thus despised the means of redemption. Even more, perhaps, than his vision of the blessed in heaven, More's matter-of-fact
description of hell defines him as a man of his day: the world he saw
here and beyond was the medieval world in every physical detail, ascribed
to the purposeful creation of God.

Of course, there was nothing original in More's 'medieval' world-
view, in his pessimism about mankind. Conventional Christianity in his
day (and after) entirely agreed with it, indeed demanded it. The last
thing More would wish to display was originality in religion. Only those
who have tried to make him an improbable saint all his life, or (perhaps
worse) some sort of a star in the liberal firmament (between, as it were,
Socrates and John Stuart Mill), can be put out by discovering that More
believed in hell and damnation. Nevertheless, a question arises. More's
faith in the conventional doctrine of his day does seem to have been
particularly complete and passionate, much more so than was found in
the men with whom he shared his life, his thought and his death. I do
not know that Erasmus spoke of hell in More's terms, any more than
that he opposed the manifestations of covetous sin with More's horrified
intensity. There is here a strong hint that More's acceptance of conventional teaching on the Fall was exceptionally personal. He does seem to
have been exceptionally conscious of sin, with the result that not
humanism but antihumanism—the relentlessly unoptimistic conception of human nature—stood at the heart of all his serious writing. Such
a powerful consciousness of sin argues a personal experience of it: envis-
aging sin in a very special, very personal way, More talks like a man who
has found and fought sin in himself.

At this point we begin to tread on dangerous ground. Entering into a
dead man's mind and private experiences (especially one so concerned
to hide himself) is at best a speculative enterprise, and the line I shall
take will in addition cause displeasure. However, I mean to do no more
than follow the signposts which More himself has left behind. Let me
list some of them. For four years in his youth More tried to find out
whether he had a vocation for the monastic life, and he did so in the
strictest order of the day, the Charterhouse. Even after he decided that
he could not abandon the world, he wore a hairshirt. There are strong
echoes of the monastic principle in the organization of Utopia, though
the Utopians knew nothing of that heart of the monastic existence, the
vow of chastity. In fact, they are unmistakably concerned with sex and
procreation, their attitudes including both the rule that engaged couples
shall see each other naked before they have taken the irrevocable decision to marry, and an off-hand likening of the carnal act to an easing of
an itch, or of the bowels—both common sense and a mild distaste. In
his private existence, too, More notoriously worked hard at combining

some of the monastic practices with a transformation of the sexual instinct into a family life pleasing to God. At the same time his merry tales evince a notable strain of distrust of women, at times rising to positive dislike. One main thread in the *Confutation* is provided by Luther's special vileness in breaking his vow of chastity, a theme that is treated with obsessional frequency, nor is Luther the only heretic whose special heinousness lies in this particular sin. In the *Dialogue of Comfort*, so generally compassionate, the kindness of God is illustrated with a very odd parable about a beautiful young woman who is saved from adultery by a heaven-sent fever which destroys her beauty—'beautifieth her fair fell with the colour of the kite's claw'—and so entirely destroys her lust that the close presence of her lover would make her vomit at the very thought of desire. It is a strangely disgusted, and rather disgusting, passage, and it is really not possible to deny that More, attentive to humanity, was more frequently than most preoccupied with the problems of sexuality, with what he would have called 'the flesh'.

Such a preoccupation was bound to come to one so deeply concerned about the human condition, about the future of mankind, the injunctions of religion and the life eternal, but once again one feels that in More the preoccupation was sharpened by personal experience. His youthful attraction to the life religious, and the manner in which echoes of that life resound throughout his later years, argue powerfully that here lay his true ambition. In that case he was bound to regard celibacy as the only condition really acceptable to God, and of celibacy he had proved incapable. More, after all, throughout his life proved himself to be a passionate man   passionate in his beliefs, passionate in his friendships, passionate in his reactions to insults and contumely, passionate in his attacks upon heresy. It would have been strange if he had not also known the passions of the flesh: and what were hairshirts for except for the mortifying of it? But his inmost convictions about the true claims of God and religion made his inability to renounce the world and live celibate into a sin, into his personal experience of the Fall of man. Being a man of sense and wisdom, he had for all practical purposes come to terms with his failure in the face of the monastic challenge: the least he could do, and the most, if he could not live in a cloistered chastity, was to beautify the consequences of his carnal nature by building a family life which transcended the original impulse of mere desire, and for the rest to come as close as possible in life and in thought to his monastic ideal. But none of these compensations can have altered a conviction that he had failed to live up to what he (that very medieval man) regarded as God's ultimate demand on man, and had thus found in himself a plain case of original sin. What indeed was the Fall all about, and what had been the fruit of the tree of knowledge? He knew about the Fall with that special intensity that came from experience and self-knowledge. He must have held that he had seen the right way and had proved incapable of it: for a man of his integrity and conscience, that knowledge could never cease to torment. If this passionate man was really never seen 'in a fume', his powers of self-control were indeed formidable; and all his life, especially his last three years, show how formidable they were. But it is to do him almost an injustice to suppose him always serene and equable, effortlessly kind and considerate, a man of ever-undisturbed balance. Such qualities had to be worked for, and outbursts had to be guarded against. The guard did slip at times—in the argument with Germain de Brie, in his often cutting remarks at the expense of inferior beings, most of all in the reckless and often untruthful vituperation of his polemics. More, I suggest, knew demons—demons whom he could subdue and tame but never exorcise. Grounds enough for withdrawing into privacy and ambiguity.

More, then, understood the problems of man's unregenerate nature because he shared them, and his deep consciousness of the implications at times overrode his sympathy. So long as he lived an active and public life he remained determined to apply coercion and judgement to dangerous sinners rather than compassion and comprehension. But we can now understand why he appeared to change so notably after he resigned the chancellorship, and especially after he began his imprisonment. The Thomas More of the 'Tower works', and of those last letters to Margaret Roper is, on the face of it, a very different person from the persecutor of Protestants, and the hammer of poor Christopher St German—even from the More who translated Lucian with Erasmus and dreamed up the island of Nowhere. No more aggression or combativeness; no more sarcasm, no more savagery; even the censoriousness of the loving father, who was also a judge, had gone. But he was, of course, not really a different man. He had displayed those qualities of calm good sense and gentle kindness often enough throughout his life, as he was to display them so remarkably at the end. Before this, however, they had cost him self-control and discipline; now, they came easily. He had found peace; the demons were gone at last. In the most splendid passage of the *Dialogue of Comfort*, perhaps the most splendid passage he ever wrote, More asked why men should so much dread imprisonment and the prospect of death. The life to which man's disobedience to God had condemned him was itself a prison, with death at the end its only certainty. What could others do to a man to aggravate that inescapable fate? 'There is no more difference between your grace and me but that I shall die today and you tomorrow.' He spoke these words to Norfolk on the eve of his imprisonment, and before the end of 1534 he knew that he meant them exactly. The Tower liberated him, because here, at last, he had reached his only possible cloister, out of the world. What others thought of as a good man's prison was to him his monk's cell. He had found the tonsure in the Tower.[1]

1. I have not burdened this essay with footnotes; the evidence used is all familiar enough.

NORTHROP FRYE

Varieties of Literary Utopias †

There are two social conceptions which can be expressed only in terms of myth. One is the social contract, which presents an account of the origins of society. The other is the utopia, which presents an imaginative vision of the *telos* or end at which social life aims. These two myths both begin in an analysis of the present, the society that confronts the myth-maker, and they project this analysis in time or space. The contract projects it into the past, the utopia into the future or some distant place. To Hobbes, a contemporary of the Puritan Revolution, the most important social principle was the maintenance of *de facto* power; hence he constructs a myth of contract turning on the conception of society's surrender of that power. To Locke, a contemporary of the Whig Revolution, the most important social principle was the relation of *de facto* power to legitimate or *de jure* authority; hence he constructs a myth turning on society's delegation of power. The value of such a myth as theory depends on the depth and penetration of the social analysis which inspires it. The social contract, though a genuine myth which, in John Stuart Mill's phrase, passes a fiction off as a fact, is usually regarded as an integral part of social theory. The utopia, on the other hand, although its origin is much the same, belongs primarily to fiction. The reason is that the emphasis in the contract myth falls on the present facts of society which it is supposed to explain. And even to the extent that the contract myth is projected into the past, the past is the area where historical evidence lies; and so the myth preserves at least the gesture of making assertions that can be definitely verified or refuted.

The utopia is a *speculative* myth; it is designed to contain or provide a vision for one's social ideas, not to be a theory connecting social facts together. There have been one or two attempts to take utopian constructions literally by trying to set them up as actual communities, but the histories of these communities make melancholy reading. Life imitates literature up to a point, but hardly up to that point. The utopian writer looks at his own society first and tries to see what, for his purposes, its significant elements are. The utopia itself shows what society would be like if those elements were fully developed. Plato looked at his society and saw its structure as a hierarchy of priests, warriors, artisans, and servants—much the same structure that inspired the caste system of India. The *Republic* shows what a society would be like in which such a hierarchy functioned on the principle of justice, that is, each man doing his own work. More, thinking within a Christian framework of ideas, assumed

† Reprinted by permission of *Daedalus*, Journal of the American Academy of Arts and Sciences, from the issue entitled "Utopia," Spring 1965, vol. 9412.

that the significant elements of society were the natural virtues, justice, temperance, fortitude, prudence. The *Utopia* itself, in its second or constructive book, shows what a society would be like in which the natural virtues were allowed to assume their natural forms. Bacon, on the other hand, anticipates Marx by assuming that the most significant of social factors is technological productivity, and his *New Atlantis* constructs accordingly.

The procedure of constructing a utopia produces two literary qualities which are typical, almost invariable, in the genre. In the first place, the behavior of society is described *ritually*. A ritual is a significant social act, and the utopia-writer is concerned only with the typical actions which are significant of those social elements he is stressing. In utopian stories a frequent device is for someone, generally a first-person narrator, to enter the utopia and be shown around it by a sort of Intourist guide. The story is made up largely of a Socratic dialogue between guide and narrator, in which the narrator asks questions or thinks up objections and the guide answers them. One gets a little weary, in reading a series of such stories, of what seems a pervading smugness of tone. As a rule the guide is completely identified with his society and seldom admits to any discrepancy between the reality and the appearance of what he is describing. But we recognize that this is inevitable given the conventions employed. In the second place, rituals are apparently irrational acts which become *rational* when their significance is explained. In such utopias the guide explains the structure of the society and thereby the significance of the behavior being observed. Hence, the behavior of society is presented as rationally motivated. It is a common objection to utopias that they present human nature as governed more by reason than it is or can be. But this rational emphasis, again, is the result of using certain literary conventions. The utopian romance does not present society as governed by reason; it presents it as governed by ritual habit, or prescribed social behavior, which is explained rationally.

Every society, of course, imposes a good deal of prescribed social behavior on its citizens, much of it being followed unconsciously, anything completely accepted by convention and custom having in it a large automatic element. But even automatic ritual habits are explicable, and so every society can be seen or described to some extent as a product of conscious design. The symbol of conscious design in society is the city, with its abstract pattern of streets and buildings, and with the complex economic cycle of production, distribution, and consumption that it sets up. The utopia is primarily a vision of the orderly city and of a city-dominated society. Plato's Republic is a city-state, Athenian in culture and Spartan in discipline. It was inevitable that the utopia, as a literary genre, should be revived at the time of the Renaissance, the period in which the medieval social order was breaking down again into city-state units or nations governed from a capital city. Again, the utopia, in its typical form, contrasts, implicitly or explicitly, the writer's own society with the more desirable one he describes. The desirable society, or the utopia proper, is essentially the writer's own society with its unconscious ritual habits transposed into their conscious equivalents. The contrast in value between the two societies implies a satire on the writer's own society, and the basis for the satire is the unconsciousness or inconsistency in the social behavior he observes around him. More's *Utopia* begins with a satire on the chaos of sixteenth-century life in England and presents the Utopia itself as a contrast to it. Thus the typical utopia contains, if only by implication, a satire on the *anarchy* inherent in the writer's own society, and the utopia form flourishes best when anarchy seems most a social threat. Since More, utopias have appeared regularly but sporadically in literature, with a great increase around the close of the nineteenth century. This later vogue clearly had much to do with the distrust and dismay aroused by extreme laissez-faire versions of capitalism, which were thought of as manifestations of anarchy.

Most utopia-writers follow either More (and Plato) in stressing the legal structure of their societies, or Bacon in stressing its technological power. The former type of utopia is closer to actual social and political theory; the latter overlaps with what is now called science fiction. Naturally, since the Industrial Revolution a serious utopia can hardly avoid introducing technological themes. And because technology is progressive, getting to the utopia has tended increasingly to be a journey in time rather than space, a vision of the future and not of a society located in some isolated spot on the globe (or outside it: journeys to the moon are a very old form of fiction, and some of them are utopian). The growth of science and technology brings with it a prodigious increase in the legal complications of existence. As soon as medical science identifies the source of a contagious disease in a germ, laws of quarantine go into effect; as soon as technology produces the automobile, an immense amount of legal apparatus is imported into life, and thousands of non-criminal citizens become involved in fines and police-court actions. This means a corresponding increase in the amount of ritual habit necessary to life, and a new ritual habit must be conscious, and so constraining, before it becomes automatic or unconscious. Science and technology, especially the latter, introduce into society the conception of directed social change, change with logical consequences attached to it. These consequences turn on the increase of ritual habit. And as long as ritual habit can still be seen as an imminent possibility, as something we may or may not acquire, there can be an emotional attitude toward it either of acceptance or repugnance. The direction of social change may be thought of as exhilarating, as in most theories of progress, or as horrible, as in pessimistic or apprehensive social theories. Or it may be thought that whether the direction of change is good or bad will depend on the attitude society takes toward it. If the attitude is active and resolute, it may be good; if helpless and ignorant, bad.

A certain amount of claustrophobia enters this argument when it is realized, as it is from about 1850 on, that technology tends to unify the whole world. The conception of an *isolated* utopia like that of More or Plato or Bacon gradually evaporates in the face of this fact. Out of this situation come two kinds of utopian romance: the straight utopia, which visualizes a world-state assumed to be ideal, or at least ideal in comparison with what we have, and the utopian satire or parody, which presents the same kind of social goal in terms of slavery, tyranny, or anarchy. Examples of the former in the literature of the last century include Bellamy's *Looking Backward*, Morris' *News from Nowhere*, and H. G. Wells' *A Modern Utopia*. Wells is one of the few writers who have constructed both serious and satirical utopias. Examples of the utopian satire include Zamiatin's *We*, Aldous Huxley's *Brave New World*, and George Orwell's *1984*. There are other types of utopian satire which we shall mention in a moment, but this particular kind is a product of modern technological society, its growing sense that the whole world is destined to the same social fate with no place to hide, and its increasing realization that technology moves toward the control not merely of nature but of the operations of the mind. We may note that what is a serious utopia to its author, and to many of its readers, could be read as a satire by a reader whose emotional attitudes were different. *Looking Backward* had, in its day, a stimulating and emancipating influence on the social thinking of the time in a way that very few books in the history of literature have ever had. Yet most of us today would tend to read it as a sinister blueprint of tyranny, with its industrial "army," its stentorian propaganda delivered over the "telephone" to the homes of its citizens, and the like.

The nineteenth-century utopia had a close connection with the growth of socialist political thought and shared its tendency to think in global terms. When Engels attacked "utopian" socialism and contrasted it with his own "scientific" kind, his scientific socialism was utopian in the sense in which we are using that term, but what he rejected under the category of "utopian" was the tendency to think in terms of a delimited socialist society, a place of refuge like the phalansteries of Fourier. For Engels, as for Marxist thinkers generally, there was a world-wide historical process going in a certain direction; and humanity had the choice either of seizing and directing this process in a revolutionary act or of drifting into greater anarchy or slavery. The goal, a classless society in which the state had withered away, was utopian; the means adopted to reach this goal were "scientific" and anti-utopian, dismissing the possibility of setting up *a* utopia within a pre-socialist world.

We are concerned here with utopian literature, not with social attitudes; but literature is rooted in the social attitudes of its time. In the literature of the democracies today we notice that utopian satire is very prominent (for example, William Golding's *Lord of the Flies*), but that there is something of a paralysis of utopian thought and imagination.

We can hardly understand this unless we realize the extent to which it is the result of a repudiation of Communism. In the United States particularly the attitude toward a definite social ideal as a planned goal is anti-utopian: such an ideal, it is widely felt, can produce in practice only some form of totalitarian state. And whereas the Communist program calls for a revolutionary seizure of the machinery of production, there is a strong popular feeling in the democracies that the utopian goal can be reached only by allowing the machinery of production to function by itself, as an automatic and continuous process. Further, it is often felt that such an automatic process tends to decentralize authority and break down monopolies of political power. This combination of an anti-utopian attitude toward centralized planning and a utopian attitude toward the economic process naturally creates some inconsistencies. When I was recently in Houston, I was told that Houston had no zoning laws: that indicates a strongly antiutopian sentiment in Houston, yet Houston was building sewers, highways, clover-leaf intersections, and shopping centers in the most uninhibited utopian way.

There is however something of a donkey's carrot in attaching utopian feelings to a machinery of production largely concerned with consumer goods. We can see this if we look at some of the utopian romances of the last century. The technological utopia has one literary disadvantage: its predictions are likely to fall short of what comes true, so that what the writer saw in the glow of vision we see only as a crude version of ordinary life. Thus Edgar Allan Poe has people crossing the Atlantic in balloons at a hundred miles an hour one thousand years after his own time. I could describe the way I get to work in the morning, because it is a form of ritual habit, in the idiom of a utopia, riding on a subway, guiding myself by street signs, and the like, showing how the element of social design conditions my behavior at every point. It might sound utopian if I had written it as a prophecy a century ago, or now to a native of a New Guinea jungle, but it would hardly do so to my present readers. Similarly with the prediction of the radio (called, as noted above, the telephone, which had been invented) in Bellamy's *Looking Backward* (1888). A slightly earlier romance, said to be the original of Bellamy's book, is *The Diothas*, by John MacNie (1883).[1] It predicts a general use of a horseless carriage, with a speed of twenty miles an hour (faster downhill). One passage shows very clearly how something commonplace to us could be part of a utopian romance in 1883:

> "You see the white line running along the centre of the road," resumed Utis. "The rule of the road requires that line to be kept on

---

1. I owe my knowledge of *The Diothas*, and much else in this paper, to the admirable collection *The Quest for Utopia, An Anthology of* *Imaginary Societies* by Glenn Negley and J. Max Patrick (New York: Schuman, 1952).

the left, except when passing a vehicle in front. Then the line may
be crossed, provided the way on that side is clear."

But while technology has advanced far beyond the wildest utopian dreams
even of the last century, the essential quality of human life has hardly
improved to the point that it could be called utopian. The real strength
and importance of the utopian imagination, both for literature and for
life, if it has any at all, must lie elsewhere.

The popular view of the utopia, and the one which in practice is
accepted by many if not most utopia-writers, is that a utopia is an ideal
or flawless state, not only logically consistent in its structure but permit-
ting as much freedom and happiness for its inhabitants as is possible to
human life. Considered as a final or definitive social ideal, the utopia is
a static society; and most utopias have built-in safeguards against radical
alteration of the structure. This feature gives it a somewhat forbidding
quality to a reader not yet committed to it. An imaginary dialogue between
a utopia-writer and such a reader might begin somewhat as follows: Reader:
"I can see that this society might work, but I wouldn't want to live in
it." Writer: "What you mean is that you don't want your present ritual
habits disturbed. My utopia would feel different from the inside, where
the ritual habits would be customary and so carry with them a sense of
freedom rather than constraint." Reader: "Maybe so, but my sense of
freedom right now is derived from *not* being involved in your society. If
I were, I'd either feel constraint or I'd be too unconscious to be living a
fully human life at all." If this argument went on, some compromise
might be reached: the writer might realize that freedom really depends
on a sense of constraint, and the reader might realize that a utopia should
not be read simply as a description of a most perfect state, even if the
author believes it to be one. Utopian thought is imaginative, with its
roots in literature, and the literary imagination is less concerned with
achieving ends than with visualizing possibilities.

There are many reasons why an encouragement of utopian thinking
would be of considerable benefit to us. An example would be an attempt
to see what the social results of automation might be, or might be made
to be; and surely some speculation along this line is almost essential to
self-preservation. Again, the intellectual separation of the "two cultures"
is said to be a problem of our time, but this separation is inevitable, it is
going steadily to increase, not decrease, and it cannot possibly be cured
by having humanists read more popular science or scientists read more
poetry. The real problem is not the humanist's ignorance of science or
vice versa, but the ignorance of both humanist and scientist about the
society of which they are both citizens. The quality of an intellectual's
social imagination is the quality of his maturity as a thinker, whatever
his brilliance in his own line. In the year that George Orwell published
1984, two other books appeared in the utopian tradition, one by a

humanist, Robert Graves' *Watch the North Wind Rise*, the other by a
social scientist, B. F. Skinner's *Walden Two*. Neither book was intended
very seriously: they reflect the current view that utopian thinking is not
serious. It is all the more significant that both books show the infantilism
of specialists who see society merely as an extension of their own spe-
ciality. The Graves book is about the revival of mother goddess cults in
Crete, and its preoccupation with the more lugubrious superstitions of
the past makes it almost a caricature of the pedantry of humanism. Skinner's book shows how to develop children's will power by hanging lollipops around their necks and giving them rewards for not eating them: its
Philistine vulgarity makes it a caricature of the pedantry of social science. The utopia, the effort at social imagination, is an area in which
specialized disciples can meet and interpenetrate with a mutual respect
for each other, concerned with clarifying their common social context.

The word "imaginative" refers to hypothetical constructions, like those
of literature or mathematics. The word "imaginary" refers to something
that does not exist. Doubtless many writers of utopias think of their state
as something that does not exist but which they wish did exist; hence
their intention as writers is descriptive rather than constructive. But we
cannot possibly discuss the utopia as a literary genre on this negatively
existential basis. We have to see it as a species of the constructive literary
imagination, and we should expect to find that the more penetrating the
utopian writer's mind is, the more clearly he understands that he is com-
municating a vision to his readers, not sharing a power or fantasy dream
with them.

* * *

ROBERT M. ADAMS

Paradise a la Mode

The first Utopia was the Garden of Eden, and the last, no doubt, will
be when all of us who deserve it will be gathered into Abraham's bosom.
As each individual is free to imagine details of those blessed conditions
for himself, there is no arguing with them as symbols, and perhaps
something more, of a blissful, timeless state. In addition the world around
us is full of good places, from the soothing Marquesas to the 6th arron-
dissement of Paris, where all good Americans are said to go when they
die—would that the greater number of them would stay away until then!
For a certain scholarly temper a quiet seat in the Bodleian library with a
decent lunchtime pub outside seems Utopia enough. There are hill towns
in Provence or Tuscany, idyllic islands in the Bahamas or off the Cali-

fornia coast, earthly paradises where if we are not exquisitely content, it must be very much our own fault. Yet in all these lyrical havens, from the highest heaven to the merest beach-resort there lurks the sinister suspicion of a deadly agent, the secret serpent of boredom.

"I'd be bored, I'd be bored"—it's the haunting refrain that led Pascal to reflect that most of the world's troubles stem from our inability to sit quietly in a comfortable room and think (*Pensée* no 139). So the true Utopia is the meditative self-occupied mind, which is everywhere and always available to us, not only in a closed garden, but just as accessible in a slum or a subway, a shanty or a shed. The active, questioning mind is an inexhaustible resource—or is it, quite? Perhaps for a while, perhaps when challenged—but in the long run, over a string of rainy, empty, companionless days? Indeed, one man's undisturbed Utopia could be agreeable enough, for a while, given a special temperament; as the poet Marvell wrote,

> Two paradises 'twere in one
> To live in paradise alone.

But as Adam himself was the first to discover, a bit of society may be very welcome—and then, with the addition of another person, especially a female person, the possibility opens up that one person's paradise may be another person's prison-chamber. There's a big rub with all Utopias, that instead of planning the paradise to gratify the people (*other* people), the proprietor is tempted to plan the people to satisfy the specifications of the paradise. It is the diabolical optimism of the Utopian architect that infuriates, or risks infuriating, its inhabitants. In an ancient phrase, the society offers the best of all conceivable worlds, and everything in it is a necessary evil. The architect sees how necessary it is, the victim only how evil it is. Especially for the planner of Utopias, hell (in the words of M. Sartre) is other people; the simplest way to escape from them is to erase the qualities that make them "other."

Procrustes, a figure in ancient Greek mythology, had a marvellous bed of exactly the right size for everybody. Travellers passing by were invited to try it out. If they were too long for the bed, convenient parts of them were chopped off till they fitted it exactly; if too short, they were stretched out to the right size. Theseus, invited to join in a demonstration of the apparatus, took exception to the process and killed Procrustes, for which he was hailed as a liberator; the story exemplifies the world's unending struggle between proprietor and client. ("Our process worked to perfection," says the one; "it produced nothing but unbearable agony," says the other.) The world's most massive experiment in a classless society has recently come to an end, amid equal quantities of thanksgiving and misgiving. The apparatus for stretching and chopping people to size worked to the complete satisfaction of the *apparatchiks*. It caused, indeed, a goodly measure of personal agony; getting rid of it was surely a good thing. But after operating, more or less, for generations, it seems to have left behind a people almost devoid of the positive motivations—such as social invention and chance-taking—that are requisite when the machine does not yet exist or has gone irretrievably bust.

More's Utopians are not devoid of initiative, and they are not indifferent to improvements in their social machinery that may come about by accident or by acts of providence; they allow particularly for a measure of change in the direction of greater efficiency, more economy. But their society is not set up to encourage innovation; rather it encourages routine and conformity. The machinery of producing food *en masse* can only inhibit experiment and for that matter quality; contempt for gold and silver can only discourage search for useful metals like copper and aluminum, and exploration of their qualities. We are not told that the Utopians put any effort into the exploitation of their resources of coal, sulphur, or salt, if indeed they have any. It is characteristic that their introduction to Greek literature prompts them to issue editions of the originals in large numbers of copies, but not to write a Lucianic satire on Utopian life—something that would give their society a special, and welcome, dimension of self-mockery.

In fact, the discipline required to make the organized Utopia hold together—a discipline tangibly symbolized by crenellated cities and intricate defenses for the island as a whole—represses not just debauchery and idleness but other competing fantasies and idealisms as well. What would be the fate of Rabelais' bawdy, sprawling book in a nation of lockstep Nosey Parkers? One shudders to think; and yet the story of Gargantua and Pantagruel contains at least three mini-Utopias with affinities to More's fantasy. Power to organize is, inevitably, power to repress. No man is free to drive his automobile unless all men are required to drive on a publicly designated and compulsory side of the road. We count on that much efficiency—i.e., sanity—in everyone, and are horrified at the destruction wrought when someone, for reason of drink or drugs, abandons it. But the necessary and severely practical rules governing traffic can be twisted—oh, so easily!—by the "authorities" to serve partisan social ends, as anyone will know who has ever walked a picket line or in an unpopular political demonstration. The more indefinite the regulations, the more amenable they are to a particular spin—witness, for example, a particularly (and no doubt deliberately) vague formula of the *Utopia*. Outside the senate or popular assembly, the Utopians are are forbidden to "consult together" on matters of public business. The expression "consult together" translates a Latin formula, *inire consilia*, which may mean several quite different things: to discuss informally, to reflect on the implications of, to consider in a public forum, or to plot secretly with the end of taking concerted action. In the penumbra of feelings surrounding these alternative meanings—unexpressed but explosively active—is the implicit addendum "leading to or resulting in the use of force and violence." Of course plotting a bloody insurrection is political light years away from considering the advantages and disadvantages of a proposed public policy. But as "inire consilia" they are all the same thing in Utopia, all subject to the penalty of the headsman's axe. Indeed, More's rule is so extravagantly vague that one can hardly doubt it is deliberately so. A ruler determined to keep the reins of public discussion in his hands would like nothing better than the power to control or permit "consilia" according to his own definition of what they are or may be. And, reading back from Huxley's *Brave New World* (below, p. 240), one sees that the same slogans could be set over More's ideal community as over the Central London Hatchery: COMMUNITY, IDENTITY, STABILITY. (Actually, the exact words matter very little; the point of the formula is a triple incantation, three interlocking affirmations.)

An organized Utopia (which some people would think a contradiction in terms) tends toward that ideal condition of the administrator where everything that isn't absolutely forbidden is positively required. Slogans, formulas, and categorical stamps are just the external signs of an inner uniformity after which the planning mentality is always striving. Better in many respects the Utopia of Robinson Crusoe, which is so full of individual challenges and strenuous achievements that it isn't generally thought of as a Utopia at all. But Crusoe has all he can do to organize his own civilization, keep track of its history, and maintain his accounts in balance with the Great Bookkeeper in the Sky. Practical necessities shield him from the inertia of solitude, and solitude protects him from the two predatory civilizations, that of Europe and that of the cannibals. Declining altogether the gambit of a money-, machinery-, and community-existence, Crusoe lowers the material standards of his life while heightening the excitement level of the survival game. His mini-bookkeeping foreshadows the comic meticulousness of which Henry Thoreau made such deft use in *Walden*; perhaps for that reason, the Pacific castaway never appears along the shores of Walden pond.

As an individual Utopia takes to itself unlimited freedom, it also takes to itself numerous menial, routine responsibilities that in organized communities are taken care of by servants or "services" or machines. Around the farm, these are chores; in big cities, they constitute for many of the workers in the "sanitary engineering" department an entire hidden world, a subculture. In recent images of city life, the feeling is of being integrated in the machinery of the metropolis—whether one is dealing with mountains of literal garbage, or human derelicts, or packs of ratlike criminals. It's not so much that mass populations are reduced to drab uniformity, as that the culture that struggles to do this ignoble job is itself subject to disintegration within and open attack from without. The constraints and constrictions of urban society are on the surface; they are

among the first things people think of when they consider civilization—
its discontents.

The appeal to modern imaginations of anti-Utopias of increasing and
deepening nastiness is a pretty good signal that utopias themselves, as
emblems of milky innocence, have about run their course. The oxy-
moron of "an organized utopia" has been strangled by its own first term.
More literally speaking, the work of setting up a new human structure
and the drudgery of keeping things going day after day provide a concentrated dose of those drab routines that made a utopia seem desirable in
the first place. Actually, the utopian spirit has been seen at its most
concentrated, recently, in the "hippy" communes that sprang up first
in America during the 1960s, and more recently in parts of Eastern
Europe. Being spontaneous, at least by original intention, these enter-
prises were not, as a rule, oppressively disciplined or rigorously organized. Though there may have been exceptions, they were more ridiculed
than persecuted. They had pretty much their own way as far as drugs
and sex were concerned; and though they declared their independence
of the industrial complex, they had access through publications like The
Whole Earth Catalogue to a wide way of intricate and sometimes
expensive technology tailored to handicraft use. For the most part, individual communes were independent ventures; and they met, accordingly, with different destinies. Statistics are lacking, and perhaps always
will be; for sure, the whole story could never be cast in statistical form.
But when we recall that Moses compared the life-span of his utopian
community with that of the Roman empire, modern communes seem
clearly to have grown from a different soil. Flung together in a spirit of
enthusiasm and defiance, the greater number of them have not lasted
through their first decade. One would like to have reports from those
still operational on the principles and adjustments that enabled them to
survive.

A communal society, producing for subsistence not profit or luxury,
is bound to be at a disadvantage when brought into close contact with a
society that produces for personal luxury and openly advertises the fact.
(Amid all the self-pluming flutter over the demise of Russian socialism,
perhaps some consideration should be given to the penetration of Eastern airspace by Western television waves advertising Western consumer
goods.) So in ever-shrinking, ever-more-remote enclaves there may survive even now bits of primitive communist societies, not built by plan
from designs in printed books, but grown instinctively out of the earth
and the folk-life flourishing on it. Such societies do not shrink from
private property as unclean, but they do not put much stock in it; they
would rather share, rather cooperate. They do not, as a rule, long survive contact with a competitive, money economy. But in the remote
Marquesas and the no-longer-so-remote (alas!) Andamans, deep in the
mountainous interior of New Guinea and perhaps among the last, shy

urvivors of an almost propertyless stone-age society, some pigmy survivors of the ancient ways may persist. As late as the Second World War the depths of the South American rain forests still sheltered a few last families of nomadic aborigines, still innocent of fire and the wheel—illiterate, furtive, not quite propertyless. They hardly represent an ideal of human life to which the most utopian-minded among us can aspire; but natural they are, or were, till the great war's insatiable appetite for rubber introduced traders (bearing civilization and its blessings) into the heart of their watery, buggy, snake-infested paradise.

Professor Elton's concluding suggestion (p. 204 above) that his terminal cell in the Tower of London provided More with a spiritual equivalent for the monastery from which since his early years he had felt excluded may include an implicit comment on the *Utopia* as well. The good place is that found or created by the mind for the working out of its own cycles. Perhaps the worst place for the agile eye, the busy tongue, or the meddling hand is the best for the slowly unfolding mind.

Insights

C. S. LEWIS

[A Jolly Invention] †

* * *All seem to be agreed that [Utopia] is a great book, but hardly
any two agree as to its real significance. We approach it through a cloud
of contradictory eulogies. In such a state of affairs a good, though not a
certain, clue is the opinion of those who lived nearest the author's time
than we. Our starting-point is that Erasmus speaks of it as if it were
primarily a comic book; Tyndale despises it as "poetry"; for Harpsfield it
is a "iollye inuention," "pleasantly" set forth;[1] More himself in later life
classes it and the *Praise of Folly* together as books fitter to be burned than
translated in an age prone to misconstruction. Thomas Wilson, fifty years
later, mentions it for praise among 'feined narrations and wittie invented
matters (as though they were true indeed)." This is not the language in
which a friend a enemy an author (when the author is so honest a man
as More) refer to a serious philosophical treatise. It all sounds as if we
had to do with a book whose real place is not in the history of political
thought so much as in that of fiction and satire. It is, of course, possible
that More's sixteenth century readers, and More himself, were mistaken. But it is at least equally possible that the mistake lies with those
modern readers who take the book *au grand sérieux* ["with deadly seriousness"]. There is a cause specially predisposing them to error in such
a matter. They live in a revolutionary age, an age in which modern
weapons and the modern revolutionary technique have made it only too
easy to produce in the real world states recognizably like those we invent
on paper: writing Utopias is now a serious matter. In More's time, or
Campanella's, or Bacon's, there was no real hope or fear that the paper
states could be "drawn into practice": the man engaged in blowing such
bubbles did not need to talk as if he were on his oath. And here we have

† From *English Literature in the Sixteenth
Century Excluding Drama*, Vol. III of *The
Oxford History of English Literature* (Oxford:
The Clarendon Press, 1954) 167–71. Reprinted
by permission of Oxford University Press. Notes
are by the editor of this volume.

1. Tyndale was the Protestant reformer with
whom More disputed. Nicholas Harpsfield
wrote a late sixteenth-century life of More; and
Thomas Wilson wrote in 1553 a *Rule of Rhe-
torique*.

do with one who, as the Messenger told him in the *Dialogue*, "used to look so sadly" when he jested that many were deceived.

The *Utopia* has its serious, even its tragic, elements. It is, as its translator Robynson says, "fruitful and profitable." But it is not a consistently serious philosophical treatise, and all attempts to treat it as such break down sooner or later. The interpretation which breaks down soonest is the "liberal" interpretation. There is nothing in the book on which the later More, the heretic-hunter, need have turned his back. There is no freedom of speech in Utopia. There is nothing liberal in Utopia. From it, as from all other imaginary states, liberty is more successfully banished than the real world, even at its worst, allows. The very charm of these paper citizens is that they cannot in any way resist their author: every man is a dictator in his own book. It is not love of liberty that makes men write Utopias. Nor does the *Utopia* give any color to Tyndale's view that More "knew the truth" of Protestantism and forsook it: the religious orders of the Utopians and their very temples are modelled on the old religion. On the other hand, it is not a defense of that old order against current criticisms; it supports those criticisms by choosing an abbot as its specimen of the bad landlord, and making a friar its most contemptible character. R. W. Chambers, with whom died so much that was sweetest and strongest in English scholarship, advanced a much more plausible view. According to him the Utopians represent the natural virtues working at their ideal best in isolation from the theological; it will be remembered that they hold their Natural Religion only provisionally "onles any godlier be inspired into man from heuen." Yet even this leaves some features unaccounted for. It is doubtful whether More would have regarded euthanasia for incurables and the assassination of hostile princes as things contained in the Law of Nature. And it is very strange that he should make Hedonism the philosophy of the Utopians. Epicurus was not regarded by most Christians as the highest example of the natural light. The truth surely is that as long as we take the *Utopia* for a philosophical treatise it will "give" wherever we lean our weight. It is, to begin with a dialogue: and we cannot be certain which of the speakers, if any, represents More's considered opinion. When Hythloday explains why his philosophy would be useless in the courts of kings More replies that there is "another philosophy more ciuil" and expounds this less intransigent wisdom so sympathetically that we think we have caught the very More at last; but when I have read Hythloday's retort I am all at sea again. It is even very doubtful what More thought of communism as a practical proposal. We have already had to remind ourselves, when considering Colet, that the traditional admission of communism as the law of uncorrupted Nature need carry with it no consequences in the world of practical sociology. It is certain that in the *Confutation* (1532) More had come to include communism among the "horrible heresies" of the Anabaptists and in the *Dialogue of Comfort* he defends private riches. Those who think of More as a "lost leader" may discount these later utterances. Yet even at the end of the *Utopia* he rejects the Utopian economics as a thing "founded of no good reason." The magnificent rebuke of all existing societies which precedes this may suggest that the rejection is ironical. On the other hand, it may mean that the whole book is only a satiric glass to reveal our own avarice by contrast and is not meant to give us directly practical advice.

These puzzles may give the impression that the *Utopia* is a confused book: and if it were intended as a serious treatise it would be very confused indeed. On my view, however, it appears confused only so long as we are trying to get out of it what it never intended to give. It becomes intelligible and delightful as soon as we take it for what it is—a holiday work, a spontaneous overflow of intellectual high spirits, a revel of debate, paradox, comedy and (above all) of invention, which whets many harts and kills none. It is written by More the translator of Lucian and friend of Erasmus, not More the chancellor or the ascetic. Its place on our shelves is close to *Gulliver* and *Erewhon* within reason. The distance of Rabelais, a long way from the *Republic* or *New Worlds for Old*.[2] The invention (the "poetry" of which More was accused) is quite as important as the merits of the polity described, and different parts of that polity are on very different levels of seriousness.

Not to recognize this is to do More grave injustice. Thus the suggestion that the acquisitive impulse should be mortified by using gold for purposes of dishonor is infantile if we take it as a practical proposal. If gold in Utopia were plentiful enough to be so used, gold in Utopia would not be a precious metal. But if it is taken simply as satiric invention leading up to the story of the child and the ambassadors, it is delicious. The slow beginning of the tale, luring us on from London to Bruges, from Bruges to Antwerp, and thence by reported speech to fabulous lands beyond the line, has no place in the history of political philosophy: in the history of prose fiction it has a very high place indeed. Hythloday himself, as we first see him, has something of the arresting quality of the Ancient Mariner. The dialogue is admirably managed. Mere conversation holds us contented for the first book and includes the analysis of the contemporary English situation which is the most serious and the most truly political part of the *Utopia*. In the second book More gives his imagination free rein. There is a thread of serious thought running through it, an abundance of daring suggestions, several backhanded blows at European institutions, and, finally, the magnificent peroration. But he does not keep our noses to the grindstone. He saw many things for the fun of them, surrendering himself to the sheer pleasure of imagined geography, imagined language, and imagined institutions. That is what readers whose interests are rigidly political do

2. *Erewhon*, a Utopia by Samuel Butler (1872); *New Worlds for Old* by H. G. Wells (1908).

ιot understand: but everyone who has ever made an imaginary map responds at once.

Tyndale's belief that More "knew the truth and forsook it" is a crude form of the error which finds in the *Utopia* a liberalism inconsistent with More's later career. There is no inconsistency. More was from the first a very orthodox Papist, even an ascetic with a hankering for the monastic life. At the same time it is true that the *Utopia* stands apart from all his other works. Religiously and politically he was consistent: but this is not to say that he did not undergo a gradual and honorable change very like that which overtook Burke and Wordsworth and other friends of liberty as the Revolutionary age began to show its true features. The times altered; and things that would once have seemed to him permissible or even salutary audacities came to seem to him dangerous. That was why he would not then wish to see the *Utopia* translated. In the same way any of us might now make criticisms of democracy which we would not repeat in the hour of its danger. And from the literary point of view there is an even greater gulf between the *Utopia* and the works which followed. It is, to speak simply, beyond comparison better than they.

J. W. ALLEN

[A Sad and Witty Book] †

The 'fruitful, pleasant and witty work, of the best state of a public weal, and of the new isle, called Utopia',[1] written in Latin and published at Louvain in the year 1516,[2] was, for sixteenth-century England, the earliest expression of that same dream. I deal with it last because, logically considered, it lies beyond the point that was reached later. Crowley felt bound to accept the form of society as it stood, for it was to him of divine ordinance. Starkey[3] was at least convinced that the existing form of society must, substantially, be accepted, if one wished to get anything done. But for the very practical character of his thought, he too might

† From *A History of Political Thought in the Sixteenth Century* (London: Methuen & Co., Ltd.,) 153–56. Reprinted by permission of the publisher. Notes are Allen's unless credited to the editor of this volume. References to *Utopia* have been changed to reflect the paging of this edition.

1. Title-page of the second edition (1556) of Ralph Robinson's translation, first published in 1551.

2. More's European reputation secured for his book a vogue on the continent it seems to have lacked in England. By 1520 editions had been published at Paris, Basle and Vienna. A German version appeared in 1524, an Italian in 1548, a French version in 1550. No English translation appeared till 1551. In the same year was printed a Dutch version.

3. Robert Crowley and Thomas Starkey wrote respectively *The Way to Wealth* and *A Dialogue between Cardinal Pole and Thomas Lupset*, mid-sixteenth-century tracts on social problems, which Allen contrasts with More's *Utopia* [Editor].

have sought his remedy in some kind of communism. As it w. proposed that government should determine rents and organize inde through officials. But More had felt no need of accepting anything as stood, because in truth he had no hope of getting anything done. It is essentially this lack of faith in the possibility of actually constructing a very and a true commonwealth, that isolates More and separates him from Crowley and Starkey. Crowley declared that the very root of all evil is the notion that a man may do as he wills with his own. Starkey hoped to find remedy and establish the true commonwealth by means of religion and reasonable and thorough regulation. Twenty years before Starkey and Pole, More had come to the conclusion that the mass of men will never become religious, that law can be but a palliative, and that, while private property exists, it is vain to hope that men will think they have no right to do as they will with their own. The inference was obvious. only in a land such as never was and such as is nowhere nor will be, can the perfect commonweal exist. With an irony and in a fantastic form that betray his scepticism, More set forth his dream of that Utopia.

It is a mistake to regard More's Utopia as an isolated work of imagination. The thought of its first 'book' is in close accord, up to a certain point, with that of Crowley and of Starkey's Dialogue. More is preoccupied with the same evils that are denounced by the later writers: the stupid brutality of criminal law, the excesses of sheep-farming [4] idleness and frivolity, extravagance and waste, unjust and unnecessary poverty, prevalent selfishness and greed. But so little hope had More that any change for the better could be effected, that he had really no remedial measures to propose. His book became a simple indictment of society. Where Crowley saw religion as a lever, More saw a vast and stupid, conservative inertia. Every proposal for change is always opposed, simply as suggesting something new.

> 'These things, say they, pleased our forefathers and ancestors; would God we could be so wise as they were: and as though they had wittily concluded the matter and with this answer stopped every man's mouth, they sit down again. As who should say it were a very dangerous matter, if a man in any point should be found wiser than his forefathers were.' [5]

While the Dialogue saw possibilities of large reconstruction by governmental action, More saw Princes 'employ much more study how by right or by wrong to enlarge their dominions, than how well and peaceably to rule and govern that they have already': Princes who suppose that

---

4. On this particular point there is a difference of opinion. The passage in the Utopia in which More speaks of sheep devouring men and houses and cities is very well known. In the Dialogue, when Lupset attacks enclosure, Pole expresses the view that more sheep are wanted.

5. See above, Utopia, p. 8.

operty of their subjects is to their own advantage. If the *Utopia* be
ry tale, it is the saddest of fairy tales. More himself says that he had
ken great pains and labour in writing the matter'. It was, obviously,
so. The book amounts to an indictment of humanity almost as terrible
as *Gulliver's Travels*, though wholly without Swift's savagery of resentment.

It is excessively difficult to get any change made, and yet everything
needs to be changed. Among the nations of Christendom More's traveller cannot find 'any sign or token of equity and justice'. The rich men
who control things

> 'invent and devise all means and crafts, first how to keep safely,
> without fear of losing, that they have unjustly gathered together,
> and next how to hire and abuse the work and labour of the poor for
> as little money as may be. These devices, when the rich men have
> decreed to be kept and observed under colour of the commonalty,
> that is to say also of the poor people, then they be made laws.'[6]

In Starkey's *Dialogue* it was implied that More had disregarded the
actual. But it was the Pole of the *Dialogue* who idealized Parliament,
satisfied with the fiction of the common law as to its representative character. He had founded on it a great hope of reconstruction. More was
possessed by no such illusion and had no such hope.

'The whole wealth of the body of the realm,' declared an anonymous
writer, 'cometh out of the labours and works of the common people.'[7]
More's thought was the same. Usurers become rich; but 'labourers, carters, ironsmiths, carpenters and ploughmen', all those who do the necessary work 'that without it no commonwealth were able to continue
and endure one year', all these labour all their lives for a pittance, with
nothing before them but an 'indigent and beggarly old age'.

For this injustice and absurdity there is, it is asserted, but one conceivable remedy. 'Where possessions be private, where money beareth
all the stroke, it is hard and almost impossible that there the weal public
may justly be governed and prosperously flourish.' For 'where every man's
goods be proper and peculiar to himself' and where every man 'draweth
and plucketh to himself as much as he can', there will a few 'divide
among themselves all the whole riches' and 'to the residue is left lack
and poverty'. So we reach the conclusion: 'I do fully persuade myself,
that no equal and just distribution of things can be made nor that perfect
wealth shall ever be among men unless this propriety be exiled and banished. . . . Christ instituted among his all things common; and the same
community doth yet remain amongst the rightest Christian companies.'

6. See above, *Utopia*, p. 83.
7. *How to Reform the Realm in setting them to work to restore Tillage, c.* 1535. Attributed uncertainly to Clement Armstrong. Reprinted in *Tudor Economic Documents* (Tawney and Power), Vol. III. See p. 115.

The evils resulting from private ownership may, indeed, be 'som eased' by law and regulation, but 'that they may be perfectly cured it is not to be hoped for, whiles every man is master of his own to hir self'.

All this is asserted by the mouth of More's imaginary traveller, not in immediate connection with the account of the isle which is Nowhere, but in the far more significant discussion that precedes that account. In his own person More makes the usual objections. 'Men shall never there live wealthily where all things be common.' Men are driven to work by hope of gain for themselves: under communistic conditions every one will idle. The dilemma is stated, but it is not resolved. It was hardly worth while attempting to resolve it; so obvious was it that the remedy proposed by the traveller, Hythloday, was impossible of application. To the doubts expressed by More, Hythloday can only answer that, if he knew the island of Nowhere, he would know better. Coming after all that has gone before, the answer is as sad as it is witty. It was no answer at all; and it reveals at once the fallacy of what follows. Proof of the assertions made in the first book of the *Utopia* is supplied in the second by means of a picture of an imaginary commonwealth, in which communism has actually resulted in all but complete contentment, prosperity and stability. The picture, obviously, is a mere assumption of what has to be proved. So conscious was More of the fallacy that, when he came to describe his island of the blessed, he let fancy loose and became little more than ingenious. He makes, it is true, in the course of this account certain far-reaching suggestions; but for the most part it seems to be calculated rather to amuse than to suggest. It appears, too, after all, that this particular land of heart's desire is not, on close acquaintance, so very attractive. 'So must I needs confess and grant,' More concludes, 'that many things be in the Utopian weal public, which in our cities I may rather wish for than hope after.' Many things, perhaps; but surely not those houses all alike, those people so much alike that they are content hardly to differ in dress, that monotony of grave entertainment and garnishing of the mind. But it did not matter. More knew that his Utopia was nowhere and proved nothing. He had declared in effect that, men being what they are, there is no conceivable remedy for social evils except, at all events, one that cannot be adopted; and as to that one, that it is doubtful what, in any case, the result of its adoption would be. His book is the work of a sceptic in politics, though of a sceptic whose mind rests in religious faith. The real land of More's heart's desire was not of this world. It was Crowley and Starkey who were the idealists in politics: it was More who had kept to the actual. His Utopia is a *reductio ad absudum* of their very and true commonweal. He had written the last word first.

ELIZABETH McCUTCHEON

Denying the Contrary:
More's Use of Litotes in the *Utopia* †

* * *

Still other effects are inherent in litotes,[1] as More uses them. Ambiguity is one, for reasons both logical and psychological. The Renaissance was well aware of the logical complications and ambiguities which result when something is affirmed by negating the contrary. Litotes and ten other figures (an important group in the *Utopia*, including antithesis, irony, paradox and paralipsis) can be specifically related to that topic of invention called opposites, of which there were thought to be four sorts in all: contraries, relatives, privatives, and contradictories. To affirm one contradictory is to deny the other, but litotes based on the first three categories may well be ambiguous. Though immediate contraries (faith/ unbelief, for example) have no species between, so that "one or the other must be affirmed",[2] mediate contraries do have a mediate or middle ground between the two extremes. "Not white" is the seemingly inevitable text-book example; as Thomas Wilson says, "if a cloth be not white, it is no reason to call it blacke. for it may bee blewe, greene, redd, russett. . . ."[3] Relatives (Isidore cites "few" and "many") and privatives (sight and blindness, for example, for which a mediate could be an eye inflammation, according to Isidore)[4] can also be ambiguous. On these grounds such common litotes as "non pessime" (48/28, 52/1, 80/16), "non exigvi" (46/8, 214/22), "haud pauca" (54/2, 244/14), "haud pauci" (218/9, 224/20–21), "nec pauci" (222/14), "haud multi" (158/5), "haud saepe" (188/25), "non saepe" (184/29), or "haud semel" (212/6) are logically ambiguous. We may, at first, think of their opposites, just as we do with white-black, yet all have one or more species between. "Non pessime" for instance, has to move from *worst* through *rather bad* and *bad* even before it can move towards *good*, *quite good*, or *the best*, if it does; "haud pauci" may mean *more than a few*, *some*, or *many*, and "haud semel" [not once] is even more open ended.

A second kind of ambiguity arises from the psychological peculiarity

---

† "Litotes: Denying the Contrary," *Moreana* 31–32 (November 1971): 116–21. Reprinted by permission of Amici Thomae Mori. Notes are McCutcheon's unless credited to the editor of this volume.

1. Litotes is the rhetorical figure by which one affirms something in the course of denying its contrary. It is a minor though persistent mannerism within More's stylistic and rhetorical gamut; but by concentrating on it, McCutcheon is able to illuminate a really important quality of More's mind *[Editor]*.

2. Sister Miriam Joseph, *Rhetoric in Shakespeare's Time*, p. 322.

3. Thomas Wilson, *The Rule of Reason; Conteining the Art of Logike* [1551] (London, 1567), fol. 52ᵛ, as cited in Sister Miriam Joseph, *Rhetoric in Shakespeare's time*, p. 322.

4. Isidorus, *Etymologiarum*, in *Patrologiae cursus completus . . . Series latina*, ed. Jacques Paul Migne (Paris, 1844–1864), LXXXII, 153–54 [Book *II*, ch. 31: 'De oppositis']. [The Latin examples which follow would translate as "not the worst," "no slight," "not a few," "not many," "not often," etc., etc. The number are references to page and line of the Yale Latin text.— *Editor.*]

of negating a negation.[5] As Jespersen has observed, ". . . it shou.. noted that the "double negative always modifies the idea, for the re.. of the whole expression is somewhat different from the simple ide.. expressed positively." He calls attention to the same phenomenon which led Puttenham to call litotes the "Moderator", though he interprets it differently, when he adds that *not uncommon is weaker than common,* . . . the psychological reason being that the *detour* through the two mutually destroying negatives weakens the mental energy of the hearer and implies on the part of the speaker a certain hesitation absent from the blunt, outspoken common . . ."[6] In fact, since litotes as a rhetorical and literary technique not only moderates but intensifies, so that, as John Smith points out, ". . . *sometimes a word is put down with a sign of negation, when as much is signified as if we had spoken affirmatively, if not more,"*[7] it may be either stronger or weaker. But it is ambiguous. We can and must depend upon the context, of course, but even so we do have to hesitate and decide to what extent a particular litotes is moderating, to what extent emphasizing, or better, attempt to hold two apparently contradictory but equally real effects in our minds at the same time. I do not think, pace Jespersen, that this necessarily "weakens the mental energy of the hearer". More probably it arouses it,[8] requiring us to linger over the construction and its context—hence its particular effectiveness as a figure of emphasis. But we are required to undergo a complex mental action; if something is, for example, *not uncommon,* to pursue Jespersen's example. we move from a *common* which isn't quite started to the *uncommon* which is, and then, because that is denied, back towards *common* again. But we do not usually know quite where to stop, a process we can visualize this way:

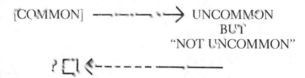

It is just this sort of ambiguous area which a recent cartoon exploits.[9] A husband and wife are standing in front of what should be a welcome mat. But this mat reads, "not unwelcome", to the chagrin of the wife, who says, " *'See what I mean? You're never sure just where you stand with them'* "

5. Litotic constructions should, logically, be part of Empson's seventh type of ambiguity, but he does not discuss double negations, although he does comment usefully on negatives in general; see Wiliam Empson, *Seven Types of Ambiguity,* 3rd ed. (London: Chatto and Windus, 1956), pp. 205–214.
6. Otto Jespersen, *Negation in English and Other Languages,* in *Selected Writings of Otto*

Jespersen (1917; rpt. London: George Allen & Unwin Ltd., n.d.), p. 63. Cf. Ch. 24 in his *The Philosophy of Grammar* (1924; rpt. Allen & Unwin, 1948).
7. John Smith, *The Mystery of Rhetorick Unveil'd* (London, 1688), sig. *a*4.
8. See also Lee M. Hollander, "Litotes in Old Norse", p. 1.
9. *The New Yorker,* February 6, 1971, p. 36.

a larger sense we're never quite sure where we stand in the *Utopia*, ~~~her. It is, of course, a commonplace to talk about ambiguity in the *Jtopia*. But on the smallest syntactical level ambiguity does exist of a sort which can never be altogether resolved, and probably was not meant to be. For this ambiguity vivifies the text, arouses its readers, and agitates its points, however casually they appear to be made, so that they neither evaporate nor solidify. We are constantly, though obliquely, tested by the many litotes already cited, not least those institutions "non pessime" ["not the worst"] (52/1) which Raphael found in the new world, or persona More's "haud pauca" (244/14) ["not a few"] in his concluding speech. Curiously, perhaps consciously, this last "haud pauca" contradicts the implications of another "haud pauca" early in Book I (54/2), which More uses in apparent and ironic antithesis to the positive "multa" (54/1) earlier in the sentence. Here More observes that Raphael did, of course, find many ["multa"] customs which were ill-advised in those new countries, "so he rehearsed not a few points from which our own cities, nations, races, and kingdoms may take example for the correction of their errors" (55/2-4).

We can sense inherent ambiguities and the potential spread of meaning in a given litotes from still another point of view by looking at various translations of the "non exigvi momenti negocia" (46/8) of More's first sentence. Ralph Robinson, thinking of litotes as an emphatic and intensifying device, doubles the idea in a positive sense; it becomes "weightye matters, and of great importaunce". Gilbert Burnet, however, preserves the litotic implications, though slightly modifying the meaning, when he renders the litotes as "some Differences of no small Consequence". Closer to our period, H. V. S. Ogden, who chiefly hears the moderating possibilities, turns the phrase into "some differences". In an attempt to reconcile the moderating impulse and the emphatic one, Paul Turner writes of 'a rather serious difference of opinion".[1] The Yale translation settles for simple emphasis: "certain weighty matters" (47/10). Burnet alone has left some of the ambiguities unresolved; all the other translators have, in a sense, made our minds up for us. But what we gain in clarity we lose elsewhere. The alternatives, and therefore any possible irony, disappear, as does the ambiguity, and with that, the tension and movement of mind, so that nuances of meaning are also dissolved. In short, this litotes becomes far less significant, both in what it says and the way it says it, as an anticipation of the *Utopia* to come. For the phrase More writes certainly calls attention, however obliquely, to the

---

1. Ralph Robynson, trans. (1551) in *The Utopia of Sir Thomas More*, ed. J. H. Lupton (Oxford: Clarendon Press, 1895), p. 21; Gilbert Burnet, trans., *Utopia: Written in Latin by Sir Thomas More, Chancellor of England: Translated into English* (London, 1684), p. 1; H. V. S. Ogden, ed. and trans., *Utopia*, by Sir Thomas More (New York: Appleton-Century-Crofts, 1949), p. 1; Paul Turner, trans., *Utopia*, by Thomas More (Harmondsworth, Middlesex, Eng.: Penguin Books Ltd., 1965), p. 37.

kind of issue being argued about in the known world. He does admittedly, spell out the details of what was a massive commercial problem,[2] but he certainly says enough to reinforce our sense of the power and splendor and pride which activates almost all states (except, as we shall discover, Utopia). Indeed, "negocia" itself has commercial overtones which are very unlike the word Raphael will later use for what he thinks of as the public welfare: "salutem publicam" (104/8). By beginning, then, with "non exigvi momenti negocia" More is able to raise, for just a moment, a question to which much of the subsequent discussion returns: what sorts of state matters are trifling? And what sorts are not? But, whatever else it does, this first "non" foreshadows the processes of negation and opposites which typify so much of the Utopia.

Like all other negatives, only more so, because now the negative is itself negated, litotes speak of a habit of mind, a tendency to see more than one side to a question.[3] Intellectual, judicial, and persuasive, they ask us to weigh and consider alternatives which the writer has himself considered. So each litotes does, then, link writer with reader, who tries to repeat, as best he can, the mental and judicial processes the figure so economically and often ambiguously encloses. As Puttenham says, litotes is a "sensible figure," one which "alter [s] and affect [s] the minde by alteration of sense".[4] The persuasive bias of Renaissance rhetoric is implicit here. Where a modern writer in the ironic mode, like Herman Melville or Henry James, will use this sort of negation to reveal hesitations, qualifications, uncertainties and ambiguous complications in the consciousness of the narrator or a major character in his fiction. More's fiction, though no less ironic, uses litotes, primarily, to affect and alter our minds. Yet it is also true that the alternatives were More's to begin with, so that litotes makes us simultaneously much more aware of his mind in action and certain divisions in it; it reinforces our sense of More himself as one who indeed, saw more than one side of a question.[5]

From this point of view, even such a seemingly conventional litotes as "haud dubie" (62/25, 86/16, 96/32, 236/3) or a more emphatic "Neque dubium est" (216/27 -28) or a "non dubito" (242/16) ["Doubtless," "There's no doubt," "I don't doubt"] implies a process of mental assessment on the part of the speaker. It suggests, as "to be sure" or "certainly"

2. In this connection see the note to 46/8, 295 in the Yale Utopia.

3. More's use of negatives in general, though beyond the scope of this study, is an important element in his style (and his thought) and needs more investigation. In thinking about negatives, I found some terse comments by Ian Watt on the negative in Henry James illuminating; he talks of what he calls "the right judicial frame of mind". See Ian Watt, "The First Paragraph of The Ambassadors: An Explication," Essays in Criticism, X (July, 1960), 250–74; rpt. in Rhetorical Analyses of Literary Works, ed.

Edward P. J. Corbett (New York: Oxford Univ. Press, 1969), pp. 184–203; the words I cite are on p. 190.

4. Puttenham, The Arte of English Poesie, p. 148.

5. An intensive example of a reading on these lines is David Bevington, "The Dialogue in Utopia.: Two Sides to the Question", S.P., 58 (1961), 496–509. Compare and contrast with this J. H. Hexter, More's Utopia: The Biography of an Idea (1952; rpt. Torchbook ed., New York: Harper, 1965).

...t, that someone has weighed the possibilities and reached a deci-
...—hence its usefulness as a persuasive figure. The same effect is mul-
...plied in one of More's favorite litotic constructions, which, unlike most,
does spell out (but qualify) its alternatives: some combination of a negative with *minus* or *minus quam*. Like the "nec minus salutaris quam
festiuus" of the title page, ["no less beneficial than entertaining"] or the
several *non minus . . . quam* litotes in the passage describing the Utopian way with gold, these constructions seem to ask us to weigh or try to
balance different ideas or values, almost as if we were asked to find the
balance point on a moving see-saw. The ideas are grammatically "equal",[6]
yet, often, the figure is weighted on one side; there is, in other words, a
kind of dynamic emphasis which requires that we hold the two elements
both together and apart. It can startle, or it can result in ironic or satiric
incongruities: things which shouldn't be "equal" are, but things which
should be, too often aren't. Raphael's description of the robber, who is
in no less danger "if merely condemned for theft" than "if he were convicted of murder as well" (75/8–9) is an instance of the first sort; his
description of the Utopian way of providing for its citizens, an instance
of the second: "Then take into account the fact that there is no less
provision for those who are now helpless but once worked than for those
who are still working" (239/22–25). But most litotes in *Utopia* do not,
in fact, spell out the alternative in this way. With litotes like "non pessime" or "haud pauca" ["not the worst," or "not a few"] it is almost as if
we saw one side of a metaphysical see-saw. So the mind is stimulated or
teased into the sort of action described earlier, having, often, to con-
struct the opposite which is denied and hold on to contraries which it
weighs, each against the other. And once again, though in a more oblique
way, we discover a weighting, a persuasive action which often favors
Utopian attitudes, however negatively they may appear to be described.
As More says, in a fine piece of understatement, which also reveals an
awareness of just how complex this sort of question is, Raphael found
nations "non pessime institutas" [not the worst established] (52/1). But
with this we come back, full circle, to Peacham's point; litotes does,
indeed, "praise or dispraise, and that in a modest forme and manner".[7]
In the *Utopia*, more precisely, it praises and dispraises, often almost
simultaneously, since to deny something about Utopia is to affirm it,
indirectly, of the world as we know it.

More ended his book with a famous wish. My own present hope is a
more modest one—that somehow litotes be more systematically retained
in translations of *Utopia*, which have, usually, made at best tepid attempts
to preserve it, often converting a litotic construction to a simple positive.
Obviously, syntactical patterns are difficult to turn from one language to

---

6. Jespersen, *Negation in English and Other Languages*, discusses *non minus quam* briefly, pp. 83–84.

7. Peacham, *The Garden of Eloquence*, p. 151.

another, and negatives are trickier still. But when, for example,
final "haud pauca" (244/14) becomes "many" (245/17), or the freq.
litotic descriptions of the Polylerites and the Utopians, which comme
via diversa on the way of this world, are transformed into straightforward
descriptions, we lose the emphasis and the understatement, the irony
and possible satire, and the ambiguity of the original. The complicated
action of More's mind is coarsened, his meaning blurred, the energy
and tension of a muscular prose relaxed. On a larger scale, we lose the
cumulative effect of a device much repeated, and we have, too often,
only one side of what is at least a two-sided vision inherent in every
denial of the contrary. In More's hands, litotes was, in fact, a superlative
tool for both the exceedingly polite gentleman, the fictional More, and
the passionate visionary who had seen Utopia. Avoiding controversy it
constantly calls attention, without seeming to do so, to the purpose and
values behind the countless delightful details with which More created
both dialogue and discourse; it truly is a figure of and for the mind.
Intensive yet understated, emphatic, often drily ironic, sometimes
humorous or wry, concealing tremendous energy in its apparent ease
and frequent brevity, litotes is not the least of the rhetorical figures in
the vision and satire we call *Utopia*.

EDWARD BELLAMY

From *Looking Backward*[†]

[A widely known and much discussed American Utopia was that of Edward
Bellamy, an early New England socialist. *Looking Backward* (1887) took its
major premise from the old Rip Van Winkle story, but in addition it managed to articulate some of the pressing problems of an industrial mass-pro-
duction society. Coming from a clerical background, Bellamy's feelings (as
distinct from his ideas) were tinged with the misty benevolent idealism of the
late Puritan movement. To modern tastes, his vision of that remote era 2000
A.D. is almost too genteel. Julian West, his time-traveler, lays eyes on no
roughnecks, no garbage collectors, no coal-miners, no criminals, no ethnic
misfits. The soft, obsequious women he meets have nothing to do but go
shopping for knick-knacks and coo over their men—who also have very little
to fill their overflowing leisure hours. Yet here and there in this idyll of
parlor socialism, elements of compulsion and regimentation make themselves reluctantly felt. As we approach in hard reality the magic year 2000,
it is amusing to see how widely most of Bellamy's prophecies missed, and
where (on occasion) they hit the target.]

† From Edward Bellamy, *Looking Backward, 2000–1887*, ed. John L. Thomas (1888; Cambridge: Belknap Press of Harvard UP, 1967).

[The Industrial Army]

The questions which I needed to ask before I could acquire even an outline acquaintance with the institutions of the twentieth century being endless, and Dr. Leete's good-nature appearing equally so, we sat up talking for several hours after the ladies left us.[1] Reminding my host of the point at which our talk had broken off that morning, I expressed my curiosity to learn how the organization of the industrial army was made to afford a sufficient stimulus to diligence in the lack of any anxiety on the worker's part as to his livelihood.

"You must understand in the first place," replied the doctor, "that the supply of incentives to effort is but one of the objects sought in the organization we have adopted for the army. The other, and equally important, is to secure for the file-leaders and captains of the force, and the great officers of the nation, men of proven abilities, who are pledged by their own careers to hold their followers up to their highest standard of performance and permit no lagging. With a view to these two ends the industrial army is organized. First comes the unclassified grade of common laborers, men of all work, to which all recruits during their first three years belong. This grade is a sort of school, and a very strict one, in which the young men are taught habits of obedience, subordination, and devotion to duty. While the miscellaneous nature of the work done by this force prevents the systematic grading of the workers which is afterwards possible, yet individual records are kept, and excellence receives distinction corresponding with the penalties that negligence incurs. It is not, however, policy with us to permit youthful recklessness or indiscretion, when not deeply culpable, to handicap the future careers of young men, and all who have passed through the unclassified grade without serious disgrace have an equal opportunity to choose the life employment they have most liking for.[2] Having selected this, they enter upon it as apprentices. The length of the apprenticeship naturally differs in different occupations. At the end of it the apprentice becomes a full workman, and a member of his trade or guild. Now not only are the individual records of the apprentices for ability and industry strictly kept, and excellence distinguished by suitable distinctions, but upon the average of his record during apprenticeship the standing given the apprentice among the full workmen depends.

"While the internal organizations of different industries, mechanical and agricultural, differ according to their peculiar conditions, they agree

1. The ladies depart from the drawing room immediately after dinner and disappear just as abruptly from the ideal society. Clearly they do not work, are not trained for any activities, and make no contribution to the society [Editor].

2. The rather complicated decisions about who gets educated, how much, and along what lines are passed over very casually by Doctor Leete [Editor].

in a general division of their workers into first, second, and third gi. according to ability, and these grades are in many cases subdivided r. first and second classes. According to his standing as an apprentice . young man is assigned his place as a first, second, or third grade worker. Of course only young men of unusual ability pass directly from appren- ticeship into the first grade of the workers. The most fall into the lower grades, working up as they grow more experienced, at the periodical regradings. These regradings take place in each industry at intervals cor- responding with the length of the apprenticeship to that industry, so that merit never need wait long to rise, nor can any rest on past achievements unless they would drop into a lower rank. One of the notable advantages of a high grading is the privilege it gives the worker in electing which of the various branches or processes of his industry he will follow as his specialty. Of course it is not intended that any of these processes shall be disproportionately arduous, but there is often much difference between them, and the privilege of election is accordingly highly prized. So far as possible, indeed, the preferences even of the poorest workmen are considered in assigning them their line of work, because not only their happiness but their usefulness is thus enhanced. While, however, the wish of the lower grade man is consulted so far as the exigencies of the service permit, he is considered only after the upper grade men have been provided for, and often he has to put up with second or third choice, or even with an arbitrary assignment when help is needed. This privilege of election attends every regrading, and when a man loses his grade he also risks having to exchange the sort of work he likes for some other less to his taste. The results of each regrading, giving the standing of every man in his industry, are gazetted in the public prints, and those who have won promotion since the last regrading receive the nation's thanks and are publicly invested with the badge of their new rank."

"What may this badge be?" I asked

"Every industry has its emblematic device," replied Dr. Leete, "and this, in the shape of a metallic badge so small that you might not see it unless you knew where to look, is all the insignia which the men of the army wear, except where public convenience demands a distinctive uni- form. This badge is the same in form for all grades of industry, but while the badge of the third grade is iron, that of the second grade is silver, and that of the first is gilt.[3]

"Apart from the grand incentive to endeavor afforded by the fact that the high places in the nation are open only to the highest class men, and that rank in the army constitutes the only mode of social distinction for the vast majority who are not aspirants in art, literature, and the

3. Gold is apparently too rich for the new society; gilt is a rather tawdry substitute [*Editor*].

ssions, various incitements of a minor, but perhaps equally effective, sort are provided in the form of special privileges and immunities
in the way of discipline, which the superior class men enjoy. These,
while intended to be as little as possible invidious to the less successful,
have the effect of keeping constantly before every man's mind the great
desirability of attaining the grade next above his own.[4]

"It is obviously important that not only the good but also the indifferent and poor workmen should be able to cherish the ambition of rising.
Indeed, the number of the latter being so much greater, it is even more
essential that the ranking system should not operate to discourage them
than that it should stimulate the others. It is to this end that the grades
are divided into classes. The grades as well as the classes being made
numerically equal at each regrading, there is not at any time, counting
out the officers and the unclassified and apprentice grades, over one-
ninth of the industrial army in the lowest class, and most of this number
are recent apprentices, all of whom expect to rise. Those who remain
during the entire term of service in the lowest class are but a trifling

---

4. The description of the industrial army
beginning with the sentence "With a view to
these two ends. . . ." on p. 123 was revised and
expanded in the second edition. The first edition reads: "With a view to these two ends, the
whole body of members of the industrial army
is divided into four general classes. First, the
unclassified grade, of common laborers, assigned
to any sort of work, usually the coarser kinds;
to this all recruits during their first three years
belong. Second, the apprentices, as the men
are called in the first year after passing from the
unclassified grade, while they are mastering the
first elements of their chosen vocations. Third,
the main body of the full workers, being men
between twenty-five and forty-five. Fourth, the
officers from the lowest who have charge of the
men to the highest. These four classes are all
under a different form of discipline. The
unclassified workers, doing miscellaneous work,
cannot of course be so rigidly graded as later.
They are supposed to be in a sort of school,
learning industrial habits. Nevertheless they
make their individual records, and excellence
receives distinction and helps in the after career,
something as academic standing added to the
prestige of men in your day. The year of
apprenticeship follows. The apprentice is given
the first quarter of it to learn the rudiments of
his vocation, but is marked on the last three
quarters with a view to determine which grade
among the workers he shall be enrolled in on
becoming a full workman. It may seem strange
that the term of apprenticeship should be the
same in all trades, but this is done for the sake
of uniformity in the system, and practically

works precisely as if the terms of apprenticeship
varied according to the difficulty of acquiring
the trade. For, in the trades in which one cannot become proficient in a year, the result is
that the apprentice falls into the lower grades
of the full workmen, and works upward as he
grows in skill. This is indeed what ordinarily
happens in most trades. The full workmen are
divided into three grades, according to efficiency, and each grade into a first and second
class, so that there are in all six classes, into
which the men fall according to their ability.

"To facilitate the testing of efficiency, all
industrial work, whenever by any means, and
even at some inconvenience, it is possible, is
conducted by piece-work, and if this is absolutely out of the question, the best possible
substitute for determining ability is adopted. The
men are regraded yearly, so that merit never
need wait long to rise, nor can any rest on past
achievements, unless they would drop into a
lower rank. The results of each annual regrading, giving the standing of every man in the
army, are gazetted in the public prints.

"Apart from the grand incentive to endeavor
afforded by the fact that the high places in the
nation are open only to the highest class men,
various incitements of a minor, but perhaps
equally effective, sort are provided in the form
of special privileges and immunities in the way
of discipline, which the superior class men
enjoy. These, while not in the aggregate
important, have the effect of keeping constantly before every man's mind the desirability
of attaining the grade next above his own,"
[Thomas's note].

fraction of the industrial army, and likely to be as deficient in sensib. to their position as in ability to better it.[5]

"It is not even necessary that a worker should win promotion to a higher grade to have at least a taste of glory. While promotion requires a general excellence of record as a worker, honorable mention and various sorts of prizes are awarded for excellence less than sufficient for promotion, and also for special feats and single performances in the various industries. There are many minor distinctions of standing, not only within the grades but within the classes, each of which acts as a spur to the efforts of a group.[6] It is intended that no form of merit shall wholly fail of recognition.

"As for actual neglect of work, positively bad work, or other overt remissness on the part of men incapable of generous motives, the discipline of the industrial army is far too strict to allow anything whatever of the sort. A man able to do duty, and persistently refusing, is sentenced to solitary imprisonment on bread and water till he consents.[7]

"The lowest grade of the officers of the industrial army, that of assistant foremen or lieutenants, is appointed out of men who have held their place for two years in the first class of the first grade. Where this leaves too large a range of choice, only the first group of this class are eligible. No one thus comes to the point of commanding men until he is about thirty years old. After a man becomes an officer, his rating of course no longer depends on the efficiency of his own work, but on that of his men. The foremen are appointed from among the assistant foremen, by the same exercise of discretion limited to a small eligible class. In the appointments to the still higher grades another principle is introduced, which it would take too much time to explain now.

"Of course such a system of grading as I have described would have been impracticable applied to the small industrial concerns of your day, in some of which there were hardly enough employees to have left one apiece for the classes.[8] You must remember that, under the national

5. In the first edition the passage beginning "The grades as well as the classes. . . ." reads: "The classes being numerically equal, there is not at any time, counting out the officers and the unclassified and apprentice grades, over one-eighth of the industrial army in the lowest class, and most of this number are recent apprentices, all of whom expect to rise. Still further to encourage those of no great talents to do their best, a man who, after attaining a higher grade, falls back into a lower, does not lose the fruit of his effort, but retains, as a sort of brevet, his former rank. The result is that those under our ranking system who fail to win any prize, by way of solace to their pride, remaining during the entire term of service in the lowest class, are but a trifling fraction of the industrial army, and likely to be as deficient in sensibility to their position as in ability to better it." [JLT].

6. This sentence was added in the second edition. [JLT].

7. In the first edition this paragraph reads: "As for actual neglect of work, positively bad work, or other overt remissness on the part of men incapable of generous motives, the discipline of the industrial army is far too strict to allow much of that. A man able to do duty, and persistently refusing, is cut off from all human society" [*Thomas's note*]. [Here a bit of iron fist is felt beneath the velvet glove. Presumably other forms of anti-social behavior (apart from sloth) are also punished by jail terms or perhaps harsher inflictions, but we are not told of them—*Editor*.]

8. By 1887 relatively little mass production had taken root in America; Bellamy clearly had handicraft industries in mind [*Editor*].

ganization of labor, all industries are carried on by great bodies of men, many of your farms or shops being combined as one. It is also owing solely to the vast scale on which each industry is organized with coordinate establishments in every part of the country, that we are able by exchanges and transfers to fit every man so nearly with the sort of work he can do best.[9]

"And now, Mr. West, I will leave it to you, on the bare outline of its features which I have given, if those who need special incentives to do their best are likely to lack them under our system. Does it not seem to you that men who found themselves obliged, whether they wished or not, to work, would under such a system be strongly impelled to do their best?"[1]

I replied that it seemed to me the incentives offered were, if any objection were to be made, too strong; that the pace set for the young men was too hot; and such, indeed, I would add with deference, still remains my opinion, now that by longer residence among you I have become better acquainted with the whole subject.

Dr. Leete, however, desired me to reflect, and I am ready to say that it is perhaps a sufficient reply to my objection, that the worker's livelihood is in no way dependent on his ranking, and anxiety for that never embitters his disappointments; that the working hours are short, the vacations regular, and that all emulation ceases at forty-five, with the attainment of middle life.[2]

"There are two or three other points I ought to refer to," he added, "to prevent your getting mistaken impressions. In the first place, you must understand that this system of preferment given the more efficient workers over the less so, in no way contravenes the fundamental idea of our social system, that all who do their best are equally deserving, whether that best be great or small. I have shown that the system is arranged to encourage the weaker as well as the stronger with the hope of rising, while the fact that the stronger are selected for the leaders is in no way a reflection upon the weaker, but in the interest of the common weal.

"Do not imagine, either, because emulation is given free play as an incentive under our system, that we deem it a motive likely to appeal to the nobler sort of men, or worthy of them. Such as these find their motives within, not without, and measure their duty by their own endowments, not by those of others. So long as their achievement is proportioned to their powers, they would consider it preposterous to expect praise or blame because it chanced to be great or small. To such natures

9. In the first edition the passage beginning "You must remember. . . ." reads: "You must remember that, under the national organization of labor, all industries are carried on by great bodies of men, a hundred of your farms or shops being combined as one. The superintendent, with us, is like a colonel, or even a general, in one of your armies" [Thomas's note].
1. [This sentence was added in the second edition [Thomas's note].
2. What the "ancients" of forty-five years old do with the rest of their lives (shuffleboard or checkers?) is not considered [Editor].

emulation appears philosophically absurd, and despicable in a m.
aspect by its substitution of envy for admiration, and exultation for regr
in one's attitude toward the successes and the failures of others.

"But all men, even in the last year of the twentieth century, are not
of this high order, and the incentives to endeavor requisite for those who
are not must be of a sort adapted to their inferior natures. For these,
then, emulation of the keenest edge is provided as a constant spur. Those
who need this motive will feel it. Those who are above its influence do
not need it.

"I should not fail to mention," resumed the doctor, "that for those
too deficient in mental or bodily strength to be fairly graded with the
main body of workers, we have a separate grade, unconnected with the
others—a sort of invalid corps, the members of which are provided with
a light class of tasks fitted to their strength. All our sick in mind and
body, all our deaf and dumb, and lame and blind and crippled and
even our insane, belong to this invalid corps, and bear its insignia. The
strongest often do nearly a man's work, the feeblest, of course, nothing;
but none who can do anything are willing quite to give up. In their lucid
intervals, even our insane are eager to do what they can."

"That is a pretty idea of the invalid corps," I said. "Even a barbarian
from the nineteenth century can appreciate that. It is a very graceful way
of disguising charity, and must be grateful to the feelings of its recipi-
ents."

"Charity!" repeated Dr. Leete. "Did you suppose that we consider the
incapable class we are talking of objects of charity?"

"Why, naturally," I said, "inasmuch as they are incapable of self-
support."

But here the doctor took me up quickly.

"Who is capable of self-support?" he demanded. "There is no such
thing in a civilized society as self-support. In a state of society so barbarous as not even to know family coöperation, each individual may possibly support himself, though even then for a part of his life only; but
from the moment that men begin to live together, and constitute even
the rudest sort of society, self-support becomes impossible. As men grow
more civilized, and the subdivision of occupations and services is carried
out, a complex mutual dependence becomes the universal rule. Every
man, however solitary may seem his occupation, is a member of a vast
industrial partnership, as large as the nation, as large as humanity. The
necessity of mutual dependence should imply the duty and guarantee of
mutual support; and that it did not in your day constituted the essential
cruelty and unreason of your system."

"That may all be so," I replied, "but it does not touch the case of
those who are unable to contribute anything to the product of industry."

"Surely I told you this morning, at least I thought I did," replied Dr.
Leete, "that the right of a man to maintenance at the nation's table

⸳nds on the fact that he is a man, and not on the amount of health
⸳d strength he may have, so long as he does his best."

"You said so," I answered, "but I supposed the rule applied only to
the workers of different ability. Does it also hold of those who can do
nothing at all?"

"Are they not also men?"

"I am to understand, then, that the lame, the blind, the sick, and the
impotent, are as well off as the most efficient, and have the same income?"

'Certainly," was the reply.

"The idea of charity on such a scale," I answered, "would have made
our most enthusiastic philanthropists gasp."

"If you had a sick brother at home," replied Dr. Leete, "unable to
work, would you feed him on less dainty food, and lodge and clothe him
more poorly, than yourself? More likely far, you would give him the
preference; nor would you think of calling it charity. Would not the
word, in that connection, fill you with indignation?"

"Of course," I replied; "but the cases are not parallel. There is a sense,
no doubt, in which all men are brothers; but this general sort of brotherhood is not to be compared, except for rhetorical purposes, to the
brotherhood of blood, either as to its sentiment or its obligations."

"There speaks the nineteenth century!" exclaimed Dr. Leete. "Ah,
Mr. West, there is no doubt as to the length of time that you slept. If I
were to give you, in one sentence, a key to what may seem the mysteries
of our civilization as compared with that of your age, I should say that
it is the fact that the solidarity of the race and the brotherhood of man,
which to you were but fine phrases, are, to our thinking and feeling, ties
as real and as vital as physical fraternity.

"But even setting that consideration aside, I do not see why it so sur-
prises you that those who cannot work are conceded the full right to live
on the produce of those who can. Even in your day, the duty of military
service for the protection of the nation, to which our industrial service
corresponds, while obligatory on those able to discharge it, did not operate to deprive of the privileges of citizenship those who were unable.
They stayed at home, and were protected by those who fought, and
nobody questioned their right to be, or thought less of them. So, now,
the requirement of industrial service from those able to render it does
not operate to deprive of the privileges of citizenship, which now implies
the citizen's maintenance, him who cannot work. The worker is not a
citizen because he works, but works because he is a citizen. As you
recognize the duty of the strong to fight for the weak, we, now that
fighting is gone by, recognize his duty to work for him.

"A solution which leaves an unaccounted-for residuum is no solution
at all; and our solution of the problem of human society would have
been none at all had it left the lame, the sick, and the blind outside with
the beasts, to fare as they might. Better far have left the strong and well

unprovided for than these burdened ones, toward whom every heart
yearn, and for whom ease of mind and body should be provided, r
no others. Therefore it is, as I told you this morning, that the title
every man, woman, and child to the means of existence rests on no basis
less plain, broad, and simple than the fact that they are fellows of one
race—members of one human family. The only coin current is the image
of God, and that is good for all we have.

"I think there is no feature of the civilization of your epoch so repugnant to modern ideas as the neglect with which you treated your dependent classes. Even if you had no pity, no feeling of brotherhood, how
was it that you did not see that you were robbing the incapable class of
their plain right in leaving them unprovided for?"

"I don't quite follow you there," I said. "I admit the claim of this class
to our pity, but how could they who produced nothing claim a share of
the product as a right?"

"How happened it," was Dr. Leete's reply, "that your workers were
able to produce more than so many savages would have done? Was it
not wholly on account of the heritage of the past knowledge and achievements of the race, the machinery of society, thousands of years in contriving, round by you ready made to your hand? How did you come to
be possessors of this knowledge and this machinery, which represent
nine parts to one contributed by yourself in the value of your product?
You inherited it, did you not? And were not these others, these unfortunate and crippled brothers whom you cast out, joint inheritors, co-
heirs with you? What did you do with their share? Did you not rob them
when you put them off with crusts, who were entitled to sit with the
heirs, and did you not add insult to robbery when you called the crusts
charity?

"Ah, Mr. West," Dr. Leete continued, as I did not respond, "what I
do not understand is, setting aside all considerations either of justice or
brotherly feeling toward the crippled and defective, how the workers of
your day could have had any heart for their work, knowing that their
children, or grand-children, if unfortunate, would be deprived of the
comforts and even necessities of life. It is a mystery how men with children could favor a system under which they were rewarded beyond those
less endowed with bodily strength or mental power. For, by the same
discrimination by which the father profited, the son, for whom he would
give his life, being perchance weaker than others, might be reduced to
crusts and beggary. How men dared leave children behind them, I have
never been able to understand."

Note.—Although in his talk on the previous evening Dr. Leete
had emphasized the pains taken to enable every man to ascertain
and follow his natural bent in choosing an occupation, it was not
till I learned that the worker's income is the same in all occupations

that I realized how absolutely he may be counted on to do so, and thus, by selecting the harness which sets most lightly on himself, find that in which he can pull best. The failure of my age in any systematic or effective way to develop and utilize the natural aptitudes of men for the industries and intellectual vocations was one of the great wastes, as well as one of the most common causes of unhappiness in that time. The vast majority of my contemporaries, though nominally free to do so, never really chose their occupations at all, but were forced by circumstances into work for which they were relatively inefficient, because not naturally fitted for it. The rich, in this respect, had little advantage over the poor. The latter, indeed, being generally deprived of education, had no opportunity even to ascertain the natural aptitudes they might have, and on account of their poverty were unable to develop them by cultivation even when ascertained. The liberal and technical professions, except by favorable accident, were shut to them, to their own great loss and that of the nation. On the other hand, the well-to-do, although they could command education and opportunity, were scarcely less hampered by social prejudice, which forbade them to pursue manual vocations, even when adapted to them, and destined them, whether fit or unfit, to the professions, thus wasting many an excellent handicraftsman. Mercenary considerations, tempting men to pursue money-making occupations for which they were unfit, instead of less remunerative employments for which they were fit, were responsible for another vast perversion of talent. All these things now are changed. Equal education and opportunity must needs bring to light whatever aptitudes a man has, and neither social prejudices nor mercenary considerations hamper him in the choice of his life work [*Editor's note*].

Anti-Utopias

ALDOUS HUXLEY

From *Brave New World* †

[Huxley's sardonic novel *Brave New World* grew out of the author's realization, sometime in the late 1920s, that most of the technical procedures for
bringing Utopia out of the realm of fantasy and into the world of practical
reality either already existed or would soon exist. Taking Henry Ford and
his newly developed assembly-line procedures as patterns for the new age,
he moved his action some five or six hundred years into the future and
assumed (very much as More had done) that the people of the new society
would have to be engineered to fit the new technology and the new social
conditions. The engineering of people, as Huxley foresees it, has to be done
inwardly as well as outwardly. His brave new world managers begin by controlling the original genetic endowment of the embryo and then conditioning it within an artificial glass womb, by means of carefully modified
environments, to develop into exactly the class and quality of creature that
society needs.

The novel opens with a group of new students being shown through the
main London Hatchery and Conditioning Center. The offensive Director
and his even more offensive Assistant patiently explain the appalling perfection of the machinery for conditioning embryos (which in 1932 it wasn't yet
fashionable to call "clones") to the exact measure required by the machinery
of society. But of course conditioning does not stop when the pseudo-persons
have been decanted from their bottles at the end of the assembly line. They
have to be shaped to the exact measures of docility and unimaginative self-
satisfaction that represent society's ideal; they have to be shaped and reshaped
for the rest of their existence. Potential problems like parental affection,
romantic love, and individual anxieties have to be conditioned out of the
population. Total promiscuity, addiction to a stupefying drug called "soma,"
organized games, and mindless entertainments are among the approved
activities of this completely "successful," completely self-satisfied community. Though it resembles both fascism and communism, the basic character
of the brave new world is managerial, i.e., bureaucratic. It isn't cheap and
grungy, like George Orwell's sullen anti-Utopia, *1984*. Everything in Huxley's fictional world glitters, and everything works, to the satisfaction of the

† All notes are by the editor of this volume.
Copyright © 1932, 1960 by the author.
Reprinted by permission of HarperCollins
Publishers. Also by permission of Mrs. Laura
Huxley and Chatto & Windus.

itants; indeed, the fact that they are perfectly comfortable with their
ond-rate selves and third-rate lives becomes before long the most infuri-
ing thing about them. Which is just what Huxley intended.]

I

A squat grey building of only thirty-four stories. Over the main entrance
the words CENTRAL LONDON HATCHERY AND CONDITIONING CENTRE,
and, in a shield, the World State's motto, COMMUNITY, IDENTITY, STA-
BILITY.

The enormous room on the ground floor faces towards the north.
Cold for all the summer beyond the panes, for all the tropical heat of
the room itself, a harsh thin light glared through the windows, hungrily
seeking some draped lay figure, some pallid shape of academic goose-
flesh, but finding only the glass and nickel and bleakly shining porcelain
of a laboratory. Wintriness responded to wintriness. The overalls of the
workers were white, their hands gloved with a pale corpse-coloured rubber. The light was frozen, dead, a ghost. Only from the yellow barrels
of the microscopes did it borrow a certain rich and living substance,
lying along the polished tubes like butter, streak after luscious streak in
long recession down the work tables.

"And this," said the Director opening the door, "is the Fertilizing
Room."

Bent over their instruments, three hundred Fertilizers were plunged,
as the Director of Hatcheries and Conditioning entered the room, in the
scarcely breathing silence, the absent-minded, soliloquizing hum or
whistle, of absorbed concentration. A troop of newly arrived students,
very young, pink and callow, followed nervously, rather abjectly, at the
Director's heels. Each of them carried a notebook, in which, whenever
the great man spoke, he desperately scribbled. Straight from the horse's
mouth. It was a rare privilege. The D. H. C. for Central London always
made a point of personally conducting his new students round the various departments.

"Just to give you a general idea," he would explain to them. For of
course some sort of general idea they must have, if they were to do their
work intelligently—though as little of one, if they were to be good and
happy members of society, as possible. For particulars, as every one
knows, make for virtue and happiness; generalities are intellectually necessary evils. Not philosophers but fretsawyers and stamp collectors com-
pose the backbone of society.

"To-morrow," he would add, smiling at them with a slightly menac-
ing geniality, "you'll be settling down to serious work. You won't have
time for generalities. Meanwhile . . ."

Meanwhile, it was a privilege. Straight from the horse's mouth into
the notebook. The boys scribbled like mad.

Tall and rather thin but upright, the Director advanced into the room. He had a long chin and big rather prominent teeth, just covered, when he was not talking, by his full, floridly curved lips. Old, young? Thirty? Fifty? Fifty-five? It was hard to say. And anyhow the question didn't arise; in this year of stability, A.F. 632, it didn't occur to you to ask it.[1]

"I shall begin at the beginning," said the D. H. C. and the more zealous students recorded his intention in their notebooks: *Begin at the beginning.* "These," he waved his hand, "are the incubators." And opening an insulated door he showed them racks upon racks of numbered test-tubes. "The week's supply of ova. Kept," he explained, "at blood heat; whereas the male gametes," and here he opened another door, "they have to be kept at thirty-five instead of thirty-seven. Full blood heat sterilizes." Rams wrapped in theremogene beget no lambs.[2]

Still leaning against the incubators he gave them, while the pencils scurried illegibly across the pages, a brief description of the modern fertilizing process; spoke first, of course, of its surgical introduction—"the operation undergone voluntarily for the good of Society, not to mention the fact that it carries a bonus amounting to six months' salary"; continued with some account of the technique for preserving the excised ovary alive and actively developing; passed on to a consideration of optimum temperature, salinity, viscosity; referred to the liquor in which the detached and ripened eggs were kept; and, leading his charges to the work tables, actually showed them how this liquor was drawn off from the test-tubes; how it was let out drop by drop onto the specially warmed slides of the microscopes; how the eggs which it contained were inspected for abnormalities, counted and transferred to a porous receptacle; how (and he now took them to watch the operation) this receptacle was immersed in a warm bouillon containing free-swimming spermatozoa—at a minimum concentration of one hundred thousand per cubic centimetre, he insisted; and how, after ten minutes, the container was lifted out of the liquor and its contents re-examined; how, if any of the eggs remained unfertilized, it was again immersed, and, if necessary, yet again; how the fertilized ova went back to the incubators; where the Alphas and Betas remained until definitely bottled; while the Gammas, Deltas and Epsilons were brought out again, after only thirty-six hours, to undergo Bokanovsky's Process.[3]

"Bokanovsky's Process," repeated the Director, and the students underlined the words in their little notebooks.

---

1. A.F. (After Ford) 632 would be, if one counted from the year of Henry Ford's birth, 1863, A.D. 2495; but, counting from the year of the incorporation of the Ford Motor Company, it is A.D. 2535.
2. Male gametes are, more simply, sperm. A thermogene is an apparatus for maintaining body heat during an operation.

3. Products of the Brave New World reproductive system are classified by intelligence from Alpha (superior) to Epsilon (minimal). Bokanovsky (an imaginary name) is the author of an artificial process for cloning (as we now call it) embryos.

One egg, one embryo, one adult—normality. But a bokanovskified egg will bud, will proliferate, will divide. From eight to ninety-six buds, and every bud will grow into a perfectly formed embryo, and every embryo into a full-sized adult. Making ninety-six human beings grow where only one grew before. Progress.

"Essentially," the D.H.C. concluded, "bokanovskification consists of a series of arrests of development. We check the normal growth and, paradoxically enough, the egg responds by budding."

Responds by budding. The pencils were busy.

He pointed. On a very slowly moving band a rack-full of test-tubes was entering a large metal box, another, rack-full was emerging. Machinery faintly purred. It took eight minutes for the tubes to go through, he told them. Eight minutes of hard X-rays being about as much as an egg can stand. A few died; of the rest, the least susceptible divided into two; most put out four buds; some eight; all were returned to the incubators, where the buds began to develop; then, after two days, were suddenly chilled, chilled and checked. Two, four, eight, the buds in their turn budded; and having budded were dosed almost to death with alcohol; consequently burgeoned again and having budded—bud out of bud out of bud—were thereafter—further arrest being generally fatal—left to develop in peace. By which time the original egg was in a fair way to becoming anything from eight to ninety-six embryos—a prodigious improvement, you will agree, on nature. Identical twins—but not in piddling twos and threes as in the old viviparous days, when an egg would sometimes accidentally divide; actually by dozens, by scores at a time.

"Scores," the Director repeated and flung out his arms, as though he were distributing largesse. "Scores."

But one of the students was fool enough to ask where the advantage lay.

"My good boy!" The Director wheeled sharply round on him. "Can't you see? Can't you *see?*" He raised a hand; his expression was solemn. "Bokanovsky's Process is one of the major instruments of social stability!"

Major instruments of social stability.

Standard men and women; in uniform batches. The whole of a small factory staffed with the products of a single bokanovskified egg.

"Ninety-six identical twins working ninety-six identical machines!" The voice was almost tremulous with enthusiasm. "You really know where you are. For the first time in history." He quoted the planetary motto. "Community, Identity, Stability." Grand words. "If we could bokanovskify indefinitely the whole problem would be solved."

Solved by standard Gammas, unvarying Deltas, uniform Epsilons. Millions of identical twins. The principle of mass production at last applied to biology.

"But, alas," the Director shook his head, "we *can't* bokanovskify infinitely."

Ninety-six seemed to be the limit; seventy-two a good average. From the same ovary and with gametes of the same male to manufacture as many batches of identical twins as possible—that was the best (sadly a second best) that they could do. And even that was difficult.

"For in nature it takes thirty years for two hundred eggs to reach maturity. But our business is to stabilize the population at this moment, here and now. Dribbling out twins over a quarter of a century—what would be the use of that?"

Obviously, no use at all. But Podsnap's Technique[4] had immensely accelerated the process of ripening. They could make sure of at least a hundred and fifty mature eggs within two years. Fertilize and bokanovskify—in other words, multiply by seventy-two—and you get an average of nearly eleven thousand brothers and sisters in a hundred and fifty batches of identical twins, all within two years of the same age.

"And in exceptional cases we can make one ovary yield us over fifteen thousand adult individuals."

Beckoning to a fair-haired, ruddy young man who happened to be passing at the moment, "Mr. Foster," he called. The ruddy young man approached. "Can you tell us the record for a single ovary, Mr. Foster?"

"Sixteen thousand and twelve in this Centre," Mr. Foster replied without hesitation. He spoke very quickly, had a vivacious blue eye, and took an evident pleasure in quoting figures. "Sixteen thousand and twelve, in one hundred and eighty-nine batches of identicals. But of course they've done much better," he rattled on, "in some of the tropical Centres. Singapore has often produced over sixteen thousand five hundred; and Mombasa has actually touched the seventeen thousand mark. But then they have unfair advantages. You should see the way a negro ovary responds to pituitary! It's quite astonishing, when you're used to working with European material. Still," he added, with a laugh (but the light of combat was in his eyes and the lift of his chin was challenging), "still, we mean to beat them if we can. I'm working on a wonderful Delta-Minus ovary at this moment. Only just eighteen months old. Over twelve thousand seven hundred children already, either decanted or in embryo. And still going strong. We'll beat them yet."

"That's the spirit I like!" cried the Director, and clapped Mr. Foster on the shoulder. "Come along with us, and give these boys the benefit of your expert knowledge."

Mr. Foster smiled modestly. "With pleasure." They went.

In the Bottling Room all was harmonious bustle and ordered activity. Flaps of fresh sow's peritoneum[5] ready cut to the proper size came shoot-

4. Podsnap's Technique, though mentioned only once in passing, is important. In Dickens' novel *Our Mutual Friend* Mr. Podsnap is the type of self-satisfaction and self-importance.
5. Peritoneum is the membrane enclosing the viscera.

up in little lifts from the Organ Store in the sub-basement. Whizz
d then, click! the lift-hatches flew open; the bottle-liner had only to
each out a hand, take the flap, insert, smooth-down, and before the
lined bottle had had time to travel out of reach along the endless band,
whizz, click! another flap of peritoneum had shot up from the depths,
ready to be slipped into yet another bottle, the next of that slow interminable procession on the band.

Next to the Liners stood the Matriculators. The procession advanced;
one by one the eggs were transferred from their test-tubes to the larger
containers; deftly the peritoneal lining was slit, the morula [6] dropped into
place, the saline solution poured in . . . and already the bottle had passed,
and it was the turn of the labellers. Heredity, date of fertilization, mem-
bership of Bokanovsky Group—details were transferred from test-tube to
bottle. No longer anonymous, but named, identified, the procession
marched slowly on; on through an opening in the wall, slowly on into
the Social Predestination Room.

"Eighty-eight cubic metres of card-index," said Mr. Foster with relish,
as they entered.

"Containing *all* the relevant information," added the Director.

"Brought up to date every morning."

"And co-ordinated every afternoon."

"On the basis of which they make their calculations."

"So many individuals, of such and such quality," said Mr. Foster.

"Distributed in such and such quantities."

"The optimum Decanting Rate at any given moment."

"Unforeseen wastages promptly made good."

"Promptly," repeated Mr. Foster. "If you knew the amount of over-
time I had to put in after the last Japanese earthquake!" He laughed
goodhumouredly and shook his head.

"The Predestinators send in their figures to the Fertilizers."

"Who give them the embryos they ask for."

"And the bottles come in here to be predestined in detail."

"After which they are sent down to the Embryo Store."

"Where we now proceed ourselves."

And opening a door Mr. Foster led the way down a staircase into the
basement.

The temperature was still tropical. They descended into a thickening
twilight. Two doors and a passage with a double turn insured the cellar
against any possible infiltration of the day.

"Embryos are like photograph film," said Mr. Foster waggishly, as he
pushed open the second door. "They can only stand red light."

6. Morula is the mass of the embryo at an early stage of segmentation. It resembled a raspberry
or blackberry (*mora* = Latin for blackberry).

And in effect the sultry darkness into which the students now follow him was visible and crimson, like the darkness of closed eyes on a summer's afternoon. The bulging flanks of row on receding row and tier above tier of bottles glinted with innumerable rubies, and among the rubies moved the dim red spectres of men and women with purple eyes and all the symptoms of lupus.[7] The hum and rattle of machinery faintly stirred the air.

"Give them a few figures, Mr. Foster," said the Director, who was tired of talking.

Mr. Foster was only too happy to give them a few figures.

Two hundred and twenty metres long, two hundred wide, ten high. He pointed upwards. Like chickens drinking, the students lifted their eyes towards the distant ceiling

Three tiers of racks: ground floor level, first gallery, second gallery

The spidery steel-work of gallery above gallery faded away in all directions into the dark. Near them three red ghosts were busily unloading demijohns from a moving staircase.

The escalator from the Social Predestination Room.

Each bottle could be placed on one of fifteen racks, each rack, though you couldn't see it, was a conveyor traveling at the rate of thirty-three and a third centimetres an hour. Two hundred and sixty-seven days at eight metres a day. Two thousand one hundred and thirty-six metres in all. One circuit of the cellar at ground level, one on the first gallery, half on the second and on the two hundred and sixty-seventh morning, daylight in the Decanting Room. Independent existence—so called.

"But in the interval," Mr. Foster concluded, "we've managed to do a lot to them. Oh, a very great deal." His laugh was knowing and triumphant.

"That's the spirit I like," said the Director once more. "Let's walk around. You tell them everything, Mr. Foster."

Mr. Foster duly told them.

Told them of the growing embryo on its bed of peritoneum. Made them taste the rich blood surrogate on which it fed. Explained why it had to be stimulated with placentin and thyroxin. Told them of the *corpus luteum* extract.[8] Showed them the jets through which at every twelfth metre from zero to 2040 it was automatically injected. Spoke of those gradually increasing doses of pituitary administered during the final ninety-six metres of their course. Described the artificial maternal circulation installed in every bottle at Metre 112; showed them the reservoir of blood-surrogate, the centrifugal pump that kept the liquid moving over the placenta and drove it through the synthetic lung and waste product filter. Referred to the embryo's troublesome tendency to anæmia,

---

7. Lupus is a tubercular disease that darkens and renders livid the skin.

8. *Corpus luteum* is material remaining in the ovary after release of an ovum.

ne massive doses of hog's stomach extract and foetal foal's liver with
nich, in consequence, it had to be supplied.

Showed them the simple mechanism by means of which, during the
last two metres out of every eight, all the embryos were simultaneously
shaken into familiarity with movement. Hinted at the gravity of the so-
called "trauma of decanting," and enumerated the precautions taken to
minimize, by a suitable training of the bottled embryo, that dangerous
shock. Told them of the test for sex carried out in the neighborhood of
Metre 200. Explained the system of labeling—a T for the males, a circle
for the females and for those who were destined to become freemartins
a question mark, black on a white ground.[9]

"For of course," said Mr. Foster, "in the vast majority of cases, fertil-
ity is merely a nuisance. One fertile ovary in twelve hundred—that would
really be quite sufficient for our purposes. But we want to have a good
choice. And of course one must always have an enormous margin of
safety. So we allow as many as thirty per cent of the female embryos to
develop normally. The others get a dose of male sex-hormone every
twenty-four metres for the rest of the course. Result: they're decanted as
freemartins—structurally quite normal ("except," he had to admit, "that
they *do* have the slightest tendency to grow beards), but sterile. Guar-
anteed sterile. Which brings us at last," continued Mr. Foster, "out of
the realm of mere slavish imitation of nature into the much more interesting world of human invention."

He rubbed his hands. For of course, they didn't content themselves
with merely hatching out embryos: any cow could do that.

"We also predestine and condition. We decant our babies as social-
ized human beings, as Alphas or Epsilons, as future sewage workers or
future . . ." He was going to say "future World controllers," but correcting himself, said "future Directors of Hatcheries," instead.

The D.H.C. acknowledged the compliment with a smile.

They were passing Metre 320 on Rack 11. A young Beta-Minus
mechanic was busy with screwdriver and spanner on the blood-surrogate
pump of a passing bottle. The hum of the electric motor deepened by
fractions of a tone as he turned the nuts. Down, down . . . A final twist,
a glance at the revolution counter, and he was done. He moved two
paces down the line and began the same process on the next pump.

"Reducing the number of revolutions per minute," Mr. Foster
explained. "The surrogate goes round slower; therefore passes through
the lung at longer intervals; therefore gives the embryo less oxygen.
Nothing like oxygen-shortage for keeping an embryo below par." Again
he rubbed his hands.

"But why do you want to keep the embryo below par?" asked an
ingenuous student.

---

9. Freemartins are neuters—sterile females, infertile males.

"Ass!" said the Director, breaking a long silence. "Hasn't it occurr
to you that an Epsilon embryo must have an Epsilon environment as
well as an Epsilon heredity?"[1]

It evidently hadn't occurred to him. He was covered with confusion.

"The lower the caste," said Mr. Foster, "the shorter the oxygen." The
first organ affected was the brain. After that the skeleton. At seventy per
cent of normal oxygen you got dwarfs. At less than seventy eyeless monsters.

"Who are no use at all," concluded Mr. Foster.

Whereas (his voice became confidential and eager), if they could discover a technique for shortening the period of maturation what a triumph,
what a benefaction to Society!

"Consider the horse."

They considered it.

Mature at six; the elephant at ten. While at thirteen a man is not yet
sexually mature, and is only full-grown at twenty. Hence, of course, that
fruit of delayed development the human intelligence.

"But in Epsilons," said Mr. Foster very justly, "we don't need human
intelligence."

Didn't need and didn't get it. But though the Epsilon mind was mature
at ten, the Epsilon body was not fit to work till eighteen. Long years of
superfluous and wasted immaturity. If the physical development could
be speeded up till it was as quick, say, as a cow's, what an enormous
saving to the Community!

"Enormous!" murmured the students. Mr. Foster's enthusiasm was
infectious.

He became rather technical; spoke of the abnormal endocrine co-
ordination which made men grow so slowly; postulated a germinal
mutation to account for it. Could the effect of this germinal mutation
be undone? Could the individual Epsilon embryo be made a revert, by
a suitable technique, to the normality of dogs and cows? That was the
problem. And it was all but solved.

Pilkington, at Mombasa, had produced individuals who were sexually
mature at four and full-grown at six and a half. A scientific triumph.
But socially useless. Six-year-old men and women were too stupid to do
even Epsilon work. And the process was an all-or-nothing one; either
you failed to modify at all, or else you modified the whole way. They
were still trying to find the ideal compromise between adults of twenty
and adults of six. So far without success. Mr. Foster sighed and shook
his head.

Their wanderings through the crimson twilight had brought them to
the neighborhood of Metre 170 on Rack 9. From this point onwards

---

1. Epsilons, as the lowest class, are systematically rendered stupid, to fit them for the menial tasks
that are their destiny.

...ack 9 was enclosed and the bottles performed the remainder of their journey in a kind of tunnel, interrupted here and there by openings two or three metres wide.

"Heat conditioning," said Mr. Foster.

Hot tunnels alternated with cool tunnels. Coolness was wedded to discomfort in the form of hard X-rays. By the time they were decanted the embryos had a horror of cold. They were predestined to emigrate to the tropics, to be miners and acetate silk spinners and steel workers. Later on their minds would be made to endorse the judgment of their bodies.[2] "We condition them to thrive on heat," concluded Mr. Foster. "Our colleagues upstairs will teach them to love it."

"And that," put in the Director sententiously, "that is the secret of happiness and virtue—liking what you've *got* to do. All conditioning aims at that: making people like their unescapable social destiny."

In a gap between two tunnels, a nurse was delicately probing with a long fine syringe into the gelatinous contents of a passing bottle. The students and their guides stood watching her for a few moments in silence.

"Well, Lenina," said Mr. Foster, when at last she withdrew the syringe and straightened herself up.

The girl turned with a start. One could see that, for all the lupus and the purple eyes, she was uncommonly pretty.

"Henry!' Her smile flashed readily at him—a row of coral teeth.

"Charming, charming," murmured the Director and, giving her two or three little pats, received in exchange a rather deferential smile for himself.

"What are you giving them?" asked Mr. Foster, making his tone very professional.

"Oh, the usual typhoid and sleeping sickness."

"Tropical workers start being inoculated at Metre 150," Mr. Foster explained to the students. "The embryos still have gills. We immunize the fish against the future man's diseases."[3] Then, turning back to Lenina, "Ten to five on the roof this afternoon," he said, "as usual."[4]

"Charming," said the Director once more, and, with a final pat, moved away after the others.

On Rack 10 rows of next generation's chemical workers were being trained in the toleration of lead, caustic soda, tar, chlorine. The first of a batch of two hundred and fifty embryonic rocket-plane engineers was just passing the eleven hundred metre mark on Rack 3. A special mechanism kept their containers in constant rotation. "To improve their sense

2. Conditioning embryos to alternate comfort and discomfort should be compared to the similar process with slightly older subjects in *Walden Two* (below, pp. 248ff).

3. Careless fiddling around with the sex objects Lenina and Fanny is part of the program of sexual promiscuity that in *Brave New World*

protects society from any undue concentration of individual feelings. Smart Mr. Foster to the contrary, human embryos don't ever have functional gills and aren't properly fish.

4. The Director and Henry share contentedly in Lenina's favors; in *Brave New World*, casual copulation is the required morality.

of balance," Mr. Foster explained. "Doing repairs on the outside ▪ rocked in mid-air is a ticklish job. We slacken off the circulation whe they're right way up, so that they're half starved, and double the flow of surrogate when they're upside down. They learn to associate topsy-turvy-dom with well-being; in fact, they're only truly happy when they're standing on their heads.

"And now," Mr. Foster went on, "I'd like to show you some very interesting conditioning for Alpha Plus Intellectuals. We have a big batch of them on Rack 5. First Gallery level," he called to two boys who had started to go down to the ground floor.

"They're round about Metre 900," he explained. "You can't really do any useful intellectual conditioning till the foetuses have lost their tails.[5] Follow me."

But the Director had looked at his watch. "Ten to three," he said. "No time for the intellectual embryos, I'm afraid. We must go up to the Nurseries before the children have finished their afternoon sleep."

Mr. Foster was disappointed. "At least one glance at the Decanting Room," he pleaded.

"Very well then." The Director smiled indulgently. "Just one glance."

B. F. SKINNER

From Walden Two†

For many years, B. F. Skinner was an academic psychologist of the behaviorist persuasion. Behaviorism, which was titled if not invented by another American psychologist, John B. Watson, built on the premise that a complete and adequate treatment of psychological problems can be given without reference to consciousness and introspection. Not only so, but by changing peoples' outer behavior, a therapist can sometimes change their inner way of thinking. They will learn to find inward, emotional reasons for wanting to do what they have to do anyway. This doesn't amount to the drill-sergeant's morality, but it may come close, and the approach has often worked best under drill-sergeant conditions. During the Second World War, for example, behaviorist principles did something to soften the edges of inter-racial conflict by encouraging the formation of mixed military units with the expectation that the men would get along together.

Skinner's academic background comes clear in his first and only novel. Walden Two is a set of rather wooden discussions among three professors, with four student listeners, on the merits of a communal society and the principles of "behavioral engineering" said to underlie it. Chief spokesman for the community is its founder, a maverick academic named Frazier; his

5. Fetuses have visible tails, which they lose about five and a half weeks after conception.
† New York: Macmillan, 1948 by B. F. Skin-ner. Copyright © 1948 by B. F. Skinner. Renewed 1976 by B. F. Skinner. All notes are by the editor of this volume.

 ̄gonist is an orthodox academic named Castle; and the narrator, referred
 ̄as Burris, is the scarcely disguised author himself, Burrhus Frederic Skin-
 ̄ ̄er. He acts ostensibly as arbiter of the arguments, though it comes as no
surprise when, at the end of the book and in the teeth of Castle's contemp-
tuous objections, he resigns his university post and joins the new community.

While Skinner draws on a number of previous Utopias for the plan of his
ideal society (Thoreau's *Walden* being emphatically *not* one of them), his
social scheme is most closely modeled on that of Thomas More. Everyone
works in *Walden Two*, but not very hard; there is a minimum reliance on
money; the standard of living, though far from lavish, is sufficient for everyone; and, most striking of all, everyone is subject to a uniform, unvarying
program of behavioral engineering. In all these ways, and sometimes in its
actual verbal formulation of them, *Walden Two* is directly reminiscent of
More's *Utopia*. But particularly in its program for conditioning children
from birth to a uniform and rigorous program of conformity, it is reminiscent of Huxley's *Brave New World*. Only one detail distinguishes the two
pictures. Huxley loathes and abominates the parody of a good society that
his social engineers produce; Skinner frankly admires the authoritarian system embodied in *Walden Two*. He has not, by any means, convinced all
his readers on this point; in fact, some have reacted to his book with horrified
revulsion. So *Walden Two* cannot be classified either as a "utopia" or as a
"dystopia"—rather it forces the reader to classify himself. And it may have
the happy result of casting him back on Walden One—Thoreau's—to test
his mind on a keen wit and the sharp air of real spiritual independence.]

"Each of us," Frazier began, "is engaged in a pitched battle with the
rest of mankind."

"A curious premise for a Utopia," said Castle. "Even a pessimist like
myself takes a more hopeful view than that."

"You do, you do," said Frazier. "But let's be realistic. Each of us has
interests which conflict with the interests of everybody else. That's our
original sin, and it can't be helped. Now, 'everybody else' we call 'society.' It's a powerful opponent, and it always wins. Oh, here and there
an individual prevails for a while and gets what he wants. Sometimes he
storms the culture of a society and changes it slightly to his own advantage. But society wins in the long run, for it has the advantage of numbers and of age. Many prevail against one, and men against a baby.
Society attacks early, when the individual is helpless. It enslaves him
almost before he has tasted freedom. The 'ologies' will tell you how it's
done.[1] Theology calls it building a conscience or developing a spirit of
selflessness. Psychology calls it the growth of the super-ego.

---

1. Frazier, the spokesman for Walden Two, must emphasize that society performs behav-ioral engineering on its members—and per-forms it badly—to set up the position of the new utopia, which does the same thing, but does it better. Note the frequent appearance in Frazier's mouth of the words "experimental" and "scientific."

"Considering how long society has been at it, you'd expect a better job. But the campaigns have been badly planned and the victory has never been secure. The behavior of the individual has been shaped according to revelations of 'good conduct,' never as the result of experimental study. But why not experiment? The questions are simple enough. What's the best behavior for the individual so far as the group is concerned? And how can the individual be induced to behave in that way? Why not explore these questions in a scientific spirit?

"We could do just that in Walden Two. We had already worked out a code of conduct—subject, of course, to experimental modification. The code would keep things running smoothly if everybody lived up to it. Our job was to see that everybody did. Now, you can't get people to follow a useful code by making them into so many jacks-in-the-box. You can't foresee all future circumstances, and you can't specify adequate future conduct. You don't know what will be required. Instead you have to set up certain behavioral processes which will lead the individual to design his own 'good' conduct when the time comes. We call that sort of thing 'self-control.' But don't be misled, the control always rests in the last analysis in the hands of society.

"One of our Planners, a young man named Simmons, worked with me. It was the first time in history that the matter was approached in an experimental way. Do you question that statement, Mr. Castle?"

"I'm not sure I know what you are talking about," said Castle.

"Then let me go on. Simmons and I began by studying the great works on morals and ethics—Plato, Aristotle, Confucius, the New Testament, the Puritan divines, Machiavelli, Chesterfield, Freud—there were scores of them. We were looking for any and every method of shaping human behavior by imparting techniques of self-control. Some techniques were obvious enough, for they had marked turning points in human history. 'Love your enemies' is an example—a psychological invention for easing the lot of an oppressed people. The severest trial of oppression is the constant rage which one suffers at the thought of the oppressor. What Jesus discovered was how to avoid these inner devastations. His technique was to *practice the opposite emotion*. If a man can succeed in 'loving his enemies' and 'taking no thought for the morrow,' he will no longer be assailed by hatred of the oppressor or rage at the loss of his freedom or possessions. He may not get his freedom or possessions back, but he's less miserable. It's a difficult lesson. It comes late in our program."

"I thought you were opposed to modifying emotions and instincts until the world was ready for it," said Castle. "According to you, the principle of 'love your enemies' should have been suicidal."

"It would have been suicidal, except for an entirely unforeseen consequence. Jesus must have been quite astonished at the effect of his discovery. We are only just beginning to understand the power of love

...use we are just beginning to understand the weakness of force and gression. But the science of behavior is clear about all that now. Recent discoveries in the analysis of punishment—but I am falling into one digression after another. Let me save my explanation of why the Christian virtues—and I mean merely the Christian techniques of self-control—have not disappeared from the face of the earth, with due recognition of the fact that they suffered a narrow squeak within recent memory.

"When Simmons and I had collected our techniques of control, we had to discover how to teach them. That was more difficult. Current educational practices were of little value, and religious practices scarcely any better. Promising paradise or threatening hell-fire is, we assumed, generally admitted to be unproductive. It is based upon a fundamental fraud which, when discovered, turns the individual against society and nourishes the very thing it tries to stamp out. What Jesus offered in return for loving one's enemies was heaven *on earth*, better known as peace of mind.[2]

"We found a few suggestions worth following in the practices of the clinical psychologist. We undertook to build a tolerance for annoying experiences. The sunshine of midday is extremely painful if you come from a dark room, but take it in easy stages and you can avoid pain altogether. The analogy can be misleading, but in much the same way it's possible to build a tolerance to painful or distasteful stimuli, or to frustration, or to situations which arouse fear, anger or rage. Society and nature throw these annoyances at the individual with no regard for the development of tolerances. Some achieve tolerances, most fail. Where would the science of immunization be if it followed a schedule of accidental dosages?

"Take the principle of 'Get thee behind me, Satan,' for example," Frazier continued. "It's a special case of self-control by altering the environment. Subclass A $_3$, I believe. We give each child a lollipop which has been dipped in powdered sugar so that a single touch of the tongue can be detected. We tell him he may eat the lollipop later in the day, provided it hasn't already been licked. Since the child is only three or four, it is a fairly diff——"

"Three or four!" Castle exclaimed.

"All our ethical training is completed by the age of six," said Frazier quietly. "A simple principle like putting temptation out of sight would be acquired before four. But at such an early age the problem of not licking the lollipop isn't easy. Now, what would you do, Mr. Castle, in a similar situation?"

"Put the lollipop out of sight as quickly as possible."

"Exactly. I can see you've been well trained. Or perhaps you discovered the principle for yourself. We're in favor of original inquiry wher-

---

2. This is not exactly the way most people have read the New Testament. One might start by looking at the Beatitudes (Matthew 5).

ever possible, but in this case we have a more important goal and don't hesitate to give verbal help. First of all, the children are urged to examine their own behavior while looking at the lollipops. This helps them to recognize the need for self-control. Then the lollipops are concealed, and the children are asked to notice any gain in happiness or any reduction in tension. Then a strong distraction is arranged—say, an interesting game. Later the children are reminded of the candy and encouraged to examine their reaction. The value of the distraction is generally obvious. Well, need I go on? When the experiment is repeated a day or so later, the children all run with the lollipops to their lockers and do exactly what Mr. Castle would do—a sufficient indication of the success of our training."

"I wish to report an objective observation of my reaction to your story," said Castle, controlling his voice with great precision. "I find myself revolted by this display of sadistic tyranny."

"I don't wish to deny you the exercise of an emotion which you seem to find enjoyable," said Frazier. "So let me go on. Concealing a tempting but forbidden object is a crude solution. For one thing, it's not always feasible. We want a sort of psychological concealment—covering up the candy by paying no attention. In a later experiment the children wore their lollipops like crucifixes for a few hours."

> ' 'Instead of the cross, the lollipop,
> About my neck was hung.' "

said Castle.

"I wish somebody had taught me that, though," said Rodge, with a glance at Barbara. [3]

"Don't we all?" said Frazier. "Some of us learn control, more or less by accident. The rest of us go all our lives not even understanding how it is possible, and blaming our failure on being born the wrong way."

"How do you build up a tolerance to an annoying situation?" I said.

"Oh, for example, by having the children 'take' a more and more painful shock, or drink cocoa with less and less sugar in it until a bitter concoction can be savored without a bitter face."

"But jealousy or envy—you can't administer them in graded doses," I said.

"And why not? Remember, we control the social environment, too, at this age. That's why we get our ethical training in early. Take this case. A group of children arrive home after a long walk tired and hungry. They're expecting supper; they find, instead, that it's time for a lesson in self-control; they must stand for five minutes in front of steaming bowls of soup.

3. Rodge is Roger, a former student of Burris; Barbara is his fiancée, who is having trouble giving up the good things of life that Walden Two will ask her to forego. The verse is a sarcastic parody of "The Ancient Mariner."

The assignment is accepted like a problem in arithmetic. Any groaning or complaining is a wrong answer.[4] Instead, the children begin at
once to work upon themselves to avoid any unhappiness during the delay.
One of them may make a joke of it. We encourage a sense of humor as
a good way of not taking an annoyance seriously. The joke won't be
much, according to adult standards—perhaps the child will simply pre-
tend to empty the bowl of soup into his upturned mouth. Another may
start a song with many verses. The rest join in at once, for they've learned
that it's a good way to make time pass."

Frazier glanced uneasily at Castle, who was not to be appeased.

"That also strikes you as a form of torture, Mr. Castle?" he asked.

"I'd rather be put on the rack," said Castle.

"Then you have by no means had the thorough training I supposed.
You can't imagine how lightly the children take such an experience. It's
a rather severe biological frustration, for the children are tired and hungry and they must stand and look at food; but it's passed off as lightly as
a five-minute delay at curtain time. We regard it as a fairly elementary
test. Much more difficult problems follow."

"I suspected as much," muttered Castle.

"In a later stage we forbid all social devices. No songs, no jokes—
merely silence. Each child is forced back upon his own resources—a
very important step."

"I should think so," I said. "And how do you know it's successful?
You might produce a lot of silently resentful children. It's certainly a
dangerous stage."

"It is, and we follow each child carefully. If he hasn't picked up the
necessary techniques, we start back a little. A still more advanced stage"—
Frazier glanced again at Castle, who stirred uneasily—"brings me to my
point. When it's time to sit down to the soup, the children count off—
heads and tails. Then a coin is tossed and if it comes up heads, the
'heads' sit down and eat. The 'tails' remain standing for another five
minutes.

Castle groaned.

"And you call that envy?" I asked.

"Perhaps not exactly," said Frazier. "At least there's seldom any
aggression against the lucky ones. The emotion, if any, is directed against
Lady Luck herself, against the toss of the coin. That, in itself, is a lesson
worth learning, for it's the only direction in which emotion has a surviving chance to be useful. And resentment toward things in general, while
perhaps just as silly as personal aggression, is more easily controlled. Its
expression is not socially objectionable."[5]

Frazier looked nervously from one of us to the other. He seemed to

---

4. This is the drill-sergeant mentality, which
believes in inflicting pain or discipline for its
own sake.

5. Frazier's paragraph invites more careful
analysis than Burris gives it.

be trying to discover whether we shared Castle's prejudice. I began realize, also, that he had not really wanted to tell this story. He w vulnerable. He was treading on sanctified ground, and I was pretty sure he had not established the value of most of these practices in an experimental fashion. He could scarcely have done so in the short space of ten years. He was working on faith, and it bothered him.

I tried to bolster his confidence by reminding him that he had a professional colleague among his listeners. "May you not inadvertently teach your children some of the very emotions you're trying to eliminate?" I said. "What's the effect, for example, of finding the anticipation of a warm supper suddenly thwarted? Doesn't that eventually lead to feelings of uncertainty, or even anxiety?"

"It might. We had to discover how often our lessons could be safely administered. But all our schedules are worked out experimentally. We watch for undesired consequences just as any scientist watches for disrupting factors in his experiments.

"After all, it's a simple and sensible program," he went on in a tone of appeasement. "We set up a system of gradually increasing annoyances and frustrations against a background of complete serenity. An easy environment is made more and more difficult as the children acquire the capacity to adjust."

"But why?" said Castle. "Why these deliberate unpleasantnesses—to put it mildly? I must say I think you and your friend Simmons are really very subtle sadists."

"You've reversed your position, Mr. Castle," said Frazier in a sudden flash of anger with which I rather sympathized. Castle was calling names, and he was also being unaccountably and perhaps intentionally obtuse. "A while ago you accused me of breeding a race of softies," Frazier continued. "Now you object to toughening them up. But what you don't understand is that these potentially unhappy situations are never very annoying. Our schedules make sure of that. You wouldn't understand, however, because you're not so far advanced as our children."

Castle grew black.

"But what do your children get out of it?" he insisted, apparently trying to press some vague advantage in Frazier's anger.

"What do they get out of it!" exclaimed Frazier, his eyes flashing with a sort of helpless contempt. His lips curled and he dropped his head to look at his fingers, which were crushing a few blades of grass.

"They must get happiness and freedom and strength," I said, putting myself in a ridiculous position in attempting to make peace.

"They don't sound happy or free to me, standing in front of bowls of Forbidden Soup," said Castle, answering me parenthetically while continuing to stare at Frazier.

"If I must spell it out," Frazier began with a deep sigh, "what they get is escape from the petty emotions which eat the heart out of the unprepared. They get the satisfaction of pleasant and profitable social relations scale almost undreamed of in the world at large. They get immeasurably increased efficiency, because they can stick to a job without suffering the aches and pains which soon beset most of us. They get new horizons, for they are spared the emotions characteristic of frustration and failure. They get—" His eyes searched the branches of the trees. "Is that enough?" he said at last.

"And the community must gain their loyalty," I said, "when they discover the fears and jealousies and diffidences in the world at large."

"I'm glad you put it that way," said Frazier. "You might have said that they must feel superior to the miserable products of our public schools. But we're at pains to keep any feeling of superiority or contempt under control, too. Having suffered most acutely from it myself, I put the subject first on our agenda. We carefully avoid any joy in a personal triumph which means the personal failure of somebody else. We take no pleasure in the sophistical, the disputative, the dialectical." He threw a vicious glance at Castle. "We don't use the motive of domination, because we are always thinking of the whole group. We could motivate a few geniuses that way—it was certainly my own motivation—but we'd sacrifice some of the happiness of everyone else. Triumph over nature and over oneself, yes. But over others, never."

"You've taken the mainspring out of the watch," said Castle flatly.

"That's an experimental question, Mr. Castle, and you have the wrong answer."

Frazier was making no effort to conceal his feeling. If he had been riding Castle, he was now using his spurs. Perhaps he sensed that the rest of us had come round and that he could change his tactics with a single holdout. But it was more than strategy, it was genuine feeling. Castle's undeviating skepticism was a growing frustration.

"Are your techniques really so very new?" I said hurriedly. "What about the primitive practice of submitting a boy to various tortures before granting him a place among adults? What about the disciplinary techniques of Puritanism? Or of the modern school, for that matter?"

"In one sense you're right," said Frazier. "And I think you've nicely answered Mr. Castle's tender concern for our little ones. The unhappinesses we deliberately impose are far milder than the normal unhappinesses from which we offer protection. Even at the height of our ethical training, the unhappiness is ridiculously trivial—to the well-trained child.

"But there's a world of difference in the way we use these annoyances," he continued. "For one thing, we don't punish. We never administer an unpleasantness in the hope of repressing or eliminating undesirable behavior. But there's another difference. In most cultures the child meets up with annoyances and reverses of uncontrolled magnitude. Some are imposed in the name of discipline by persons in authority. Some, like hazings, are condoned though not authorized. Others are merely accidental. No one cares to, or is able to, prevent them.

"We all know what happens. A few hardy children emerge, partilarly those who have got their unhappiness in doses that could be swlowed. They become brave men. Others become sadists or masochist. of varying degrees of pathology. Not having conquered a painful environment, they become preoccupied with pain and make a devious art of it. Others submit—and hope to inherit the earth. The rest—the cravens, the cowards—live in fear for the rest of their lives. And that's only a single field—the reaction to pain. I could cite a dozen parallel cases. The optimist and the pessimist, the contented and the disgruntled, the loved and the unloved, the ambitious and the discouraged—these are only the extreme products of a miserable system.

"Traditional practices are admittedly better than nothing,' Frazier went on. "Spartan or Puritan—no one can question the occasional happy result. But the whole system rests upon the wasteful principle of selection. The English public school of the nineteenth century produced brave men—by setting up almost insurmountable barriers and making the most of the few who came over. But selection isn't education. Its crops of brave men will always be small, and the waste enormous. Like all primitive principles, selection serves in place of education only through a profligate use of material. Multiply extravagantly and select with rigor. It's the philosophy of the 'big litter' as an alternative to good child hygiene.

"In Walden Two we have a different objective. We make every man a brave man. They all come over the barriers. Some require more preparation than others but they all come over. The traditional use of adversity is to select the strong. We control adversity to build strength. And we do it deliberately, no matter how sadistic Mr. Castle may think us, in order to prepare for adversities which are beyond control. Our children eventually experience the 'heartache and the thousand natural shocks that flesh is heir to.' It would be the cruelest possible practice to protect them as long as possible, especially when we *could* protect them so well."

Frazier held out his hands in an exaggerated gesture of appeal.

"What alternative *had* we?" he said, as if he were in pain. "What else could we do? For four or five years we could provide a life in which no important need would go unsatisfied, a life practically free of anxiety or frustration or annoyance. What would *you* do? Would you let the child enjoy this paradise with no thought for the future—like an idolatrous and pampering mother? Or would you relax control of the environment and let the child meet accidental frustrations? *But what is the virtue of accident?*[6] No, there was only one course open to us. We had to *design* a series of adversities, so that the child would develop the greatest possible self-control. Call it deliberate, if you like, and accuse us of sadism; there was no other course." Frazier turned to Castle, but he was scarcely

---

6. Nobody tries to answer the question about accident, but there seems to be a real difference between pain inflicted coldly and systematically by an authority figure and pain that happens incidentally while doing an agreed-upon task. Or so a more articulate opponent of the distinctly cranky ideologist might say.

_nging him. He seemed to be waiting, anxiously, for his capitula-
_. But Castle merely shifted his ground.

"I find it difficult to classify these practices," he said. Frazier emitted a disgruntled "Ha!" and sat back. "Your system seems to have usurped the place as well as the techniques of religion."

"Of religion and family culture," said Frazier wearily. "But I don't call it usurpation. Ethical training belongs to the community. As for techniques, we took every suggestion we could find without prejudice as to the source. But not on faith. We disregarded all claims of revealed truth and put every principle to an experimental test. And by the way, I've very much misrepresented the whole system if you suppose that any of the practices I've described are fixed. We try out many different techniques. Gradually we work toward the best possible set. And we don't pay much attention to the apparent success of a principle in the course of history. History is honored in Walden Two only as entertainment. It isn't taken seriously as food for thought. Which reminds me, very rudely, of our original plan for the morning. Have you had enough of emotion? Shall we turn to intellect?"

Frazier addressed these questions to Castle in a very friendly way and I was glad to see that Castle responded in kind. It was perfectly clear, however, that neither of them had ever worn a lollipop about the neck or faced a bowl of Forbidden Soup.

Suggestions for Further Reading

The first biography of More was written by his son-in-law, William Roper, shortly after More's execution and during the reign of Mary Stuart; but it could not be published till 1635, well after the reign of Elizabeth. It is a major source of all later biographies, including the "standard" one by R. W. Chambers, publication of which coincided with the canonization of More in 1935. Though heavily riddled by criticism, the portrait of More painted by Chambers remains genial and ingratiating; it has served as the basis of a successful play by Robert Bolt titled A Man for All Seasons (1960). A more recent biography by Richard Marius (1984) is neither genial nor ingratiating, but in important respects is closer to the historic truth.

Serious students of More will have to have access to, even if they do not read every page of, the Yale edition of More's Complete Works, in fifteen volumes and counting. Utopia is in volume 4, under the joint editorship of J. H. Hexter and Father Edward Surtz. A "Modernized Series" supplementary to the Complete Works provides easy access to More's sometimes antiquated English and knotty Latin. Another useful appendage to the Yale edition is A Concordance to the Utopia of St. Thomas More, ed. L. Bolchazy (Hildesheim, 1978). Elizabeth Rogers edited the Correspondence (in Latin) for Princeton (1947) and Selected Letters (in English) for the "Modernized Series" in 1961. In 1963 Stanley Morison assembled under the title The Likeness of Thomas More the various portraits and representations of his person. "Thomas More and the Painter's Eye" is a careful, cogent article by Warren Wooden and John N. Wall, Jr.; it relates the woodcuts placed before the text of Utopia to the details in the text itself, and appeared in The Journal of Medieval and Renaissance Studies 15 (1985): 231–63.

A wide-ranging survey of the field is that of Frank and Fritzie Manuel, Utopian Thought in the Western World (Cambridge, MA, 1979); it unfolds before the serious reader long perspectives of exploratory possibilities. For less comprehensive study there are numerous samplers and studies of Utopian writings such as those by Lewis Mumford (1922), Frances T. Russell (1932), Harry Ross (1938), V. F. Calverton (1941), G. Negley

SUGGESTIONS FOR FURTHER READING

M. Patrick (1952), Richard Gerber (1955), W. H. G. Armytage ...1), T. Molnar (1967), and A. O. Lewis, Jr. (1971). The assemblage ...ost closely focused on Thomas More is that of R. S. Sylvester and G. Marc'hadour, *Essential Articles for the Study of Thomas More* (1977).

Collecting exotic Utopias is like collecting wild mushrooms: there is no fixed limit. A preliminary sampling might include Etienne Cabet, *Voyage en Icarie* (1840); Th. Hertzka, *Freeland* (1891); Paul Goodman, *Utopian Essays* (1964); Evgeny Zamyatin, *We* (1928); J. V. Andreae, *Christanopolis* (1619); Gabriel de Foigny, *La Terre Australe Connue* (1676); William Morris, *News from Nowhere* (1891); H. G. Wells, *A Modern Utopia* (1905); George Orwell, *Nineteen Eighty Four* (1949); F. M. C. Fourier, *Le Nouveau Monde Industriel* (1892); Sebastien Mercier, *L'An Deux Mille Quatre Cent* (1770); and E. R. Curtis, *A Season in Utopia: The Story of Brook Farm* (1961).

In addition to the books and articles excerpted in the present collection, the reader will want to consult studies often antiquated, specialized, or otherwise marginal, but still valid, of which a few examples are Frederic Seebohm, *The Oxford Reformers* (1867); Karl Kautsky, *Thomas More and His Utopia* (1880); P. A. Duhamel, "The Medievalism of More's Utopia," in *Studies in Philology* 52 (1955): 99–126; and Marie Delcourt, "Le Pouvoir du Roi dans l'Utopie," in *Mélanges offerts a M. Abel Lefranc* (1936).

Among more detailed and extensive listings, students may avail themselves of R. W. Gibson, *St. Thomas More: A Preliminary Bibliography of His Works and of Moreana to the Year 1750*, with a supplementary listing of Utopiana by R. W. Gibson and J. Max Patrick (New Haven, 1961); also Frank and Madjie P. Sullivan, *Moreana: Materials for the Study of St. Thomas More* (four vols., 1964–66, with an index, 1971). Germain Marc'hadour with assistants edits the quarterly *Moreana*, updating More-related events throughout the world.